The Lives of Dalhousie University

VOLUME ONE

George Ramsay, ninth Earl of Dalhousie (1770–1838), copied by Charles Comfort from the portrait by Sir John Gordon.

The Lives of Dalhousie University

VOLUME ONE, 1818–1925

Lord Dalhousie's College

P.B. WAITE

McGILL-QUEEN'S UNIVERSITY PRESS

Montreal & Kingston • London • Buffalo

© The Governors of Dalhousie College and University 1994
ISBN 0-7735-1166-0
Legal deposit second quarter 1994
Bibliothèque nationale du Québec

Printed in Canada on acid-free paper

Canadian Cataloguing in Publication Data

Waite, P. B. (Peter Busby), 1922–
    The Lives of Dalhousie University
    Includes bibliographical references and index.
    ISBN 0-7735-1166-0 (v. 1)
    1. Dalhousie University – History. I. Title.
    LE3.D32W34 1994   378.716'22   C94-900118-X

End papers: Watercolour of Halifax from Dartmouth
Cove. Artist unknown. Courtesy J. Ross Robertson
Collection, Metropolitan Toronto Central Library
T16318.

This book was typeset by Typo Litho Composition Inc.
in 11/13 Sabon.

Contents

List of Illustrations

Acknowledgments

The photographs in this book are mostly from Dalhousie University Archives. Dr Charles Armour, university archivist, was able to provide some negatives; but for others the professional skill of Findlay Muir, of Dalhousie's Audio-Visual Services, has been essential in re-doing old photographs. The overall selection of pictures is basically mine, but I have had excellent advice, generously tendered, from Karen Smith, in charge of the Killam Library's Special Collections, and from Mern O'Brien, director of the Dalhousie Art Gallery.

A word about the Arthur Lismer sketches. He was principal of the Nova Scotia (then the Victoria) College of Art and Design in Halifax from 1916 to 1919. When Dalhousie was considering celebrating its centennial in 1918, it commissioned Lismer to do sketches for its historical booklet. Not all the original sketches were published, nor have all the published ones survived; but some of both have been reproduced here.

P.B.W.

Preface

In 1986, near the end of his term as president of Dalhousie University, W.A. MacKay invited me to write Dalhousie's history. His successor, Howard Clark, agreed. Submission of the manuscript we established as 31 December 1992.

In that time I believed it possible to master the main sources of Dalhousie's history. I was partly right, but only partly. Dalhousie's official records are substantial; they, and the *Dalhousie Gazette*, were canvassed, as well as collections of private papers such as those of the ninth Earl of Dalhousie (1770–1838) and Archibald MacMechan, professor of English here from 1889 until 1931. What was impossible to master, save as the work of two lifetimes, was Dalhousie in the Halifax newspapers. The references to newspapers are but samples drawn from a sea of information. There were eleven newspapers in Halifax in the 1860s, and if in time they became fewer, they also got thicker.

I once cherished the idea that Dalhousie's history could be written in one volume, that the current fashion of writing universities' histories in two volumes, such as those of Queen's, McGill, McMaster, Mount Allison, was simply lack of control on the part of the author. Ruthless principles of selection could surely get Dalhousie's history within the covers of one convenient volume. So indeed it could; but it would have been a stiff, dried-up book, full of charters and statutes, stones and buildings, the humanity baked out of it. No reader, unless he be a monster of determination (and digestion), would be able to read so dense a book as that would have to be. So what has emerged has been, to continue the metaphor, a Christmas cake: flour, butter, and eggs to be sure (the building materials of cakes), but with cherries, raisins, candied fruit, and brandy mixed up in it. Thus the reader will encounter poetry, real and doggerel, flippant remarks from the *Dalhousie Gazette*, nasty (and elevating) comments from legislators, as well as usual accounts of buildings, finances, appointments, and curriculum. A university is a place where human beings meet and work, where professors teach students, and students even teach professors, and their lives and thoughts are worth trying to recover.

Dalhousie was, and is, a university in Halifax, and it seemed essential, right from the start, to give something of Halifax's character and history. Dalhousie was also, for its first forty years and more, a creature of Nova Scotian politics, at the centre of the one-college idea in the 1840s – an idea it never quite abandoned. A little of the history of that imperialism, as it may well have been regarded by other colleges in Nova Scotia, was also inevitable.

This is a narrative history of Dalhousie. Analysis there is, but it is derived mostly from the work of others on the social backgrounds and careers of Dalhousie, and other, students. I have used their research with gratitude.

I have reason to be grateful to many people in this long process. Dr Charles Armour, Dalhousie University archivist, put the full resources of the Archives at my disposal, and I have imposed myself and my exigencies upon his good nature and that of his staff. Allan Dunlop of the Public Archives of Nova Scotia has often suggested material relevant to Dalhousie that I would not have found. The staff of the Public Archives of Nova Scotia, that wonderful place, have been unfailingly helpful. Mrs Carolyn Earle of the Maritime Conference Archives at Pine Hill introduced me to papers that I should certainly have missed otherwise. Many professors, students, members of the Board of Governors, alumni, and others have given me their time and their recollections. They have been acknowledged more specifically in the notes and bibliography.

The manuscript has been read by the doyen of Nova Scotian historians and political scientists, Murray Beck, professor emeritus of Dalhousie. His Lunenburg background, experience of Acadia University, eighteen years as Dalhousie's professor of political science, and especially his comprehensive knowledge of Nova Scotia's history and politics, have been brought to bear on this manuscript. I have taken his points unreservedly.

Dean Judith Fingard, of Dalhousie's Graduate Studies, herself an expert on Dalhousie's history, found time to read the manuscript and make several suggestions which I trust I have incorporated, not too imperfectly. Dr T.J. Murray, dean of medicine from 1985 to 1992, has been good enough to read and comment on sections where I deal with the Medical School and has saved me from several pitfalls. Denis Stairs, vice-president academic of Dalhousie, 1988–1993, to whom this project reports, has been a great help. In the midst of far more weighty responsibilities he has answered requests quickly and dexterously.

Two anonymous reviewers evaluated the manuscript for McGill-

Queen's University Press. Thankless labour that, for only a modest reward; but they made valuable suggestions. Mary Wyman typed the
whole manuscript into the History Department's word processor,
chapter by chapter, revision by revision. Efficient, quick, amiable, she
is a paragon. Diane Mew edited the manuscript from end to end. She
is the best editor in Canada I know, whose information ranges from
Caesar to Shackleton, whose travel from Shetland to South Africa;
best of all she is armed with an impatient disdain for prosy writing. She
has spruced up the whole text.

My wife, Masha, has read it all in draft and in proof and I have con-
tinually relied on her judgment and good taste.

P.B.W.
Halifax, Nova Scotia
June 1993

Lord Dalhousie's College

· I ·

A Brave Beginning
1816–1821

Lord Dalhousie comes to Nova Scotia. Halifax in 1816. The Castine Fund. Presbyterian rivalries. Lord Dalhousie's College approved. Scottish educational traditions. Laying the corner-stone, 1820.

Dalhousie Castle lies a dozen miles southeast of Edinburgh, not far from the village of Bonnyrigg, but out in the Scottish countryside, as befits an ancient establishment that dates from the thirteenth century. Of that original building only the foundations and dungeon remain; the main structure now visible was built about 1450, using the salmon-red stone quarried across the South Esk. The castle stands between the South Esk and the Dalhousie burn that flows into it, two streams where salmon and trout still run.

The rivers flow north in this part of Midlothian. The whole country-side, Edinburgh included, fronting on the Firth of Forth, is backed against the Moorfoot hills and the hills of Lammermoor. The history of this Midlothian countryside is shot through with legend, and with the wars against England. Sir William Ramsay de Dalwolsey swore fealty to the English king, Edward I, at Dalhousie Castle, when Edward stayed there on his way to defeat William Wallace at Falkirk in 1298. The Ramsay family were raised to the peerage in the time of the Stuart king, James VI of Scotland and James I of England (1603–25); that did not prevent the first Earl of Dalhousie from fighting with his regiment in 1644 at Marston Moor, down in Yorkshire, on the side of Oliver Cromwell. Cromwell himself wrote despatches from Dalhousie Castle in 1648, a few months before the execution of Charles I in London in January 1649.

After the Union of England and Scotland in 1707, the Ramsays and other Scots became soldiers in the service of Great Britain. The fifth earl fought in the War of the Spanish Succession, 1702–13; another Ramsay signed the agreement for the surrender of Quebec on 18

3

September 1759. The ninth earl, George Ramsay, ours, fought with Wellington in Spain in 1812–14, and at Waterloo in 1815. Watching the ninth earl's panache that terrible Sunday, 18 June 1815, Wellington said of him, "That man has more confidence in him than other general officer in the army." That confidence was not always justified; the ninth earl's compaigning in Spain did not earn him accolades from historians, who pictured him as slow and methodical rather than decisive. Yet he must have been well regarded at the time, for during and after the war he received honours from king and Parliament – a KB in 1813, after Waterloo a GCB, and the official thanks of Parliament.[1]

All that did not help much to repair Dalhousie Castle, which Lord Dalhousie set about after his return from Waterloo. He got an architect to help restore it to its original form, which cost more than he had readily available. Like many British officers after the Napoleonic Wars, he sought a colonial appointment to preserve his military rank and pension. His idea was to follow Sir John Coape Sherbrooke as lieutenant-governor of Nova Scotia and thence as governor general of British North America to which Sherbrooke had been appointed in April 1816. The colonial secretary was Lord Bathurst, the longest serving colonial secretary in the nineteenth century, from 1812 to 1827. His actual title was secretary for war and colonies, a significant combination of responsibilities. He also found it easy to reward service in the Peninsular War with positions in the postwar colonial service. Lord Dalhousie got his appointment to Nova Scotia in July 1816. With his wife and the youngest of his three sons he sailed from Portsmouth on 11 September in HMS *Forth*, a forty-gun frigate. It was a good passage, via Madeira as was common in westward sailings, and she ran into Halifax harbour on the morning of 24 October. Lord Dalhousie came ashore in state the same afternoon.

Lord Dalhousie took to Halifax and to Nova Scotia almost at once. He liked his house and he noted that the "natives," as he at first called Haligonians, "good quiet and plain Burgesses, are inclined to show us every attention."[2] He was forty-six years old, fit, intelligent, and active, driven by considerable curiosity about the world around him. He was a man trenchant of mind and inclined to be authoritarian of decision, though cautious until he had duly weighed up the options. He was experienced and knowledgeable on farming, and was much given to improving old and slack methods in both farming and politics. In his early travels around Nova Scotia he noted much land unfarmed, not because it was not owned, but because the owners did not live up to the terms of the grant, holding it for opportunity to sell it for a fat, but unearned, profit. With the help of Richard J. Uniacke, his attorney general, Dalhousie was able, over the next year or so, to get some

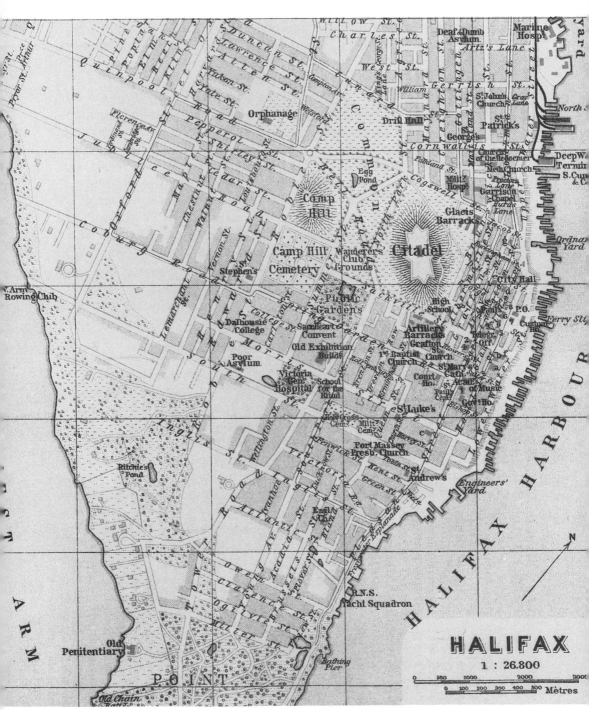

Halifax in 1900. Reproduced from Baedeker's *Canada*, 1907 edition.

100,000 acres returned to the crown for non-performance of the terms of the land grant.[3] His quest for knowledge of his domain is detailed in his journal, and it opens up fresh and interesting vistas on the Nova Scotia of 1816–20, a period not otherwise well served by newspapers and other records. Nothing seemed to give Lord Dalhousie more satisfaction than to mount his horse and explore the Nova Scotian countryside, or to get the admiral on the Halifax station to take him on a voyage around the coasts. Sometimes, as in 1817, he combined both, taking a naval ship around to Pictou, and then riding back to Halifax via Truro. Few governors have been so assiduous at seeing and describing their colony. And he grew to be very fond of it. He wrote to Sir John Sherbrooke, now governor general of British North America, in June 1818, "a more quiet, contented and kind people does not exist, nor can there be a more interesting situation than that which sees a beautiful country and a happy people bursting into prosperity by hard labour."[4]

Nova Scotia had a population at that time of some eighty thousand of mixed origins; Lunenburg County's German settlers came there in 1753, but otherwise the inhabitants of the South Shore and the Annapolis valley were of Yankee background, from both before and after the American Revolution. As Sam Slick once said, those parts were "near about half apple sarce, & t'other half molasses, all except to East'ard, where there is a cross of the Scotch."[5] In religion they were Baptists, Congregationalists, and Presbyterians; the new waves of immigrants that came after 1815 were also Methodists, Catholics, and various splintered branches of Presbyterians. Only one-fifth were Anglicans, and the proportion would get smaller; Nova Scotia was on the eve of a considerable expansion of population that would rise by the 1850s to three hundred thousand.

Halifax had a more pronounced Anglican and British flavour, having both a major military garrision and a large naval base. There were troops enough in Halifax to line both sides of the street from the dock to Government House when Dalhousie arrived, and in the summer months Halifax was the principal British naval base for the whole northwest Atlantic. (In winter they sensibly moved to Bermuda.) There were some handsome buildings already in place: Admiralty House in the dockyard; Government House, finished in Sir John Wentworth's time seven years before; Province House under construction; the Town Clock on the side of the Citadel Hill. The hill itself, at 275 feet above sea level, was some twenty feet higher than it is now; it had yet to undergo the big renovations of 1828–60. Halifax was also a city of churches. There is a handsome watercolour painting of Halifax by an unknown artist done for T.C. Haliburton's 1829 history of Nova

Scotia, the artist having set up his easel just above Dartmouth Cove. Below the Citadel, the steeples marked the skyline of the town: to the left, St Matthew's Presbyterian; then St Paul's Anglican, the style and construction taken straight out of Boston, literally in pieces, in 1750; then the Town Clock, and finally, on the right, the round church, St George's Anglican, that reflected the taste of the Duke of Kent.[6]

Halifax was a town of great contrasts – an amalgam of military, naval, governmental, and commercial enterprises, all gathered together around a large and spacious roadstead. The town itself had been founded only seventy years before. The opulent and the poor, the stone buildings and the wooden ones, lived side by side; social and economic segregation did not yet exist. The town still got its water from wells; in 1817 the Halifax Water Company was formed to supply the town with water by pipes, from a reservoir on the Common. It failed, however; Halifax would get water mains in the 1840s. In 1818 the Assembly passed an act establishing a watch at night in Halifax "for the better preservation of property." A few years later the Assembly passed a traffic act. No one was allowed to gallop a horse on any public highway in Halifax or any other town faster than "a slow or easy trot." Sleighs in winter were to have bells (otherwise you could not hear them coming), and everyone was to drive on the left hand side of the road.[7]

There was a good deal of military and naval pomp and ceremony in Halifax. When Lord Dalhousie's ship left Halifax three weeks after his arrival, she was saluted officially as she made her way down the harbour. Lord Dalhousie rode down to Point Pleasant to watch:

The scene was very beautiful – the Grand Battery [the Citadel], George's Island, Fort Clarence [Dartmouth at Eastern Passage], Point Pleasant, followed each other. The *Forth* was then abreast of the North point of McNab's island, hove to & backed her topsails, so as to lay herself right across the stream, returned the salute, in the most magnificent style, & then filling handsomely stood down to York Redoubt where the Battery again saluted her.

But there were other sides to military life. Alexander Croke, a vice-admiralty judge in Halifax from 1801 to 1815, irascible, conservative, and literary, poked fun at wicked Halifax, all in heroic couplets. A Halifax party in 1805:

> Great Harlots into honest Women made,
> And some who still profess that thriving Trade;
> Great Accoucheurs, great Saints and greater Sinners,
> And all who love great Dances and great Dinners;

Great Ladies who the chains of home despise
And Pleasure's Call *above* decorum prize;
Red Coats, and Blue Coats altogether squeeze
Buzzing and humming, like a Swarm of Bees.[8]

It was only twenty years since Prince Billy (to become William IV in 1830) and his ADCs could drink themselves under the table at Government House. Gentlemen who could manage it went up to visit the brothels on Citadel Hill, concentrated on the two upper streets, Barrack Street (now Brunswick), and Albemarle (now Market). It was a drinking society at all levels. Lord Dalhousie noticed in his travels around Nova Scotia heavy indulgence in rum, especially in the evening when the farm labourers were coming home, "staggering along the roads, noisy & roaring like ill-doing blackguards."[9]

It was a rough and violent society. Richard J. Uniacke's son killed a Halifax merchant in a duel in July 1819. His father, as attorney general, could not prosecute, but told the court that whatever his feelings, they must be subservient to the laws of the land, which he was sure would be administered with both justice and mercy. Young Uniacke got off, but the episode shocked the city, and it began the trend away from duelling.[10] It was not the end of it, however; Joseph Howe was compelled to fight a duel in 1840, but it ended without either antagonist being hit. Howe's opponent missed; Howe, a good shot, fired into the air.

Halifax had been a war town built out of the discovered necessities of one war – the War of the Austrian Succession – and in preparation for others; the Napoleonic Wars with France and the War of 1812 with the Americans were fresh in the minds of every inhabitant. It was only three years since young Thomas Chandler Haliburton slipped from the afternoon church service at St Paul's to run down to the waterfront to see HMS *Shannon* with the captured USS *Chesapeake* behind her, sailing past the Halifax wharves to anchor at the dockyard. The commander of the American ship, Captain James Lawrence, died in Halifax of his wounds, and was buried in St Paul's cemetery with full military honours a few days later.[11]

Effects of the War of 1812
The aftermath of the War of 1812 in Nova Scotia fell on Dalhousie's predecessor, Sir John Sherbrooke, a fellow officer from the Peninsular War. Wellington thought highly of him. "Sherbrooke is a very good officer, but the most passionate man I think I ever knew."[12] Sherbrooke had become lieutenant-governor of Nova Scotia in 1811. When Napoleon abdicated in April 1814, the War of 1812 against the

Americans took a new and decisive turn. British troops were sent across the Atlantic, and some of them came to Halifax. On instructions from Lord Bathurst, the colonial secretary, Sherbrooke was told to occupy "so much of the District of Maine as will ensure uninterrupted communication between Halifax and Quebec." Sherbrooke believed that it would be done best by control over the Penobscot River. That in turn was determined by possession of Castine, a small port that lay right at the mouth of the river on the east bank. Sir John Sherbrooke put together a small fleet of warships and transports and brought two thousand British regulars from Halifax. Castine gave up with hardly a shot being fired, and this was followed a few days later by the surrender of Bangor. Maine from the Penobscot to the St Croix was soon in British hands.

British military administration of the territory was mild and gave little offence to the inhabitants. American laws were left in place, administered by American justices of the peace. Castine became the main clearing port for the whole district. The customs rules were the same as those that obtained at Halifax. The Peace of Ghent in December 1814 required the evacuation of the British, which they duly complied with in April 1815, bringing the Castine money with them to Halifax, some £12,000 Halifax currency.* Lord Dalhousie described it as a large sum of money, the spending of which would certainly need mature consideration.[13] The story has been set down in poetry by Archibald MacMechan, in "The Castine Fund":

> Sir Johnny Coape Sherbrooke's the hero I mean,
> He sail'd off and captur'd the town of Castine,
> The Yankee head-centre for smart privateers
> That had bothered our merchants for nearly three years.
>
> And six months Sir John in that port did remain
> Saving work for collectors of customs in Maine,
> When peace was declared and the war it was o'er
> With ten thousand pounds he sail'd back to our shore.

---

* Halifax currency was a system of reckoning colonial accounts, already established by 1820, that started in Nova Scotia and spread to the other British North American colonies. One pound Halifax currency equalled four dollars American. Thus a shilling was the same as twenty cents. The Newfoundland twenty-cent piece, still prevalent in 1949, was a remnant of this old system. One pound sterling equalled $4.86 American.

The Earl of Dalhousie was governor then,
The bravest and wisest of Scotch gentlemen,
He said, "With this money we got at Castine
We'll found the best college that ever was seen."

Now the ends of the earth and the province have heard
How well and how wisely my lord kept his word;
And on the Parade, where the grass it grows green,
He built old Dalhousie with funds from Castine.[14]

Sherbrooke turned over the money to the imperial treasury in Halifax. Military man that he was, he was a little puzzled what best to do with it. The colony had no public standing debt to be discharged; Sherbrooke's own inclination was towards public works. There was no time, however, to decide upon so weighty a matter, given the slow sea communications between Halifax and London. Thus it remained for Dalhousie to decide. Sherbrooke had left suggestions: a possible Shubenacadie canal, that would open water communication between the south and the north shores of Nova Scotia; an almshouse; a workhouse.[15] Dalhousie noted these ideas.

Within a week of his arrival in Halifax, at a meeting of his Council on 31 October 1816, he asked for an official statement as to the actual amount of the Castine duties and where the money was. The amount was £11,596 and it had been credited to the British government by the commissioner general.[16] A few months later, on 20 February 1817, Dalhousie asked his Council for their suggestions. They were numerous and diverse. S.S. Blowers, president of the Legislative Council and chief justice of Nova Scotia since 1797, suggested the canal or an almshouse; he also suggested a form of shopping mall on the Grand Parade, a colonnade with shops inside it. The Anglican bishop suggested an almshouse. Michael Wallace, the provincial treasurer since 1797, offered no opinion. Of the views around the Council table that day, R.J. Uniacke alone suggested the possibility of a new college.[17]

Lord Dalhousie kept his own counsel, planning to bring down a matured scheme in due time. An almshouse was certainly something the Assembly could well provide for. A few months later Lord Dalhousie wrote to Lord Bathurst:

I would earnestly entreat your Lordship would not require me to appropriate the sum of Castine duties to this purpose [roads and bridges], it would go little way & would soon be lost sight of, whereas there are two or three objects of the highest importance to the Province which that sum would cover & prove of lasting benefit to the Province; but I am not yet sufficiently decided which of these objects to recommend to be adopted. I shall report in the course of the Summer.[18]

Dalhousie's first idea was to spend the money bringing King's College to Halifax. King's had been founded in 1789 at Windsor, Nova Scotia, far from the wickedness and garrison glitter of Halifax. With a good show of unanimity, the Assembly had voted £500 to buy the property at Windsor and £400 sterling annually in perpetuity for the college's upkeep. King's got a royal charter in 1802 and with it an annual grant of £1,000 from the imperial Parliament. Its charter compelled all its students to keep terms of residence and to subscribe on graduation to the thirty-nine Articles of the Church of England. The more Lord Dalhousie learned about King's the less he liked it or the idea of moving it to Halifax. In September 1817 he made an official visit to the college, attending the annual meeting of the Board of Governors. He was much displeased. The president and vice-president were the only professors and they were in violent and open war. The Board of Governors' proceedings were mostly, Lord Dalhousie noted, recriminations, "extremely indecorous and unpleasant." There were only fourteen students, who liked the mild and agreeable vice-president, William Cochran, and hated the strict and ill-tempered president, Charles Porter. They were ill-disciplined generally, riotous in their rooms and amusing themselves, when not at lectures, in careering about the countryside on horseback. They played tricks even on the bishop, their official Visitor. Bishop Inglis came out after one such visit to discover the tails of his horses had been given a close haircut, hanging lugubriously behind them "like a new washed pudding." The state of the building was "ruinous; extremely exposed by its situation, every wind blows thro' it ... The expense of living is very heavy, as there is no butcher market or fish [market] at Windsor. In short there are a thousand objections to it."[19] Although Lord Dalhousie was not in a position to note it, students were educated somehow, on the principle that good students can work almost any system. A few, such as Thomas Chandler Haliburton (BA, 1815) and E.A. Crawley (BA, 1820), were of ability and distinction.

Altogether, Dalhousie's visit persuaded him that there was no good in importing such an institution, with such a charter, into Halifax. It would merely transfer its problems and its exclusivity from one place to another. Besides, a residential college with walls around it, either literally, or metaphorically from having strict terms of residence, was not at all what he wanted. What he had in mind was quite different. It could not be grafted onto that King's root; it would have to be developed from the beginning, with its own roots.

There was another institution Lord Dalhousie had to consider, chartered a few months before he arrived – Pictou Academy. In Pictou County, Presbyterian clergymen, in addition to their regular duties, often instructed promising boys in the branches of higher education. Pictou Academy grew out of this ethos and out of the energy and talent of Thomas McCulloch. He had arrived in Pictou in 1803, a minister sent from Scotland; he soon came to the conclusion that Nova Scotia would not be able to wait for those few ministers from Scotland who were willing to endure the trials of life in the North American woods. The colony would have to grow her own ministers.[20] The upshot was a request to the Nova Scotian legislature in 1815 asking for the right to exist as an academy with no denominational restrictions. The Anglicans who controlled the Council did not like the look of it; it struck them as the beginning of open competition with King's and the Anglican establishment. The Council cleverly (or diabolically, as some thought) amended the act of incorporation so that the trustees of Pictou Academy had to be either Anglicans or Presbyterians. Since Anglicans presumably would not wish to be trustees of such an institution, Pictou Academy was in effect hived off as Presbyterian. The friends of Pictou Academy in the Assembly deplored this result, but they had no choice; they had either to accept the amendments or lose the bill altogether. Under these circumstances Pictou Academy opened in 1818. It began to look and act like a college – its students were soon wearing the red gowns and caps familiar to McCulloch from the University of Glasgow – but the academy had not, as yet, asked for or received the right to grant degrees.

Lord Dalhousie did not think much of Pictou Academy's aspirations to become a college. His preliminary opinion was reinforced when he visited Pictou in September 1817, and discovered to his surprise that Pictou was not the considerable town represented to him but a very inconsiderable village. He later told Edward Mortimer, the chief magistrate of Pictou at whose house he stayed, that a non-denominational college was very desirable for Nova Scotia, "but not in a distant corner of it, at Pictou."[21]

Dalhousie's attitude was shaped by his strong sense of reality, of what was possible. Pictou was, it is true, the centre of a vigorous, litigious, not to say combative Presbyterian community, with the Scottish drive for education both in its ministers and its adherents. But the academy could never acquire, as far as Lord Dalhousie could make out, the weight of population needed to sustain the form and the life proper to a college.

But there was something else. Presbyterians were anything but united. Scottish immigrants to Pictou imported into their settlements in the new world the rich feuds that had marked the old one. The splits and rivalries within the Presbyterian church were not about theology but over the relations between church and state. The first major split developed in 1733 over lay patronage. Who had the final authority to appoint a minister to the living – the lay patron of the district whose lands had helped to subsidize the church or the congregation? In case of dispute, who had the last word?

The Seceders broke away from the Kirk of Scotland on that issue in 1733. Within a decade the Seceders themselves split over the burgess oath: was it lawful or sinful to take the oath required in certain Scottish cities subscribing to the Presbyterian church by law established? Thus came into existence the Burghers (those who did so subscribe) and the Anti-Burghers (those who did not). The Seceders, of both persuasions, were men of sturdy independence; their ministers were often men of humble origin who had been subsidized by their parishes into schools and universities.[22]

Thomas McCulloch was one of these, a Seceder and Anti-Burgher. This group gradually became more numerous in Pictou County, simply because the ministers of the official Church of Scotland, the Kirk, were anything but enthusiastic about emigration to the wilds of North America. In Nova Scotia the two Seceder branches, the Burghers and Anti-Burghers, united in 1817, forming the Presbyterian Church of Nova Scotia. The Kirk Presbyterians called themselves the Church of Scotland.

There was no love lost between the Kirk and the Seceders. In Scotland, the Kirk was composed in the main of moderate, easy-going, civilized men of quiet, unostentatious piety, and often considerable culture. The Seceders were strong on zeal and messianic fervour, but tougher and more strenuous altogether. It was not surprising that more Seceder ministers had come out to Nova Scotia. Those few Kirk men who were in Nova Scotia were apt to be much less gentle and civilized; some were fierce and rabid partisans. They were also Conservatives whereas the Seceders were liberal, sometimes radical. They would become a driving force, when the time came, behind the Reformers of the 1830s.

McCulloch was against the Kirk and much that it stood for. He came to the view that Nova Scotia would have to prepare her own ministers, and began to teach a small select group of students divinity. It was, naturally, anti-Kirk divinity. The Kirk men were thus anti-McCulloch and anti-Pictou Academy.[23]

McCulloch was not a great preacher; he did not have the Gaelic, as his great friend and contemporary, James MacGregor, did, and that in Nova Scotia where Gaelic was much spoken. McCulloch's strength lay in his scholarship; his writing was sinewy, biting, polemical. He himself was apt to be testy and difficult. He was not one who "accepted a few dinners and became a harmless man."[24] Those social seductions were not for him. He relished a fight. He had taken on the Roman Catholics a decade before and published his outspoken convictions on that subject. He fought the Kirk with the same indefatigability. For a man of allegedly indifferent health, McCulloch had a fund of energy. Lean and hard, he drew adrenalin from the vitality of his hatreds: the Kirk, cant, hypocrisy, indifference, and pretence. He was a tough man with a fund of sarcastic humour, even about himself. "Like a beast in winter," he once told his Glasgow friend James Mitchell, "I am living on my grease and that as you know is not very abundant."[25] Little grease, little oil, only a bare minimum of hypocrisy, Thomas McCulloch was a formidable antagonist.

Origins of Dalhousie College

These were the circumstances of Nova Scotian education that Lord Dalhousie had to consider in thinking about a new institution in Halifax. He brought the whole question before his Council in the form of a draft despatch to the colonial secretary on 11 December 1817. Lord Dalhousie dismissed earlier suggestions by Sherbrooke and others for eleemosynary institutions. They were admirable enough in their way, but they seemed to Dalhousie to "rather offer a retreat to the improvident than encouragement to the industrious part of society." There spoke the Scot! Nor would moving King's from Windsor to Halifax help.

At Edinburgh University professors were appointed at modest salaries, with the privilege of lecturing to any who bought an admission ticket from the professor. Such classes were open to all sects of religion, to strangers spending a few weeks in town, to the military, the navy, to anyone in fact who wanted to spend a useful hour or two during the forenoon. The Edinburgh system made professors both diligent and interesting,

as on their personal exertions depend the character of the class and of the individual himself who presides in it.

Such an institution in Halifax open to all occupations and to all sects of Religion restricted to such branches only as are applicable to our present state and having power to expand with the growth and improvement of our society would I am confident be found of important Service to the Province.

Lord Dalhousie proposed £1,000 of the fund to improve and extend the library of the British garrison. It was, after all, the Nova Scotia command that had produced the Castine fund in the first place. The rest, £9,750, would go to support a new college. Lord Dalhousie proposed to put up £2,000 to £3,000 at once to begin a building, leaving the rest as a fund which, duly invested, would produce interest annually to pay professors. He expected that the Nova Scotia legislature would in due time provide a grant matching this annual income. The site for the college would be the Grand Parade. Any present military use he proposed to move to the immediate area of the barracks.

Lord Dalhousie proposed a small interim Board of Trustees, men in Halifax who would be accessible by virtue of offices already held: the lieutenant-governor himself, the chief justice, the bishop (Anglican, of course), the treasurer of the province, and the Speaker of the Assembly. This selection had some obvious weaknesses; three of those dignitaries were already on the board of King's College and might be said to have prior interests. All of them were busy men. But it was not as casual as it looked. Lord Dalhousie already knew how difficult it was to convene meetings in Windsor of the King's College board; one of his chief concerns was that the officers of the new college would be accessible and in Halifax.

The clear point of beginning of a university is not always easy to discern; but Dalhousie College (it did not yet have this name) does have a precise one: that submission of Lord Dalhousie to his Council of 11 December 1817. The eight members of Council gave it their unanimous approval, and it was so entered upon the minutes.[26]

The despatch that went to Lord Bathurst three days later varied only slightly from that submission. To the trustees Lord Dalhousie added the minister of St Matthew's, the Kirk of Scotland church in Halifax. The Grand Parade he defined as "that Area in front of St. Paul's Church."[27] Lord Dalhousie elaborated in writing to Sir John Sherbrooke. The actual college building, he said, would be at the eastern extremity of the Parade, facing St Paul's Church; but the foundations would of course be down on Duke Street; there shops would be set up, to be leased out and which would provide some modest income for the college. (It was in effect an early version of the present Scotia Square.) Lord Dalhousie envisaged a single-storey stone building. Sir John Sherbrooke was enthusiastic; a purpose "so judicious," he said, "cannot but help meet with the approbation of the Secretary of State."[28]

It did. Lord Dalhousie's suggestions Lord Bathurst laid before the supreme authority in Great Britain, the Prince Regent, acting for the incapacitated King George III. The Prince Regent had extravagant habits and a flamboyant taste; once a handsome young man, by 1818 he was gross and fat from years of indulgence. Nevertheless, he had great love for the arts; Brighton Pavilion was rebuilt by him after 1817, and still stands as a remarkable achievement by the Prince Regent's architect, John Nash. That, Regent's Park, and Regent Street, represent only a part of Nash's work under the Prince Regent's lavish if idiosyncratic patronage. The prince's approval of the college proposed for Halifax must have been nearly immediate; Lord Bathurst's despatch is dated 6 February 1818, and it may be properly set down as the official beginning for Dalhousie College:

having submitted them [Lord Dalhousie's proposals for a College] to the consideration of the Prince Regent, His Royal Highness has been pleased to express his entire approbation of the funds in question being applied in the foundation of a Seminary in Halifax, for the higher Classes of Learning, and towards the Establishment of a Garrison Library.

That despatch arrived while Lord Dalhousie was in Bermuda in April 1818, but on his return he was delighted to find that the founding of a college in Halifax had such prompt and unequivocal approval. He asked Council for suggestions in framing a charter for the college, and it was agreed to submit a draft to London. In the meantime work could be started in laying out the ground.[29]

Lord Dalhousie lost no time in seeking information and support from the one quarter he best knew, the University of Edinburgh. He had attended it himself as well as the Edinburgh High School, where he had sat beside the young Walter Scott. Dalhousie never took a degree; in 1787 when he was seventeen years old, he felt obliged to take up a military career after the death of his father. He now solicited the views of an Edinburgh professor of belles lettres who knew Halifax well, the Reverend Dr Andrew Brown. Brown had come to Halifax in 1787 as the Kirk minister for St Matthew's Church, where he stayed for eight years. A brilliant preacher and a leading figure in Halifax society, he did much to try to heal the divisions among Presbyterians. He was well known in Nova Scotia and in the United States as a historical researcher, a scholar unusual for his time in sympathizing with the Acadians. Returning to Scotland in 1795, he travelled back in the same ship as Prince William (later William IV) and so impressed him that the prince recommended him for the Regius Professorship in Rhetoric and Belles-Lettres when it became open in 1801.[30]

Lord Dalhousie wrote to Brown asking him to deliver a letter enclosed to the principal of Edinburgh University, Dr George Husband Baird, also asking for information and suggestions. Dalhousie explained to both men the current state of Nova Scotian education, the

The Grand Parade in 1817, looking south from the site of the future Dalhousie
College. Two of buildings in this drawing still stand: St Paul's Church (1750),
and to the right the National School (1818), now a restaurant.

problem with King's College, how it operated to exclude 80 per cent of the population. The Halifax college would operate under the principles of the University of Edinburgh, with lectures open to all the religions admissible at Edinburgh.[31]

Traditions of Scottish Education
Behind the character and standing of the University of Edinburgh in 1818, and other Scottish universities, there lay a substantial tradition of Scottish religion and education. The essential element of it was the Scottish belief that everyone should have his chance. Going to school was something as important as going to church on the Sabbath, valued as much for itself as preparation for work. The Scottish parish school helped to define the worth of the student in ways that were relatively independent of class and circumstance. John Locke's argument in his 1690 *Essay Concerning Human Understanding* that man is born as *tabula rasa* on which was written experience may have been accepted in England as a philsophical principle; in Scotland that idea came from other origins – parish schools, Presbyterianism, oatmeal and whisky perhaps,

> The rank is but the guinea's stamp
> The Man's the gowd for a' that...

There is much in Robert Burns's "The Cottar's Saturday Night" that speaks to this argument:

> From scenes like these, old Scotia's grandeur springs,
>   That makes her lov'd at home, rever'd abroad,
> Princes and lords are but the breath of kings,
>   "An honest man's the noblest work of God."[32]

In the lecture halls of Edinburgh, Glasgow, Aberdeen, and St Andrew's this came to be a democracy of the mind – that a man's intelligence was what mattered and it should have opportunity to develop. It was not a doctrine for the weak, the lazy, or the faint-hearted: hard work was, the Scots believed, good for minds, as exercise and stress was for muscles and bones. It was achievement that signified.

The beginning of this process of education, the parish school, was expected among other things to prepare an élite for the university and the professions. It provided the necessary instruction in Latin, but it joined to that such utilitarian subjects as surveying or bookkeeping, while still keeping the basic focus on intellectual and moral training. The effect was to allow recruiting of business and the professions from

a wider cross-section of the population than in England, enough to justify the pervasive expectation that careers were open to talent.

The Scots had early organized a system of scholarships that opened
their universities to good students. As a start it was essential to recruit
for the ministry. Every presbytery that contained at least twelve parishes was obliged by a 1645 law to provide an annual scholarship. It
did not meet all a student's expenses; it enjoined frugality; but a poor
student could manage by ekeing out his resources with summer work
as tutor or farm hand. Entrance examinations were unknown at most
Scottish universities. Students were tested in course.

Compared to English universities, the classics were neglected; but
because classics did not occupy the central position they did in Oxford
or Cambridge, university education in Scotland had a more philosophical, scientific character. It is not surprising that alone in Great
Britain the Scottish universities possessed original schools of philosophy. By 1800 the dominant theme of them came to be called the philosophy of common sense, rejecting the metaphysical conclusions of
Bishop Berkeley and David Hume.[33]

Philosophy was thus the first of the university subjects which
Scottish students got their teeth into, their first big adventure in university. If, in doing ethics on the one hand and logic on the other, students
got a double dose of philosophy, the Scottish view was, so much the
better.[34] Philosophy of course included natural philosophy – that is,
science – and the Scots did much with that. It was entirely reasonable
that Thomas McCulloch's interests comprehended theology and medicine and science. His range owed much to his natural genius, but not
a little to his philosophical training at the University of Glasgow.

There was a wholesomeness, a vitality, an intense empirical curiosity
about these Scottish intellectual traditions. That was what Lord
Dalhousie was thinking of when he sought advice from Andrew Brown
and George Baird. He received a long reply signed by both men,
though written by Andrew Brown, giving a history of the university,
how it began with one professor in 1583, and grew as need and funds
allowed. As to qualifications for admission, Baird and Brown made
clear,

The Gates of the University are open to all persons indiscriminately from
whatever Country they may come or to whatever modes of faith or Worship
they may be attached. In fact we do not know that any other disqualification
for admission to the privileges of the University exists, than the brand of
public ignominy or a sentence of Expulsion passed by another University.
Nothing further in the shape of pledge or engagement is exacted from the general Student, than that he take the Sponsio Academica, binding himself to ob-

serve the regulations relative to Public Order, to respect his teachers, and maintain the decorum becoming the character of a Scholar.[35]

They saw advantages in Halifax for teaching by volunteers in professional fields such as law, medicine, and religion. The University of Edinburgh's experience was decidedly in favour of the principle of private lecturing; at Edinburgh, far from being injurious to full-time professors, private voluntary lecturers tended to augment the number and the range of students.

Baird pointed out in a private letter written shortly after that the University of Edinburgh had no power to nominate any of its own professorships: "This total want of power and patronage, I hold to be, without exception, the greatest excellence of the University system. Give the Senatus academicus a right to these and on every vacancy there would be party canvassings and contentions excited which would be equally destructive of our peace, comfort and prosperity." Thus, while Senate ran the internal affairs of the university, the election to chairs and professorships should be vested either in the crown or in some body totally distinct from the college itself. There was much good sense in this; the in-fighting over professorial appointments at Oxford and Cambridge was well known even then.

Professorial salaries at Edinburgh were quite modest. The professor of chemistry was paid only £30 a year. But he drew fees from students; in the 1817–18 session he had five hundred students, and thus his gross income, at two thousand guineas, was more than adequate. Of course Halifax could not produce nearly as many students, and the salaries paid to professors would have to be much more generous; still, Baird said, "your Lordship will not lose sight of the importance of allowing a Professor to depend in some degree on the popularity required by his learning [,] talents and exertions."[36] That idea was salutary for all professors.

Andrew Brown knew a good deal more than Baird about Halifax. He was sure, he wrote Lord Dalhousie, that only a literary institution like a college would promote classics, science, and religion in Halifax. But it was important to remember that the University of Edinburgh was basically at arm's length from the Kirk. The university left religion up to the students, except for those in theology. It made no attempt to determine how students should spend the Sabbath; it had never even had divine service within its walls.[37]

Starting the College Building

Lord Dalhousie submitted most of this correspondence to the trustees of his proposed college – it was called St Paul's College for a short time

– and at the same meeting on 12 November 1818 he produced three different sets of plans for a building. Under Lord Dalhousie's directions an architect, a Mr Scott, was to be employed to prepare a final set of plans embodying, as the board saw it, the best features of each. A month later a minute of Council formally registered the handing over of the Grand Parade as the site and grounds for the new college.[38]

The Grand Parade had been reserved for militia purposes when the town was laid out in 1749, though it had never been military property as such. Locals did not much like it; they felt it got in the way of progress up and down George Street. Paths across it were inevitable. One went on an angle, from George Street across down to the corner of Duke and Barrington streets, descending in its last fifty yards very abruptly. When the Duke of Kent was general commanding at Halifax from 1794 to 1798, he had had the Parade levelled off by having support walls built along the sides facing Duke and Barrington streets. Thus the corner of the two streets was some fifteen feet below the level of the Parade. Those support walls were built with space behind them, used for storing ice. To put a college building at that northern end of the Parade required some structural reinforcement to support the weight of the building and to develop shops from ice houses, but no major changes of alignment and scale were needed.

The session of the legislature of 1819 was the first in the new Province House, which had been under construction since 1811. Lord Dalhousie delivered the Speech from the Throne on 11 February, in the Council chamber, under the portraits of George III and Queen Charlotte. He congratulated the legislature on their meeting for the first time in such a handsome building, and hoped that Nova Scotia, "this happy country," would continue to be blessedly ignorant of the influence of party or faction. After all, the purpose of any legislature, was "the prosperity, the improvement, the happiness of the land you live in." Lord Dalhousie emphasized improvement, but roads and bridges – an Assembly preoccupation – was not Lord Dalhousie's idea of what improvement really meant. "I will submit to you the plan of an institution at Halifax in which the advantages of a collegiate education will be found within the reach of all classes of society, and which will be open to all sects of religious persuasion."[39] By April the Assembly had agreed to match Lord Dalhousie's £3,000 of Castine money, reserved for building, with £2,000 of its own. It professed its warmest thanks for Lord Dalhousie's initiative and hoped that "this Institution may flourish, and continue to the Inhabitants of Nova Scotia a lasting monument of the enlightened policy of Your Excellency's administration."[40]

The *Royal Gazette* of 28 April solicited tenders for supplying the "best iron rubble stone, best white lime, and hard fresh sand" for a building at the north end of the Parade, and for tenders for the masonry work. Plans were available for inspection at the office of Michael Wallace, the provincial treasurer. Wallace had had considerable experience in building; he had been the official mainly responsible for the elegant but costly work on Government House, and was on the committee for building Province House. He was old-fashioned in dress and style, irascible, always on the boil about something, and very much at the centre of things in Halifax. He was connected closely with King's College; he sent his sons there, and married off his daughter Eleanor to President Charles Porter in 1808.[41] He had already been authorized, in March 1819, to buy square timber for construction and there was £5,000 to build with. Given the prices that prevailed in Halifax after the war, that might not go far enough. But Dalhousie was confident that that sum, with £7,000 invested in British Consols, and with a promise of £500 a year from the Assembly, would make a substantial beginning.[42]

In December 1819 the interim Board of Trustees officially applied for a royal charter for the Halifax College, as it was now called. The rules would be those of the University of Edinburgh, in principle taken from the Baird-Brown letters of 1818. Three professors, it was expected, would be appointed, in classics, mathematics and natural philosophy, and moral philosophy. The papers covering this were despatched to the Nova Scotian agent in London, Nathaniel Atcheson, who was instructed to get Bishop Robert Stanser, the only trustee not in Halifax, to sign the official application as the others had done. Bishop Stanser was then on the Continent, but returned to London early in January 1820. The proposal to establish a college at Halifax, and the fact that he was nominated to its Board of Trustees, came to the absentee Anglican bishop as a complete and painful surprise. He would not sign the requisition. As a governor of King's College he was bound to King's; he had been reliably told that King's was in "a ruinous state, and that Funds are immediately wanted for an entire new Building," and he was bound, as official Visitor, to take cognizance of that fact, above all else. He would sign nothing for a Halifax college. So the request to the secretary of state went forward without the signature of the Bishop of Nova Scotia.[43] Though nominated to it, he was never to be a member of the board. That was both a reality and a symbol.

Royal charters were a gift of the crown, but they came with fees for engrossing, sealing wax, and parchment. King's had paid £370 sterling for its charter in 1802; Halifax College would require something like £570 – that is, about £700 currency. When Lord Dalhousie heard that, he and his board called off the royal charter. The price was too heavy; they had better things to do with that kind of money. The building was going to be rather more expensive than expected; it would be cheaper to allow the Halifax College to be established under a simple statute of Nova Scotia.[44]

Lord Dalhousie also sought suggestions, indeed nominations, from Professor James Henry Monk of Trinity College, Cambridge, Regius professor of Greek, for a principal for the Halifax College. The same growing perception of limitation of means animated this request; instead of three professors proposed six months before, it was now, for the moment at least, only one, who would be principal and would combine the teaching of classics and mathematics. The salary offered was £300 a year, with the prospect of it being doubled by fees. The college was now being built, Lord Dalhousie said, and might be ready by December 1820, but the new principal would not be needed before March or April of 1821. The building, though large, would not have accommodation for staff or students, but house rents in Halifax were moderate.[45]

By this time, May 1820, Lord Dalhousie's own career had taken a new turn. He had been bitterly disappointed, indeed extremely angry, when in May 1818, contrary to promises made by Lord Bathurst, the governor generalship of British North America had gone to the earl's impecunious brother-in-law, the Duke of Richmond. Dalhousie was deeply chagrined, and wrote the colonial secretary accordingly: "I have now served my Country 21 years, chiefly on foreign service, I have followed up a Military life without shrinking from any duty or any climate, I have sacrificed every comfort of an independent fortune, every happiness that man can desire in his family ... to serve my Country with distinction." He privately decided that he would serve out his term in Nova Scotia, then retire to Scotland. So he told the Duke of Richmond when on a visit to the Canadas in the summer of 1819.[46] Then in August 1819, when hunting near Sorel, the Duke of Richmond was bitten by a fox. The wound healed, but the rabies he received began its terrible work, and he died agonizingly a few weeks later.

Lord Dalhousie heard the news in Halifax. He made no representations to London; he let the British government decide whether he would go to Lower Canada as governor general or retire to Scotland. He knew enough of the Canadas by that time to suspect that governing them would not be easy. He was told of his promotion in late November 1819; Quebec was quite inaccessible until May 1820, and he was content to winter in Halifax. There were things to be settled, not least the reannexation of Cape Breton to Nova Scotia that had al-

ready been decided in London. Basically he was pleased with his so-
journ in Nova Scotia and with his work; he could deliver his province
to his successor without any basic problems. It was "overflowing with
the necessaries of life, and roused to a spirit of Industry that gives the
fairest promise of happiness and prosperity." So he told himself in his
journal.[47]

There would be some vexations to come in the session of 1820. But
in his prorogation speech on 3 April 1820, Lord Dalhousie was able
to point proudly to the new college rising now above the level of the
Grand Parade.

I earnestly recommend to your protection, the College now rising in this
town. The state of the Province requires more extended means of education;
and this College, open to all classes and denominations of Christians, will afford these means in the situation best suited to make them generally available.
I am myself fully convinced that the advantages will be great even in our time,
but growing, as it will grow, with the prosperity of the Province, no human
foresight can imagine in what extent it may have spread its blessings, when
your children's children shall compare the state of Nova-Scotia to what it is
now.[48]

There was more to this than encomiums and good wishes. Dr John
Inglis, minister of St Paul's Anglican Church, and in effect the coadju-
tor bishop in Bishop Stanser's long absence in England, had been hard
at work arousing the Church of England clergy, and anyone else who
would listen, against a college at Halifax. Inglis was a King's man; he
was the first student to register there in 1788, and he had married
Cochran's daughter in 1802. He had always taken the position that in
Nova Scotia one college was enough, and more than enough "for several centuries," as he put it. In the light of the actual condition of
King's, he was even more fearful and resentful at the building of the
"quite needless and romantic" college at Halifax.[49]

Lord Dalhousie had good reason to have the laying of the cornerstone of Halifax College done with every bit of ceremony, military and
masonic, that the old town and his own energy and power could muster. On Monday, 22 May 1820 troops from the garrison formed a lane
from the Granville Street side of Province House to the Parade and to
the railed enclosure at the northern end. There was already formed a
square manned by the Masons. In ceremonial procession from the
Province House came Lord Dalhousie, the admiral, the chief justice
and all the Council (except for Bishop Stanser) at a few minutes before
two o'clock in the afternoon. There was a vast assemblage of people,
among whom was a reporter from *Royal Gazette*, perhaps young John

Howe, or his half-brother Joseph, then sixteen years of age. Before laying the cornerstone, Lord Dalhousie felt that he owed it to himself and to the college to tell those present:

I have never yet made any public declaration of the nature of the Institution I am here planting among you; – and, because I know that some part of the Public imagine, that it is intended to oppose the College already established at Windsor.

This "College of Halifax" is founded for the Instruction of youth in the higher Classics, and in all Philosophical Studies: – It is formed in imitation of the University of Edinburgh: – Its doors will be open to all who profess the Christian Religion; to the Youth of His Majesty's North American Colonies, to strangers residing here, to Gentlemen of the Military as well as to the Learned Professions, to all in short who may be disposed to devote a small part of their time to study. It does not oppose the King's College at Windsor, because it is well known that College does not admit any student unless they subscribe to the tests required by the Established Church of England and these tests exclude the great proportion of the Youth of this Province ... it is founded on the principles of Religious Toleration secured to you by the Laws, ... and if my name as Governor of the Province can be associated with your future well-being it is upon the foundation of this College that I could desire to rest it. From this College every blessing may flow over your Country: – in a few months hence, it may dispense blessings to you whom I now address; may it continue to dispense them to the latest ages! Let no jealousy disturb its peace, let no lukewarm indifference check its growth.

Protect it in its first years, and it will abundantly repay your care.[50]

The cornerstone was then laid. The grand master of the Masons gave Lord Dalhousie the corn, wine, and oil which were duly poured upon the newly laid stone. A royal salute was fired from the guns at Fort Charlotte, on George's Island; this was followed by three times three cheers from the crowd. It was unforced enthusiasm; there it was, a Halifax College being started, and Lord Dalhousie himself was much liked.

Ten days later, Lord Dalhousie's successor, Sir James Kempt, another middle-aged soldier from the Peninsular Wars, sailed up the harbour and took the oath of office. Lord Dalhousie's tenure of Nova Scotia was at an end. His things were already packed on board HMS *Newcastle*, a Royal Navy frigate anchored off the dockyard, waiting to take him to Quebec. Kempt had been asked particularly to keep a fatherly eye on the new college building on the Parade and, honest soldier that he was, he would follow instructions. That care would be needed more than ever now that Lord Dalhousie was far away in

Quebec City. For, among the cheers of the Halifax crowd at the laying of the cornerstone, Dalhousie could already discern the sound of the grinding of axes.

· 2 ·

New Building, Silent Rooms
1821–1837

Divisions between Nova Scotian colleges. Sir James Kempt. Finishing the building. Proposal to unite Dalhousie and King's College, 1823–4. Nova Scotia's Executive Council and Colonial Office pressure for college union.

Like Julius Caesar's Gaul, Nova Scotia's college geography in 1821 was divided into three parts, all different. King's in Windsor had a fine royal charter and a decrepit wooden building; it was also riven by personal feuds rather more damaging than its building. The second, Pictou Academy, had no charter as a college, but had a useful building and great ambitions. The third part was Dalhousie College, with a handsome new (and expensive) stone building right in the middle of Halifax, almost finished, but having neither principal, staff, nor students – nothing in fact except £8,289.9s.6d. invested in London, a growing debt in Halifax, and that fine property on the Grand Parade.

Sir James Kempt knew this only too well. But he was of Lord Dalhousie's mind, that a metropolitan college in the capital was the best, the only, answer to the potential of a three-way split. Sir James was not perhaps as intellectually vigorous as Dalhousie; the long correspondence between them is like that between the head groundsman and the lord of the manor. Still, Kempt had strengths that Dalhousie had not: he was affable, tractable, sensible, disposed now and then to be disarmingly hypocritical. He thus worked well with local politicians, especially with Simon Bradstreet Robie, the Speaker of the Assembly, whom Lord Dalhousie had sometimes thought of as a low, conniving fellow. Kempt was not a bad hand at conniving himself, when needed.

He was a fifty-five-year-old bachelor, born and raised in Edinburgh, with a fine military record. In Halifax he developed a reputation as rather a gay (in the old-fashioned meaning) blade, disposed to having pretty women around Government House, one of whom was a famous

27

and beautiful grass widow, Mrs Logan. He was liked for his parties and his vivacity. High-toned he was not. Like his predecessor, Kempt was also a great traveller, but rather more practical, having a penchant for making good roads. The Kempt Road in Halifax marks that proclivity.[1]

Lord Dalhousie remarked from the heights of the Quebec Citadel that in only two respects had the Assembly of Nova Scotia disappointed him. They had secretly opposed his wishes on militia appropriations; and their same "want of candour and honesty" was evident with his new college. What he meant was that the Assembly's willing acceptance of his initiative in creating the college was followed by a lamentable lack of support for proceeding with it.[2] Lord Dalhousie had wanted it to be *the* college of Nova Scotia, with King's hived off for that 20 per cent Anglican constituency. The Assembly, riven by its own loyalties, prejudices, and fixations, became difficult, if not impossible, to arouse on the subject of a non-denominational college.

Kempt had been asked to keep a close eye on the building. He did more than that; he positively badgered the engineer, Lieutenant Gregory of the Royal Engineers, and the treasurer of the province, Michael Wallace, to get on with the work, and, even more, to present accounts. By the end of the 1820 working season in November, the stone work was finished, both wings were roofed and slated in, and all that remained was the slating of the centre roof, which could not be finished until the pediment was up. By now it was obvious that the costs would outrun the money available in Halifax, notwithstanding attention to economy – consistent, that is, with the magnitude of the work. Kempt thought the whole building looked very handsome, and it was going to be "a great ornament to the town."[3]

By January 1821 it was clear that the building was about £3,000 beyond the money available. Kempt called a meeting with S.S. Blowers, the chief justice, Michael Wallace, and Speaker Robie, to consider ways and means. With debt now accumulating it was expedient to incorporate the governors of the college. These now were: Lord Dalhousie, Sir James Kempt (or the lieutenant-governor of Nova Scotia, whoever he was), the Anglican Bishop of Nova Scotia, the chief justice, the treasurer of the province, the Speaker of the Assembly, and a president of the college, yet to be named. The 1821 bill for incorporation passed the Council first, then went to the Assembly. The original bill had incorporated in it a promise to donate a further £2,750, above the £2,000 given in 1819, but the Assembly deleted that. £2,000 was enough. At that point two MLAs brought forward a petition from Pictou Academy asking for government aid. Nor was that all: "the

Dalhousie College in 1825, looking north

Windsor people are as clamorous to get some aid to King's College –
in short, there is a general scramble for the *three* Institutions at one and
the same time, and there are many persons who now express the interests of Dalhousie College in a very *lukewarm manner*, who were, when
your highness was here, its firmest supporters."[4]

The 1821 statute was passed, incorporating the governors of "the
Dalhousie College." The chief justice sent a copy of the incorporation
to Lord Dalhousie at Quebec. "You have," Lord Dalhousie replied,
"as you threatened me, placed my name in the front rank, and to that
post of honour I cannot possibly have any objection – my only dislike
to be so put forward, was in the apparent presumption which the
world will ascribe to me." The costs were making him uneasy. So far,
so good; but what of the next stage?

[I]s this child of my hopes to be cut off in its birth? I should be inclined to
charge my good friends Wallace and Gregory with the murder, if it so happens. I was well aware that we were working beyond our means, and I earnestly pressed those gentlemen to a serious calculation of what we had done,
and what we were going to do this last Summer. Nothing of that sort was
done, and now we are deep indeed in difficulties, although I trust not quite
beyond our depth.[5]

Dalhousie College's official legal existence began during the coldest
January in living memory. The harbour was frozen over as far out as
McNab's Island. Ships could come in no further than York Redoubt;
one ship had to be cut out of the harbour for two miles by a military
working party. Sleighs went everywhere over the harbour ice.[6] It was
a chill that seemed to affect the Assembly. Kempt urged them in a special message in February 1821 to vote money for Dalhousie College.
Robie was willing enough, but he had to fight what Kempt called "a
great indisposition" on the part of the Assembly. The best they could
do was to revive an offer made in 1820. As a parting gesture the
Assembly had in April 1820 offered Lord Dalhousie £1,000 to buy the
Star and Sword for his GCB, which were both expensive, the Star especially. At that point Lord Dalhousie was angry with the Assembly for
omitting, surreptitiously, an appropriation for militia inspection and
had refused the gift. Kempt ingeniously suggested that this £1,000 be
given to Dalhousie College instead, a dignified way of disposing of the
money, and one that would gratify Lord Dalhousie. That was done.
Still, it annoyed Kempt that the Assembly gave £400 to Pictou
Academy without any urging from him at all. Technically he could
have blocked it, but to have done so would have created great irrita-
tion and ill-humour. That was not Kempt's style.[7]

Negotiations about a principal for the college went forward as slowly as the building. In October 1821 Lord Dalhousie learned that it was a matter of money; able men could make much more money in England without having to emigrate to the colonies. Lord Dalhousie's correspondent added that "certainty of church preferment would be a great inducement."[8] It was just this that Lord Dalhousie wished to avoid.

For a time Kempt had hopes that the colonial secretary could be persuaded to give the crown's coal revenues from Nova Scotia to aid what should become the main provincial college and university, but Lord Bathurst demurred. Kempt suspected the hands of John Inglis and Bishop Stanser in helping to kill that excellent idea. Inglis was, in Kempt's opinion, a most cunning ecclesiastic, whose indefatigability equalled his guile; as for Bishop Stanser, he had been living in England since 1816 on his bishop's salary doing nothing at all.[9]

By this time, January 1823, some £5,000 was needed to pay the debt on the Dalhousie building. Kempt tried to force the pace with his Board of Governors, but they were not having it. They felt they ought to rest on their oars now that the building was finished, at least until some way might be devised for getting rid of the debt. This was not to Kempt's mind a very sound way of going forward; he gloomily reflected that the building of the college had been done most injudiciously. It was not that the building was not well made – it was; but it had been done with little regard for time and money.

Lord Dalhousie in Quebec agreed. He too was gloomy and disappointed. He thought the very worst thing for the college was to stand still. Perhaps the whole thing should be abandoned. The debt was in any case secured by the capital fund invested in London. Giving that up would mean the end to a noble dream, but perhaps, he said, Nova Scotia was not ready for it:

If the idea of a College in Halifax is pronounced to be premature, be it so. Make that building then a Grammar School, or anything so that it may in some way be useful ... when the parents of Halifax shall see the advantage of an Institution more comprehensive for education than a common school then the College charter may venture to raise its head from the grave, to which the present generation has committed it ...

In all the share that I have had in that Institution, there is only one point, which gives me any regret, and that is, that I was over persuaded by the good Chief Justice and Mr. Wallace to allow my name to be given to it in the Charter. I always felt and thought it an impropriety, and I am convinced it has produced ill-will and opposition to it. From the interest I shall ever feel in its progress, I cannot but be vexed, and disappointed in its premature decay.[10]

It was not quite as bad as that. Robie pulled together some support in the Assembly and Kempt fired off a bold message on 25 March 1823, asking that a loan or some other means be given to Dalhousie College to allow it to pay the debts incurred in its building. It would be, after all, a college open to all denominations; it was not the rival of any other college. It was, said Kempt, "the friend and co-relative of all. I cannot but flatter myself," he concluded, "that it will not be suffered to be stifled in its infancy, and so promising an object, after the great expense already incurred on it, to be rendered useless and abortive." [11]

Kempt hoped that would rally the Assembly, though he warned Lord Dalhousie the next day that no great confidence should be placed in a lower house "subject to be veered about by every wind that blows." And the opposition to Dalhousie College now met with in Halifax, he added, "is not to be believed." John Inglis had, Kempt thought, poisoned the institution's whole constituency. [12]

The Assembly took its time. The question of more money to Dalhousie College was postponed for ten days; finally on 4 April there emerged from Committee of the Whole a resolution that £5,000 should be loaned, not given, to Dalhousie, for five years, without interest. Repayment would be secured by the capital fund of the college invested in England. It passed the Assembly by a vote of twenty-three to eleven. The opposition to any money being offered at all came mainly from the Annapolis valley. [13]

This seems to have tipped the scales in King's consideration of a possible union with Dalhousie. King's with a dilapidated building did have professors and students, though not many of either; Dalhousie College with a handsome new building had neither professors nor students. It was obvious policy to think of uniting the two colleges. Such a union would certainly forestall the ambitions of Pictou Academy! Thomas McCulloch of Pictou Academy had already been warning Dr Inglis about the danger to King's of Dalhousie College, that it would affect King's far more than Pictou Academy ever could or would. Kempt now promoted union actively, and being on the boards of both colleges, he could do something about it. [14] A King's committee was struck in September 1823; they met a committee from Dalhousie, and this was followed by a joint meeting at Government House, Halifax, in January 1824.

The resolutions that emerged from that meeting envisaged a wholly new college, with a new name, "The United Colleges of King's and Dalhousie," in Halifax. The structure was very like that of King's, the president to be an Anglican clergyman, and three or more fellows were also to be Anglican (and unmarried). Those were concessions the Dalhousie board made. On the other hand, Dalhousie College got the professorships, and students, open to any qualified person, of whatever religion; there were also no rules requiring student residence in college. The general aim was to put an end to King's-Dalhousie rivalry. As Inglis put it, to keep up that rivalry would keep both institutions in "poverty and insignificance, because it must be evident that one college will be ample for the literary wants of Nova Scotia, and perhaps of the adjoining provinces, for several centuries."[15]

Lord Dalhousie was delighted with these discussions. Now that union was proposed, he was willing that his own name should disappear and the new united college be called only King's. He felt his name, and that of King's, should not be equated by thus being put in apposition.[16] But Lord Dalhousie's enthusiasm for union was not matched by some governors of King's, notably the chief justice. Blowers stressed the Oxford traditions behind King's, how Oxford enjoyed learned leisure, in peace and tranquillity, far from noisy crowds, far from "the hurry and bustle of trade – and the dissipation, extravagances and bad example of the idle." His other objection was more philosophically pertinent: that the union was an attempt to engraft King's upon a college of quite dissimilar design. Classics was the core of the King's curriculum; at the joint college, classics might well be made subservient to more diffuse interests, that "classical education may be lost in the more showy and dazzling employment of [scientific] experiments and amusing pursuits."[17]

Lord Dalhousie scoffed at these objections. That the morals of King's students would suffer in Halifax, he simply dismissed out of hand. In his experience, Windsor and its surroundings were not remarkable for moral tone. "And I maintain, as proof of my argument, that the studious and quiet habits of the students in the City of Edinburgh form a striking contrast to the gay, hunting, riding, driving, extravagant expenses of the young men at the English universities."[18]

Notwithstanding the objections of the chief justice, the majority of the King's governors were in favour of union. Early in 1824 a bill was drafted to join the two colleges. It would not go to the legislature yet; drafts would be sent to the Archbishop of Canterbury and to Lord Bathurst. John Inglis went over to help things along. Kempt thought Inglis was sincere in the cause of union. After all, King's had officers, energy, and a religious constituency; now it would have a building and metropolitan students. But the Archbishop of Canterbury had other advisers, not the least of whom was Sir Alexander Croke. Croke, of Oriel College, Oxford, had been vice-admiralty court judge in Halifax and had lived on an estate in the Halifax western suburbs, overlooking the North-West Arm. He was an unrelenting Anglican. It was he, with Bishop Charles Inglis and Chief Justice Blowers, who had once put into the King's rules that all entering students had to subscribe to the thirty-nine Articles. The archbishop was thus relying upon a person who had succeeded in making himself the most unpopular man in the province.[19] From whatever influences, or perhaps from his own convictions, the Archbishop of Canterbury refused to accept the proposed union of King's and Dalhousie. When Lord Bathurst concurred in that refusal, the union was dead, at least in the lifetime of those two officials.

Sir James Kempt had not given up hope for the coal-mine revenues for Dalhousie College, and his importuning finally bore fruit late in 1823. The colonial secretary offered £1,000 to both King's and Dalhousie from that source. It was on one condition: that the Assembly match both grants with equal amounts. This offer the Assembly received with considerable coolness. It got Kempt's message in January 1824, and replied to it on the very last day of the session, two months later. The Assembly said it was proposing to review all education grants in the 1825 session, and Lord Bathurst's despatch would be considered then. Then nothing was heard of the subject from the Assembly for five years.

To What Purpose?
By 1824 the Dalhousie College building stood completed at the north end of the Grand Parade, but it stood empty. The governors left matters at a standstill while union with King's was being proposed, ventilated, and eventually rejected. They kept hoping for money, encouraged by Kempt's ineradicable belief that Lord Bathurst could be persuaded to part with the crown revenue from the Nova Scotia coal mines. In the meantime, the Dalhousie College board hired no one, and opened nothing; they did not have sufficient income from endowment with which to pay any salaries. Dalhousie's capital fund was £8,289.9s.6d. invested in 3 per cent Consols in London. It brought in precisely £248.13s.8d. per annum, not enough remuneration for any good principal. As of 12 June 1822, the cost of the building was £11,806.2s.0d.; the final cost was £13,707.18s.3d.[20] An accurate estimate of what this means in contemporary 1990s terms is virtually impossible, but since something is better than nothing, the final cost would represent something like $3 million.[21] It was a great deal of money for one building.

Kempt, in London in the summer of 1825, reported that the Archbishop of Canterbury was still obdurate against any union of the colleges. He also noted that Inglis, since March of 1825 Bishop of Nova Scotia, had in that capacity collected about £2,000 for King's. The failure of union was a great triumph, Kempt reported, to Thomas

McCulloch "and his Gang" at Pictou. Old Michael Wallace, of the Auld Kirk, who hated McCulloch and all his works, would, said Kempt, have a heart attack when he heard that result.[22]

McCulloch had not been idle; he never was. He wrote Lord Dalhousie at Quebec in September 1823, urging that Dalhousie College, if it were to prosper, would have to be attached to some religious denomination. The Anglicans, he warned, would never give Dalhousie College a fair shake, in or out of union, on any matter academic or otherwise, that might interfere with King's needs or King's welfare. Why not, urged McCulloch, put Dalhousie College under the guardianship of the Nova Scotia Presbyterians? Lord Dalhousie replied that to do that would put King's and Dalhousie in a state of perpetual war. His object, he told McCulloch, was to erase all distinctions in higher education in Nova Scotia, so that Protestant and Catholic, Presbyterian and Episcopalian, would all be accepted on the same terms.

But there was more to McCulloch's argument than Lord Dalhousie would allow. It goes to the heart of the difficulty his college was now facing. McCulloch emphasized:

Indeed no well regulated church will be disposed to receive its teachers from a seminary for the soundness of whose principles it can have no guarantee. And it appears to me that the Dalhousie College is most likely to be under the control of persons who with views and feelings inclined to the established Church will not be very apt either to consult the success of the seminary which seems to interfere with the favorite institution of their own religious society ... Thus it would seem that while that seminary [Dalhousie College] is unconnected with any religious body having an interest in its prosperity it is exposed to the attacks of those who are both enterprising and powerful.[23]

The truth was that right across British North America the influence of the churches in education was pervasive and powerful. A college with no denomination behind it, in a world where denominational rivalries and loyalties were a fundamental way of life, was almost doomed. In an age of such intense religious convictions, upon whose loyalty and support could an open, tolerant, non-aligned college depend?

So Dalhousie College languished. A room for a steward is recorded as having been established in December 1825, and in the summer of 1826, by some unrecorded informal arrangement, it agreed to rent out vacant rooms. John Leonhard, a confectioner, rented the northeast corner rooms on the Barrington Street level. In the Assembly session of 1827 Thomas Chandler Haliburton, a King's graduate be it remembered, referred in a fit of temper to "the Pastry Cook's shop called

Dalhousie College."[24] The air of almost deliberate negligence annoyed Philip John Holland, editor of the *Acadian Recorder*, and his impatience showed in an editorial on 27 October 1827:

Months and years have passed and our ears have again and again greeted the joyful report that this institution would very soon open its doors ... We [now] pass it without thinking of the purposes to which it should be applied and for which it was built ... Where, we ask, lies the fault? It was planned, wisely in our opinion, by Lord Dalhousie. If those who supported him thought otherwise, and determined at a future time to withdraw that support, they betrayed the interest of the province most shamefully ... If the design be good, why has it not been forwarded? and why has so large a sum been expended to no purpose? ... As to the utility of a college in Halifax no serious objections have been stated openly or candidly; nor do any seem to be entertained except by those who are fearful of its interference with other institutions, and who in an indirect manner oppose its success. Of its injuring the Windsor or Pictou institutions there cannot be the smallest apprehension ... is Halifax to be the only place considered unworthy of possessing a learned institution?

Thus it was that D.C. Harvey felt impelled to write the oft-quoted sentence in his 1938 Dalhousie history: "Dalhousie College was an idea prematurely born into an alien and unfriendly world, deserted by its parents, betrayed by its guardians, and through its minority abused by its friends and enemies alike."[25]

It is not difficult to contrive conspiracies out of this strange tale of cost overruns and delays, with nothing to show for it after a decade and £13,000 but an empty building with a pastry shop in the bottom corner. The great expense of the building itself, the apparent absence of any strong, positive, active interest on the part of the Board of Governors, makes it look as if Lord Dalhousie, Philip Holland, and D.C. Harvey were right in suspecting something was very much amiss. Was it not true that of the six-man Board of Governors, the chief justice, and the Anglican bishop were vitally interested in that other institution, King's? Was it not evidence of Lord Dalhousie's incapacity as a judge of men to appoint men to the Dalhousie board already on the King's board? These are baleful questions that lie unquiet in the mind and are not easily put to rest.

The expense is undeniable; the college could have been built at least one-third cheaper had it been started in 1823 instead of 1819 just after two major wars, when prices were still high. There is also good evidence that Lord Dalhousie was persuaded to expand the original plan of a one-storey design, as hopes for union with King's developed in 1820 and 1821. That probably explains the rather attractive second-storey addition, giving life to an otherwise low and not very distinguished front.[26]

Nevertheless straightforward answers are possible. Lord Dalhousie did not want an absentee board of governors, but preferred people in Halifax who could act and work. He also seriously underestimated the importance of religious affiliation, of local resistance to a "godless" college, and how difficult it would be for a college with no denominational backing whatever to develop roots of its own. Even the new University of London, created for the same reasons as Dalhousie College, had difficulties; after it was started in 1828, it was forced to create King's College, an Anglican establishment, within it. In short, Lord Dalhousie could command, could create; he could not furnish an enthusiastic or loyal constituency for his college.

But there is something more. Lord Dalhousie had received some support for his ideas from his Council, and tacit, though grudging, support from the Assembly in 1820. The real problem with his college may well have been in the Council. Lord Dalhousie was conservative by habit and thought; Nova Scotia was his first posting as a civil governor and in the coinciding of his ideas with his Council's at many points, he may well have misread the men themselves. He got along well with them; they were of his world and manners, and that made his misreading all the easier. Most of them had been in office, and would so remain, for a long time. Blowers had been on Council since 1797 and would stay until 1833. Richard Uniacke was attorney general from 1797 to 1830, treasurer Michael Wallace the same. They and their nine other colleagues *were* the government; no one got an appointment to office without being nominated by one of them. Of the twelve members of Council in 1830 at least five were related by marriage and family. Judge Brenton Halliburton, perhaps its ablest member, was appointed to Council in 1815 by Sir John Sherbrooke; he was married to Bishop Charles Inglis's daughter. By 1830, Halliburton's father, two uncles, his father-in-law, two brothers-in-law, his son-in-law (plus three other assorted relations) had all had seats on the Council at one time or other, and five were members at the same time.[27] Halliburton's boisterous abilities were well liked by Lord Dalhousie; he was distinguished, as Dalhousie pointed out, "by great fluency of conversation, and a loud and vulgar laugh at every word." His law was not extensive but, like his wine, it was of the very best quality.[28] Halliburton's group knew each other well, and they shared views about politics and society. Most were Anglicans, although Wallace was a Kirk Presbyterian; they had seen several governors come and go, each with their own penchants and peculiarities.

The Council thus knew perfectly well how to handle governors. Give them their head a bit, let them gallop around with their own peculiar interests for a while; if they press something they want very much, let them have it – on principle. But take care that the Council control the practice. Dalhousie College is a case in point. Lord Dalhousie had found his Council accepting his ideas; they would not set their will against the governor's. They did not have to. They could recover any ground in their own sweet way, in their own good time, and there was lots of that. Thus it was that Dalhousie College was betrayed by its guardians, for its guardians neither really believed in it, nor were sincere in wanting it. The Council had simply bided its time, allowing natural difficulties their way, even abetting them from time to time. A few years later, in 1843, Joseph Howe commented on this very point:

It appears to have been the fate of this Institution [Dalhousie College] to have had foisted into its management those who were hostile to its interests; whose names were in its trust, but whose hearts were in other institutions. These, if they did nothing against, took care to do nothing for it – their object was to smother it with indifference.[29]

The Assembly was not much more charitable, though a good deal more open. In 1829 a resolution was proposed that the £5,000 loan of 1823 be called in. Beamish Murdoch, historian and lawyer, moved in amendment that the £5,000 be left with Dalhousie, provided the college be put into operation according to its original design within some reasonable period. Murdoch's amendment was defeated, and the original motion passed by eighteen votes to nine.[30]

This put the governors of the college fairly up against it. They did not have £5,000 on hand, except that endowment in London. They had made efforts to find a principal; the most promising candidate was Dr J.S. Memes of Ayr Grammar School, Scotland, recommended by Lord Dalhousie. Correspondence with Dr Memes opened in 1828; but the Assembly resolution forced the governors to back away for the time being, though still holding out hopes that they would be able to open the college ere long. Lord Dalhousie, now in England and about to leave as governor general of India, wrote the governors that he could raise £500 himself, and might be able to promise £500 annually. But in the autumn of 1829 they authorized the secretary to put any rooms in the college that were vacant and unoccupied out to rent to the highest bidder.[31]

At the 1830 session of the Assembly Michael Wallace gave a long-awaited report on the college. On the east end of the building there was a grammar school of fifty-five boys, on the west a painting school. The pastry cook remained. There was income from those rentals. The capital sum of the endowment was, however, not under the control of the governors, but under a triumvirate: Lord Dalhousie, Chief Justice Blowers, and Michael Wallace himself. The governors were only authorized to receive the dividends from the London agents, Morland, Duckett and Co. If the Assembly were to insist upon getting their £5,000, the sale of the building and the Parade adjoining would probably bring in that much; but Wallace could not bring himself to believe that "the Assembly could be disposed thus to annihilate the plan adopted by Lord Dalhousie for the promotion of useful learning in the Town of Halifax." He asked the Assembly to postpone collecting the money until a more propitious time. Indeed, said Wallace, the college was about to start; a principal had already been selected and was waiting to come out to Halifax.[32]

The Assembly was none too willing. Lawrence Hartshorne moved that the £5,000 be forgiven Dalhousie College, but that went down overwhelmingly. James Boyle Uniacke moved that the loan not be called in, since hope now was that the college would open in a year. That, too, was defeated. Alexander Stewart (liberal but shifting gradually to the right) moved that Dalhousie be given three years to pay its debt. That the Assembly accepted.

With three years' grace now available to them, the Dalhousie governors took only four days to decide to ask Dr Memes to come as principal, and as soon as possible. His salary was to be £300 a year plus an estimated £100 or so from student fees. A delay then ensued, and there is some evidence that the Dalhousie governors wanted Dr Memes ordained first. He was a lay person, not a divine; he was famous for his books, the *Memoirs of the Empress Josephine*, and a *Life of Canova*, the Italian sculptor. These works, estimable no doubt, did not have the right ring to them. In British North America, college principals then (and later) were usually men of the cloth. McGill broke this tradition in 1852 when it appointed a lawyer as principal, and more dramatically in 1855 when it appointed J.W. Dawson, a scientist, of Pictou County, who would remain until 1893. But in 1830 ministers were the rule; ordination for Memes was a form of insurance. Dr Memes gave up Ayr Grammar School as of 1 October 1831, and was proposing to embark for Halifax on the 12th.[33]

The Colonial Office Intervenes
But he never did sail. The Colonial Office intervened; it now revived the idea of Dalhousie's union with King's. The old Archbishop of Canterbury, Charles Manners-Sutton, had gone to his heavenly reward

in 1828, and the former colonial secretary, Lord Bathurst, had gone to being president of the Council. Sir George Murray, the new colonial secretary, now determined that King's would be united with Dalhousie. The weight of his opinion – and of his four successors in that office – now swung portentously behind the project. If that were to happen, it had always been understood by King's (and Dalhousie) as a prior condition that Dr Charles Porter, president of King's since 1807, would be president of the united college. Porter was, more-over, Michael Wallace's son-in-law, and that connection helped to strengthen his present, and future, position. It also left Dr Memes in Ayr.

The Colonial Office had fat files on the two Nova Scotia colleges, and on Pictou Academy, not all of it accurate, some of it naive, and most of it grossly underestimating the strength of intense religious loyalties in Nova Scotia. As administrators often would, the Colonial Office officials assumed that the rationality of their proposals would automatically recommend them to any thinking legislator or voter. Sir George Murray in 1829 opened up several options. One was selling Dalhousie College lock, stock, and barrel, and after its debts were paid, giving the funds that remained to King's. Alternatively, he suggested that King's could move to Halifax into the Dalhousie College building. Amid these brutal options he pointed out the great inconvenience of college schemes that were too expensive for the purpose, "so strongly exemplified in the case of Dalhousie College."[34]

His successor, Viscount Goderich, was more decisive. The annual £1,000 British parliamentary grant to King's would be halved in 1833 and terminated altogether in 1834. He thought the Assembly should not ask for, nor expect, repayment of the £5,000 from Dalhousie College. The boards of governors of the two colleges met in January 1832 in Halifax to consider the full implications of this verdict. Union proposals emerged on virtually the same basis as those of 1823. The Speaker of the House, S.G.W. Archibald, on both boards, dissented from this decision, not liking the contradictions of two quite different systems patched together, arguing that a constitution of the two colleges would need legislation.[35]

Sir Peregrine Maitland, lieutenant-governor from 1828 to 1832, was thin, austere, and Methodist. But he was also a realist, and was quite certain that a union between King's and Dalhousie was essential, and the sooner the better. Dalhousie College, he said, "possesses a substantial building in a state of great forwardness, and a Constitution ... well suited to the wants of the Province and to the opinions which are prevalent in British North America." The Assembly was becoming clamorous for the repayment of the Dalhousie loan, and it has not so far shown much disposition to be indulgent to a college which, after all, was "to be perfectly open to all religions."[36]

King's was also getting a union on virtually its own terms. As in 1823, union was conditional on its Anglican exclusiveness being transferred to Halifax. In effect, Dalhousie would be made a non-sectarian section of King's College, Halifax, with Charles Porter as president. To those King's terms, Lord Goderich was unhelpful and unrepentant. Never mind that the Dalhousie College board had been willing to give up its individuality to King's; in effect Goderich agreed with S.G.W. Archibald, that the Nova Scotian legislature would have to be the arbiter of such a college union, and that union was not to be saddled with terms the legislature could not or would not accept. Goderich's successor, Lord Glenelg, was even more firm, deploring King's resistance to the only measure that, in Glenelg's view, could put colleges in Nova Scotia on a sensible basis. Glenelg even talked of recommending to William IV that the King's royal charter be annulled. It was, said Glenelg, a question of "the existence of any College at all in the Province."[37]

King's now fell upon dark days. In vain was Dr Porter sent to England to plead its cause. By 1834 the parliamentary grant was cut off, and all King's had left was the annual £400 sterling from the Nova Scotia legislature. King's went on determinedly, with four students. It reminded G.G. Patterson of the story of the bull that attacked an oncoming railway engine: courage admirable, judgment wanting![38]

Dalhousie, King's, and Pictou Academy

The lieutenant-governor now on the scene in Halifax was Sir Colin Campbell, who came in July 1834. Like his predecessors, Sir Colin was a military man who had served in Spain and at Waterloo. He was fifty-eight years old, gregarious and hearty. His weakness was his political baggage: he had too many old prejudices; he was not skilled enough to deal with questions on their merits, and he preferred to rely on local advice which was too often self-interested and strongly conservative. He was, in short, naive, friendly, and in some circumstances dangerous. At first he enjoyed a good deal of local popularity, and was soon the patron of a host of local organizations. He braved the cholera epidemic of 1834, and won plaudits for visiting its victims at the Dalhousie College cholera hospital and elsewhere.

The cholera epidemic had been brought to the Maritimes by immigrants in festering ships, and not even isolation on McNab's Island could contain it. It was spread by unclean drinking water, especially in summer. Halifax still got its drinking water from wells; good fresh water from Long Lake would be brought to town only in 1847.

Cholera was an ugly and dangerous disease, striking with little or no warning; by the time you knew you had it, it was often too late. It broke out in August 1834, and by the end of that month there were thirty-five new cases and fifteen deaths every day. About one-third of the cholera victims were treated at the Dalhousie College cholera hospital, the rest at home. By the end of September the epidemic was waning, but by then some four hundred people, out of Halifax's population of fourteen thousand, had died.[39]

Two large rooms at the west end of the Dalhousie building had been rented to the Mechanics Institute in 1833, to be given up on a week's notice, as doubtless they were during the cholera epidemic. But the Mechanics Institute returned, and through organizing and sponsoring lectures and meetings on a great variety of subjects, became what Howe was to call the "University of Halifax." By the end of the 1830s it had become the Halifax community centre, not a bad function. When Dr Thomas McCulloch came to lecture at the Mechanics Institute on affinities between chemicals, fifty people had to be turned away.[40]

McCulloch was already anticipating that Pictou Academy might not be able to go on in its present form. It had fallen upon darker days, too. In the past its difficulties owed much to the hatred of it by the Auld Kirk in Pictou and their influential ally in Halifax, Michael Wallace. Wallace died in October 1831, aged eighty-seven, irritable, unyielding, but powerful to the end. Lord Goderich had judged the lobbying for and against Pictou Academy correctly, and in July 1831 had instructed Maitland that a bill should be passed giving Pictou Academy some permanent support. That was easier said than done. Maitland found it impossible to reconcile McCulloch with his Kirk enemies. Pictou town was in a state of war between those hard Presbyterian rivalries; the 1830 election had produced riots that shocked and pained Joseph Howe, and convinced him that the real villains were the Kirk men, no matter whether they had a reverend in front of their name or not.[41]

The 1832 act "to Regulate and Support Pictou Academy" was a compromise, initiated by a Council weary of the war in Pictou. The academy was given £400 per annum for ten years, £250 of which was to go to McCulloch as annual salary. It was given on condition that five of the original Seceder trustees resign and allow the lieutenant-governor to nominate others. Several of the best did resign, and Maitland appointed Kirk men in their place. The purpose was to broaden Pictou Academy's base of support; but the effect was to transfer the war to inside the Board of Trustees. Maitland hoped that it might work itself out. But disputes so deep rarely work themselves out;

if anything, they are apt to grow worse. Feuds continued, the academy suffered, students fell off; McCulloch was disheartened. Had all his years of work, of self-sacrifice, come to this? But he was tough and philosophical:

To maintain it [Pictou Academy] in existence I drowned myself in debt and for years kept my family labouring for nothing and nobody said, Thank you. After a grievous struggle I have neither debt nor wealth but the world is before me and though at my time of life folks get a little stiff about the joints mine I must put to the test ... Pictou has very little appearance of being much longer a place for me ... To begin the world again my whole stock is health and determination...[42]

The fate of Dalhousie College was also uncertain. The Assembly had by 1835 become impatient. The three years' postponement of Dalhousie's £5,000 debt had, with two years' more of grace, lengthened to five years. William O'Brien moved on 4 February 1835 that the House exact payment, that the attorney general take the necessary steps. John Johnston went further and demanded that the endowment in London be made over, and that some useful building, a poorhouse or a lunatic asylum, be established in Halifax with the money. The Johnston amendment was defeated overwhelmingly, but O'Brien's carried, twenty to sixteen. The Dalhousie Board of Governors called a meeting on 20 April, and addressed the two surviving trustees of the Endowment Fund – Lord Dalhousie and Chief Justice Blowers – asking them to transfer the funds to Halifax to meet the £5,000 now required by the province, to pay some expenses owing to the estate of Michael Wallace for building, and to pay for some repairs "now absolutely required."[43]

It sounded desperate and decisive, but it wasn't. Both Sir Colin Campbell and Lord Glenelg feared that paying the £5,000 back would require either the sale of the college or alienating most of the endowment; if either went, union of the colleges – still a hope – would become impossible. So they devised a means of once more putting off the evil day of reckoning. In the Speech from the Throne opening the 1836 session, the lieutenant-governor appealed to the House to relinquish its claim of 1835, so that there might be sufficient funds "for establishing and maintaining an United College upon liberal principles." The House was willing to listen. It asked for and got extensive accounts and correspondence of both colleges, which were laid before the House on 7 March.

Dealing with them created considerable discussion. Alexander Stewart moved that while the House approved of having only one college, the governors of King's had stoutly refused to give up their charter, and that as the session was already advanced, further decision should be put off. For the time being the £5,000 claim would be suspended. Stewart's comprehensive resolution created a divisive debate. A sweeping amendment was proposed by a leading Methodist, Hugh Bell, newly elected for Halifax: that since every Nova Scotian had an equal claim to education, the House could not acknowledge "the rights of any particular Church or Denomination whatever to preference or predominance of any kind," and that the House was grateful for the recognition of that basic egalitarian principle by Lord Glenelg and his predecessors. Such even-handed non-denominationalism was more than the House was prepared to stand for, and Bell's amendment was decisively defeated by thirty-one votes to five. In the end, when the House voted on Stewart's main motion, the result was a tie, which the Speaker broke by voting in favour of it. Sir Colin Campbell was not pleased. Closing the 1836 session he urged the Assembly to take action next year, for there was not, he said, "means within the Province for maintaining two Colleges."[44]

But the Assembly did not take action in 1837, and when action did come, in 1838, it took a quite different form. In truth, the project for uniting King's and Dalhousie, accepted by Lord Dalhousie, urged by Lieutenant-Governor Kempt and his successors, insisted upon by every colonial secretary after Lord Bathurst, had finally come to an end. It was defeated by the indomitable will and indefatigable energy of the Anglicans in Windsor and Halifax, defending an increasingly anachronistic status quo. King's and its supporters were not malicious; it is proper to say they were interpreting their rights and their duties as they saw them.[45] But there was a world of fighting in those narrow perceptions of rights and duties. King's was the first college in Nova Scotia; it was also the first to repel, successfully as it turned out, the dangerous idea of One College. In its 1823–4 form, which Lord Dalhousie himself accepted, union may well have been unworkable. At the least, the result might have been two colleges on one campus, perhaps shaking down eventually into one institution, or perhaps ending like King's College in the University of London after 1828. That would have been better than what did happen. In any case, the Archbishop of Canterbury killed the 1823–4 proposal, and by the 1830s neither colonial secretaries in London nor the Legislative Assembly in Halifax were willing to accept union on King's terms. By 1838 the Assembly had acquired a new sense of itself and its purposes, and was imbued with a growing and restless distrust of the Council's stifling, octopus-like grip on the province's institutions. King's had been part of that. The new movement to energize Dalhousie College was part of a broader political struggle that came to be called responsible government. Those initiatives came from reform-minded men of the Assembly.

· 3 ·

One College or Several?
1838–1847

Joseph Howe and radical politics. The 1838 Pictou Academy
Bill. Failure to appoint Edmund Crawley. Thomas McCulloch
comes and Dalhousie College opens, 1838. The rivals,
Queen's College and Dalhousie, 1840. The Reform party and
"One College." McCulloch's death, 1843. Dalhousie becomes
moribund.

Little of radical politics had been seen in Nova Scotia until 1827 when
the Pictou *Colonial Patriot* first appeared, with Jotham Blanchard
as its editor and Thomas McCulloch contributing editorials. Joseph
Howe at first disagreed with both, but the more he read, the more he
came to their point of view. Howe expressed himself differently, with
more patience and tolerance, not being as pugnacious as Blanchard or
McCulloch, and still basically a moderate. His Halifax *Novascotian*
was growing steadily in circulation and influence simply because it sur-
passed the others in useful information. Howe was the first editor in
Nova Scotia to take seriously the reporting of Assembly debates. What
the *Acadian Recorder* and other Halifax papers did was to offer small,
irregular summaries. Howe began reporting debates in 1828, doing it
all himself, and increasing the range and comprehensiveness of the reports as their popularity grew. They were a remarkable education for
everyone who read the *Novascotian*, or had it read to them. Not least
was it an education for the editor himself. Nor did Howe confine himself to that. His press published T.C. Haliburton's *History of Nova
Scotia* in 1829, and *The Clockmaker* was serialized in the *Novascotian*
in 1835. The latter was so popular that Howe put it out as a book in
1836. This is what D.C. Harvey referred to in a famous *Dalhousie
Review* article in 1933, as "The Intellectual Awakening of Nova
Scotia."[1]

That, of course, comprehended politics as well. There had always
been friction between the Assembly and the Council, inevitable in any

two-chamber government. But it was only after the election of 1836 that it became more serious. When the Assembly met in 1837 there was for the first time a number of reform-minded members, dissatisfied with the way political institutions in Nova Scotia had been working. How big that group was depended on the issue and the men, but the division on Howe's Twelve Resolutions of 1837, which severely criticized the working of the Council (in both its modes), was twenty-six to twenty. That forced Lord Glenelg to order the complete separation of the Council into its two functions, legislative and executive. The Assembly had won a major victory.

The Dalhousie College victory followed the next year. Most Reformers were behind that move too. Two men were the moving spirits: S.G.W. Archibald, the Speaker of the House, and his son, Charles Dickson Archibald. At sixty years, Archibald senior was suave, handsome, well-mannered, and spoke with great ease and authority. He was a Seceder Presbyterian, a man of convictions who deployed them without cant or aggression. He had long supported Pictou Academy, as he had opposed the exclusiveness of King's, but he was well capable of judging Thomas McCulloch's weaknesses as well as strengths. Archibald in later years grew too conservative for Howe and his Reform friends, but they always got along well and Howe liked him to the end.[2]

His son, Charles Dickson, was born in 1802, the eldest of fifteen children in what was a singularly happy marriage. Charles sat for Truro from 1826 to 1830 when his father was Speaker of the Assembly. The young man married an English heiress in 1832 and moved to England four years later. But he was back and forth to Nova Scotia a good deal, and he may have been as influential as his father in devising the ingenious idea of bringing McCulloch's restless energies to the service of Dalhousie College.

McCulloch was now feeling his sixty-two years. Although he had lived most of his adult life in Pictou, the triumph of his Kirk enemies within Pictou Academy, an institution he had founded, nurtured, and bled for, was hard and bitter. Pictou, he told his Glasgow friend, James Mitchell, in November 1834, "has very little appearance of being much longer the place for me." A year later, S.G.W. Archibald was trying to nudge him in the direction of Dalhousie College; still McCulloch clung to Pictou. Halifax was to him a hotbed of toryism; if he went there, he would be, he said, "a presbyterian among church [Anglican] bigots and a Seceder among Kirk [Presbyterian] bigots"; hardly very enviable. At this stage in his life he had no great ambitions left; in 1818 it would have been different, being principal or president of Dalhousie College, but of course that would not have happened under Lord Dalhousie.[3]

The Archibalds, father and son, knew that story. Though S.G.W. Archibald was educated in the United States, Charles was a product of Pictou Academy and admired McCulloch for his talent, pluck, and perseverance amid privations. McCulloch's situation now was worse than in former years, though at no time within Charles Archibald's recollection had "your worldly circumstances rendered you an object of envy." What animated young Archibald and his father was not charity but respect: "Without flattery I can say that the course of Lectures on Chemistry which you were delivering when I left Halifax [for England] nearly six years ago [February 1830], would bear comparison with any I have ever attended."[4]

The bill to effect the change in McCulloch's circumstances was called "An Act to Alter and Amend the Act to regulate and support Pictou Academy." The old act of 1832 gave £400 to Pictou Academy, with £250 of it specified as salary to McCulloch. The new act split the £400, leaving £200 to the academy, and the other £200 going to the Dalhousie Board of Governors to pay McCulloch as principal. The bill created a considerable stir in the Nova Scotia legislature. It went through first and second reading on 21 March 1838 without a word of opposition. It went through Committee of the Whole in the same way. Then the opposition struck. The Anglicans were led by J.B. Uniacke, and the Roman Catholics by Lawrence Doyle, both of whom noisily denounced the bill; it was being smuggled through the House, they said. Speaker Archibald remarked he had no objection to having the bill sent again to Committee of the Whole if certain members wanted their objections heard. Meantime, a seven-year-old libel against McCulloch was published and sent to members of both houses. The opposition included the Anglicans, the Roman Catholics, who had never forgiven McCulloch for his anti-Catholic diatribes of thirty years earlier, and most, if not all, of the Kirk men. Young Archibald went to work on the Baptists. They were assured privately that they would have their man, the Reverend Edmund A. Crawley, as the Dalhousie professor of classics. There was no express agreement or contract but, as Charles Archibald said, "there certainly was an implied contract and coalition entered into with that party [the Baptists]." Archibald's letter to McCulloch reveals much about the pressures for and against the Dalhousie College idea:

We find the Church of England, the Kirk and the Roman Catholics leagued together to defeat this Measure and why? – purely because it contemplates a little honour and moderate provision for you – Against such an alliance your friends and party cannot stand and it is not only in reference to this matter, but to an immense variety of other subjects that I consider a good understanding between the leading Sects of Dissenters to be highly politic and indeed indispensable. Should you come to preside over Dalhousie College you must endeavour as far as possible to plan all denominations on an equal footing, but in the circumstances of the Country and in the nature of things, it must become essentially a Dissenting Institution – and it is not one of the least advantages which I foresee that its Establishment will unite the Presbyterians of your Church and the Baptists and the Methodists. I do not wonder that the Bishop has always opposed the opening of this College, for it requires no great prescience to enable one to predict that it will concentrate into one focus the scattered Bands which singly he has hitherto been able to put down.[5]

In the end the Pictou-Dalhousie bill passed the Assembly by twenty-six votes to seventeen, a surprisingly large majority. "This is a queer world," wrote Thomas Dickson, the MLA for Pictou, "and I verily believe that some of both branches of the Legislature are some of the queerest people in it."[6]

It was just as queer in the Legislative Council. Its basic instinct was to postpone the whole bill; the Kirk men canvassed for that idea, but they were fought off. Pros and cons were heard at the bar of the Legislative Council. The Reverend D.A. Fraser, a staunch Kirk man, said the bill had been produced in secret and had he known of it sooner he could have got thousands of signatures against it. That led the Seceder minister Hugh Ross to remark that if the reverend gentleman brought forth a petition to remove George's Island from Halifax to Pictou he could have got signatures for it! The treasurer of Dalhousie, Charles Wallace, bearded James Tobin, a member of the Legislature Council, over breakfast on 10 April to try to get him to oppose the bill – anything to keep that Seceder McCulloch out of Dalhousie, even if it meant not opening it. Notwithstanding all that, the bill emerged unchanged on 10 April and became law a week later.[7]

As this was being accomplished the Reverend Edmund Crawley was already writing McCulloch with suggestions for the proper curriculum in a college of three professors, in particular about classics, to which professorship he considered himself already appointed. Crawley had graduated from King's in 1820, became a lawyer, and in 1827 helped to lead the split from St Paul's Anglican Church to found Granville Street Baptist Church. He then went to the United States to study for the Baptist ministry, graduating eventually from Brown University. He was able, knowledgeable, energetic, high-handed, and he carried with him no small estimate of his own capacity. His application for a professorship went to the Dalhousie board before the bill had even come up in the Assembly. Crawley was more importunate than greedy. He offered to serve as professor of classics with little or no salary, if that would help. But he wanted, indeed it seemed that he required, the appointment. He saw Charles Wallace a couple of days before the appointments were to be made and received from him flattering assurances and best wishes for his success.[8]

McCulloch was surprisingly patient with all of Crawley's importunities. He knew how much the passage of the Pictou-Dalhousie Act had depended upon Crawley and his influence with the Baptists. Still, McCulloch said, Crawley was premature, and his allusions to the importance of Latin and Greek at the University of New Brunswick and at King's magnified the role of classics too much. Nova Scotian opinion was not ready for it, nor was McCulloch. There is much good sense in McCulloch, and nowhere does it show better than in his long letter to Charles Archibald on this point:

[T]hat boys should in Halifax or elsewhere spend six or seven years upon Latin and Greek and then four more in College partially occupied with the same language is a waste of human life adapted neither to the circumstances nor the prosperity of Nova Scotia ... If Dalhousie College acquires usefulness and eminence it will not be by an imitation of Oxford but as an institution of science and practical intelligence.

Any fourth professor, McCulloch said, should be a natural scientist, teaching geology, mineralogy, zoology, botany; whatever the province produced naturally should have an echo in the splendour of Dalhousie science. McCulloch added a postscript about the nomination of the professors. He did not care who was nominated, but "I mentioned to your father I view the nomination of the existing candidates as a business which should be carefully weighed."[9]

The Dalhousie College Board of Governors met on 6 August 1838. It was not that difficult to arrange; it was now down to a rump of three – the lieutenant-governor, the treasurer of the province, and the Speaker of the House. Lord Dalhousie had died earlier in the year, at Dalhousie Castle, blind and decrepit; the bishop was away, and that spring the chief justice had retired from the board. Sir Colin Campbell and Charles Wallace were not happy with McCulloch, forced upon them by the Assembly; they fudged his appointment, saying he was "for the present appointed President." McCulloch would teach moral philosophy, logic, and rhetoric, and would be paid £400 a year plus student fees, £200 coming from the Assembly and £200 from Dalhousie's funds.[10] Public advertising was authorized for the two other professorships, which were to be in classical languages, and mathematics and natural philosophy. There were seven applicants, of whom the most important were Crawley (Baptist) and Alexander

Romans (Kirk) for classics; James McIntosh (Kirk) and Thomas Twining (Church of England) for mathematics.

The Kirk was bitter about the McCulloch appointment. It published a remonstrance stating that appointing McCulloch would be "an act of injury, injustice and insult to every well educated man in the province." It had also learned, with astonishment it said, that appointments to the college professorships might be contrary to the intentions of Lord Dalhousie, which were to have Dalhousie College in the style of Edinburgh University. That style was, the Kirk robustly asserted, that all professors be members of the Kirk of Scotland!

What the Kirk claimed had been true once; but it was a rule long fallen by the wayside, as recent appointments to Edinburgh indicated. And, of course, it had never been a consideration in Lord Dalhousie's mind, as his search for a principal through an Anglican professor at Cambridge showed. But by August 1838 Lord Dalhousie was dead, and the genial but obtuse old Highland soldier who ruled at Government House in Halifax was persuaded by Charles Wallace and his Kirk friends that the iniquity of appointing a Seceder as president of Dalhousie was bad enough without compounding it by appointing a Baptist as professor. Thus when the time for decision came, at the board meeting of 15 September 1838, the lieutenant-governor and Wallace proposed, and carried, first, for the professorship of mathematics and natural philosophy, the Reverend James McIntosh, a Kirk man, of talent sufficient to justify the appointment; and second, for the professorship of classics the Reverend Alexander Romans, a Kirk man, against the greater claims and more substantial candidacy of Edwin Crawley. Speaker Archibald opposed this, speaking as bluntly as he could. But he had been unwell since April, and may not have been as effective as usual. In any case he was simply outvoted.[11]

The Baptists were furious and felt betrayed. At the head of their fury was Crawley himself. He hit the newspapers twelve days later with a series of articles on the history of his arrangements with Dalhousie College, ringing the changes about his and the Baptists' betrayal.[12] Members of the Assembly, and the Archibalds, were taken aback by the blatant disregard of their promises of six months before. Certainly an articulate group of the Assembly were dismayed, and in the session of 1839 would give that strange Dalhousie board its comeuppance. The Baptists would have even sterner resolves.

Thomas McCulloch was not happy either with Dalhousie's refusal to appoint Crawley. Crawley would no doubt have been a difficult, even intractable, colleague, but McCulloch wished to make friends for Dalhousie and not make enemies when it could well have been avoided. He left Pictou for Halifax in mid-October, his friends from various Pictou congregations accompanying him on his journey as far as Truro. He was rather pleased with himself, despite the row over the two professorships. He did not mind rows: he had lived, thrived, on them. His own appointment to Dalhousie had occasioned a fearsome one. God had at last given him, as he put it, "to possess the gate of my enemies." His pride was gratified to see his foes so humbled.

Lord Dalhousie who for the sake of his college hated me built it for me [.] Our Bishop in the expectation of making it his own was I believe the principal means of preventing it from going into operation till I had need of it. The Kirk clergy his tools effected the destruction of the [Pictou] Academy ... Government placed me at what I may fairly term the head of the education of the province. This I neither coveted nor sought...

Perhaps best of all, his Kirk enemies had not prospered. The most determined of them, the Reverend Kenneth MacKenzie, was dead, "a fearful monument to an ill spent life. In Pictou it is a common remark that no man who opposed the [Pictou] Academy ever prospered in his deed." There was some little *Schadenfreude** in all of this; perhaps McCulloch's essential greatness can be allowed that very human, and not very Christian, weakness. There was a residual toughness about him; he would not be suborned.

He had no great enthusiam for Halifax. But it was the metropolitan centre of the province, things went on there that had to be taken cognizance of, and a college there was going to be important. He had even less respect for Halifax after reading in the Pictou papers about a two-day Halifax riot in August in the streets and houses a couple of blocks up the hill from Dalhousie College. A discharged sailor claimed he had been robbed by prostitutes in one of the houses on the Hill, so his friends, and soldiers, sacked houses on upper Duke Street. It was no secret that they were going to finish their work the following night, and this time locals joined in. Most of these were what the Halifax *Times* described as "the lowest characters," but more respectable onlookers were delighted to see the terrible nuisance of those houses being got rid of, even by a mob out of control. It took old Sir Colin Campbell himself, who in brisk, military fashion, ordered the streets cleared. The riot confirmed ancient prejudices at King's, that Halifax was a wicked place, where young men, in acquiring the best of knowledge, could imbibe the worst of it.

---

* *Schadenfreude* is a word for which we have no short English equivalent. It means malicious enjoyment of others' misfortunes.

Dr Thomas McCulloch in the 1840s, a pastel drawing by Sir Daniel MacNee, now in the Atlantic School of Theology. "He carried the whole college on the strength of his power and reputation."

The College Opens

Dalhousie College opened on 1 November with a dozen students and more expected. McCulloch thought some of the rooms as big as a palace. And three professors in arts was at that time regarded as a more than adequate complement for a provincial college. There was little equipment and no library, but McCulloch was confident that Dalhousie must eventually be "the leading seminary of the province."[13]

He was still a prodigious teacher, his mind clear and vigorous. He was a stickler for grammar but he especially abhorred wordiness. Any word not absolutely necessary to convey meaning weakened the sentence. George Patterson recalled "how mercilessly his big pencil went through our superfluous adjectives!" The students thought he carried it too far, that his own style was bare and devoid of ornament, rather the way he was. But he trained minds to exact thinking, and to correct, if rugged, writing. His philosophy was developed from the Scottish common-sense school and especially from Thomas Reid, the critic of Hume. Physically, however, McCulloch was showing his years; his movements lacked vigour, and his eyes often had a worn and weary look. But his indomitable will remained. Sick or well, he was at class, sometimes to totter home to Argyle Street to bed. He carried the whole college on the strength of his power and reputation. It was not easy, for his two subordinate professors, Romans and McIntosh, were not strong academically and were worse in the classroom. McIntosh too easily found time to indulge in Halifax social life and the drinking that went with it.

The students who came from the country, especially the half-dozen or so who had followed McCulloch from Pictou, were hard-working and diligent. Some from Halifax were too, but there was a proportion of Halifax youths more bent on amusement. Since the lowest age was fourteen, that meant a good deal of high spirits and low cunning had to be suppressed, diverted, transformed, perhaps something of all of those. Romans and McIntosh could not manage this group; McCulloch could. Students were rather in awe of McCulloch, and he repaid their attention and progress with abundant interest. Even the unruly calmed down, except once, recalled by a student, when someone rebelled against him in class. McCulloch "bowed his head, if I mistake not, let fall a tear, at all events said in tones in which the expression of pain overcame anger, 'This is the first time I have been so insulted ... in a class-room in my life.'" Everyone felt the weight of that reproof, perhaps even the miscreant.[14]

The official Dalhousie timetable for the autumn of 1838 was as follows:

1. Latin, 8–9 AM, Prof. Romans
2. Greek, 10–11 AM   "
3. Greek & Latin, 12 noon to 1 PM Prof. Romans
4. Algebra, 10–11 AM Prof. McIntosh
5. Logic, 11–12 AM, Dr. McCulloch
6. Rhetoric, 1–2 PM   "
7. Mathematics, 8–9 AM, Prof. McIntosh
8. Moral Philosophy, 10–11 AM Dr. McCulloch
9. Natural Philosophy 12 noon to 1 PM, Prof. McIntosh

The Dalhousie terms were set on the Scottish style, having one term from October to April inclusive. King's followed the Oxford system, spreading their work more evenly over the year. The Scottish system suited the country boys, who worked on farms from May to September, but city parents found it intolerable to have their sons idle all that time. Some families sent their sons to Dalhousie in the winter and in the summer to new and popular lectures at St Mary's school.

The enraged Baptist constituency lost no time. In the autumn of 1838 Crawley followed up his Dalhousie College articles in the *Novascotian* with three on Horton Academy and hopes for its college expansion. In November the Baptist Education Society met in Wolfville to discuss what they would do. The Baptists now agreed to found a college and a petition went to the legislature to grant a charter. Crawley's personal animus gave voice and leadership to a movement in the Baptist community that was already burgeoning.[15]

The Assembly opened in mid-January of 1839, recent events at Dalhousie and at Wolfville in the forefront of their deliberations. It immediately appointed a three-man committee of Joseph Howe, William Young, and Lawrence Doyle to ask the lieutenant-governor for documents, proceedings, accounts of Dalhousie College. How had the incredible events of 15 September 1838 actually come about? Doyle spoke for the astonishment most MLAs felt at references by the lieutenant-governor and others to Lord Dalhousie's alleged legacy of Presbyterian exclusiveness. It had always been understood, said Doyle, that Dalhousie College was to be altogether unrestricted, open to anyone. If that were not so, then the sooner the House insisted on getting its £5,000 back the better.

Joseph Howe was more specific. Had he known what would happen in September (he was overseas in Britain from May to October), had he believed that anyone "would be mad enough to endeavour to make Dalhousie College a Sectarian Institution," he would have opposed the Pictou-Dalhousie Act of 1838, even though it had wakened Dalhousie from "its death-like sleep." Certainly Dalhousie College must not continue in its present form.

Rather than see it established for the exclusive benefit of any church he would prefer that a party of artificiers should be brought down from the barracks, and should be directed to mine it, and blow the structure into the air ... The effect of these narrow views was, to keep classes of christians – which should respect each other, and live in charity – in a state bordering on enmity, harrassed [*sic*] by conflicting and angry feelings.

William Young said much the same, moderately as was his wont, judging the September appointments "most unwise and impolitic." There must not be, he said, four or five colleges in the province – if so, their degrees would become a laughing stock.[16]

Speaker Archibald reported on Dalhousie's funds. The accounting had been complicated by Michael Wallace's death in 1831, and by Lord Dalhousie's, and by the fact that the agents in London, empowered to receive dividends, had failed. Still, about two-thirds of the income on capital could be reclaimed by affidavit, some £786 sterling. That was done in the nick of time. And the money would meet the costs of current repairs.[17]

On 9 February 1839, the Bill for the Incorporation of Queen's College (the first name chosen for Acadia) was given first reading, and on 15 February Howe presented the bill to amend the Dalhousie College Act. The two bills now proceeded roughly in tandem. On the second reading of the Queen's College Bill Crawley appeared at the bar of the House. He said much that clarified the events of September last. Two or three days after the Dalhousie appointments had been made, Sir Colin Campbell asked to see Crawley. In that interview, Crawley asked the governor if it were not true that his (Crawley's) failure to get the professorship of classics was due to Crawley's religion, not his competence? In other words, if he'd been a Presbyterian, would he have got the job? "His Excellency hesitated, but after a while said, Certainly – that such was the fact."

Then Treasurer Charles Wallace was called to the bar, and his testimony went directly against that of Crawley:

Mr. Howe – Do I understand Mr. Wallace to say that Mr. Crawley was not rejected because he was a Baptist.
Mr. Wallace – Certainly not.
Mr. Howe – Do I understand Mr. Wallace aright, that although he had promised Mr. Crawley, the peculiar circumstances under which he was placed

with Mr. Romans was a reason sufficiently strong to abrogate those promises.

Mr. Wallace – Yes.

Mr. Howe remarked that the house would now perceive, why he had been anxious to have this examination. The statements of the gentleman [*sic*] heard at the bar were directly contradictory.

The following day Crawley was again heard in connection with Queen's College. Nova Scotians, he said, had waited for fifteen years for Dalhousie College, and what had appeared had simply not justified expectations. Some members of the House hoped that the Queen's College Bill would not be pressed, that new legislation to clear out the old Dalhousie board and establish a new one would allay inflamed feelings and satisfy the Baptists. J.B. Uniacke (Anglican) made that appeal. Why should there be, he said, several inferior establishments in the province instead of one good one? As for Howe, he was sympathetic to Crawley and his talents, but

he would not say, therefore, that another College should be endowed. If it was determined to have a College at Horton, much as he wished to see a College in Halifax, and believed it to be the best site for one, he would say, Down with it, let us get our money from it, and if one sect must have such an establishment, let it be respectable, and let not two inefficient institutions go into operation. In these matters Nova Scotia acted with a degree of profusion that no other country attempted.[18]

The Queen's College Bill came out of the Committee of the Whole with a recommendation that it be given the three-months' hoist. A motion to overturn this recommendation, and thus keep the bill, was defeated. This first attempt to incorporate Queen's College failed.

The Dalhousie College Amendment Bill passed the Assembly that same day but it did not fare so well in the Legislative Council, coming back with amendments that the House could not accept. In a conference between the two houses the Assembly insisted on its point

that the object this House had in view in passing that Bill was to place Dalhousie College under the management of a body of Gentlemen, selected from the various Religious Denominations in this Province, carefully excluding Clergymen, in order that those jealousies which had marred the usefulness, and arrayed the feelings of portions of the Population, against the interests of other Institutions might, in this case, be avoided, and all classes combined in support of a College offering equal privileges to all; that these amendments made by the Council, which are now the subject of Conference, strike at the vital principle of the Bill, a principle upon the value of which, there exists in the Assembly no difference of opinion.[19]

A further snag occurred on a money question in the bill, and the Assembly put forward a new bill with the contentious money clause avoided. It was given third reading in the House but was thrown out on a technicality by the Legislative Council. Thus neither the Queen's College nor the Dalhousie bill succeeded in 1839. Both were to do so in 1840.

The Dalhousie Act of 1840 did what had been intended in 1839; it broke the old Dalhousie trust, as Howe and others had wanted. Abolished was the old board established by Lord Dalhousie and the Act of 1821. The governor general of British North America as member, a holdover from Lord Dalhousie's days, was deleted as impracticable; the chief justice was dropped; indeed, all ex-officio officers were dropped except the lieutenant-governor and the president of Dalhousie College. Twelve new members across a religious and political spectrum were named. Future vacancies were to be filled by a curious system of selection: the Legislative Council would choose three, from which the Assembly would select two, and from which the Council would nominate one. Two further sections of the 1840 act must be quoted:

v. That the said College shall be deemed and taken to be an University, with all and every the usual privileges of such Institutions, and that the Students in the said College shall have the liberty and faculty of taking the Degrees of Bachelor, Master and Doctor...

vi. That no Religious Tests or Subscriptions shall be required of the Professors, Scholars, Graduates, Students or Officers of the said College, but that all the privileges and advantages therefo shall be open and free to all and every person and persons whomsoever, without regard to religious persuasion.[20]

The act went through the Assembly without recorded division, but was subject to British approval.

In 1840, too, the Queen's College Bill was accepted by the Assembly, twenty-seven to fifteen. Howe spoke against the college but voted for it, one of several who did. Howe regretted the fact that Queen's was created at all, deplored "making five great roads, where only one should be"; but since Crawley had been rejected by the old Dalhousie board on religious grounds (he plainly concurred with

Crawley's estimate of the reasons), he felt he had no option. But for that circumstance, nothing would have induced Howe to vote for the incorporation of Queen's College.[21]

It met with similar reactions in the Legislative Council. As it passed third reading, a protest was entered by Mather Almon and L.M. Wilkins; if the Queen's College Bill were to become law, they said, "it is reasonably to be anticipated that similar Institutions, connected with other Religious Denominations in this Province, will be required ... and thereby to prevent the ample endowment, from the same source [i.e., public revenue] of some *one* central and efficient College, perfectly open and unrestricted, and operating equally for the benefit of all classes of the People." With that appeal to posterity, the Legislative Council passed the Queen's College Bill.[22]

Queen's College did not keep its name. Lord John Russell, the colonial secretary, reported that the Queen did not wish her name associated with the college (probably because it was Baptist), and in 1841 it was given the name Acadia College, a happy choice. Russell also objected to the way that future vacancies on the Dalhousie board were to be filled, in particular having nominations and choices given to the popular body. In 1841 that was changed too, giving the power to the lieutenant-governor-in-council.

The creation of Acadia College so quickly, so resolutely, was remarkable; it showed what could be done within a strong religious constituency, driven by determination, anger, and self-sacrifice. It showed, indeed, what Dalhousie did not have: substantial and committed public support from a closely knit section of the province, in this case the Annapolis Valley, whose farms had been started only seventy years before by New England dissenters, mainly from Connecticut and Rhode Island. On the other hand, there was a clear sense among a minority in both the Assembly and the Legislative Council that this development was unfortunate, that it was the result of a concatenation of circumstances that might well have been avoided had there been better management, or even a little plain common sense, in the two critical members of that Dalhousie rump board. Rarely in history are there clear points of departure; rarely can one say this, or that, came from such and such an event. But this one is unmistakable: the Dalhousie board's refusal to appoint Edmund Crawley as professor of classics in September 1838. It had distinct and momentous consequences for university education in Nova Scotia. Within five months of that refusal, the Queen's College Bill was before the Assembly, failing in 1839 by only two votes, and passing the following year. Even in 1839 it was already late; the only person who could have averted that progress was Crawley, and he would have none of it.

Crawley's determination and outrage carried with it suspicion that perhaps he was glad the way things had turned out. He would have been bound to accept the office of professor of classics at Dalhousie College had it been offered, and he made a fine display of indignation when he did not get it; but was he sincere? Herbert Huntingdon, the MLA for Yarmouth, alleged in 1849 he was not. Huntingdon's furious accusation created a sensation in the Assembly, and was denied by Tory leader J.W. Johnston as a gross lie, but Huntingdon reiterated that Crawley and the Baptists were secretly delighted when he was excluded from Dalhousie in 1838.[23] In 1841 St Mary's College – Roman Catholic – was granted a charter by the legislature. All four of Nova Scotia's little colleges were thus under way – King's, Dalhousie, Acadia, and St Mary's. Despite appearances, however, the Assembly did not accept this as a *fait accompli*; in 1842, 1843, and after, there were major efforts to revert to, and establish, "One Good College."

In 1842 the issue arose over how the newly created colleges of Acadia and St Mary's were to be funded. King's had long had a permanent annual grant of £444. One awful weekend in March of 1842 the funding question oscillated precariously back and forth, impelled by bad temper and shifts on both sides. Eventually the House gave £444 to Acadia and St Mary's, £400 to Dalhousie. The grants would be for three years, except Dalhousie's, which was for two. All were to begin on 1 January 1843.[24]

The question of funding was a difficult and anguished one, and the Baptists did not make it easier for themselves, by pushing hard for what they wanted. They had a case: they had dug into their own pockets to help create Acadia, and it was now doing well enough to need, and to ask for, a capital grant for more space. In their view, Dalhousie College had done nothing for itself; there it sat on the Grand Parade, but what had built it was Castine money and a legislative loan. King's was not much better, though at least it made exertions on its own behalf. But the Assembly was not at all certain it was right to have created Acadia. Many who had opposed it in the first place now rolled their eyes, and said, "Ah! did I not tell you that they [the Baptists] would harrass [sic] you every year for money? You wouldn't believe it – now are you satisfied?"[25] Howe, who had supported the Acadia charter, was not pleased either. That mattered; since October 1840 Howe had been on the Executive Council and Speaker of the House since February 1841. The Baptists thought Howe's principle of not favouring any denomination, of making all colleges equal, loaded the dice against Acadia. It was, as Murray Beck pointed out, a question of different conclusions drawn from different premises. The Baptists were anything but even-handed; they turned on Howe and others in April and May 1842 in their powerful weekly, the *Christian Messenger*. They threatened Howe and Young, both new members of the Executive Council, with dire consequences if they had the temerity to oppose a capital grant to Acadia College. By the end of 1842 Howe was beginning to wonder if Acadia was not in league with his Tory rivals. That meant increased strain in the relations between Howe and J.W. Johnston, the Baptist Tory who was attorney general.

Since October 1840 Nova Scotia had had a coalition Executive Council put together by the magic wand of the governor general, Charles Poulett Thomson, who came down from Quebec to work it out with Lord Falkland, the new lieutenant-governor. The Executive Council was made into a combination of Tories and Reformers, with a Tory preponderance. Working under that arrangement was not going to be easy, with the college question at the boiling point and the attorney general an active Baptist.

The college question thus came before the Assembly in 1843 compounded and exacerbated by utterances in the newspapers, and by some intemperateness on both sides. The *Novascotian* put it in the context of the whole educational system of Nova Scotia: of a population of two hundred and fifty thousand, probably thirty thousand children were growing up without the basic rudiments of education, and here was the legislature squandering £1,800 a year on four colleges. And the worst of it was that everyone knew the Methodists and Presbyterians were waiting, thinking in due course that they, too, would get their slice of the cake. Richard Nugent, the Catholic editor of the *Novascotian*, became more annoyed the more he thought about it:

We must confess ourselves astonished at the credulity or infatuation of our Countrymen, and lament the mistaken policy of our public men which gave rise to the present deplorable state of the Educational affairs of the Province...

What is to be done? Shall we go on, *ad infinitum* creating College after College...? Or, shall we pause here, and enquire, seriously, – where the evil will end?[26]

That certainly stirred up a row. The Assembly opened a debate two days later to consider the whole question of colleges. Tory J.J. Marshall argued that it was impossible to support a general college and suppress the others. The best policy was to wait until such a college were asked for. For the present, two-thirds of Nova Scotia would be against it. Howe replied that in 1842 all the colleges were put on the same level, and all were satisfied but Acadia. The Baptists had made the table groan with petitions for more money, and now the

Methodists and Presbyterians were getting restless. What did Nova Scotia need with so many colleges? Switzerland had one college for every four hundred thousand people. From Committee of the Whole came the following: "Resolved, that the policy, heretofore pursued, of chartering and endowing Collegiate Institutions, of a Sectarian or Denominational Character is unsound, and ought to be abandoned." Attempts were made to stop that decisive declaration. Fairbanks of Queen's County, a Tory, agreed with Marshall; he proposed that however desirable it might be to have one college free of sectarian control, yet "experience has shown the impracticability of uniting the various denominations of Christians in such a manner, and that a different Policy having been forced upon the House, and hitherto recognized and adopted ... it would be unwise and unjust to prostrate those Institutions." That was defeated, and the main motion carried. A committee of Howe, William Annand, Huntingdon, and others was charged with drafting a bill that would establish the One College principle once and for all. The Baptists sought vainly to be heard. A motion "founding one General College upon the ruin of all others ... unless sanctioned by the cordial feelings and wishes of the population, cannot be effected" received the three-months' hoist. That was after midnight on 27 March 1843, and the debate finally adjourned at 1:30 AM.[27]

It was a wrenching debate, with little charity and no quarter given. The Baptists were disposed to rail at anyone who got in their way, who might choose to advocate establishing common schools as against, as the *Novascotian* bluntly put it, "a set of worthless denominational Colleges with half-read Professors." The legislature was becoming a battleground of friends and supporters of each. The more the Baptists rose in their wrath, the more Howe became aroused. Some Baptists, he said, were worse than Roman Catholics when it came to persecution. Indeed, if we had to have a pope, he went on, he would rather have one in Rome than in Wolfville; and one who would look the part, in gorgeous and solemn robes, not a Baptist one in black coat and tights.[28]

The debate ended because the committee could not agree on where that single college would be, so that, finally, nothing was done. The Legislative Council had accepted none of it; the grants passed in 1842 were still intact; they would expire in another two and a half years, in Dalhousie's case in one and a half. The question would now go to a broader forum.

"One College" in the Election of 1843
The discussion about One College went on that summer and fall of 1843 in the newspapers and ultimately on the hustings. On Wednesday, 25 September 1843 a large meeting was held in Mason's

Hall, Halifax to discuss establishing one "liberal and respectable Provincial College." G.R. Young had visited McGill during the summer, and concluded that it was important to consider having a medical school in Halifax. It was not an impossible dream, he said. Let each sect train its own clergy, by all means, but let general education, classics, mathematics, law, medicine, be taught at one good central college. The Nova Scotian denominational colleges were already costing £5,000 to £6,000 a year; it was a system that went "against the spirit of the age."

Howe, too, pointed out the advantages of size, substance, and the power that went with them. King's, he said, although it had been in existence for half a century, was nothing. A degree from King's had no weight at all; outside of Nova Scotia it was worth no more than the parchment it was written on. It was time, he said, to call a halt to building up these feudal, sectarian, power centres. Why, they "were like feudal castles in the olden time, each the rallying point of a party whose only object was to strengthen their own position ... and levy contributions on the public." Howe particularly deplored the spectacle of "these peripatetic, writing, wrangling, grasping Professors" riding over the countryside, stirring up trouble. No old Baptist, not even Henry Alline, said Howe, stirred up so much strife as arrogant professors of philosophy and religion had done in the past six years. Edmund Crawley, lean, tall, dressed in black, had been seen in so many places around the province that he was called "Galloping Tongs."[29] There were a number of resolutions put before the Mason's Hall meeting, but the most important one, which went forward with others to the Assembly, was as follows:

Resolved, therefore, that this meeting earnestly suggest a concentration of the energy and means of the true friends of Education, both in the Capital and the Country to oppose a system which is intended to lead to the erection and support of five or six weak and inefficient Institutions under the name of Colleges, and to encourage the Legislature to endow one Central College, which from the number of its professors, the branches of varied learning taught, its Library and Museum, will enable the Youth of Nova Scotia to receive a liberal education at home, instead of being sent, as under the present and contemplated Sectarian system, to be educated abroad.[30]

Public meetings in a similar vein went on into October. One of the biggest was Onslow, on Monday, 9 October. The *Novascotian* counted 113 wagons, gigs, and saddle horses tied up outside the Presbyterian meeting house to hear speakers on the One College question. There was another at Stewiacke that same day, and at Londonderry a fortnight later. The debates raged on and went straight into the general election, called at the end of October.[31]

The election call was mainly Lord Falkand's doing, for he now despaired of being able to carry any government measures through the Assembly. That election was also where the One College movement flagged and failed. Where the issue surfaced, as it did in a number of central constituencies, the arguments used by the *Christian Messenger* came home to roost – that is, if Howe and the Reformers won, Acadia College would get nothing from the Assembly but the odd crumb, and the new Roman Catholic college of St Mary's would fare no better. King's would get the same treatment. It was in some ways a battle of the periphery against the capital, and the capital lost; where the college question intruded, the Reformers and the One College principle lost ground. In the election that November the Reformers lost their majority in the Assembly to the Tories, who now had a majority of one. Eight of the new Tory seats were in the Baptist belt, from Annapolis through Kings into Colchester. After the appointment to the Council of J.W. Johnston's brother-in-law, Mather Almon, in December, Howe resigned from the Council, and the coalition regime was at an end.[32]

The Last Years of McCulloch's Dalhousie

Dalhousie College carried on valiantly, even hopefully. In December 1842 it struck a code of rules to govern the college. The terms were changed to accommodate local tastes and exigencies. The BA was now laid down as three years of two terms each, the terms beginning in the fourth Tuesday of January to 1 July, and from 1 September to 15 December. The admission age was set at a minimum of fourteen years. Students were to wear caps and gowns, after the King's College fashion. Dalhousie College was to be conducted on the principle that "entire liberality in point of Religion" was compatible with cultivating "sentiments of piety and virtue." The professorships were to be open to "any religious denomination"; there were to be no religious tests; and "all the awards and honours of the Institution will be open to all classes without distinction." Internal governance of the college was vested in the professors collectively.[33]

These rules were drawn up by a committee of the new seventeen-member Board of Governors that had been appointed in May 1842 pursuant to the new 1841 act. It was rather large and clumsy, but certainly more representative than the rump of three hitherto existing. The new board reduced salaries. The president's would be £300 as of 1 January 1844. Romans, whose appointment in 1838 had created so much of the trouble in the first place, had not worked out well. He was

Meeting of the Halifax Tandem Club, on the Grand Parade in front of Dalhousie College, about 1840. A coloured version of this engraving was presented to Dalhousie in 1950.

retired as of 31 December 1842, with six months' pay. McIntosh would take over classics as well as the mathematics he already taught with an increase in salary to £200. A professor of modern languages (mainly French, Italian, and Spanish) would be added at £150.[34]

The new board also wanted to establish clear title to the Grand Parade. The new Halifax City Council had passed a resolution stating that the railing on the upper, Argyle Street side of the Parade was a hazard and should be fixed. Dalhousie had thought it was the city's responsibility, but the city demurred, so Dalhousie undertook to get the work done. The military still had occasional parades there, which got in the way of lectures from time to time, but the board thought it would not interfere with this ancient use, at least for the present. The attorney general was asked about the title to the Parade; J.W. Johnston's report is not extant, but it must have given the governors pause, for they agreed to ask for a new grant of the "college lands."[35]

In early August 1843 Lorenzo Lacoste, the new professor of modern languages, arrived from New York. He was the most promising candidate, the board evidently finding his New York references satisfactory. He was a quiet man, well liked in his Halifax boarding house, unobtrusive, of regular habits, his books and clothes in good order. On 22 August he came home in mid-afternoon, walked in the garden with the owner for half an hour, then went out after dinner. He did not return. He was found at first light by a North-West Arm farmer, who discovered Lacoste floating in the water, his throat cut, evidently self-inflicted. One or two witnesses at the inquest testified that they had seen him acting strangely. The coroner's jury concluded that he had committed suicide while "insane and distracted." The cause was probably some private agony that Lacoste found too hard to bear. It might have been Dalhousie College itself, although Lord Falkland said that Lacoste was pleased with his situation. Lord Falkland also asked his London friend, rather laconically, that since Lacoste had committed suicide, could another professor of modern languages be recommended?[36]

At that time McCulloch was in western Nova Scotia gathering minerals and other specimens for his natural history collection. He had sold his first one in the 1820s and was building a second. His summer collecting time was shortened now, Dalhousie opening on the first Monday in September. McCulloch avoided the polemics of his old days in Pictou; he went about his business without apparent rancour, even amid the bitter debates of 1842 and 1843 about One College. He said nothing against the Baptists; he had preached more than once at Granville Street Baptist Church. He told a friend he was getting like an old mare he remembered in Truro: she hated to move so much that the only way to persuade her to do so was to stick a pin in her shoulder; when the pain of the pin was worse than the pain of progression, then would the mare move.[37] He had gone to Scotland in the summer of 1842 to see old correspondents and friends for the first time since 1825–6. As often happens with returning emigrés, he discovered soon enough that the river is never the same twice, that the world he had known had changed beyond his comfortable accommodation with it. Scotland was no longer home. He was glad to come back to Halifax, bringing with him his young niece to marry his son William.

Dalhousie College opened on Monday, 4 September. McCulloch was taken ill the Friday before. He went to his classes on opening day but came home exhausted. Dr Grigor of the Dalhousie board was called the next day, and thought McCulloch had symptoms of typhus. He slowly got weaker, and died on the Saturday evening of 9 September, as the five o'clock gun from the Citadel sounded. His son, holding him, felt his "father's last breath pass gently over my hand."[38]

McMulloch's dying was more peaceful than most of his living. His energy, confidence, ability, combined to make him formidable; as the *Acadian Recorder* put it, he was "gifted with masterly wit and reasoning powers of the highest order; few writers were able to cope with him." That gets precisely at his eristic style; his was not a tender soul, and his integrity made compromise difficult. Mercy was a Christian virtue he recognized rather than practised. The real power of his mind is felt in his *Stepsure Letters*, that ironic, often sardonic comment on men, women, and manners in Nova Scotia. It is also seen in his students. The best epitaph came from one, many years afterward: "I didn't know his greatness until I heard the professors at the University of Edinburgh."[39]

Dalhousie College recognized the necessity of appointing a successor as soon as one could be found. They would need at least £300 annual income to do so. They agreed to appeal to the city, each member of the board taking on one of the six wards, to induce the inhabitants to "contribute liberally towards its [Dalhousie College's] support." It was not successful; the 1840s were a difficult and narrow time financially, and everyone seemed pinched by it. By the end of 1843 Dalhousie College seemed to be unravelling at the edges. It was lacking that strong coherence that McCulloch's presence, his mind, his range, his reputation, had given the college. Then Professor McIntosh applied for and got leave to return to Scotland, ostensibly on business, in reality to look for another post. He was also asked to look for a new president in Scotland. Ultimately McIntosh pushed his demands for leave too far, and was allowed to resign. He had been replaced with McCulloch's son Thomas, much less decisive than his father, and by no means presidential material.⁴⁰ At the time of McCulloch's death the college was living close to the bone, its financial stability precarious. Ere long something had to happen: the grants given by the Assembly in 1842 would terminate for Dalhousie on 1 January 1845. The One College principle had been decided in March 1843 by seven votes, but it had never received legislative approval and it had been a lively issue all that year and into the November general election. The House left it alone in 1844; it was divisive enough without opening it up gratuitously.

By 1845, however, the House could not avoid dealing with the question. The Reformers who had provided the basic support for One College, who had carried it in 1843, now found themselves at a disadvantage. They had lost control of the Assembly. College grants were renewed in 1845, at about two-thirds their former level, but with no grant at all to Dalhousie. Joseph Howe tried to stop all the grants by an amendment condemning sectarian colleges, but it was defeated decisively. Votes of money to Acadia, St Mary's, Pictou Academy, and to Sackville Academy in New Brunswick (the future Methodist college of Mount Allison), were passed mostly by solid majorities. Attempts by Huntingdon to rescind them the next day failed narrowly; the rescinding of the permanent grant to King's failed by one vote.⁴¹

The Dalhousie Board of Governors now had little choice. Their 1845 assets were £9,342.11s.1d. sterling, in 3 per cent Consols in London, yielding an annual income of £280 sterling. They had, since 5 April 1845, the British Post Office paying £100 sterling annual rent for the lower corner at Duke and Barrington. The Mechanics Institute occupying the west wing had had it rent free since 1833, as did the Infant School. Thus Dalhousie's gross annual income was now £380 sterling, (£450 Halifax currency). Salaries took up £650. This was not the arithmetic of success. With the legislative grant ended on 31 December 1844, with McCulloch dead, there was little hope of carrying on. It had not in fact been doing well. It had no library. Its scientific apparatus was valued at £100. It had perhaps sixteen students. The other colleges looked better than Dalhousie: Acadia had twenty-seven students, St Mary's forty to eighty, depending on how they were counted; King's had twenty-two. All had libraries, St Mary's reporting fifteen hundred books, Acadia, five hundred. So the Dalhousie board's resolution of 3 June 1845 was sensible, timely, and devastating: "That in consequence of the discontinuance of the Provincial Grant it is expedient to shut up the college for the present and not to fill up the vacancies in the professorships. And that it is advisable to let the Funds of the Institution to accumulate."⁴²

Thus did the 1838 opening of Dalhousie College come, ingloriously, to an end. G.R. Young, William Young, Huntingdon, and Howe had tried to buttress Dalhousie. All had failed. What lay behind that failure was Dalhousie's liberal and unsectarian character. It had no constituency. As Gaius Lewis, Liberal MLA for Cumberland put it, "it seemed [that it was] not owned by any." What he meant by that was painfully obvious: the others – King's, Acadia, St Mary's, and now Mount Allison in New Brunswick – were "owned," by Anglicans, Baptists, Catholics, and Methodists, respectively. As for the Presbyterians, they had never "owned" Dalhousie, had never professed to, though the first appointments of 1838 had given that impression. By 1847 Dalhousie College was a community centre and a government office building, its college state neatly summed up in a report to the Assembly that year:

Professors. – None
Students attending Lectures. – None.

· 4 ·

Through the Shallows
1848–1864

Halifax in the 1840s. New government, new Dalhousie Act, 1848. Dalhousie Collegiate School, 1849–54. Dalhousie High School, 1856–60. Presbyterians, education, and J.W. Dawson. What to do with Dalhousie? George Grant, the Kirk, and the two synods' agreement. The Dalhousie Act of 1863. Attempts to repeal it, 1864.

As the 1840s ended, Halifax was beginning to feel the accelerating pace of change. It began with steamships. Howe met up with one on his way to England in May 1838. He was twenty days out of Halifax with several hundred miles to go, his sailing ship, the *Tyrian*, was rolling about in a dead calm, when out of the west, underneath a pillar of black smoke, came a steamship. "On she came," reported Howe, "with the speed of a hunter, while we were moving with the rapidity of an ox-cart loaded with marsh mud." She was the *Sirius*, fourteen days out of New York on a trial run. Samuel Cunard's steamers began regular runs from England to Halifax and Boston two years later. RMS *Britannia* arrived in Halifax at 2 AM, 17 July 1840, and after a few hours went on to Boston.[1] She was carrying mail – letters with the first new postage stamps issued in May 1840, the penny black and the two-pence blue.

It was a Cunard steamer that in 1842 brought Charles Dickens to Halifax. Howe met him and escorted him rather breathlessly around the sights during the brief stop the steamer made. It happened to be the day of the opening of the legislature. Howe was the Speaker of the House; Dickens accompanied him and described the scene:

[I]t was like looking at Westminster through the wrong end of a telescope. The Governor [Lord Falkland], as Her Majesty's representative, delivered what may be called the Speech from the Throne. He said what he had to say manfully and well. The military band outside the building struck up God Save

70

Halifax in 1860, from the Dartmouth side of the harbour, painted by William Hickman

the Queen before His Excellency was quite finished; the people shouted; the in's rubbed their hands; the out's shook their heads; the Government party said there never was such a good speech; the Opposition declared there never was such a bad one...

The market is abundantly supplied and provisions are exceedingly cheap ... The day was uncommonly fine, the air bracing and healthful, the whole aspect of the town cheerful, thriving and industrious. I carried away with me a most pleasant impression of the town and its inhabitants.[2]

Halifax got gas street lighting in 1843–4, its eighty or so lamps lighted every night by hand, save when there was moonlight, when the inhabitants had to find their way by that source. By the end of the 1840s a telegraph line was in place from Halifax to the New Brunswick border. It was built by the Nova Scotian government at Howe's urging and duly denounced by the Opposition as an extravagant waste of money. Within a year it was paying 5 per cent on its investment, an early example, of which Howe was very proud, of government enterprise.[3]

Halifax was starting to develop business from its ports. Its wharves were spreading along the harbour, and the warehouses and banks were built just inland from them. Its motto when it was incorporated in 1841 was, and is, *E mari merces*, "From the sea, commerce." Its population in 1851 was 20,749, up 44 per cent from 1836. Hugo Reid, who would become principal of Dalhousie College School in 1856, found Halifax people "all thriving, they are very lightly taxed ... But they have demagogues who want places, fiery religious zealots who want power, and universal suffrage for those to delude and make a tool of. The great struggle is for the loaves and fishes ... without any hypocritical disguise as a homage of vice to virtue."[4]

Dalhousie Collegiate School
From 1845 onward the legislature, in particular the Reform party, was too busy with the politics of responsible government to worry about the divisive subject of college education. The general election of August 1847 returned twenty-nine Reformers and twenty-two Conservatives. The Tory government resigned after losing a vote of confidence at the end of January 1848, and a Reform government came into power with J.B. Uniacke as premier, Howe as provincial secretary, and Herbert Huntingdon eventually financial secretary. Legislation to revive Dalhousie (without money) was soon put in place. The 1848 Dalhousie Act was brought in by Howe; Dalhousie College remained much the same as before, but the board was trimmed from seventeen to no more than seven, no less than five, appointed by the governor-in-council, to hold office during pleasure. They were to

take such steps as they could to render Dalhousie useful and efficient. The legislation passed the House, all three readings in three days. In September 1848 seven board members were appointed: William Young, Joseph Howe, Hugh Bell, James Avery, William Grigor, Andrew MacKinlay, and John Naylor. William Young was made chairman.[5]

The new board met in November to receive a report prepared by Young on the current state of Dalhousie; it was approved unanimously and ordered to be published. Dalhousie's building, said Young, was "central, airy and convenient," with six excellent classrooms, besides the lower storey, at Barrington and Duke streets, occupied by the General Post Office. Dalhousie's capital was £9,342 sterling (£10,043 currency). If that were taken out of Consols and put into provincial bonds, it would earn 5 to 6 per cent instead of 3 per cent. (That in fact would be done in 1855–6.) Young said it was unnecessary to refer to the various unsuccessful attempts to make Dalhousie College into what Lord Dalhousie had designed it to be. The board certainly did not want Dalhousie College to remain "a melancholy memorial of well intended and patriotic efforts defeated, and large funds unproductive and neglected." Hence, they decided on something Lord Dalhousie had thought of – that is, failing a college, why not a grammar school? William Young had recently been in the United States, had looked at high schools in Boston, Philadelphia, and elsewhere, and other members of the board had made inquiries about the state of education in Halifax. With good teachers and low fees, a Dalhousie school could offer high school education for all denominations, to which parents could look with confidence to supply "a want so justly complained of and so deeply felt in this community." Pupils were not to exceed forty per teacher and each teacher would be given a "proportion" – usually half – of fees. Five pupils per class were to be allowed to come free, so that children "who displayed extraordinary ability in the common schools may be advanced, and their minds developed and improved."[6]

Before Dalhousie Collegiate School could be brought into operation, a massive row developed in the 1849 session of the Assembly over, once more, the sectarian colleges. W.A. Henry started it, perhaps innocently, though having been through the wrenching debates of 1843 he might have known better. He moved that the permanent grant of £444 per year to King's be abolished, that King's should be put on the same basis as the other sectarian colleges, St Mary's and Acadia. That set the cat fairly among the pigeons. Henry's purpose, so J.W. Johnston alleged, was to destroy King's; after that he could get the Assembly to destroy the others.

The Uniacke government decided, perhaps unwisely, that this renewal of the college question would be open, that there would be no specific administration policy. That allowed everyone to air their prejudices and their memories. Howe said, sensibly enough, that he did not like the sectarian colleges, but there they now were. Although his basic preference for one free unsectarian college still stood, it would "not be wise to revive sectarian bitterness in the country again." Even if Dalhousie was not at present a college, its basic resources, its central position in a city of twenty thousand, would in the long run assert themselves. It could well be that young men trained at Sackville, King's, Acadia, and St Mary's would go on to Dalhousie to finish their education; "these Seminaries will, in fact, become feeders from which the central Institution will be ultimately strengthened and nourished." One thing abundantly clear to Howe from his experiences from 1843 to 1849 was

that we may make education a battle ground, where the laurels we reap may be wet with the tears of our country, – that we may outvote each other by small majorities, to have our decisions reversed every four years. But without mutual forbearance, and a spirit of compromise, we can do little good, and make no satisfactory and permanent settlement of these questions.

Uniacke agreed with Howe, that to uproot the sectarian colleges would never rally the public around Dalhousie.[7]

Henry observed that his little bill, with one clause in it, created a great deal of fuss. The sectarian colleges were certainly the seeds of discord for the future. Even Uniacke, himself educated at King's, decided to send his sons abroad for their college education. Did not that prove something? Henry pointed out, aptly enough, that Maine with six hundred thousand people seemed to manage with three colleges; Massachusetts, with eight hundred thousand got along with Harvard, and unless Nova Scotia made a start, by getting rid of the permanent grant to King's, any hope of a strong central college with one hundred students was gone, "and the sickly seminaries now existing would be fastened on the province." Let us, he said, get rid of this mongrel system. "This mongrel system, as the speaker calls it," said J.W. Johnston, "is one which enables the yeomanry in this country to educate their sons at moderate expense."

Henry's bill passed, only to be defeated in the Legislative Council with the help of Bishop Inglis, and the House ground on to another massive debate on the general state of education in the province. It was not a pretty performance; the Uniacke administration were divided among themselves, and upbraided each other. The *Novascotian* said bluntly, on 5 March 1849:

We have had no Collegiate Instruction in the Country – we have had nothing but a number of sickly and inefficient Schools drawing largely from the Treasury ... We have seen the Country agitated from one extremity to the other by interested red hot sectarians. We have seen Ministers of the Gospel and itinerating Professors, converted into active political agents coursing the Province, preaching politics instead of peace and good will among men.

Those colleges should be nurtured by their own friends, not by the Nova Scotia legislature.

When that debate had wound down, and the ruffled legislators had gone home, the Dalhousie Collegiate School opened on 11 April 1849, with Thomas McCulloch, Jr as headmaster, and three other teachers. There were 117 pupils enrolled that year, four of whom were free scholars. The overall average age was twelve years. For the next three years the Dalhousie board struggled to make the school a success. There were difficulties: arrears of fees made it difficult to pay teachers; McCulloch wanted to resign in April 1850 on account of ill health and was persuaded to continue against his better judgment; there was lack of harmony among the teachers. By 1854 the number of pupils had fallen to sixty-one, and in October the school was closed.

Dalhousie High School, 1856 and After

The public function of Dalhousie's building and grounds grew. If requests for use of the Parade and the Dalhousie College building are anything to go by, it became a community centre of the time. City Council in 1853 wanted to use the south end of the Parade as a temporary market while a new market building was being built. The board said no, but the city pressed the point and the board relented, since the market was temporary. In 1854 there was a request to use the Parade for a circus; the board replied that they did "not deem themselves authorized to let the Parade Ground for such an object." In the spring of 1856 the governors decided, as part of a new Dalhousie School, to enclose part of the Parade. The public had always used the Parade as a crossing between Argyle Street and Barrington. It was the centre of the city, it was the place where Haligonians when young played hopscotch or later baseball or cricket, as their fathers and grandfathers had done. Who were these Dalhousie governors to assert such claims? The governors' action stirred up the wrath of the local papers, not least the *British Colonist*, the principal Conservative paper: "We consider it to be of the smallest possible importance whether the grant of Governor Parr or that of the Earl of Dalhousie be recognized as a valid one; in either case the property belongs to the citizens of Halifax ... *That fence must not be tolerated*!" But the fence was built. The Liberal *Morning*

Dalhousie College about 1875, looking northwest from Barrington Street. The basic configuration of the Grand Parade still stands. The tracks along Barrington Street are for the horse-car line established in 1872. It would become a tram-line in 1895.

Chronicle defended Dalhousie School, its fence, and its board for trying to give Halifax people a good high school and inexpensive education.[8]

There was more to the *British Colonist's* animus than just the Parade. It did not like the new Dalhousie School either. Staff for it had been hired in England in 1855, its head an experienced headmaster, Hugo Reid, who brought two other teachers with him. There had been some difficulty in getting good lay teachers – the best and most available ones were clerics – but the Dalhousie board insisted on laymen, remembering the row of 1838. Hugo Reid was forty-six years old, an active author and educator, a graduate of Edinburgh High School, and formerly principal of Liverpool High School before coming to Halifax. Dalhousie High School opened on 15 January 1856. The *Morning Chronicle* visited the school a week after it opened and found everything excellent – principal, teachers, curriculum. Reid and his staff were good teachers, and engendered enough enthusiasm to suggest that this was, perhaps, the right niche.

Hugo Reid had certain ideas of his own. One was school uniforms, familiar in England but not in Halifax. They were soon the butt of local jokes and mischief. As the *British Colonist* put it, Dalhousie High School had "monkeyfied the pupils ... until the poor sinners are hunted like rabbits by all the ragamuffins in the city." Reid also found his Nova Scotian students intelligent but declared them bone lazy. They were good-natured but utterly ignorant about the geography and history of North America, their arithmetic outdated and clumsy. Reid wanted to push them harder, but found that the discipline available to him – homework or staying after school – was not sufficiently stern. He wanted corporal punishment, as he was used to in England, but he told the governors ruefully, "the spirit of the age seems against the latter." The school proceeded nevertheless, with about eighty students by the end of 1856, from the middle and upper classes of Halifax.[9]

Presbyterian Overtures

At the same time as the Dalhousie School was opening, the Presbyterians were trying to combine forces, ecclesiastical and educational. On 6 February 1856 three committees met in solemn conclave in Poplar Grove Church in Halifax, representing the three separate Presbyterian synods in Nova Scotia – the Presbyterian Church of Nova Scotia, the Free Church of Nova Scotia, and the Kirk of Scotland. The Free Church was new on the scene, having been created by the great disruption of 1843 in Britain, which had spilled over into North America. This upheaval, the last major Presbyterian row over church organization, was over the question of whether a congregation had the right to refuse a pastor presented lawfully to it. The issue had been brewing for a decade, and broke into the open in 1843. The Free Church asserted the congregation's right to veto, if it chose, any such presentation.

Nova Scotians aimed to reunite what in Scotland had been sundered. The chairman of the three committees was the Reverend James Ross, professor of biblical literature at the West River Seminary, near Pictou. Aside from union, the other main concern was the deeply felt Presbyterian need for education in science and literature. To this end, "the original constitution of Dalhousie College ... seems fitted to supply this want," said the three-committee group, and they agreed to call on the Dalhousie board. That was done two days later at St Matthew's Presbyterian (Kirk) Church. William Young, for the Dalhousie board, replied that Dalhousie's present annual income was only £800 currency, of which £570 was reserved for the three teachers of the Dalhousie School, with £80 for annual repairs. Dalhousie, thus, had no money for an additional chair, nor did Young, at that point premier of Nova Scotia, hold out any hope of getting money from the legislature. Could the Presbyterians themselves endow a chair or two? If they could, Dalhousie would offer space in the college building.[10]

Young's offer was made, so the *Presbyterian Witness* said, on two conditions: that no clergyman be appointed professor, and that any professor be subordinate to Hugo Reid, the principal of the school. There was criticism of William Young for the first condition, though the second was largely accepted then and later. The Presbyterians pointed out, sensibly enough, that in Nova Scotia, and in British North America, the only highly educated class *were* the ministers. Anyway, said the *Presbyterian Witness*, the time was past when "a clerical Professor would swamp a college."

This question was not a new one. It is recorded in the Assembly *Journals* for 1839 in the debates over the new Dalhousie bill, the result of the row over Crawley. But it had never been part of Dalhousie regulations and there is some doubt that William Young, who could hardly be described as precipitate, would have put it that bluntly. Joseph Howe informed the secretary of the Dalhousie board that he had never assented to any such restriction at any Dalhousie meeting he had attended. "We can no more close the Institution [Dalhousie] against Clergymen than against Printers or Lawyers, Doctors or Booksellers." Even had the board the power, said Howe, it would be unwise:

Much of the little learning that there is in this Province is in possession of the Clergy, and though I quite admit their propensity to wrangle and fight about Education as they do about Religion, still I am not sure that an Institution that admits them, with all their faults to its highest honors and distinctions, will not more surely prosper.

Moreover the Presbyterians, of all the sects, had always been zealous friends of education. Howe had no wish to inflame the Presbyterians against Dalhousie, or against the Liberal government of William Young. To exclude Presbyterian ministers would create feelings akin to those aroused by the Crawley exclusion of 1838; worse, indeed, for the church was more numerous and powerful than the Baptists.

It is clear from Howe's remarks that Dalhousie College was not, perhaps had never been, politically neutral. Like the Sleeping Beauty, she had been awakened in 1838 by a fair prince carrying the shield of Reform; she had been put to sleep again by the wicked Tories, and brought to half-life after their defeat in 1848. Dalhousie was a Reform/Liberal institution; in the 1850s it was defended by the leading Reform/Liberal newspaper, the *Morning Chronicle*; and it was criticized by the leading Tory/Conservative newspaper, the *British Colonist*.

William Young was also persuaded to be flexible by a man who knew a great deal about colleges, education, and Nova Scotia: the new principal of McGill University, John William Dawson, of Pictou, appointed to McGill in September 1855. Dawson was a promising geologist in 1850 when Joseph Howe appointed him superintendent of education for the province. Aged thirty, Dawson threw himself into his work with apostolic zeal, for three years criss-crossing the province, and producing comprehensive and searching reports. He resigned in 1853 from ill-health (and frustration with the Liberal government), and was appointed to a New Brunswick royal commission on the future of King's College, Fredericton. The subsequent creation of the University of New Brunswick owed much to Dawson.[11] He wrote to William Young in December 1854, urging the latest New Brunswick recommendations as "an admirable argument for a *central college* on the most modern principles ... I wish, above all things," he told the premier of Nova Scotia, "you could get a grant of £1,000 per annum to Dalhousie, and let us try the same experiment here. With the great local advantages of Halifax, it must do even better than Frederickton [*sic*]." But a premier whose working majority was volatile could not bring that about. A year later Young, discouraged with his efforts to energize Dalhousie College, got solace from Dawson. Take heart, said Dawson; McGill's conditions were worse. Get a new charter that allows other institutions to affiliate with Dalhousie, on the New Brunswick plan. Then Dawson read in the Halifax *Presbyterian Witness* accounts of the rapprochment of February 1856, and its failure. His letter to Young with its basic good sense must be quoted:

You will I am sure excuse me for suggesting a way in which this may be turned to good account.

Let the [Dalhousie] governors give by resolution, or if necessary by getting a short act of the legislature, a University character to the college, and open negotiations with the Presbyterians or other churches offering to take their professors with such endowments or grants as they have, giving them the use of the building, the co-operation of your teachers, and the benefit of University degrees with free scholarships for students for the University. These would be material advantages to them, and would at once elevate your college to a position that would soon enable it to command legislative aid.

Do not fear clerical professors; in a non-sectarian provincial institution with a public trust they will be quite harmless, and proscribing them will cause only mischief.[12]

Young and the governors paid attention to Dawson's suggestions. They drew up a minute, dated 18 March 1856, embodying them. As Young put it to Dawson, "I have [had] passed a minute throwing open its [Dalhousie's] portals and not excluding clerical professors. This movement may lead to important results." It did. The important results were to come in two stages, 1856 and 1862. Discussions with the Congregationalists and Presbyterians were renewed. The Presbyterians were, however, still unhappy with the Dalhousie School, even if the rule against clerical professors was dropped. The Synod of the Free Church regarded "Dalhousie College in its present condition as a sham, a mockery and a disgrace. Its funds have been perverted from their original intention. It is now merely a rival (and not a very formidable rival either) to the Free Church Academy." The Dalhousie governors were, however, reluctant to part with their new high school, and preferred to try a college tier on top of it.[13]

The Congregationalists were less choosy than the Presbyterians, mostly because they couldn't be anything else. The Congregationalists were part of a New England group from which the Nova Scotia Baptists had developed. They were Puritans who had insisted upon the autonomy of the congregation, not unlike the Free Kirk, as against the aristocracy of Presbyterianism which exercised its control through an ascending series of ecclesiastical courts. Groups with these beliefs came to Liverpool, Nova Scotia, before the American Revolution. Old Yankees they were, with fish, molasses, and rum in their business and a stern and Protestant God in their hearts. One of them, James Gorham, left £3,000 to found a college; Gorham College in Liverpool

opened in 1851, with an English principal, the Reverend Frederick
Tomkins, MA, of University College, London. It was going, with prospects of success, when on 7 February 1854 the building burned to the
ground. A building fund was started, growing slowly, when the possibility of amalgamation with Dalhousie College opened up.[14]

Congregationalist Addition, 1856–71
The new policy of Dalhousie – the result of advice from Howe and
Dawson and action from Young and the Dalhousie board – was set out
on 18 March 1856, and is of some importance. Dalhousie would
admit any body of Christians maintaining a denominational seminary
on the following terms:

1 Any body willing to combine its funds with Dalhousie College's
would have represention on the Dalhousie board.
2 All future funds acquired to be added to the common pool.
3 Chairs of professors, and all classes, would be open to all creeds,
"merit only being considered in the selection."

The arrangements with Gorham College were worked out on an
amended basis. Two professorships were established: the Reverend
Frederick Tomkins as professor of mathematics and principal, and the
Reverend George Cornish professor of classics, both paid by Gorham.
The Dalhousie board decided there would be no amalgamation of
funds until the union of Dalhousie and Gorham College had had
chance to develop.[15]

This college section of Dalhousie was opened officially on 20
October 1856, with an inaugural address by Hugo Reid, who was
made dean of faculty. This departure was praised by the *Presbyterian
Witness*, the two Gorham professors especially. But other newspapers
were less sanguine. The *Acadian Recorder* complained that Dalhousie
College had taken over the least numerous of all the denominations.
The *Morning Chronicle*, the Liberal spokesman, defended the governors and their idea as a useful first step. Nevertheless, this university
stage did not prosper. Cornish resigned in the spring of 1857 and went
to McGill, where ultimately the Congregationalist funds followed him.
Then ill-health compelled Tomkins to return to England, and the university section of the Dalhousie School was forced to discontinue.[16]

Reid reported eighty-eight pupils in the high school at the end
of 1857, but personal quarrels developed with his assistant, James
Woods, which the board found it impossible to resolve. Woods
resigned and set up his own school, Spring Garden Academy, in
competition. By 1859 attendance at Dalhousie was down to fifty.

Reid resigned in January 1860. One other professor, Count George d'Utassy, professor of modern languages, was given six months' notice. Athletic but diminutive, Count d'Utassy, besides languages, had specialized in fencing, dancing, and horses.[17]

At this point the minutes of the Dalhousie Board of Governors close down for two years. When the governors resurfaced in February 1862, it was to consider whether the college should be turned into a museum; its income could be used to arrange the McCulloch collections and buy new exhibits, and thus become the Provincial Museum of Nova Scotia. The governors had all but come to the end of their tether; their high school experiment had come and it had gone; their union with Gorham College had dissipated. What could they now do with the place? The new University of New Brunswick Act of 1859, establishing a provincial university in Fredericton, seemed in striking contrast to Halifax. The handsome sandstone building, set in its ample acres on the hillside on the edge of Fredericton, had been reconstituted by the energy, interest, and talent of an unusually able lieutenant-governor, Sir Edmund Head, and the royal commission he had sponsored.[18] The university's thirty-three students were a comment on the now moribund Dalhousie College building on the Grand Parade in downtown Halifax.

The Dalhousie governors were well aware of these difficulties. Perhaps the most concerned was the premier of Nova Scotia himself, now in 1862 Joseph Howe. One of Howe's Presbyterian friends was the Reverend Peter MacGregor, the minister of Poplar Grove Presbyterian Church, Halifax, since 1843. A Pictou Academy graduate, vigorous and well thought of, MacGregor, fourteen years younger than Howe, talked with Howe from time to time about Dalhousie's problems. In June 1862 Howe set down some frank suggestions that MacGregor could show to his Presbyterian friends.

There were now, said Howe, only four Dalhousie governors left: the chief justice (William Young), Andrew MacKinlay (the bookseller), Dr Avery, and himself. The Dalhousie College building was solid and could easily be put in good repair. The income from its invested funds, and from rents, amounted in all to £900 currency a year. Fifty students at £10 each, or one hundred at £5, would give another £500. If you Presbyterians, said Howe, have any funds for secular education – say another £300 a year – then the total, £1,700, would found a decent university with five or six decently paid professors. Having laid this out, Howe went on: "If this can be done now is the time. If it cannot we must turn the College into a Provincial Museum or risk the confiscation of its funds by some hostile movement for which the present condition of the property furnishes a fair excuse."[19] That was plain talking; it carried an unmistakable ring of authenticity. It is a neat summary of the condition of Dalhousie in June 1862, presented on the very eve of critical meetings of the two Presbyterian synods. Howe's letter was undoubtedly intended for that specific purpose.

The Presbyterians Rally

Had the Presbyterians believed in bad omens, they could well have taken the view that Dalhousie College was an ill-starred venture. Its history over the forty-four years of its existence had comprehended indifference, prejudice, chicanery, timidity, occasionally boldness and courage; it had been and was still a political issue. As Howe noted, some action to make it operational had now to be taken or Dalhousie would have to be thrown to the wolves, its endowment given away to causes ostensibly more worthy, its building made more useful than a private high school or a post office. Dalhousie's funds, the *Christian Messenger* suggested, had been contributed by the whole community, and to the community they might properly return. The Reverend George Grant noted in the Kirk periodical, the *Monthly Record*, that if Dalhousie were not revived, "the last hope for the higher education of the country on a liberal basis would be lost forever." The college had "never yet had a fair trial; let us give it one."[20] He urged the same message privately with Charles Tupper, the Conservative party's strong and able first mate. Grant protested to Tupper against any proposed subversion of the Dalhousie charter and of the intentions of its founder, and he assured Tupper of the support of the Kirk in any effort to revive Dalhousie.[21]

George Monro Grant was a Kirk minister out of Pictou County who knew from hard personal experience those bitter Presbyterian rivalries. He was a man who fought against divisions, and for unions. He used to say that in the Presbyterian religion all the splits were made in Scotland and all the unions in British North America. Grant's ally, the Scottish-born Allan Pollok, was sent out to Nova Scotia and became the pastor of St Andrew's Church, New Glasgow, in 1852. Grant and Pollok both took an active role in the Kirk Synod, and early came to the conclusion that the most important issue facing the Kirk in Nova Scotia was that of producing a native-trained ministry. The Kirk needed something better than a system of sending Nova Scotian students off for six or seven years to Glasgow, Scotland, or to Kingston, Canada West.

The Kirk Synod met at St Andrew's Church, New Glasgow on 25 June 1862. It passed the following resolution: "Whereas there has not hitherto existed any unsectarian institution in Nova Scotia for the higher education of the country," and since provision for such was made in the constitution of Dalhousie College, a committee should be appointed to recommend action. The Kirk committee agreed on a number of points. First, that in the past the Kirk had not taken the interest in Nova Scotian university education "that she ought to have taken, and which from the history of her Mother Church she would be expected to take." Second, that a sound curriculum of literary and scientific education might be established at Dalhousie College "with any or all of the religious denominations of the Province." That very evening the Kirk committee met with Peter MacGregor and Professors Ross and King, members of the committee of the Presbyterian Church of the Lower Provinces, also in session in New Glasgow.[22]

The "Presbyterian Church of the Lower Provinces" was the union of the Free Church of Scotland and the Presbyterian Church of Nova Scotia. Four years in the making, it was effected in 1860. The Free Church had founded an academy and divinity school in Halifax, headed by George Munro of Pictou; the Presbyterian Church of Nova Scotia had established a seminary at West River, transferred to Truro in 1856. The union of the two Presbyterian churches produced a rationalization, by which academic work was done in Truro and theology in Halifax. This latter unit would eventually become Pine Hill Divinity College. Altogether the Presbyterian Church of the Lower Provinces was a stronger body and had better institutions than any the Kirk could muster. The Kirk Presbyterians in 1861 were nineteen thousand in all, or 6 per cent of the total population of Nova Scotia; the new Presbyterian Church of the Lower Provinces boasted sixty-nine thousand adherents in Nova Scotia, 21 per cent of the population.

There were thus several groups that combined in 1862: Howe and the Liberal government, urged on by Peter MacGregor and William Dawson of McGill; Grant, Pollok, and the Kirk, who made their views known to Charles Tupper of the Conservative opposition; and the United Presbyterians, among whom was the Reverend George Patterson, of Salem Church, Green Hill, in Pictou County.

George Patterson was the education spokesman for the United Presbyterians. He, too, was a product of Pictou Academy, and had in fact followed Thomas McCulloch to Dalhousie, where he had been until McCulloch's death in 1843. Patterson was thoroughly acquainted with Dalhousie's difficulties. He wrote to his friend E.M. McDonald, former editor of the New Glasgow *Eastern Chronicle* and now in 1862 the Queen's Printer at Halifax, asking him to use his influence with Premier Howe to prevent Dalhousie from degenerating into an "old curiosity shop," as opponents of the museum idea were wont to call it. Patterson was certain that the United Presbyterians could be persuaded to cooperate in re-establishing Dalhousie.[23]

George Monro Grant, a Lismer sketch reproduced from Harvey's *Dalhousie*. "Our colleges [are] ill-equipped, half-starved, narrow, petty and sectarian."

A special committee was struck to confer with one already established by the Kirk Synod. Meetings between the Kirk and the United Presbyterian committees went forward with unusual harmony. They agreed they would continue to meet after the closing of their respective synods. The main object of both committees, said the *Presbyterian Witness*, was the same: "to secure a more complete course of Classical, Literary and Philosophical instruction than can be afforded in Nova Scotia by a Seminary supported by a single denomination." There were risks in giving up a working seminary at Truro, but more important was "the prospect of seeing established a College for the whole Province, capable of furnishing a course of Education for young men aspiring to fill the different professions." The *Witness* did not mention it in this context, but the Presbyterian buildings in both Truro and Halifax were outmoded, cramped, wooden, and in need of repair.[24]

George Grant agreed. The greatest defect of the Nova Scotian educational system was "Our Colleges, Universities falsely so called, ill-equipped, half-starved, narrow, petty and sectarian." Dalhousie would be a provincial university, denominational only because it would receive support from religious bodies. There was nothing strange about that, "for no University has ever been able to stand in America unless it was so supported."[25]

The main point for the Presbyterians was to ensure all-party agreement to any proposed legislation. There was no sense in making Dalhousie, once again, the creature of the Liberal party, to be shoved into the cold when the Conservatives came into power. That possibility virtually disappeared when the Conservative *British Colonist* came out with an editorial supporting Dalhousie College. It represented the influence of Charles Tupper, the rising man of the Conservative party. People would be glad to learn, the *Colonist* said, that there was now a prospect of Dalhousie College being at last put into efficient operation in 1863. Readers did not need to be reminded of its history; it was well known that the current governors had done their best to bring life to the college and had signally failed. But a month ago, in mid-July, delegates from the two Presbyterian synods had met the Dalhousie College board, and a scheme had been worked out. The *British Colonist* looked forward to seeing Dalhousie College in operation side by side with the other valuable colleges of the province. And, it added, "The jealousy which at one time existed between the different Colleges, has, we are happy to say, given place to a generous emulation with each other." That effusion was the triumph of hope over experience. On the other hand, Conservatives were bound to represent that the colleges they had been mainly instrumental in creating were, indeed, valuable.

The terms were these. Dalhousie had annual income from its funds and from rents of £900 currency, enough to fund three professors. The United Presbyterians would fund two more, and the Kirk one, also for a total of £900 per annum. Each professor the Presbyterians funded required a capital sum of £5,000, invested at 6 per cent, to produce £300 a year. The *quid pro quo* for that substantial gift was the right of the Presbyterians – or any other body – to nominate the professor to the chair, and with it the right to a seat on the Dalhousie Board of Governors. The stipulation of the two Presbyterian committees was that Dalhousie governors not be removable at the pleasure of the lieutenant-governor-in-council. They wanted some protection against the wilfulness or arbitrariness of a provincial cabinet. The consent of the Board of Governors was required to any resignation.[26] In the meantime the three empty seats on the Dalhousie board were filled, at the end of July 1862, by three ingenious nominations, representing three quite other denominations: Charles Tupper, a Baptist; S.L. Shannon, Halifax lawyer and Methodist; and J.W. Ritchie, Halifax lawyer and Anglican.

These public appointments generated not a little suspicion in Methodist and especially in Baptist quarters. The three new governors were put in, said the Baptist *Christian Messenger*, "as decoy ducks to the denominations they represent." The metaphor speaks volumes. The Methodists would have preferred Shannon almost anywhere else than where he was; as for Tupper, he was more a guarantee of political than ecclesiastical balance. So said the Halifax *Evening Express*, a Catholic paper.[27]

The Dalhousie bill was introduced to the Assembly by Howe on 10 March 1863, and went through very quietly. It was carefully framed and, if anything, deliberately understated. "An Act for the Regulation and Support of Dalhousie College," had as its preamble:

Whereas it is expedient to extend the basis on which the said College is established, and to alter the constitution thereof, so as the benefits that may be fairly expected from its invested capital, and its central position may, if possible, be realized, and the design of its original founders as nearly as may be carried out.

The key provision was that whenever any body of Christians, of whatever religious persuasion, would endow one or more professorships "for any branch of literature or science, approved of by the Board," to the extent of £300 (or $1,200) a year, then the right of nomination to the chair, and the right to nominate a governor was given.

The governors had the power to appoint the president, professors, and other college officers. Dalhousie College "shall be deemed and taken to be a University, with all the usual and necessary privileges of such institutions," giving bachelor's, master's, and doctor's degrees. No religious tests were to be required of professors, students, or officers of the college. The internal government was to be in the hands of the Senatus Academicus, formed by the professors, and whose rules were subject to board approval.

The 1863 act repealed all previous Dalhousie College acts save one – that of 1823, lending £5,000 to Dalhousie College. That stood, still a too tender subject to be gratuitously waved in front of the Assembly. The Dalhousie bill came up for second reading six weeks later; there was no debate. It received a minor amendment in the Legislative Council that the Assembly accepted without demur, and so the new Dalhousie College Act became law on 29 April 1863.[28]

The Dalhousie Act was clever for what it did not say. The word Presbyterian was not mentioned. "The plan is to be, as it were," offered the *Evening Express*, "a stroke of genius, combining the beauties of both the sectarian and non-sectarian systems. It is to be in fact a system altogether *sui generis*." It was regrettable, said the *Express*, that the result might well be failure, failure more signal than any that had "yet overtaken this ill-starred Institution." If three or four denominations were to league together against the Presbyterians' "appropriation of Dalhousie funds," the institution could well be in danger, act or no act. The other denominations would never give up their own colleges; hence the Presbyterians, knowing that, could found their own college, using public money by calling it a non-denominational university. The Baptists and the Methodists took the view that to call Dalhousie a provincial university was nothing "but a transparent misnomer for appropriating £900 of Provincial money."[29]

This was the rough weather brewing outside. And even if the act was now passed, the Presbyterians, inside, did not regard Dalhousie College as a *fait accompli*. The act was, rather, a perimeter within which to conduct further negotiations. Indeed, the issues had not been settled. The synods had not yet approved the actions of their committees. Each synod would have to find money, the Kirk £5,000 currency, the United Presbyterians double that, and they would have to dun their constituents to get it.

The two committees added several conditions after the Dalhousie Act was passed. They wanted Dalhousie to keep in mind the future establishment of medical and law faculties; they asked that in arts there be at least six professors: classics, logic and metaphysics, mathematics, moral philosophy, natural philosophy (i.e., physics), and the physical sciences of chemistry, geology, and botany. If all went as planned, urged Allan Pollok to his Kirk readers, "there is nothing to prevent Dalhousie College becoming a University like the University of London, McGill College, or the University of Toronto."[30]

Pollok, himself a graduate of Glasgow, extolled the virtues of size. The denominational colleges of Nova Scotia were, he said, too small; fifteen students per professor was the average. In actual fact the colleges *were* small: UNB had thirty-four, Acadia thirty-two, King's fifty-two students, not distinguishing between part-time and full-time; St Mary's had 108 and St Francis Xavier 102, though those larger figures may comprehend academies. What Pollok was looking for can be put in a mid-twentieth-century metaphor, namely, critical mass:

Young men learn most from those with whom they study ... The conflict of mind with mind constitutes an important influence in mental and moral training. But for this, science might be more effectually learned in the closet from suitable handbooks than from the prelections of Professors. A large attendance also infuses energy into the Professors and enlivens their work .... It is needless to say that our denominational colleges can never have a large attendance.[31]

A further difficulty developed. Dalhousie had originally agreed to pay £200 from its own funds to a teacher of modern languages, plus an extra £50 to Professor James Ross of Truro for his function as principal of Dalhousie. At that point the government announced that they were going to build a new post office, and thus ere long, Dalhousie College would be deprived of £200 per annum in rent. Thus Dalhousie would need the £250 grant that the government gave to the United Presbyterian College, now in Truro.

In short, nothing went easily. At the Kirk Synod in September 1863 Pollok found that he was in a minority. He stoutly maintained that the Dalhousie proposal had the support of 90 per cent of the laymen, whatever the Kirk Synod might think. James Ross, the moving spirit with the United Presbyterians, thought it would be a hard road; he found opposition not only in Truro, which resented the loss of the Presbyterian College, but "extreme and violent opposition" among the Kirk people in Pictou. The worst of it was that those two counties, Colchester and Pictou, were the ones Ross was counting on for financial support. Ross asked the Dalhousie board whether the Presbyterians could keep the £250 until the opposition died away and the advantages of Dalhousie had become more patent. If so, "all might yet be well. Without it I am afraid we cannot."[32]

Ultimately both groups of Presbyterians won through. Allan Pollok and George Grant – now in Halifax as minister of St Matthew's

Church – got approval for the Dalhousie venture through the Kirk Synod, without dissent. In the United Presbyterian Synod there was a vote, and the Dalhousie resolution carried finally by forty-one to seventeen.[33]

The Presbyterian synods had to tax themselves, a capital sum of $20,000 in the Kirk's case, and $2,400 a year in the case of the United Presbyterians. The latter would also have to give up their Truro college. Both synods made real sacrifices to go into the Dalhousie scheme. Pollok and Grant, Ross and his colleagues were greatly helped, however, by the fury unleashed by the Baptists and the Methodists against the new Dalhousie College. To the *Christian Messenger* and the *Provincial Wesleyan*, almost the worst aspect of the Dalhousie proposal was the Presbyterian claim to make Dalhousie into *the* provincial university – exactly what made the scheme acceptable to the broad reach of the synods' constituencies. For years Dalhousie had been nothing, had been "in a state of suspended animation," as the *Express* put it, and the question mainly before the public had been, "What shall we do with it?" It still had nothing in 1863, no library, no scholarships, no scientific apparatus. Not only would the Baptists not support it, but they "will resent it as a wrong, its being called a Provincial Institution at all." For Baptists read also Methodists, Anglicans, and Catholics. Call Dalhousie what you may, said the *Evening Express*, it will be a Presbyterian college, with Presbyterian students, and for the most part Presbyterian professors. It won't be any the worse for that: but let us call things what they are.[34] A convention of Baptists was held in Amherst at the end of August 1863, where it was resolved that the Acadia Board of Governors should take such measures as in their judgment would ameliorate the alleged preferences, financial and otherwise, given to Dalhousie College. Jonathan McCully, editor of the Halifax *Morning Chronicle*, opposed this departure. When nothing was happening with Dalhousie, McCully noted, nothing was said; the moment Dalhousie took on the appearance of life, "the Baptists came forth with a bludgeon to dash out its brains." When the Acadia College board met on 1 October, it went straight for repeal of the Dalhousie Act. No one need be surprised, said the *Messenger*, that the Baptists were taking this strong ground. It was only twenty-five years since they were rejected by Dalhousie; now, after hard work and self-sacrifice, with their own college working efficiently, they are invited by those "who spurned them from their doors to sacrifice the very Institutions which their [Dalhousie's] injustice made indispensable!"[35]

The Methodists were of much the same mind. That Methodists could ever consider abandoning their own college, said the *Provincial Wesleyan*, "to help build up Dalhousie, is, *to us*, quite inconceivable."

That any one denomination should monopolize Dalhousie, "which from its foundation was designed to be Provincial, and to have available for denominational ends all the Funds and property of such institution ... is not to be tolerated." By all means let the Presbyterians have their own college, but call it what it is. The Presbyterians should have refused Dalhousie's offer from the start, saying, "No, we cannot accept it. Other denominations, situated as they are cannot reasonably be expected to fall in with this project. At all events they should be consulted." To those who said that Dalhousie ought to be given a fair trial, the *Wesleyan* answered that neither Dalhousie nor its supporters were in any position to make such a demand.[36]

When the 1864 session of the legislature opened, this accumulated opposition broke in upon it, represented by forty-eight petitions against Dalhousie, manufactured mostly in the Annapolis Valley, including one from the trustees, governors, and fellows of Acadia College, to repeal or amend the Dalhousie Act. The serious move was on 23 March; Avard Longley, the Conservative MLA from Annapolis, moved repeal of the act. Charles Tupper, now provincial secretary after the election of 1863 and virtual premier, moved an amendment that the House go into committee to consider education generally. As the debate developed, a number of resolutions and amendments were offered, demanding repayment of the 1823 £5,000 loan, or giving the Dalhousie College building to the Presbyterians and sequestering the Dalhousie endowment, now estimated at some $51,590, dividing it equally among the Baptists, Methodists, Anglicans, Roman Catholics, and Presbyterians.

Tupper was good, as he always would be, at bold defences of unpopular positions. He hated, he said, to put himself, a Baptist, in opposition to Mr Longley, a member of Tupper's own party and a co-religionist. Still, it would have been better had Longley demonstrated his opposition in 1863, not 1864. The House felt in 1863, said Tupper, as no doubt it did now, that there was no reasonable ground on which to oppose the Dalhousie Act. Every intelligent man grasped the good sense of it. Dalhousie now had forty full-time students, twenty part-time. Tupper concluded that, "possessing, as I may confess to do, some fondness for public life, I would infinitely prefer the fate which he [Longley] threatens me [i.e., being defeated] to the highest post my country can offer, if it must be purchased by an act so unpatriotic, so unjust, as the resolution which he has moved would involve."

S.L. Shannon, Conservative MLA from Halifax and the only other member of the Dalhousie board in the legislature, said the reason why petitions against Dalhousie College were so widely signed was the be-

Charles Tupper

Charles Tupper, *c.* 1880. "Make Dalhousie worthy of our fine province. It will do no harm to [Acadia] or to any other College."

lief, sedulously fostered, that the denominational colleges would be swept out of existence by Dalhousie. He too would have opposed Dalhousie had that been so. He suspected that "the old feeling of revenge still rankled in some bosoms, and the wish to destroy the [Dalhousie] College because the governors who were dead long ago had done injustice to a distinguished Baptist!" But there is no way Dalhousie could injure Acadia, or any other college. "Dalhousie was in reality," Shannon said, "a scheme to assist in the education of the middle class of Halifax."[37]

On 29 March, Tupper's amendment to go into committee to consider education passed by a vote of thirty to fourteen. Thus was the Longley move to repeal the Dalhousie Act rejected. This apparent decisiveness is misleading. None of the fourteen MLAs who wanted the repeal of the Dalhousie Act were from the opposition Liberals; they were all of Tupper's own Conservative party. His victory in the 1863 election had been sweeping: forty seats in a fifty-five-seat House. It was as well that the Dalhousie Act commanded Liberal support, for one-third of Tupper's own party deserted him on that issue, and voted for repeal. That included all four MLAs from Kings, three from Hants, two from Digby, and a sprinkling of others. Had they been joined by the fifteen Liberals, the Dalhousie bill would have been dead. It was saved by Tupper and a bipartisan majority. Of course, the Liberals had put through the 1863 act in the first place. They had long supported Dalhousie, but until 1862 they had not been able to find the means, or the support, to make it work. Now it was in operation once again; what it had to do now was prove itself. Charles Tupper went into the enemy's camp in Wolfville in June 1864 and made a strong speech. Sustain Dalhousie, he said, "and make it worthy of our fine province. It will do no harm to Dr Cramp's really fine institution upon this beautiful hill here, or to any other College." All Dr Cramp of Acadia could say that day was, "I am still for war!"[38]

Lord Dalhousie's Experiment

Lord Dalhousie in 1818 tried to do what had hardly yet been attempted in British North America, or for that matter in the United States: develop a college that had no religious or denominational base. In many ways he was right; Methodist mathematics, Presbyterian physics, Anglican classics, was ridiculous on the face of it. A university where all creeds may be taught the arts and sciences was plausible and high-sounding, but it had not had much success. Even UNB, formed in 1859, was, said the *Evening Express*, "struggling against fate." In Nova Scotia the denominational colleges had got their way. The tide of 1838 had been missed; Crawley and the Baptists had been rejected by Dalhousie and that had led in turn to the failure of the One College idea. One might even argue, as the *Evening Express* did in a perceptive editorial, that the reason for the failure of Dalhousie in the past had not been its governors, nor its professors: "An attempt was made to raise up a general College or University on the model of those in Scotland, without sufficiently taking into account the very different relative conditions of the two populations."[39]

There is something in that. Until the 1860s Dalhousie had simply not commanded popular support; its success had not mattered. In 1863 it would make its own way, this time with the strong support of Presbyterians of both major camps. That Presbyterian habit, internecine wrangling, had largely disappeared with the union of the Seceders and Free Kirkers in 1860 as the United Presbyterians. As for the Auld Kirk, it too supported Dalhousie; its man on the Dalhousie board was George Grant. The Presbyterians were powerful, energetic, spartan; they, of all the denominations, cherished education the most. Dalhousie was non-denominational in appearance, in its laws and practice. But the vital energy that would now inhabit its heart would come from the Presbyterian love of learning and the Scottish habits of self-discipline and diligence that came with it.

· 5 ·

Great Talent, Little Money
1863–1879

Halifax in 1863. Opening of Dalhousie College. James Ross
and his five professors. Charles Macdonald. James De Mille.
Curriculum of the 1860s and 1870s. Dalhousie's students.
Faculty of Medicine, 1868–75. The University of Halifax,
1876–81. Penury.

The afternoon of Tuesday, 10 November 1863 was overcast; the wind
from the northeast seemed to make the old wooden houses of Halifax
huddle together as if for warmth. The grey smoke from the chimneys
was blowing out toward the grey sea; there would be snow before
morning.[1] Dalhousie College was opening once more, for the third
time.

The half-century-old grey stone building on the Grand Parade
looked out upon a Halifax slowly expanding and improving. Fire has-
tened the process. Granville Street was devastated by fire in 1859, and
it was then rebuilt in stone, a streetscape that is still attractive. The harbour's forest of masts and yards was bigger, as were the wharves and
the warehouses behind them. Halifax was still very much a military
place, and it showed in the red uniforms of the British soldiers, in the
blue of the navy, enjoying, or enduring, their lives in the most important military and naval station on the northwest Atlantic.

It was still dominated by the Citadel. The British army had started
rebuilding it in 1828; it was at last finished in 1860 at a cost of
£242,122, double the original estimate. After having strained the abilities, and as one historian suggests, the sanity, of a generation of military engineers, the rebuilt Citadel was rendered virtually obsolete by
technology, by the hitting power of the new, rifled artillery. Few military men were fully aware of that yet, and the Citadel would remain
occupied by British troops until 1907.[2]

Hugo Reid said in 1861 that it was the army and the navy that kept
Halifax alive. While that was partly true, Halifax was no longer so de-

95

pendent on military expenditure, although it would profit from wars for many a year yet. Reid suggested that the greatest danger to the British army in Halifax was not the enemy, whoever they might be, but something more insidious and longer lasting: Halifax daughters. "The merchants are rich, and their daughters are fair, and the mingled charms and dollars have a powerful effect on her Majesty's Service." In summer there were those delightful picnics and excursions in the environs, which were followed, often enough according to Reid, by a very old church service with the lines, "Who giveth this woman to be married to this man?"[3]

If they survived those dangers, the soldiers and sailors found Halifax much like other garrison towns. Occasionally angry at being victimized by bad rum and bad women, they would break out in frustration, as they had in 1838. There was an even bigger riot in 1863, a week before the Dalhousie bill was given second reading. Some soldiers were beaten up in a tavern on Barrack (now Brunswick) Street, so the soldiers took their revenge by setting fire to the place. Rioting broke out and two nights later some three hundred soldiers armed with sticks and slingshots took possession of the downtown streets for over an hour. Finally the military authorities from the Citadel brought things under control. The local newspapers were severe on the rioters, but the *Presbyterian Witness* suggested that the soldiers had over the years been mostly peaceable, that the cause was "the mean and miserable civilians" who were to blame, drugging and poisoning the soldiers with bad rum. Indeed, some strange concoctions were brewed up in those grim houses just two blocks above Dalhousie College.[4]

Edmund Burke once described the court of France before the Revolution as a setting where "vice itself lost half its evil by losing all its grossness." That was rarely true in Victorian Halifax. It was the theme of an editorial in the *Presbyterian Witness*, unhappy over the desecretion of Halifax's Sunday by military and naval bands. Music was bad enough on such a sacred day; the tunes they played were much worse, jocular airs too often, with highly unsuitable verses. "Pretty employment this...! Pretty preparation this for eternity!" It also descanted against Halifax theatres. The *British Colonist* replied that the Presbyterians seemed to be a group who enjoyed sullen hatred of anyone outside of "their own sanctimonious and hypocritical society." After all, said the *Colonist*, the Queen went to the theatre, and often. To which the *Witness* replied, "If the Queen frequents theatres the more's the pity!" It was not alone in its Puritan views. The *Provincial Wesleyan* was upset with the new dance that had been imported from wicked Europe in the 1850s, the waltz, that had been taken up in Halifax. The worst of it was, young ladies who ought to have been repelled by its lascivious and seductive rhythms seemed willing, recklessly, to enjoy it.[5]

Halifax in the 1860s, with grog shops and taverns everywhere with plenty of patrons, was anything but a staid place. In the view of some religious papers, it could have stood a deal of starching. Temperance movements had been steadily gathering strength since the 1840s, and it was not difficult to understand why. One could hardly walk a few hundred yards in Halifax, complained the *Witness* in 1856, "without meeting a staggering 'Crimean hero!' – and very frequently these heroes are to be seen lying full length in the gutter or on the muddy street."[6] No one could safely allege that Halifax was puritan; there were newspapers ready to try to make it so but it was uphill work.

Dalhousie College Opens

Dalhousie College was fairly in the midst of all of this. Its first concern was to shake off the dust and the mice of the past four years. The *Morning Sun* called it a "mouldering memorial" to Lord Dalhousie, hoping, despite that, it might turn into a provincial university whose professors were, for once, "up to their work." Save us, it said, from another sectarian college, with its "interminable propagation of polemical divinity." There was still plenty of that; Dalhousie would open amid the burgeoning antipathy of the religious papers, especially the Methodist and Baptist ones; even the Anglicans could not resist pointing out how Dalhousie could never be the provincial university "so long as the institution at Windsor retains the Royal Charter which so long ago constituted it as the University of Nova Scotia." Nor was there much disposition on the Dalhousie governors' part to make it a triumph; Dalhousie's opening was low key, as befitted a college whose history had been, as the chairman remarked, "a list of failures." In 1863 Dalhousie confronted considerable opposition. As James De Mille was later to remark, it started "without prestige, but on the contrary with a past history of failures ... and there were not wanting those who prophesied a new failure."[7]

Nevertheless, on that November afternoon the east room of the building was crowded, so much so that the reporter for the *Morning Chronicle* had no room to make notes, and recorded what he heard by memory. The proceedings were opened by Major-General Sir Charles Hastings Doyle, administrator of the province in the absence of the lieutenant-governor in England, and commander-in-chief of the British troops (and militia) from Bermuda to Newfoundland.

Sir Charles presented an olive branch to the phalanxes of religious warriors. "I am informed," he said, "that this College will, in no respect, be hostile to the other Educational establishments in the province." He, too, mentioned failures. Dalhousie College had

hitherto failed to obtain the patronage of the public; but I sincerely believe that the steps now taken to obtain Professors of high repute, and the exertions which have been made to remove the causes which have led to previous failures, success may attend its future efforts; and I trust it may turn out that the retrograde movements which have occurred have been simply the *reculer pour mieux sauter*. Let *aucto splendore resurgo* be its motto henceforth."[8]

The chief justice, William Young, chairman of the Dalhousie Board of Governors since 1848, gave a history of Dalhousie, rehearsing its failures. Yet, he said, "its funds had not been diverted from their legitimate object, but were yet available to commence with, [and] they had a fine building in perfect order." The new principal, James Ross, who followed Young, felt he had to enter a caveat to that point. Whatever the exterior may have been, the building was deficient in interior accommodation. There was no room suitable to perform chemistry experiments, and precious little apparatus to do them with. Perhaps the citizens of Halifax could make donations that might help remedy some of these more patent deficiencies. He hoped that the Law Society of Halifax would consider soon establishing a chair in law, and that a medical school would not be far behind. Lectures began at ten o'clock the next morning, the first students walking across the Parade through the light snowfall.

Dalhousie College in November 1863 was an experiment. No one quite knew if it would work. Students came, but much of its future depended on its staff, and their reputation had yet to be essayed or developed. It would have to make its own way by its own virtues, whatever those might turn out to be. The first motto of Dalhousie, appearing on the first *Dalhousie Gazette* of 1869, began with the word "Forsan" (Perhaps). It was from Virgil's *Aeneid*, Book 1, line 203, "Forsan et haec olim meminisse juvabit" (Perhaps the time may come when these difficulties will be sweet to remember).

The following year a more confident motto, from the Earl of Dalhousie, was adopted, "Ora et labora." There seems to be a modern impression, owing to the great diminution of Latin literacy, that these are pious nouns. Quite the contrary; they are verbs, and stern Presbyterian imperatives at that: "Pray and work." Five of the six professors first appointed were Presbyterians, used to both. Six professors had been appointed by this time, of whom five had arrived. The two nominated by the United Presbyterians were James Ross, professor of ethics and political economy, and principal, and Thomas McCulloch,

Jr, professor of natural philosophy, both formerly at Truro. The Kirk nominee was Charles Macdonald of Aberdeen, whom George Grant knew and respected, professor of mathematics. For the three appointments available to them, the Dalhousie governors had the happy idea of appointing William Lyall, also of Truro, as professor of metaphysics, regarded by many as pre-eminent in British North America.

All of that was decided by early August 1863. Advertisements were placed in the Toronto, Saint John, and Charlottetown papers for applications to the chairs of classics and chemistry, and for a tutor in modern languages. There were eleven applicants for the chair of chemistry, including Abraham Gesner, the inventor of kerosene. The governors chose George Lawson of Queen's University, Kingston, whose specialty was botany as well as chemistry. All five appointees so far were Presbyterians. The sixth chair was classics. Dalhousie would have liked to appoint the Reverend Dr John Pryor, former president of Acadia, and now minister of the Granville Street Baptist Church. But he would not accept the basic condition of giving up his pastoral charge, so John Johnson, MA, an Anglican and Irish, was appointed.[9]

The one person who was not there was Charles Macdonald, whom the governors had not notified directly, assuming that his friend and Dalhousie governor, George Grant, would have done that. The board only found out at the end of October that Macdonald was awaiting formal notification. The day he received it, he resigned his Aberdeen charge; he would sail for Halifax in December, and would be ready for duty on 4 January.[10]

Dalhousie and Its Staff

The old Dalhousie building seemed positively palatial to the forty students who came that first session. Viewed from the north it was a big building, four stories high at the Duke Street level, even though at the Parade level it was only two. At the lowest level, with entrance only on Duke Street, were the vaults of Oland's Brewery. Students were jocular about the brewery. Parents in the country, said the *Dalhousie Gazette*, who worried about sending their sons to Dalhousie and their not being able to get enough beer, could rest easy.

"The Brewery," reasoned the Governors of the College, "will be a great help to our College, as it can afford to pay a good rent." "The College," reasoned the Governors of the Brewery, "will be a great help to our Brewery, as the students can afford to pay well for good beer." Thus they are mutually dependent on each other.

There was also a shop facing Barrington Street. On the second level, still below the Parade, were student rooms, accessible from above, a reading room, and a lounge where, as one student remembered, "all the mischief going was planned."[11] The janitor and his family occupied the other rooms on that floor. Errol Boyd had been in his position since February 1824; forty-four years of rent-free accommodations may have given him and his family a sense of owning the place. From the smells working their way to the floors above, it seemed to the professors that Errol Boyd was running either a cooking school or a boarding house; the smells of cooking, in the mornings especially, were so strong, professors were "so overpowered with the odoriferous energy as to be on the point of ... dismissing their classes." Who could concentrate on quadratic equations if one's mid-morning hunger were tempted by the luscious smell of roast beef, or even corned beef and cabbage? Boyd was told about it, but couldn't or wouldn't change. A new janitor was engaged, a quaint and likeable character named John Wilson.

On the Parade level, the college's main entrance and the two entrances on either side bridged a deep moat that gave light to the basement story where the postmaster and his family lived. Dalhousie's main entrance gave onto a large T-shaped hall eight feet wide that went the full thirty feet to the back of the building, past a large semi-circular staircase; at the back it branched twenty feet each way, east and west, into two large wing rooms. There were smaller rooms off the main corridor. The building was heated with beehive stoves[12] in each room, which were fed from a vast four-foot-high coal box placed into the window recess at the junction of the T. The hall was the main student meeting place, where songs and what were called "scrimmages" took place. A scrimmage is defined by the Oxford English Dictionary as "a noisy contention or tussle." Both songs and scrimmages were not infrequent, but seem to have been confined to times when lectures were not being given. Professors did not positively prohibit them but there were attempts to restrain their excesses. Charles Macdonald used to say, "There is nobody more tolerant of fun than myself when it reveals the presence of genius, and nobody less so when it is guided by stupidity." Where scrimmaging lay between those polarities was not always easy to discern. One student exercise was to see that every freshman was elevated onto the coal box, where they had to make a speech. One strong, six-foot freshman bragged that he would like to see sophomores try to elevate *him*. It was being duly done by a group of them, when who should walk by but Professor John Johnson. Just as D.C. Fraser was depositing his end of the load on the coal box Johnson, his Irish eyes sparkling with merriment not severity, said, "A little less energy, Mr. Fraser; much less energy."[13]

On the second floor were two rooms, the west one initially being the chemistry room, and the east occupied by Principal Ross who lectured on ethics and political economy three days a week. Under the roof, and giving access to it, was an attic, reached by a ladder. Eventually it would be converted into a chemistry laboratory. In winter excellent fun was to be had getting out onto the roof and pelting the passers-by below with snowballs. The pupils of the National School across the way, described by James Ross as the "rising savages of Halifax," were a tempting target.[14]

James Ross, the first principal of Dalhousie, was born at West River in 1811 and educated at Pictou Academy under McCulloch. His school mates had been J.W. Dawson, William McCulloch, and J.D. MacGregor. He was himself the product of a minister's home, one of fifteen children. He was about to go to Edinburgh University when he was urged to replace his father, who had died in 1834, at the West River Church. Duty triumphed, and eventually the West River Seminary evolved. Ross taught everything – Latin, Greek, mathematics, logic, moral philosophy, and in alternate years, physics and chemistry. He was named by the United Presbyterians as their appointee to the professorship of ethics and political economy at Dalhousie, and was made principal by the Dalhousie board, partly owing to his role at the college at Truro of which he had been principal.

He was now fifty-two, a useful and varied teacher rather than a scholar. He had stopped formal education when he was twenty-two, but he had learned much from McCulloch that stood him in good stead, and they remained in touch. There was no hypocrisy in McCulloch's comments to Ross when he was a young man. Your father was good, he said, but lacked fire. It is probably constitutional in your family, and for that reason "I have the more frequently impressed upon yourself the importance of energy."[15] There is evidence from Dalhousie students that James Ross never quite overcame this torpidity. His beautifully neat lecture notes came from a neat mind, but were delivered with a marked absence of vigour. As if to compensate for the absence of fire in his classes, he was a generous marker of examinations.

Ross took nothing for granted. If he took on a subject, he started at the foundations, deploring easy generalities. The students complained that he too often treated them like schoolboys. In some ways that was true, but it had virtues. G.G. Patterson said that while he had written many essays in Latin, and some in Greek, he had written none in English until one in metaphysics for Lyall in his third year (which was not returned) and two for "Jimmie" Ross in the fourth (which were returned, and closely marked). Like McCulloch, Ross hated superfluity.

James Ross, *c.* 1869, Principal, 1863–85. "He had steered Dalhousie through some very difficult water ... if he lacked flair, he had great moral strength."

There was also a certain taciturnity in Ross. Benjamin Russell, later jurist and teacher at Dalhousie Law School, went to Ross's very unpretentious house on Maitland Street in August 1864 to inquire about admission to Dalhousie. Perhaps even then one did not go to the principal's house with such questions, or Ross was wakened from a nap, for when he crossly came to the door without collar, he grumbled to Russell that most matriculation students did not know their Latin conjugations well enough. Russell, who did know, found him so disagreeable that he decided to go to Mount Allison instead. Certainly Ross had no great place in students' affections. He seems to have been conscious of two things especially: how much the success of the college depended upon him, and how short of money Dalhousie really was. Dalhousie lived on the edge of financial disaster for two-thirds of his presidency. Ross may well have been one of those unremembered presidents who are better at preventing evil than creating good.

Charles Macdonald, professor of mathematics from 1863 to 1901 had taught for some years in high schools in Edinburgh and Aberdeen before coming to Dalhousie at the age of thirty-five. He was a gifted teacher. Not only did he have a wide and trenchant knowledge of his subject but singular brilliance in its exposition. He was accurate and precise, but far from being coldly logical or pedantic. He loved his work, and it showed. He positively revelled in what he was doing. "Gentlemen," he would say in effect, "I am ravished with the thought of introducing you into the delightful mysteries of mathematics, in which recreation I am confident we shall both enjoy ourselves." That invitation students found irresistible. "Lead on," they would say, "we long to follow such a charismatic leader." There would he stand, his coat covered with chalk dust (for he did not wear a gown), his massive, leonine head thrown slightly back, his face radiant with the idea of opening up to those young minds a new field of knowledge, wholly certain he would carry most of them with him. He did not overburden his courses, but preferred discussion across a fairly narrow range. Thoroughness was what he was after. He had his touches of theatre. After a particularly good class he liked to throw the chalk backwards over his head and hit, more often than not, the waste basket in the corner. The students loved that stunt, and would cheer and clap with delight.[17]

Charlie, as the students called him behind his back, could say harsh things, more so than his colleagues, but he would say them with such humour and raciness, and with such a genial smile, that his remark would have the edge taken off it. When some student was flying too high, assuming too much, Macdonald would interrupt with a few coughs and say, "Euclid thought differently but he must have been mistaken." A student was grinning at something private one day, and Macdonald, who did not like such disruptions in his class, asked the student what he was grinning at. To get laugh from his fellows, the student said, "My own folly!" Macdonald could always go one better. "You'll find it," said he in a flash, "an inexhaustible source of amusement." All this with his Aberdeen accent. A student was giving some exposition of Euclid. "Your arguments," said Macdonald, "lack cogency, it's a spley method of speech ye have. It's not gude ... Use the first equation as a sort of sledgehammer to break up the others." He did not like his mathematics closed in by too vulgar an emphasis upon the practical applications of it. Asked by a student if he were going to teach "practical mathematics" (by which the student meant things like navigation, or surveying), he replied, "Practical Mathematics! You are here, Sir, to learn a modicum of *Mathematics*."

New students were apt to fear him. Dalhousie entrance examinations in mathematics were partly oral, which had the virtue of allowing Macdonald to become acquainted with his students. One entering student was not very big and was much in awe of Professor Macdonald at close quarters. Macdonald asked him a question about parallel lines, and then, hearing the student was from the Eastern Shore, went on to talk about fishing in the Salmon River. A pat on the shoulders, and the dread ordeal was over.

Life would be intolerable, Macdonald used to conclude, but for its fun. He had no great confidence in the immediate victory of merit, wisdom, justice. In the short run, he would say, humbug, pretence, and brazen self-assertion can often prevail against wisdom and "widehorizoned thought." In the long run, the latter win out, but it is a very long run.

He had his touches of whimsy. An invitation to tea to a lady student in the 1880s:

> Carissima Puellala
> March 2
> Will do
> At 6 p.m. for Miss B. and you
> C.M.

Of medium height, with a strong, well-knit frame, he liked to begin his Saturdays with a walk around Bedford Basin, a good fifteen miles. He was a great fisherman, and worked every good stream in convenient reach of Halifax. When James De Mille came in 1865, the two became boon companions, talking of their favourite subject – trout and salmon – in Latin. The most popular professor on staff, Macdonald carried the

Charles Macdonald, *c.* 1869, Professor of Mathematics,
1863–1901. "Far from being coldly logical or pedantic,
he was full of fire. He loved his work and it showed."

whole formidable mathematics curriculum on his broad shoulders from 1863 to 1901.

The other pillar of the Dalhousie curriculum was, of course, classics. John Johnson was twenty-eight years old, an MA from Trinity College, Dublin, as Irish as Charlie was Scottish. He had wit and charm, but he was less forthright; his shafts were more delicate, the way he was, crafted more gently. He was professor of classics from 1863 to 1894. His manner was at once cool and precise. One student remembered him skating by himself up at the far end of Second Lake in Dartmouth, where he fell heavily and broke his leg just above the ankle. He had to be got to the foot of First Lake somehow. A rude conveyance was made from a young spruce tree and thus he was dragged the three miles over the ice. Not a groan escaped him; he seemed more cheerful than anyone.

Johnson's classes could never be taken for granted, nor his examinations, for he was a close marker. You could not work off some glittering generality on him. If your answers were not to the point you might just as well forget it.[18] His classes were terrors to those reluctant to work. One student, trying to pass a Greek examination, used a translation, regarded then, and one hopes now, as counsel of desperation. It worked, and he received a better mark than many in class who were better Greek scholars. At the beginning of next term, asked questions in Greek class, the student gave such idiotic answers that Johnson, tightening his gown around his shoulders as he did when he was angry, said, "Dear me, Mr. X, how *did* you pass your last examination?" Then realizing what had happened, he added, "My lad, I will look after you at the next." No professor likes being hoodwinked.

Being Irish, Johnson was fond of rugby and followed the fortunes of the Dalhousie team rain or shine. Few were as faithful as he to the fortunes, good or bad, of Dalhousie rugby.

The oldest member of staff was William Lyall, professor of logic and metaphysics from 1863 to 1890. Lyall was born in 1811, educated at Glasgow and Edinburgh, and had been a tutor at Knox College at the University of Toronto. He then went to the Free Church Academy at Halifax, and so to Dalhousie via Truro. McGill gave him an LL. D. in 1864, and he was elected a charter member of the Royal Society of Canada when it was started in 1882. Lyall's philosophy derived mainly from the Scottish common-sense school and, like Thomas McCulloch, he was much influenced by Thomas Reid and Dugald Stewart. His first book, *Intellect, the Emotions, and the Moral Nature*, was published in 1855 and is one of the first written in Canada in the field. In that book philosophy was set down as the handmaiden of religion. "Philosophy may speculate: the Bible reveals..." was the way

John Johnson, *c.* 1869, Professor of Classics
1863–94. "He had wit and charm ... There was
something fine yet tough about 'Johnnie'
Johnson."

George Lawson, *c.* 1869, Professor of Chemistry,
1863–95. "Big, bluff, rather easygoing in class ...
A professor's duty was to teach willing students."

Lyall put it. He was unusually self-effacing, having what one student called "the transparent innocence of a pure mind." He often forgot to check his watch. On one occasion, noting the class was running late, the students silently agreed between themselves to let him keep going, to see how long he would go on. After a further hour, one of the hungrier of the class could stand it no longer and began to shuffle his feet. Much embarrassed and disconcerted, Lyall stopped. But the students gave him a fine round of applause just the same. Sensitive, shy, quiet, Lyall was one of the truest scholars of the Dalhousie sextet, and one who much enjoyed his teaching. He was, in his range of interests, as someone remarked, "a whole faculty of arts."[19]

George Lawson, professor of chemistry from 1863 to 1895, came from Fifeshire and graduated from Edinburgh. He lectured at one time in science at Edinburgh, took his PH. D. at Giessen, the only Dalhousie professor of 1863 to have one of those new-fangled German degrees. Lawson was widely published and, like Lyall, was among the original members of the Royal Society of Canada, of which he became president in 1887. His real work was in botany, but he had great interest in agriculture, and was for twenty years secretary of the Nova Scotia Central Board of Agriculture. Lawson was big, bluff, rather easy-going in class. If you did not pay attention to what he was saying and doing, that was your problem, not his. He gave the inaugural address at the fall convocation of 1877 and touched on this theme. A professor's duty was to teach willing students, to set the subject before them in ways that would enable them to grasp it with the exercise of their own wits. The unwilling, or the careless, fell behind. Such students were apt to develop what every professor disliked in class, "bodily activity combined with mental indolence." That he hated.

Lawson had the power of rousing the enthusiasm of his students, teaching them to use their own powers of observation. He was a good man in the field, and he conducted his own field research classes in the summer, at his farm at Sackville and elsewhere. His major contributions to botanical research were on the Canadian east coast and the Arctic. His influence was such that by 1890 most if not all the leading botanists in Canada had been trained by him.[20]

The sixth professor was Thomas McCulloch, Jr, professor of natural philosophy. He was the third son of Thomas McCulloch but was not quite a chip off the old block. After being principal of Dalhousie briefly in 1849, he was appointed to the West River Seminary under James Ross. He duly moved to Truro in 1856, where he taught natural philosophy and mathematics. He had never been physically strong, and he died in March of 1865, at the age of fifty-four.[21]

William Lyall, *c.* 1869, Professor of Logic and Metaphysics, 1863–90. "He was unusually self-effacing ... He was in his range of interests ... a whole faculty of arts."

After the death of McCulloch, a committee of the Board of Governors was struck to see what best to do. An ingenious change was worked out with the United Presbyterians, whose professor McCulloch had been. Their Synod now resolved, through the Rev. Peter MacGregor, that as exchange for Dalhousie's courtesy in originally appointing Lyall on Dalhousie money, they would take Lyall now upon their charge, thus freeing a chair. The Dalhousie board then turned in an unexpected direction. Perhaps in their canvass of Dalhousie offerings, they reasoned that Lawson could carry some physics, that Macdonald could handle some mathematical physics, that Lyall might manage some psychology, and hence the professorship of natural philosophy (physics) could wait for a time. The board advertised simply a position, while they were working out what best to do. An early applicant was James De Mille, professor of classics at Acadia College. He had many other talents, and on 11 September 1865 he was appointed to the new chair, called rhetoric and history.[22]

James De Mille came from Saint John, New Brunswick, from a family of Dutch origin that had migrated to New York in 1658. A branch came to Saint John with the Loyalists in 1783, where James was born fifty years later. The family were Baptists, sober and diligent, and were sufficiently well off to see that James went to a good Baptist school, in this case, Horton Academy in Wolfville. De Mille attended Acadia for a season, then took a six-month tour of Europe, most of it, sensibly enough, in Italy. He then went to Brown University in Providence, Rhode Island, graduating in 1854. After a stint as a bookseller in Saint John, he was appointed to Acadia as professor of classics in 1860. He did well there. Why he resigned in 1865 to come to Dalhousie is not clear. The Dalhousie pay was certainly a little better; or De Mille may have preferred teaching history and rhetoric to classics, or Halifax to Wolfville. The Dalhousie board went to some trouble with his appointment, for it required a rearrangement of the whole curriculum to enable them to appoint him.

He was liked from the start. He was dignified, handsome, from which not even a heavy pair of glasses detracted. He was a little aloof perhaps, which was compounded by his short-sightedness. He did not always recognize his students; Patterson remembers how he was passed by unnoticed on the Grand Parade, but immediately after De Mille, prompted by his son, turned and greeted Patterson with great warmth. De Mille was something of an outdoor man, loving to swim in the North West Arm and skate on the Dartmouth Lakes. He was a great fisherman; trout and salmon streams allowed him, with his son, or with Charles Macdonald, to combine two happy avocations. De Mille was a charming talker, especially in small company, for he

James De Mille, *c.* 1869, Professor of History and Rhetoric, 1866–80. "Most students liked his infectious and sprightly performances, and if a lecture were to be sloped [skipped] ... it was not apt to be Professor De Mille's."

had a wealth of historical and literary allusions at his fingertips, and a singular facility at imparting them.

His lectures did not always claim his full attention. There was occasionally a mechanistic, perfunctory element in them that led one student, Edwin Crowell, to think that De Mille's real interests were elsewhere. Nevertheless, most students liked his infectious and sprightly performances, and if a lecture were to be skipped ("slope" was the verb used in the 1870s), it was not apt to be Professor De Mille's. He had a richly modulated voice, a capacious grasp of English; his history was never static, but dialectical; it was, as one student remembered, "a moving, living panorama." In 1878 he offered a special fourth-year course in the history of Canada. This was probably the first time such a course was offered in English Canada. For most students De Mille's lectures always ended too soon. All students studying for the BA had to take his first-year class in rhetoric; many general students registered for his class alone, not least among whom were W.S. Fielding (who became premier in 1884) and Charles Hibbert Tupper, the vigorous son of a redoubtable father. Students were proud of De Mille, proud of his fame, and many treasured him as a friend.[23]

At the same time as De Mille was appointed, James Liechti was hired as tutor in modern languages. Liechti was Swiss, a Lutheran, who had taught French and German in the Halifax Grammar School for six years. He was liked by students, patient, kind, hardworking. In 1883 he became McLeod professor of modern languages. He survived longer than any of the original old guard; he retired in 1906 to Lunenburg and lived until 1925.

Curriculum of the 1860s and 1870s

The Dalhousie curriculum of the 1860s and 1870s was conventional enough for the time, laying great stress on mathematics and classics; but it was developed and laid out with Scottish rigour. First of all, matriculation examinations were required for entrance, all of them three hours long, and formidable enough. The French entrance examination, for example, gave a quotation from Voltaire's *Charles XII* for translation into English: "Le czar, qui dans de pareilles saisons faisait quelques fois quatre cents lieues en poste, à cheval, pour aller visiter lui-même une mine ou quelque canal, n'épargnait plus ses troupes que lui-même." Those were just three out of twenty-five lines for translation, plus detailed questions of selected points of grammar. The German paper was similar. In classics, translations were required from "one easy Latin" and "one easy Greek" author. These were usually Caesar, Virgil, Cicero, or Horace; Xenophon, Homer, Lucian, or the New Testament. The mathematics exam comprehended arithmetic and Book 1 of Euclid. A further examination included English grammar and composition, the history of England, and geography. Students took examinations in October, two or three days prior to the opening of lectures.[24]

Once past that hurdle, the student settled into his first year. By the 1870s this was classics and mathematics, plus rhetoric, all three of them daily. This regimen continued in the second year, with chemistry, logic, and psychology added. In the third year classics and mathematics were continued, plus experimental physics, mathematical physics, metaphysics, French or German, Greek or chemistry. The fourth year gave Latin, ethics and political economy, history, French or German, astronomy and experimental physics. That meant four courses in the first year, five in the second, six in the third, and five in the fourth. Failing more than two classes in any year meant the year had to be repeated. In 1866 the Senate brought in a rule that classics and mathematics were *each* reckoned as two subjects! Students were allowed a supplemental examination in the autumn. One historian of Nova Scotia, David Allison, thought the Dalhousie regimen positively draconian, but he was not a Dalhousie man. Dalhousians were proud of it, and believed it the basis of Dalhousie's reputation. Johnson and Macdonald, the classicist and the mathematician, had between them established that powerful, and exigent, tradition. And though in later years more flexibility was added to the curriculum, that core of classics and mathematics would remain, if in a gradually more attentuated form, until the 1960s.[25]

Dalhousie examinations were printed and published as an appendix to the calendar. These examination papers offered a guarantee, as nearly as could be managed, of a university's standing. There you displayed what you had to do for the degree. Of course, the next question was, how were the examinations marked? Dalhousie offered no figures itself, but the students did, and they were proud of them. One of the medical professors had charged that all the arts colleges in Nova Scotia were lax in examination standards. The *Dalhousie Gazette* corrected him:

Now if the [medical] gentleman had excepted our college by name his statement would have been perfectly correct; for it is a notorious fact, admitted by themselves that plucking is almost unknown in the other colleges of Nova Scotia. But it is altogether vain for any man to decry the strictness of our examinations in the face of the evidence afforded by their results. More than once twenty per cent. of our undergraduates have failed to pass, a proportion not exceeded in any college on the continent. Why, last year our examiners plucked nearly as many men as attended King's College. Least of all ought the charge to have come from any member of the Medical Faculty whose students, though we have personal knowledge that they study not a whit harder than we do, make from 80 to 95 per cent. on their examinations.[26]

As the students put it in the *Gazette*, 11 January 1873,

Dalhousie claims for herself no indulgence and wants no man to believe in her professions without sufficient proof. What she promises to teach she does teach thoroughly and this her examination papers prove beyond all dispute. They are open to public inspection, and every man in giving his son as a foster child to Dalhousie knows exactly how that son is to be trained, because he has proof positive.

Dalhousie Students of the 1860s and 1870s

Dalhousie students were usually recognizable. The Senate required that all students wear mortar-boards and gowns, not only while at Dalhousie but going to and from as well. A common sight around the Parade was a "black angel," mortar-board on head, hurrying to class, his gown blowing in the wind. Mortar-boards were more honoured in the breach than the observance, however, and outside the college grounds gowns tended to become scarcer after the first term. They were the target for every ragamuffin who had any latent combative instincts. Duncan Fraser ('72) and a friend were walking to Dalhousie one cold winter morning and were accosted by a gang of city boys, who taunted them about their garb. To Fraser's surprise, his companion hit out right and left and of course Fraser had to join in. In the end, as Fraser put it, "the oatmeal in our systems prevailed." Gowns acquired their own patina of age and experience; the more tattered and battered the better.[27]

Dalhousie students did have minor wars with the locals. The *Dalhousie Gazette* found that crossing the Parade one risked getting mixed up in their games and the target of ordinary balls, snowballs, or even rocks. It was not always war. The *Gazette* felt sorry for some of the little fellows; imps they were, but it was not their fault: "Your mother suckled you on gin, and your father patted you with the leg of the chair, you were turned out on the streets when you could toddle." What pious Halifax did for such scamps, said the *Gazette*, was to send them to prison at Rockhead, through the unsympathetic ministrations of Judge Pryor.[28]

Students usually entered Dalhousie at the age of twenty or twenty-one in the early days. The reason was partly the scattered and feeble character of the secondary schools, with no uniform curriculum. Halifax itself did not have a public high school until 1879. Duncan

Fraser of New Glasgow came to Dalhousie when he was twenty-three. Many students had been part-time or full-time teachers before coming to Dalhousie. R.B. Bennett ('93) was a characteristic example, arriving at Dalhousie at the age of twenty after having taught school since he was seventeen.

Students tended to lodge together. Each would take turns cooking; one would buy the food, the coal, the candles or kerosene for a week, the next week another would take over. The diet was oatmeal porridge, saltfish, corned beef, lots of bread. Two enterprising Pictou County students, who came to Dalhousie in 1868 and roomed together north of the Citadel, brought with them three barrels that stood in the hall outside their room – one each of oatmeal, apples, and potatoes. Entertainment was the Debating Society on Friday nights, and Saturday afternoon rugby. Every student took part in the debating society. High-flown oratory was discouraged, and classical allusions considered pedantic. As to rugby, no one prior to about 1867 had ever seen a game. A book of rules was bought, a portion of the North Common pre-empted, and the Saturday afternoon rugby was started, usually going on until snow and ice compelled capitulation.[29]

There were few Halifax-Dartmouth students in the twenty-seven regular undergraduates in 1865–6; twelve came from New Glasgow, Pictou town or Pictou County, two from Halifax-Dartmouth, three from the Annapolis Valley, and three from Prince Edward Island. In 1871–2, of forty-eight undergraduates, twenty-seven came from Pictou County, nine from Halifax-Dartmouth. That year there were twenty-five general students as well, of whom ten were from Halifax-Dartmouth.

Dalhousie also had a diversity of religions. It did not call itself a Presbyterian college, though its detractors did. The *Dalhousie Gazette* pointed out in 1875 that the Board of Governors, Senate, and student body all had representatives from every denomination in Nova Scotia. Although a majority of students were, indeed, Presbyterian, there seems to have been little animosity between different religious denominations. The four editors of the *Gazette* were elected annually by the student body; the *Gazette* was proud to boast that in 1874–5 two were Wesleyan Methodists, and that in 1873–4 one editor was a Roman Catholic.

The Faculty of Medicine

The Faculty of Medicine was opened for the first time in early May 1868, its first session running to the end of July. It had been talked of as early as 1843, but held up by lack of clinical facilities. By 1859 there was a hospital; after a decade of attempts, Halifax City Council in

1855 voted £5,000 for it. It was completed in 1859, on a site between Morris and South streets, west of Tower Road, where the Victoria General Hospital now stands. Local doctors welcomed it, not only to help the poor – its main patrons then – but as a place where clinical work could be carried on.[30] As early as November 1863 the secretary of the Dalhousie board wondered if the Nova Scotia Medical Society was interested in discussing a possible Faculty of Medicine. One great difficulty was the lack of local expertise to teach clinical subjects. Another was the absence of any law authorizing dissection. An Anatomy Act was mooted in 1858 but public opposition was too strong. "An Act Respecting the Study of Anatomy" was passed in 1869, despite strong opposition from outside Halifax. It gave the doctors the right to dissect men who died in the poorhouse at the corner of South and Robie streets. Even after the Anatomy Act, there was a shortage of bodies. A young hospital attendant told police in 1874 that the body of a young man, Michael Gleason, who died in February, had been delivered to the Dalhousie Medical Faculty; that the coffin, over which a funeral was held, had nothing in it but rubbish. It was true; the coffin was found to be full of old hospital bedding. Cordwood was another favourite replacement. Such stories tended to confirm public suspicion of hospitals, medical schools, and dissection. Nevertheless, there was a real public need.[31]

The moving spirit in the creation of the Dalhousie Medical Faculty was Dr A.P. Reid, a man of considerable experience and distinction, and also eccentricities. Born in London, Upper Canada, in 1836, he graduated from McGill in 1858, doing postgraduate work in Edinburgh, London, and Paris. He had many adventures, not least going to the west coast of British North America, before ending up in Halifax as dean of medicine. In August 1870, after a trial of two years, it was agreed that a full medical school should start as of 1 November. The original plan was that students would do two years in Halifax and then go off to Edinburgh, London, Harvard, or Pennsylvania to complete their medical training. Some did, but five of the original twelve stayed at Dalhousie and were thus its first medical graduates. Medical degrees would carry the seal of Dalhousie College and the signatures of Sir William Young, chairman of the Dalhousie Board of Governors, Principal Ross, and Dr W.J. Almon, president of the faculty. The Medical Faculty functioned virtually as an autonomous unit; the relations between it and Dalhousie were as loose as possible consistent with any affiliation at all. In effect, Dalhousie granted the space and the use of its name for the degrees.[32]

There was difficulty with space. The board finally got the provincial government to remove the museum from the East Room so that the medical students could have a lecture room. The Dalhousie attic was converted into a dissecting room, with the light bad and the ventilation worse. In summer it was a good place to avoid; an old cadaver and a month of heat under the roof produced disconcerting results. The faculty was also a drain on funds for chemicals and apparatus, now deemed indispensable.

Medical school ambitions were difficult to contain. Dalhousie principals and presidents were not the first, nor the last, to find their medical deans were more to be feared than loved. They needed more money for their work and they needed more space. Space could have been arranged in another building by means of a trust, or by an act of incorporation for that single purpose. What emerged in 1873 was an act creating the Halifax School of Medicine that gave powers to its governors to appoint professors and make by-laws. "As the law stands the [Dalhousie] Governors cannot see how it is possible for them to affiliate with any independent institution so as to legalize their degrees." So they said in May of 1873. The Medical Faculty replied that they did not wish to separate from Dalhousie, and had not thought the 1873 act would have that effect. But Sir William Young was also chief justice of Nova Scotia, and his view was that under the 1863 act Dalhousie could not confer degrees on students of the Halifax School of Medicine, and that if the faculty were organized under the 1873 act, separation from Dalhousie would follow. The Halifax Medical School sought to avoid the full ramifications of this, not wanting to give up that Dalhousie imprimatur. But they still needed a new building, and wanted Dalhousie to help bear the expense. At that the Dalhousie board virtually threw up their hands: "Your Colleagues must be aware that the [Dalhousie] Board cannot possibly accede to these proposals. From the beginning they have never once been left in doubt as to what the Board could do and what it could not do." Those who were dissatisfied with the existing and well-defined relationship with Dalhousie should resign from it. That was a reference to divisions of opinion within medical ranks, about what best to do.

In 1875 the Dalhousie board agreed to allow medical students to have their own convocation, with Dalhousie degrees; but that year, a further Act of Incorporation created the Halifax Medical College giving additional powers, including that of conferring degrees. Separation was now inevitable. In the Dalhousie calendar for 1876–7 all reference to the Medical Faculty was omitted; Halifax Medical College granted its own degrees until 1885.[33]

The Colleges Question Revived
Joseph Howe, who had been on the Dalhousie Board of Governors

since 1848 and had given yeoman service, died on 1 June 1873. His successor on the board was the Reverend George W. Hill, rector of St Paul's Anglican Church in Halifax, the brother of P.C. Hill who would become premier in May 1875. At his first board meeting on 23 January 1874, Hill raised the question of a more ample provincial grant, and furthermore, of the necessity of getting the other colleges to think seriously about the advantages and possibilities of a central university for Nova Scotia. The previous May the board had sent a circular letter to Acadia, King's, St Mary's, St Francis Xavier, and Mount Allison, suggesting that their several boards nominate delegates to meet and discuss the question. Dalhousie got short shrift for its pains; the idea was turned down. `

That having failed, the Dalhousie board next struck a committee to prepare a submission to the legislature for more money. It was a good state paper, presenting a short history of the college, its present position, and its needs. The gist of the argument was financial. The other five colleges each received $1,400 from the legislature; all Dalhousie got was $1,000, inherited from the old Assembly grant to the Free Church College. Had the Presbyterians not combined to help resuscitate Dalhousie, chances were that they might have been given $1,400 each for two colleges, the way the Roman Catholics had with St Mary's and St Francis Xavier. It looked to Dalhousie as if "no matter how many small colleges you choose to establish, we shall give $1,400 a year to each; but attempt to combine your resources and we shall give you nothing." Should not Nova Scotia now take up a policy similar to that in Ontario (the University of Toronto), or New Brunswick (the University of New Brunswick)? Was it not obvious that no denominational college in Nova Scotia was strong enough "to fully equip a university"? Surely, said the Dalhousie petition, "the time has come for the Legislature to take its stand on one principle or the other: on the Denominational or the Provincial ... At present Dalhousie suffers injustice because neither the one nor the other is allowed." The salaries to its professors, first set in 1863, were now inadequate. Enrolment at the college was growing; in the session of 1874–5 Dalhousie had eighty-seven students in arts, thirty-three in medicine – larger than all the other Nova Scotian colleges combined.[34]

The government recognized the validity of Dalhousie's argument and increased the grant to $1,800 for 1875–6. But the following year a new act was brought in, establishing, though in an odd way, what Dalhousie looked forward to – a central university for Nova Scotia. This was the University of Halifax.

The college question was a little like measles or whooping cough, breaking out every now and then in the body politic of Nova Scotia.

The University of Halifax was a pet project of the premier's. P.C. Hill was a graduate of King's, urbane, civilized, but politically naive. His act of 1876 was courageous. Its preamble stated:

Whereas it is desirable to establish one University for the whole of Nova Scotia, on the model of the University of London, for the purpose of raising the standard of higher education in the Province, and of enabling all denominations and classes, including those persons whose circumstances preclude them from following a regular course of study in any of the existing Colleges or Universities to obtain academical degrees.

There was real idealism in the proposal, in effect setting up a central examining body with the existing colleges doing the teaching. The trouble was, the Hill government had courage but not enough strength to effect what was really needed: to draw the teeth of the six colleges by abolishing their degree-granting powers. Probably the government knew it could not do that and live. On 10 March 1876 it came close to losing the bill altogether, surviving a Conservative motive for the three months' hoist by only three votes. According to the *Halifax Evening Reporter*, the whole measure was a compromise to give those who wanted a non-sectarian institution five years' time to "to work up an agitation in favour of one central teaching university." It can also be said, as the Pictou *Standard* did, that the creation of the University of Halifax was an admission that the government would not do what it also might have done – give its $8,000 university grants to Dalhousie, the one college that was central, that professed to be, and was in principle, non-denominational. That course, said the *Standard*, "Catholics, Baptists, Episcopalians and Methodists would have resisted ... to the last extremity." That was what Samuel Creelman, commissioner of public works and mines, said in the Legislative Council in 1881. The reason why the University of Halifax had to be created, instead of using Dalhousie, was because the other colleges would not have it. They would not send any students to Dalhousie.[35]

Dalhousie's position had long been that university education in Nova Scotia was too important to be left to the vagaries of "Church, Chance or Charity." This did not endear it to those colleges so created. According to the *Gazette*, Dalhousie was "a kind of modern Ishmael, – hating and being hated by the other five colleges." In Professor Lyall's address to convocation, in 1874, he had pointed out, "We have existed under a kind of protest. A portion of the community has frowned upon us; rival institutions have been jealous of us." One correspondent in the *Halifax Evening Reporter* deplored Dalhousie-bashing, and claimed it originated mainly in Wolfville. Surely, said

"One of the People," the Crawley affair could have been forgotten by now? Dalhousie, the "People's College," had done much in the last ten years to atone for past sins, "by the numbers taught, by the acknowledged excellence of its teaching, by the liberality of its government."[36]

The *Dalhousie Gazette*'s criticism of the University of Halifax was based on the false premise under which it was started. England at the time the University of London was established had excellent teaching facilities but, outside of Oxford and Cambridge, no power of conferring degrees; "in Nova Scotia we have most admirable arrangements for conferring degrees but wretched facilities for imparting a good education." "The new Paper University will be almost helpless" to remedy that. It might give unity to study; it may expose shams "lurking in the examination-paper-less obscurity" of some colleges; but it can do little to strengthen the universities where they need it: in teaching.[37]

Dalhousie mounted a longer and more serious criticism in 1877 (anonymously but probably by Charles Macdonald), in a twenty-two-page pamphlet. It likened the sectarian colleges to "sturdy beggars hustling with shout and menace a simple-minded gentleman from whose fears more is to be expected than from his pity." The simple-minded gentleman, the Nova Scotian government, had been handing over money, being "incapable of a manful No." One university for the province was, indeed, highly desirable; to achieve that, degree-granting powers had to be withdrawn from the others. But,

when it is known that the Colleges are to continue to grant Degrees as before, with all the laxity and indiscriminateness with which they are, justly or un-justly charged, we may ask, what evil does the University of Halifax cure? What is it more than an additional *Graduating nuisance*? It is the old story, the fifth wheel to the carriage, coals to Newcastle, more Christmas-pie to the already surfeited Jack Horner, or whatever else is superfluous and absurd.

The author condemned outright, as did Dr Cramp of Acadia, the strange provision in section 15 of the act: that the University of Halifax's Senate had no power to recommend or urge that any student should study "any materialistic or sceptical system of Logic or Mental or Moral Philosophy." The author ran a coach and horses through that provision. All he had to do was to mention Lucretius, Hobbes, Hume, Comte, Darwin, Spencer. He concluded that the net effect of the University of Halifax would be to leave the idea of a provincial university still further off than before.[38]

So, in fact, it proved to be. In 1878 and 1879 the University of Halifax examined some fifty-seven candidates in arts, science, law and medicine. Some 30 per cent failed. In 1880 only twenty applied for its degree. In 1881 the University of Halifax came to an end.

That was the strangest part of the story. Its funding of $2,000 a year was to continue until 31 December 1880, after which its functioning, role, and refunding would be considered. By that time Hill's government had been defeated and replaced by a Conservative one which had much less sympathy with the University of Halifax. There was a good deal of ferment in the autumn of 1880; both leading political papers, the *Morning Herald* (Conservative) and the *Morning Chronicle* (Liberal) published a series of articles on the university question. Dalhousie's position was further stated by J.G. MacGregor, professor of physics, in ten letters to the *Morning Herald*, from December 1880 to February 1881. The University of London's example could not be transferred to Halifax. London had large numbers of well-trained students, well-trained specialists to teach them, and no accessible degree-granting university. In Nova Scotia it was the other way. There was no dearth of colleges but a great shortage of specialists. It was the teaching that was weak, and there was nothing the paper University of Halifax could do about that. It ought not to have been founded and should be abolished.

In the 1881 session the Assembly repealed the University of Halifax Act, putting in its place a grant of $1,400 a year to each of the six existing colleges, on condition that they be inspected regularly by the superintendent of education. This bill passed the Assembly by the overwhelming majority of thirty to one. But it got very different treatment in the Legislative Council. The Anglicans were unhappy: King's College to be *inspected* by a government official! The Presbyterians thought Dalhousie was being penalized. Others did not like the double grant to the small Roman Catholic colleges, St Mary's and St Francis Xavier. A few wanted to keep the University of Halifax. A motion for the three months' hoist caught the government off guard; the government leader, Samuel Creelman, desperately tried to adjourn the debate. That failed by three votes, and the three months' hoist passed by one vote. The Colleges bill was in ruins. This had two effects: it stopped the college grants, and not just in 1881, but for nearly eighty years, and it kept the University of Halifax alive. It was buried anyway.[39]

In 1871 Dalhousie's need for money had forced the governors to do their own campaigning. Sir William Young, George Grant, W.J. Stairs, and William Doull agreed to try to raise $1,200 a year for five years. They succeeded. It may also have been the origin of the Dalhousie Alumni Association that began in 1871 and was incorporated in 1876. Even so, Dalhousie lived from hand to mouth. Its total annual income in 1875 was $4,600: $3,000 from investments, $600 rent, and the government grant of $1,000. The arithmetic was fearfully simple. Dalhousie paid the three professors for which it had responsibility $1,200 a year each. They paid Liechti $500, and the janitor got his free apartment and $25 a year. It was very thin going. True, in 1876 Dalhousie got $1,800 from the government, which in 1876 went up to $3,000 for five years. That helped. Dalhousie's annual income was now $6,600.[40]

That allowed Dalhousie to do what it had been anxious to do for some time: appoint a teacher in physics. James Gordon MacGregor, (BA '71, MA '74) was one of Dalhousie's most brilliant graduates, who had gone on to do graduate work at Edinburgh and Leipzig, taking a D.SC. from the University of London in 1876. He offered himself for a lectureship in physics in 1876. George Grant had urged that a lectureship in physics be established. Unfortunately Dalhousie could spare only $400. Grant volunteered to find another $300, for one year anyway.[41]

The following year MacGregor resigned to take a post as physics master at an English public school, presumably for better pay. The Dalhousie board then appointed Dr J.J. MacKenzie in 1877. He was another Dalhousie graduate, from Pictou County, (BA '69, MA '72), who had taken his PH. D. in Germany. At his urging, the board made a great effort to strengthen Dalhousie's science. Led by Sir William Young, some $2,500 was collected to enable MacKenzie to buy some physics apparatus in Paris and Berlin in the summer of 1878. A former assistant of Lawson's, H.A. Bayne, was made professor of organic chemistry, with the Reverend D. Honeyman as lecturer in geology and paleontology. Dalhousie thus began in September 1878 with some hopes that, having strengthened its science curriculum, an increase of students would result.

Sir William Young was concerned to keep the Presbyterian Synod fully informed of Dalhousie developments. He wrote in September 1878 that "no greater misfortune could befall the Presbyterian Body than the failure or degradation of our College." One current difficulty was Principal Ross's health. Ross's strength was much shaken, said Young, and his capacity to teach so doubtful that the question of his retirement on half-pay should be considered by Synod. Synod made non-committal noises to this, but before any decision had been made, MacKenzie died of pneumonia on 2 February 1879, at the age of thirty-one.[42]

The board found the greatest difficulty in replacing him. What they really wanted to do was to retire Ross, and get the Presbyterians to fund a chair of physics, while Dalhousie took on the support of ethics and political economy that Ross taught. Young put it diplomatically in May 1879:

The Governors are sensible that in urging the Synod to accept the Principal's resignation and in assigning to Physical Instruction [Physics] a prominence it has not hitherto enjoyed, they may be asking some of its members to modify or to surrender cherished opinions but the Governors are pressed by a strong conviction that the course they venture to recommend is of the first moment to the College, and that the delay of even a year, may defeat their object.

But the Dalhousie board now lacked the pulling power of one of the most redoubtable and devoted of its governors, George Grant. He was offered the principalship of Queen's University at Kingston, Ontario, in October 1877. His congregation of St Matthew's were in despair, and his friends tried to persuade him to stay. The new Dalhousie was in no small way the result of Grant's brimming energy and his enthusiasm for education. After a month of thinking, Grant left Halifax for Queen's on 26 November 1877. He would be its principal for the next twenty-five years. Grant remained on the Dalhousie board until 1884, giving his advice by mail and on occasional visits to Halifax. [43]

On 9 October 1878 the board appointed in his place an energetic Presbyterian minister, the Reverend John Forrest, of St John's Presbyterian Church, Brunswick Street. Forrest was untried, but at thirty-five young and vigorous, and in a decade he had made St John's into a large and flourishing congregation. [44] He was the driving force behind much charitable work in the Halifax community. His appointment came at a critical time. Dalhousie was desperately looking for money from a grudging, hesitant, and impecunious Synod to appoint that essential professor of physics. Principal Ross was ill and old, and had never had talent for collecting money. The $3,000 government grant would run out in two years, at the end of 1880. Expenses were pared wherever they could be. Where could Dalhousie go for money? The Presbyterians had done their best, and more; Halifax had not yet taken up Dalhousie as its own college. Then, in the summer of 1879, Forrest had a visit from his sister Catherine and her husband who lived in New York. The husband was very rich, he was Nova Scotian and Presbyterian, and he knew Halifax well. His name was George Munro.

· 6 ·

George Munro and the Big Change
1879–1887

Munro's professorships. John Forrest. Women students. Student celebrations. Founding the Law School, 1883. Retirement of Principal Ross. Fighting the city over the Parade. Failure of union with King's, 1884–5. Getting the new building on the South Common, 1887.

George Munro was born near Pictou in 1825, apprenticed to a printer at twelve, and became a teacher at Pictou Academy at nineteen. In 1850 he went to the Free Church Academy in Halifax to teach mathematics and physics, becoming principal two years later. He had brought the academy to a flourishing condition when, amid much regret, he resigned in 1856. The reason he gave was health, but a private one was his uncertainty about his vocation; he had been preparing to be a Presbyterian minister – that calling for many intellectually minded young men in the nineteenth century. Rumour had it that after preaching one sermon he resolved never to preach another. He had no joy in eristic discourse from the pulpit. He was reserved, even shy, and in later life never sought, indeed retreated from, the limelight. He sailed for New York in October 1856, at the age of thirty-one.[1]

He spent his first years in New York working for Appleton's, the publisher, learning the business of magazine and mail order publishing from the ground up. In 1866 he started on his own with the *Fireside Companion*, a weekly family paper, which was highly successful both in the United States and in Nova Scotia. By that time on various trips back to Nova Scotia – Halifax was an easy two-to-three-day trip by steamer – he had met and married his second wife, Catherine Forrest, sister of the Reverend John Forrest, and of James Forrest, a Halifax business man. Munro sent his son by his first marriage to Dalhousie College in 1874. By 1877 Munro was publishing The Seaside Library, a reprint series of British books – and thus free from copyright – of high quality: Dickens, Thackeray, Bronte, as well as history, biography, and travel.[2] He amassed a good deal of money, investing some of it in well-chosen American stocks, some in a printing plant on Vandewater Street, New York. A main source of wealth turned out to be New York real estate. A friend was later to remark of him, "Business was his play and his passion and he brought to bear upon it such sagacity, such keenness of vision, such skill in devising his plans and such promptitude in their execution as would in other fields have won battle or founded states."

Ill from overwork, Munro found time at last in 1879 to take a long summer holiday in Halifax, living with his brother-in-law John Forrest on Brunswick Street. They talked and walked much. Forrest knew the needs of Dalhousie all too well after six months on its board. Desperate is not too strong a word for Dalhousie's financial condition. Talk of closing Dalhousie down was heard on every side. The most pressing need was to find the money to replace J.J. MacKenzie in physics. One day, as Forrest was explaining this, Munro looked at him and said quietly, "If you will find the man for the chair of Physics, I will find the money." Forrest took him at his word, and announced the offer to a stunned Board of Governors on 21 August 1879. It was the scale that made them gasp: $2,000 per annum! Even the premier of Nova Scotia was only paid $2,400 per year. To fund $2,000, assuming 5 per cent interest, required a capital of $40,000. The Board of Governors' enthusiasm, in their thanks to Munro, was understandable:

Mr. Munro's liberality is on a scale that is without parallel in the Educational History not of Nova Scotia alone but of the Dominion of Canada and his action in giving the patronage of the Chair to the Governors instead of availing himself of the privilege secured to him by Statute by nominating a Professor, enhances their sense of indebtedness.

It would be called the George Munro Chair of Physics. The professor would be J.G. MacGregor, appointed that very autumn of 1879, brought back from the English grammar school whither he had gone in 1877.[3]

This great gift did not solve Dalhousie's problems, but it gave hope, where previously there had been little, that it might be possible to overcome them. That it could not solve them was illustrated a few months later. One day – it was 18 January 1880 – there was a knock on the door of the West Room, where Charles Macdonald was lecturing. He was called out. His back was hardly turned before the students turned to high jinks, throwing notebooks about. But one of the students near the door overheard something and shouted above the din, "Be quiet

John Forrest, *c.* 1896, President, 1885–1911.
"He had a prodigious memory for people and
faces, and a shrewd judgment of them."

George Munro, a Lismer sketch reproduced from
Harvey's *Dalhousie*. "Reserved, even shy, and
never sought the limelight."

boys – there's bad news about De Mille." The silence that followed was intense. When Charlie came back he said in a broken voice, "I cannot go on, gentlemen; my beloved colleague Professor De Mille is dead." De Mille had died of pneumonia that morning, at the age of forty-eight. He was given a university funeral and buried in Camp Hill cemetery. His death left a tremendous gap; worse, Dalhousie found it impossible to find the money to fill his chair of history and rhetoric.[4]

In October 1880 George Munro was back in Halifax. He visited the college in the company of John Forrest, and met the governors, who greeted him, as well they might, with some enthusiasm. Two weeks later it was announced, through the Reverend Robert Murray, editor of the *Presbyterian Witness*, also on the board, that Munro was offering a second chair, in history, at $2,500, on condition that John Forrest resign his church of St John's and accept duty at Dalhousie as professor of history. It was this second gift that really lifted Dalhousie from despair. Principal Grant of Queen's, still on the Dalhousie board, could scarce contain his elation:

You simply take away my breath. I have just read your letter and do not know what to say first. Munro must be going to die. Evidently he is too good for this world. His first [1879] gift saved Dalhousie. His second will turn the tide of ambitious students that was setting in to the larger institutions up here and make it flow to Dalhousie.[5]

When the proposal was first made to Forrest he had hesitated, but friends pressed, and Murray suggested to the board that a word from them might just do the trick. It did. Forrest was appointed as George Munro professor of history on 15 March 1881. John Forrest was tall and straight, in figure and in manner; forthright he was, without many half-tones or pretence. One student thought of him armed with a claymore going into battle with his Scottish clan. Forrest had talents that can be described as political: a prodigious memory for people and faces, and a shrewd judgment of them, that reminded others of his great and otherwise very different contemporary, Sir John A. Macdonald. Ere long the students came to call him "Lord John." Some sentimental doggerel, referring to his later years as president, gets him about right:

> Fine me again, Lord John, fine me again,
> Please soak me for sups and swat me for ten,
> But grasp my hand firmly, say it out loud,
> "Of course I know you, you're Donald MacLeod."

Lord John and Athletics

Forrest was the first governor, and the first professor, who was fully conscious of how little Dalhousie did for its students. He had seen enough of American colleges to be well aware of what Dalhousie did not have, and did not do. His inaugural address of 1881 was preoccupied with it. Student life, he said, had plenty of trials; there was much to make it dreary and miserable. Most students were strangers to Halifax and desperately needed a good reading room and, even more, a good gymnasium. "During the past nothing, absolutely nothing, has been done to make student life enjoyable ... To me the wonder is that Dalhousie has attracted as many students as she has." As a governor he pushed for a gymnasium in the teeth of resistance from his board colleagues. They thought it an expensive luxury. He got his way by offering to pay for fitting up a gymnasium in the old brewery. The board gave up the rent, and Forrest guaranteed any shortfall between expenses and receipts. It cost him $31.36 in 1882–3, and $130.72 in 1884–5. Then the worst was over.[6]

Urged on by Forrest, the students formed the Dalhousie Athletic Club (DAC) in 1884. Out of that came the Dalhousie rugby team. One of its first games was against Acadia, played in a gale on the South Common on 15 November 1884. The wind benefited Acadia in the first half and then, unobligingly, died down for the second. The DAC gave full marks to the Acadia team, which won by one point; the Dalhousie minutes proudly pointed out that such a narrow defeat, against such a team, was no disgrace to any team in the province. "You did nobly Acadians, and deserve credit for it! And, although, it would have been an advantage to us if you had read the rules a little more carefully, and acted up to them a little more closely, yet we make no complaint for perhaps you also saw imperfections in us." Altogether, a civilized performance, at least as written! After the game the players repaired to the Halifax Hotel, where they bathed wounds and satisfied hunger, and no doubt slaked thirst.

The rugby team led to debate in the club about college colours for the football jerseys. There was sentiment briefly for garnet and blue, but a committee sensibly arranged to see samples of jerseys and the result was the official adoption in 1887, of black and gold (or yellow as it often turned out to be) as the Dalhousie colours. Dalhousie's colours were thus chosen by the rugby players, not by either board or Senate. Whatever official impetus there was came from John Forrest.[7]

A Touch of Hubris

With John Forrest as Munro professor of history in 1881, Dalhousie had acquired two high-salaried chairs, physics and history, and

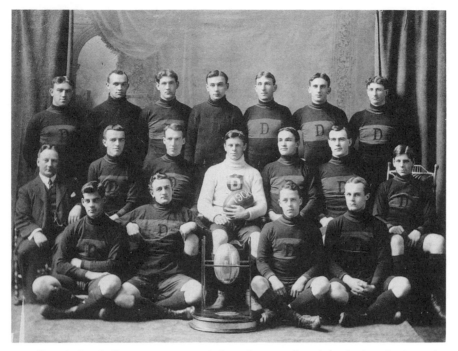

Dalhousie football team, 1908. English rugby was played until after the Second World War, when Dalhousie mounted its first Canadian football team.

Munro's quarterly cheques to keep them so. At this point, in February 1881, Conservative Premier Simon Holmes asked Dalhousie if it would be willing to surrender its degree-granting powers to a general examining body, in return for getting the government grant. To Holmes's blunt question – he was never long on tact – the Dalhousie board and its Senate returned an equally decided answer. On 10 March 1881 the Senate unanimously resolved:

That for this College to resign its University powers, would in any circumstances be a serious loss of prestige; that it would by many be thought equivalent to taking rank with those denominational colleges, if any[,] which may accept the proposal of the Government; and that it would in view of the recent additions to the teaching staff of the College and the encouragement offered to students, be a discouragement not only to prospective but also to past benefactors whose generosity may be supposed to have been elicited by the expectation that Dalhousie College was about to occupy a prominent place among the Universities of the Dominion.

That there are strong objections well understood by practical educators, to any central and degree-conferring Board, such as that which the Government proposal seems to contemplate ... that independence and originality on the part of the teacher ... are sacrificed to the *cram* of text-books...

That the Senate at the same time cordially approves of the object the Government has in view *viz.* to secure that the Educational fruits of the college Grants should be certified as satisfactory, but is of opinion that the proposal of the Government would for many reasons fail to attain its laudable object.

There was some pride, even hubris in this; certainly the gifts of George Munro had given the college a new confidence, a refurbished sense of itself and its role in Nova Scotian education. Still, it has to be remembered that Dalhousie was not rich, nor were its problems with what would now be called cash flow much altered by Munro. He gave endowed chairs and money tied to student bursaries; that did not mean accessibility to working cash. When Professor Macdonald was ill in April 1882, Professor Johnson, mathematics McGill, prepared the Dalhousie honours mathematics examinations. The board were grateful, as well they might be, for they could only pay Johnson by drawing on capital account, hence "they feel forced to accept his generous offer to give his services gratuitously."[8]

Women Students, 1881
Hardly less important than Munro professorships was a new departure in 1881: the admission of women students. The moral and phil-

osophical foundation of this change was in the *Zeitgeist* of the later 1860s and 1870s. When young John Thompson and Annie Affleck were courting in Halifax in 1867 they talked much, even argued, about "work and woman's position." Nor should one forget Henrik Ibsen's *A Doll's House*, written in 1879. Its theme, the right of a woman, in this case married with children, to pursue her own self-expression and development, created a storm in Europe and elsewhere. "I have been your doll-wife," Nora Helmer told her husband, "[now] I must try to educate myself..." How this was to be done in Nova Scotia in the 1870s was raised by Principal Ross opening the eighth session of Dalhousie, on 1 November 1870. He suggested the building of a college for women students at the south end of the Parade. That was looking to American examples, such as Vassar, the woman's college at Poughkeepsie on the Hudson River, established in 1865. In the American mid-west there were coeducational colleges, notably Oberlin in Ohio, founded in the 1830s. John Clark Murray, professor of moral philosophy at McGill, urged the latter option – the admission of women students into male colleges – and at once. Woman, he said, was immorally subjected to man because of being deprived of the education she needed in order to support herself. "It was," said Murray, "but a cruel jest to preserve social usages by which vast numbers of women must either marry or starve, and then jeer at them for the eagerness with which they choose the more tolerable of these fates." Coeducation, what Murray was aiming at, did not happen at McGill so soon. In the 1880s McGill established "separate but equal" classes, which had the virtue neither of a completely separated college like Vassar, nor of coeducation. The McGill student paper did not think much of the system. It wanted coeducation.[9]

The *Dalhousie Gazette* urged coeducation too. It opposed the conventional wisdom, repeated in the *Halifax Evening Reporter* for 1877, that sewing and cooking were more important in a girl's education than geometry. The *Gazette* took the position that to be a useful member of society a young lady should be given a proper academic education. Finishing schools, like "Mrs. Fitzflummery's," that taught exquisite manners, bad French, and ear-torturing performances at the piano, were better left to those who had some talent. The *Gazette* thought Pictou Academy an excellent example of coeducation at the grammar school level.[10] Coeducation at Dalhousie was taken up with more vigour as the 1870s drew on. Almost all the stock objections centred, said the *Gazette* in 1876, on boarding colleges. Dalhousie wasn't one. There was nothing in Dalhousie's charter to prevent admission of women students. All they had to do was to apply: "We doubt very much if any serious resistance would be offered."

So, in fact, it proved. The question came before the Board of Governors in July 1881. Could lady students be admitted? Could they compete for Munro bursaries? Munro himself was in favour, Principal Ross strongly so, as were also Forrest and Lawson. Young women were to be placed on the same level as the young men. The *Presbyterian Witness*, puritan though it often was in many ways, much approved Dalhousie's admitting women. The board did not bother to inform the Senate, assuming the Halifax papers would do that; the secretary, Charles Macdonald, also secretary of the Senate, was asked in mid-summer by a prospective lady student, Alice Cameron, whether she needed to read all seven books of Caesar's *Gallic Wars* for entrance, or would the first four suffice? (In 1892–3, and probably also in 1881, the requirements for matriculation into Dalhousie were Books IV and V of the *Gallic Wars*, and Book III of the *Aeneid*.) Macdonald got the letter while he was down at St Margaret's Bay; he answered her as best he could, noting that all he knew officially about women students was from newspapers and local comment. By that time, September 1881, Dalhousie had had inquiries from all over the province, and from as far away as Ontario. On Macdonald's return in October, he brought before Senate the board's resolution, which Senate copied and approved,

that application having been made to this Board on behalf of several young women for leave to matriculate and enter the College as undergraduates and it being desirable to grant such application and to make a general regulation as to the admission of women to all the rights and privileges of this College, Be it therefore resolved that female students shall hereafter be entitled to attend lectures and after passing the prescribed examinations to be admitted as undergraduates of this College, and to compete for and take all such prizes, honours and exhibitions and Bursaries as are now open to male students, so that hereafter there shall be no distinction in regard to College work or degrees between male and female students.[11]

Senate also exempted lady students, at their request, from having to wear academic gowns.

Principal Ross greeted the women undergraduates that November, all two of them, with a graceful speech at convocation. They had both taken Munro bursaries. The only problem Ross foresaw was the difficulty of making "staid, stern 'bachelors' out of bright lively young ladies." What would happen, he asked jocularly, when they took masters of arts degrees? "I would prefer to call them masters of *hearts*." On this flat but characteristic pun, and with a benediction, the 1881 session formally opened.[12]

Senior class, 1885. Margaret Florence Newcombe, Dalhousie's first woman graduate, became principal of the Halifax Ladies' College.

Eliza Ritchie, Bachelor of Letters, 1887, Dalhousie's first woman graduate to go on to a PH.D. She became professor of philosophy at Wellesley College.

Women students wanted to be equal to men in both standards and scholarships. Dalhousie saw to it that they were, and they would do extremely well. Still, young ladies seriously bent upon their business are apt to estimate insufficiently the distracting power of their presence. There is a delightful poem from University of Aberdeen, *c.* 1930, that suggests the problem:

> When I was a begent,*
> A beardless young begent,
> And you wore a tassel of blue,
> I toyed with my Latin,
> And played with my Greek,
> But all that I studied was you.

The *Dalhousie Gazette*, looking to the future, suggested in 1878 that restless looks and nervous actions in male students would be inevitable; nevertheless it promised to "make these halls as attractive and pleasant as possible. Smokers take warning! Ladies, we bid you welcome within the precincts of Dalhousie College." If women did come, the *Gazette* suggested in 1880, it would repress "every tendency towards rowdyism among the boys." That was more than male human nature could deliver; still, three years later the *Gazette* concluded that the presence of women students had already "raised the tone of college life"; and, contrary to some male expectations, they were clearly equal to the work.[13]

Eliza Ritchie (BL '87) found Dalhousie's doors opened ungrudgingly: "no fight, inch by inch, had to be fought, as in other places." On the contrary, she said, the early women students at Dalhousie could never forget the courtesy and kindness of professors, who strove to "relieve the apprehensions of the timid, and to encourage the efforts of the ambitious." She was impressed, too, with the fact that two-thirds of Professor Schurman's classes in English literature were women. She stressed the importance of college life for intelligent young women:

The girl whose education is pronounced finished at sixteen or seventeen years of age when she leaves school, is at that time too immature to carry on by herself the studies for which she may have a natural aptitude. Too often she becomes a mere pleasure-seeker, restless and discontented ... Her active brain has been refused its right to healthy work, and loss inevitably follows.[14]

---

* The Aberdeen word for freshman.

Munro Bursaries and Munro Days

Many women students, perhaps 40 per cent, came with bursaries. Dalhousie had not had many of those. That, too, came from Munro, in 1880. He wanted to upgrade not only the salaries of Dalhousie professors, but, more important, raise the diverse standards of the high schools. There were three good ones: Pictou Academy, Halifax High School (started in 1879), and Prince of Wales College in Charlottetown. The original Munro bursaries were distributed regionally, so as to vitiate the unfair competition of those three good high schools. By 1885 it was agreed that the system was too cumbersome, and the Munro bursaries were then thrown open to all comers. At first junior bursaries were included, but after Sir William Young offered five first-year bursaries or scholarships, the Munro exhibitions and bursaries settled into a pattern: five senior exhibitions at $150 a year for two years, plus ten senior bursaries at $100 a year for two years, all for students entering the third year of a four-year program. Since Munro scholars' fees, about $40 a year, were paid by the board, and living in Halifax ran about $18 a month, a senior exhibition covered most expenses. They were worth working and writing examinations for. Forrest remarked in 1886, to a reporter from the *Gazette*, "They have had the effect of elevating the standard. This is one of the most marked results. The students who compete for bursaries are much better prepared for college work than those who merely go up for matriculation."[15]

In 1881 the students asked for a special university holiday in honour of George Munro. Their suggestion to the board was that the third Wednesday in January be designated the George Munro Memorial Day. By 1885 it had migrated to the last Friday in January, and later moved into February. In the 1890s it would appear in November. Munro Day in 1883 was celebrated, as it often would be, by a sleigh-ride to a Bedford hotel. Wednesday, 17 January was a brilliant day, clear and cold, that encouraged even waverers to go. Over fifty Dalhousians (of a total full-time undergraduate enrolment of sixty-six) awaited the arrival of the three four-horse sleighs that drove up on the Parade in front of the college, amid a jingle of bells. The nine miles to Bedford along Bedford Basin was done at a rattling good pace – about eight miles an hour. Students could sometimes measure their speed against a railway train which then, as now, came between the road and the water. They disembarked at the local hostelry. Dinner was served at six o'clock, a scene, said the 1885 reporter, "of carnage and consumption," through soup, fish, meat, and desserts of all kinds. At length the chairman, "with a fatherly regard for the welfare of his companions ordered a cessation of hostilities" and the toasts and speeches began. In 1883 the toast to Munro came first, followed by a dozen or more others with proposers and responders for each. Speeches were supposed to be both witty and edifying, not easy to manage with a quantity of beer or wine on board. After the last toast, to "Our Next Merry Meeting," singing invariably followed. Of course, there were always some voices, as the *Gazette* observed, reminding one of the old rhyme,

> Swans sing before they die
> 'Twere no bad thing
> Should certain persons die
> Before they sing.

After an hour or so of this, the drivers called "all aboard" and the sleighs started back for Halifax. In 1885 they had moonlight all the way, so enjoyable indeed, that everyone was sorry when the college was reached, after only an hour and five minutes.[16]

The Munro Day sleigh-ride was the big event of the students' year in the mid-1880s. Students could not much share the amusements of the Halifax public; the best they could manage was skating – outdoors at Chocolate Lake or indoors at the Halifax rink – on winter Saturday afternoons. They were at church on Sunday. Students were expected to go to church; those under twenty-one, not living with parents or guardians were required to inform the president by mid-October which churches they would attend during the session. The ministers of such churches were then given the names and addresses of these students. It was a form of control, *in loco parentis*, but with amenities added. After church service students could often be observed outside the church door; there were two possibilities – walking home a young lady, or an invitation to Sunday dinner or Sunday tea. Students were invariably hungry and boarding-house fare not usually appetizing.

Board and room in Halifax then cost from $3.50 to $5.00 a week, about $100 per annum. One of the many difficulties for students was to find a suitable boarding house. One student averred, with feeling, "that the bill-of-fare in the majority of those places is the most uncertain thing of earth." Another said that boarding-house keepers were only too consistent, supposing students were possessed of iron constitutions that needed only "hash and india-rubber beefsteak" to survive.

Whether he enjoyed Dalhousie for the four years depended greatly on the student himself. Women students often boarded at the Halifax Ladies' College on Barrington Street, and thus enjoyed a form of collective life; but the male students were scattered all over the city, and found it hard to meet outside of class. Student societies existed: the

Debating Club met every Saturday night. Later, in the 1890s, there was the Philomathic Society, meeting every fortnight to discuss literature, science, and philosophy, though it disappeared after the turn of the century. The YMCA came in the later 1880s, meeting every Saturday night, to be followed a decade later by the YWCA, meeting Monday afternoons at five o'clock. The Delta Gamma Society, to which "all lady students" were eligible, was a fixture by the end of the 1880s.

While it could be argued that for male students the deficiences of boarding-house life would encourage greater vitality for their societies, it does not seem to have done so. Two decades later the *Gazette* noted: "Dalhousie students, from the fact that they are scattered throughout the city, find it easy to neglect the advantages to be derived from association. Moreover her societies are few. Hence we stand in danger of a too restricted college life."[17] In the 1880s, the era of Munro's benefactions, that would have been thought all to the good. Restricted social life usually had as concomitant hard-working students, the kind Munro remembered and approved.

Munro kept on giving. In June 1882 he offered to found a third chair, in English literature and rhetoric. For this he nominated a Prince Edward Islander, Dr Jacob Gould Schurman. He was a graduate of Prince of Wales and Acadia, who had taken his doctorate in Edinburgh, and then studied for two years in Germany. He had returned in 1880 to teach literature, psychology, and political economy at Acadia. Perhaps Munro already knew that the twenty-eight-year-old Schurman was acquainted with his daughter Barbara, for she married him in 1884. Schurman it was who settled what seems to have been a vexed question in the 1880s – the pronunciation of "Dalhousie." Schurman had the bright idea of writing to Lord Dalhousie, the thirteenth earl, who replied as follows:

My Dear Sir, – I have always pronounced my own name as if the "ou" in it were sounded like the "ow" in "now." An uneducated Scotchman, talking very broad Scotch, would probably pronounce it like ... "Dalhoossie." What the ancient pronunciation may have been, I don't know, but all educated Scotch people would pronounce my name in the same way that I do, and would have no hesitation about it.[18]

Founding the Law School
In 1883 Munro launched the fourth of his chairs, in constitutional and international law. "It is generally conceded," read Munro's letter to the board, "that the success of Dalhousie imperatively demands that a Faculty of Law be established ... Professor Weldon of [Mount Allison

College] Sackville is recommended by competent judges as most suitable to be at the head of a Law Faculty and he is willing to accept." The salary was to be $2,000. The board accepted at once and struck a committee to organize a law faculty.[19]

In 1883 most Nova Scotian lawyers had a bare minimum of training. Only a quarter of them had university degrees; most went straight from school to apprenticeship. If it was to a busy practice, the lawyer running it often did not have time for teaching an apprentice; if the lawyer had ample leisure for teaching, odds were he wasn't fit for anything. After a few years of that came the bar examination, a two-hour paper covering the whole range of English jurisprudence. Benjamin Russell, later a law teacher himself, remembered how he was invited to cram for that examination. He was taken, confidentially, to a friend's and there introduced to a washtub full of papers, the accumulated examination questions from a generation of law students. A diligent perusal of these, Russell was assured, and the candidate would certainly pass, and very likely with high marks.[20]

In 1874 a group of Halifax lawyers was incorporated under the name of the Halifax Law School, not unlike the Halifax Medical College in organization and purpose. But it never really got off the ground. In 1881, at the time of the failure of the University of Halifax, John Thompson, by then the attorney general of Nova Scotia, had an act passed to allow the establishment of a law faculty of Dalhousie College. Munro's money would not establish a faculty, but it would set up one full-time professor. Such a man would gather around him a group of unpaid lawyers and judges, each of whom would receive $100 a year for the privilege of lecturing to Dalhousie students.

The moving spirit of the faculty was well chosen; Richard Chapman Weldon, aged thirty-two, was professor of mathematics (and occasionally political science) at Mount Allison. Weldon was a farm boy brought up near Sussex, New Brunswick, who was positively cajoled by his father into going to Mount Allison. There he met Benny Russell, up from Halifax, and they became lifelong friends. Russell recalled how Weldon stood head of everything, a man who took all knowledge for his province, and who got his BA at age seventeen to prove it. Weldon taught school, then came back to Mount Allison to teach mathematics. After that he went, on the thinnest savings possible, to Yale to do a PH.D. in law. He was back at Mount Allison in 1873, then again went abroad to study at Heidelberg for a year, again returning as professor of mathematics, from 1875 to 1883. Thus Weldon came with experience from several academic worlds; he wore all of it effortlessly, guilelessly, luminously. He was one of the few people of whom it may be said that his outward appearance was an accurate reflection

Dean Richard Weldon, Dalhousie's first dean of law, 1883–1914. "He was a clear, even brilliant teacher, and he impressed a whole generation of students ... with his mind and character."

of his mind and spirit. As A.S. MacKenzie described him, "Nature cast him in her noblest mould ... his large well-proportioned, erect figure, handsome leonine head and flashing eye commanded immediate attention. One instinctively felt here was a great man. His intellect matched his exterior." He was a clear, even brilliant teacher, and he impressed a whole generation of students not only with his mind and character, but with his charm of manner and his basic kindliness.[21] It ought to be remembered, more often than it is, that the Dalhousie Law Faculty in 1883 was an experiment. The idea of a university school of law was an innovation in Canada. French Canada with its civil law tradition needed and expected legal training in universities, hence the law schools at Laval, Université de Montréal (then a branch of Laval), and McGill; but Osgoode Hall in Toronto, established in 1889, with "its hard-nosed practitioners' slant" was a sharp contrast to Dalhousie where law was not merely a technical craft, but a liberal education.[22]

There is one aspect of the Dalhousie Law Faculty so central it must be noted – Weldon's emphasis on public service:

In drawing up our curriculum we have not forgotten the duty which every university owes to the state, the duty which Aristotle saw and emphasized so long ago, of teaching the young men the science of government. In our free government we all have political duties some higher, some humbler ... We may fairly hope that some of our students will, in their riper years be called upon to discharge public duties. We aim to help these to act with fidelity and wisdom.

Of all Munro's great gifts to Dalhousie, perhaps the choice of Weldon in constitutional law was the most fruitful one of all.[23]

The first thing the Dalhousie board did, within three weeks of accepting Munro's offer, was to send three able lawyers with academic interests to Boston and New York. They were to see what the law schools there actually did. The three were John Thompson, by then on the Nova Scotia Supreme Court; Wallace Graham, a lawyer in Halifax private practice; and Robert Sedgwick, an early Dalhousie graduate ('67) and a member of the Dalhousie board. What impressed Thompson and his colleagues was not so much the Harvard method of legal education; Dalhousie was not to adopt it anyway, or Columbia's, but would rather put the emphasis on public, constitutional, and international law. What impressed the three lawyers were the American libraries, legal as well as general. The juxtapositions even now are striking, when Dalhousie's law library is substantial enough. What it was then, when its total books were zero, was almost intimidating. Professor Forrest's inaugural of 1881 dwelt on this very point: "Going from Canada and visiting any of the leading institutions of the United States we feel at first like giving up in despair. Looking at their beautiful grounds, their spacious and elegant buildings, passing through their well filled libraries and museums." He held out hope, however; nearly all American institutions had to contend with poverty at the start. The Dalhousie lawyers' committee set to work the moment they returned, dunning lawyers and judges for donations and for books. By the end of 1883 some 2,800 law books had been acquired, with personal money and effort by Thompson, Graham, Sedgewick and others.[24]

There was no room any more for the law library and classrooms in the Dalhousie College building on the Parade. Instead they were in two large ground-floor rooms in the new Halifax High School, at the corner of Brunswick and Sackville streets. The building is still there. After a couple of years, when the high school needed the rooms, Russell and Weldon, the two old friends, acquired Sir Brenton Halliburton's house on Morris Street. He had been chief justice of Nova Scotia from 1833 to 1860, and his son John (of the duel with Howe) owned it until his death in 1884. The Dalhousie board had no money for that kind of undertaking, so Russell and Weldon bought it themselves for $4,000 on their own personal mortgage, and rented it to Dalhousie for $400 a year. They also spent the summer of 1885 personally putting up shelves for the books. The law students liked Halliburton Hall, its cosiness and seclusion, and regretted giving it up, as they were to do in 1887.[25]

Munro Professor of Metaphysics
But there was one more chair to come; in 1884 Munro established the chair of metaphysics. It is to be noted that the two last chairs he established were legal and philosophical, as if, having met the needs of physics, history, and literature, he felt law and philosophy were the next most obvious of Dalhousie's weaknesses. This time Munro chose a professor already at Dalhousie, whose specialty happened to be Kantian ethics, his future son-in-law, Jacob Gould Schurman, another protean intellectual, and already Munro professor of English literature and rhetoric. William Lyall, professor of logic and metaphysics, would now become professor of logic and psychology, the latter an interest he had long had.

To the now vacated Munro chair of English literature came an Ontarian, W.J. Alexander, of Hamilton. He took his BA at the University of London, and a PH.D. from Johns Hopkins. He too had spent time in Germany, at the University of Berlin in 1883 and 1884, going straight from there to Halifax at the age of twenty-nine.

Alexander's specialty was Browning. He was to marry a Halifax girl, Laura Morrow, in 1887. Several other Dalhousie professors married Halifax girls. Schurman probably met Barbara Munro in Halifax. Charles Macdonald married Mary Stairs in 1882. Lawson had married a Halifax widow, Mrs Caroline Knox, in 1876.

The five Munro professors were exceptional men. All but Forrest had done postgraduate work in Germany. Two of the five, Forrest and MacGregor, were Pictou County and Dalhousie. But the three others were from outside Dalhousie and it was not accidental. After the failure of the University of Halifax, Dalhousie made a deliberate choice to turn efforts at consolidation in a different direction, to combine strengths rather than to comprehend weaknesses. The idea seems to have come from Robert Sedgewick, whom the alumni elected to the Dalhousie board in 1883. Munro agreed that Dalhousie, while recruiting her own ablest men, should cast her net as widely as possible.

From 1880 to 1894 Munro also provided some $83,000 in exhibitions and bursaries. Half of the first twenty-five women graduating from Dalhousie were supported in this way. And if one capitalizes the $12,500 income of the five Munro professors on the basis of 5 per cent, the capital sum needed to endow the professorships was $250,000. That plus the $83,000 meant that Munro gave Dalhousie something like $333,000. In 1993 terms that would mean about $8 million, and that at a time when gifts to universities were rare. It is small wonder that contemporaries were amazed at the magnitude and range of Munro's donations to Dalhousie. Actually, Dalhousie did not get that capital at once. For a number of years Munro covered the salaries with quarterly instalments, sometimes of stock. In 1893, however, he set up a trust fund to support the chairs. There were no more gifts after 1884, nor were there any in Munro's will. However, Dalhousie held $82,000 in promissory notes, covering the balance of the endowment for the five chairs, which were duly honoured over a period of two years after Munro's death in 1896.[26]

Munro's tremendous example started others thinking along the same lines. Alexander McLeod was a wealthy Presbyterian businessman who ran a thriving wholesale wine and grocery business on Hollis Street. In 1881, by then a childless widower of ninety, McLeod drew up a will giving $200,000 for numerous bequests, the residue to go to Dalhousie to establish a special fund to endow at least three professorships. McLeod died on 15 January 1883; what finally came to Dalhousie was $62,000 (in 1993 terms about $1.5 million). Johnson, Lawson, and Liechti were all taken off Dalhousie money and made McLeod professors, in classics, chemistry, and modern languages respectively.[27]

Death of Principal Ross

Munro's brother-in-law, John Forrest, was now about to become president. Principal Ross had been visibly failing over the past several years. The board had struck a committee on the principalship in 1878, about the time of Forrest's appointment to the Board of Governors. That inquiry seems to have had no immediate effect, presumably because Ross was not ready to retire if he could help it. He had made financial sacrifices over the years, giving up his farm at West River to go to Truro, and giving up his house in Truro to come to Halifax in 1863. His wife died in the later 1870s and his daughter Helen, married to Joseph Howe's son William, died then too, leaving Ross with his little Dartmouth farm, an unmarried daughter, and two grandchildren to look after. Pensions were meagre. In December 1883, Ross agreed to resign both his chair of ethics and the principalship; pressure was coming not only from the board, but from the Presbyterian Synod which needed the money. Ross retired on 1 May 1885. He was then nearly seventy-four, and there was a general, if largely unvoiced, impression that his retirement was overdue. He died suddenly at home in Dartmouth, in March of 1886. The Senate passed a resolution usual in such cases, but it was stiff and formal. What Ross did for Dalhousie may not seem significant, but in the early years he had steered it through some very difficult water. He was a stout captain when the going was tough; if he lacked flair, he had great moral strength. G.G. Patterson, one of Ross's students and no mean authority, claimed that it was Ross who established Dalhousie's emphasis on teaching, for which it was already famous. In the context of the development of Dalhousie in the 1880s Patterson could say Ross was *felix opportunitate mortis*, happy in the fitting time for his death.[28]

When Ross retired, the name "principal" retired with him. Forrest seems to have preferred "president," and Dalhousie's chief executive officer has been president ever since. At Forrest's accession the Parade question, and with it Dalhousie's next life, was reaching its final phase.

Dispute over the Parade

Dalhousie College had had the Parade since it was deeded in 1818 by Lord Dalhousie. He had not consulted the city magistrates when he did it, nor did he have to. Still, the city claimed it had always been a public square, used for military and public gatherings since 1749. In fact, between 1749 and 1818 it was reserved by the crown for military purposes, but without denying public access. Its very name, Grand Parade, testified to its old military function. The Duke of Kent had put a fence around it in 1796 to delimit and beautify it, and since 1818 the fence had been kept, more or less as funds allowed, by Dalhousie

College. When Halifax was incorporated in 1841, the act specified what land was transferred to its jurisdiction; the Grand Parade was not included.[29]

By the 1870s the place was an eyesore. Dalhousie's fencing and finances were both broken down, and the walls facing Barrington Street were positively dangerous. The editors of the *Dalhousie Gazette* were sure that their grandchildren in the 1920s would still be floundering through the mud of the Grand Parade on their way to classes on wet mornings. To the many complaints, Dalhousie said it had no money for expensive repairs. If the city and its public wanted the improvements effected, then let the city and the public pay for them. The city replied that it wouldn't do so without title. The issue became more heated in the 1870s because Halifax really needed a new city hall. The old one was an 1810 brick courthouse at the bottom of George Street. The antiquated place leaked rain at the top and sewage at the bottom. In March 1874 City Council agreed that the best place to build a new city hall was the south end of the Parade, opposite Dalhousie College. Legislation was drafted. The question of the title would be cleared by legislative fiat. The bill passed the Assembly but ran into opposition in the Legislative Council. St Paul's Anglican Church was not at all happy about a city hall just outside its doors, nor was Dalhousie College much taken with losing one-quarter of its Parade. The Legislative Council defeated the bill.

The City Council then chose another site, one-third of a mile further north along Barrington Street. This was unpopular and it failed. The city and public really wanted the Parade, and neither was very scrupulous about getting it. Why should a private corporation, Dalhousie, block the well-understood wishes of the public, and for a patent public need? The answer was that the private corporation had title. If so, there were three choices: Dalhousie College could be bought out; the legislature could be persuaded to legislate them out; or the title could be disputed before the courts. The city did not want to spend the money on first option, especially as a number of aldermen believed it was the city's anyway; they had had no luck with the legislature; thus litigation was the only option open.

The Dalhousie board had no interest in litigation to test a title they believed, on good grounds, valid. They preferred negotiation. The college and the city were close to an agreement in January 1877. The title of Dalhousie to the north end of the Parade would be confirmed, with enough of the Parade to exclude noise; the rest would go to the city for $10,000. The city would agree to maintain and beautify the whole Parade. That compromise was actually recommended by the city's

Committee of Laws and Privileges to City Council. It passed by a vote of eight to seven, but was put down for reconsideration and then defeated. Finally the mayor wrote in February 1877, enclosing a resolution of City Council, and asked Dalhousie, almost like a duellist, to name their counsel for litigation. Judge Ritchie on the Dalhousie board moved that that be done, provided "all previous offers by way of compromise are withdrawn."[30]

A new complication was a legacy from Miss Isabella Cogswell of $4,000 to beautify the Grand Parade, to go to whoever had title, on condition it be open to the public in perpetuity. She died in December 1874; her solicitors naturally refused to release the money when title was in dispute, and there was a time limitation after which the money would revert to charity.

Negotiations were still pending when, in April 1879, the City Board of Works deposited a large quantity of granite on the northern end of the Parade, near the college. If that was intended to get litigation started, it did. When the case came up in the autumn of 1879, the city, perhaps owing to newly discovered doubts about its claim to title, took advantage of some minor irregularity and the case was delayed until 1880. It was tried in the autumn of 1880 by Justice Weatherbe, a graduate of Acadia. Weatherbe charged the jury strongly in favour of Dalhousie, mostly on the ground of Dalhousie's undisturbed possession of the Parade since 1818. But five jurors were not persuaded; the jury split, and thus the law case failed. According to the *Presbyterian Witness*, the city was trying to get its way by bluster and force. Litigation was then abandoned, and resort was had to what the issue had long needed, compromise and open-minded negotiations. The new compromise was embodied in an act of the legislature in April 1883. All of the Grand Parade south of a line fifteen feet from the front of the college was given to the city, free of encumbrances. There was one condition: the city had no right to sell or lien any of the Parade that lay north of the northern line of George Street. The part of the Parade on which Dalhousie stood, and the fifteen feet in front, was wholly vested in the Dalhousie College. The city would also pay the college $500 a year in perpetuity, as long as the college stayed within the city limits of Halifax.[31] That settled the dispute over the Parade. The city collected the Cogswell money and then set conscientiously to work, rebuilding the stone walls and putting in iron railings. The Grand Parade began to look more like its name.

Sir William Young, chairman of the Dalhousie Board of Governors since 1848, found the busyness and complications of the 1880s more than he could manage. He was now eighty-five, and resigned in

September 1884. The board wanted him to reconsider; he agreed to stay on the board, and let someone else be chairman. The Dalhousie board were grateful and said so.

Sir William Young was in a position to render invaluable service to this institution. His practical sagacity, his brilliant talents, his cautious statesmanship, his unfailing prudence were laid under tribute to advance the interests of this college. He stood by it loyally in its days of weakness and to his counsels is due much of its strength today.[32]

That eulogy was laying it on with a trowel, but it gets at Sir William's careful approach to education and politics. He was succeeded as chairman by Adams G. Archibald, lieutenant-governor of Nova Scotia from 1873 to 1883, who had been particularly helpful in negotiations with city and government over the Parade. Archibald was appointed in December 1884, and faced almost at once some new questions. One of them was the prospect of union with King's College.

Union with King's Proposed
King's had been badly hit by the end of the government grants in 1881. Professor J.G. MacGregor of Dalhousie came to a King's Alumni meeting, probably in 1882, urging King's to appoint a committee to discuss with Dalhousie the possibilities of union. That move was then defeated by the King's Alumni by one vote. But negotiations later resumed and early in 1885 Archibald and President Forrest met with King's College representatives at the Old Dutch Church. Bishop Binney, hitherto strongly opposed to any move to Halifax, was taken by surprise at the range and generosity of Dalhousie's terms. The proposal was to establish at Halifax a new university, under a new name. Dalhousie would sell its existing Parade building, and put up a new one. All Dalhousie exhibitions and bursaries would be open to students from either institution. King's would endow one chair. Like Dalhousie, it would give no further arts degrees, but King's would retain its divinity degree. The King's group was rather pleased by the Dalhousie proposals, for King's financial picture was bleak. The deficit for 1884–5 was $1,340 more than King's income of $6,300, and savings had to come from somewhere. In Bishop Binney's view it could only come from reduction in staff and King's staff was already too small.[33]

The results of these discussions came eventually to the King's board and the alumni. The King's Alumni Association was peculiar in that it allowed admission of members who were not actually alumni. All they had to do was to pay the two-dollar fee, and they could become semi-official and vote using a member's proxy. At the meeting in Windsor on 24 June 1885, there were 105 alumni votes and thirty-two proxies. Most of the proxies were, it was said, Windsor residents, sworn to keep the college in Windsor. The bishop moved union with Dalhousie, somewhat reluctantly indeed, but believing there was no viable alternative. Dr Mather Almon moved the three months' hoist to it. Judge De Wolfe, who seconded the hoist, maintained that Dalhousie was in poor financial condition compared to the other colleges, and that it was liable to complete collapse owing to its dependence on George Munro. The Munro chairs, De Wolfe emphasized, were not yet endowed; they were paid for by cheques drawn on New York from time to time. At any moment Munro's business might fail. Not only that, but he was the publisher of "cheap and not always wholesome literature."[34] Add to that the danger of going to Halifax. Who knew where Dalhousie would put its new building? Think, said Dr Almon, of the Halifax High School, "bounded on one side by brothels and another by grog shops." When the vote came, the King's alumni turned down the union proposal by a two-thirds majority. The Halifax papers of both political parties jumped on the alumni. "Demagoguism and prejudice," said the *Morning Herald*, "will never long succeed in keeping students at a weak and decaying college." What the King's alumni did do, said the *Morning Chronicle*, was to make way for "the virtual destruction of the college they pretend to love so dearly."[35]

Dalhousie Needs a New Site
With or without union with King's, Dalhousie needed changes and they could not be too long delayed. The city engineer, E.H. Keating, was inclined to prefer the Dalhousie College part of the Parade to the south end of it. He made an inspection of the college building to see if it would do as a city hall. He asked Dalhousie to name a price. Even now Dalhousie College might possibly stay put; its problem was space. If Dalhousie stayed on the Parade, expansion of premises was going to be necessary. The governors were inclined to sell out and move. They replied in September 1885 to Keating that they would sell for $30,000 plus suitable space on city land, provided the $500 annual income, from the act of 1883, were left intact. The city were not pleased at this asking price; they offered $25,000 and no land.[36]

At this point the Miller property became available. This was a generous tract of land in the south end of the peninsula, backing onto Point Pleasant Park, from Tower Road to the harbour. The Board of Governors called in the Senate, to debate the best course of action. President Forrest said the professors could accommodate themselves to any site, but it was the students that concerned him. He dreaded moving the college so far from the centre of the city, beyond easy access by horse-car routes. Professor Lawson and Liechti did not want to go anywhere. The present building had many advantages and it would not be difficult to effect enlargements that would meet Dalhousie's needs for some time to come. Macdonald feared a move too. It would be some time, he said, before Dalhousie could put up any accommodation for students; currently Dalhousie was relying much upon the boarding houses of the North End. Thus the Miller property would be a great disadvantage; where were the boarding houses? Weldon and Alexander both wanted the Miller site, perhaps for its inherent attractiveness. Lyall wanted space, wherever it could be found. At the end of that meeting the board agreed to buy the Miller property if it could be got reasonably. But reasonable the owners were not; they asked at least $25,000. That seemed to Dalhousie grossly overpriced.[37]

By March 1886 a faculty committee decided that the expansion of the old building would not provide sufficient space. Dalhousie would have to provide for the Law Faculty, for the expansion of the library, for future staff, and for laboratory space. Thus the Parade site could not longer be thought of as permanent. At that point the committee was thinking of a time in the future when perhaps one or more of the denominational colleges might want to be on the Dalhousie campus. Faculty used the example of Melbourne University in Australia under the Colony of Victoria Act of 1881; that allowed the University of Melbourne affiliation with Anglican, Methodist, and Presbyterian residential colleges. Here the recent negotiations with King's undoubtedly had influence on Dalhousie's thinking.[38]

Several Dalhousie governors had been looking at a city property on what was then called the South Common, land north of the poorhouse at South Street and Robie, five acres of open land, at the corner of Morris (University Avenue) and Robie Street. Would the city give this land to Dalhousie and $25,000 for the Parade site?[39] The offer was predicated on a behind-the-scenes promise of Sir William Young. The $25,000 the city might pay Dalhousie for its Parade site would not be enough for a new building. If the old Dalhousie had cost £13,000 (i.e., about $52,000), how much would a new one cost that would have to be at least treble the size? True, no one seems to have been thinking of stone. The new Halifax High School of 1879 was of brick. It was at this juncture that Sir William Young offered to fund the difference between $25,000 and a new building with $20,000 of his own money. It was offered on one condition: that the new Dalhousie be built on free city land. Sir William was not putting up $20,000 simply to buy a piece of Halifax real estate.

In April 1886 the City Council accepted the Dalhousie offer, and legislation went forward that very session of the legislature. The act confirmed at last the city's full title to the whole of the Grand Parade, and the gift of the Morris and Robie streets property to Dalhousie. There was one condition to the gift: the land would revert to the city if it were sold out or leased by Dalhousie. The city would continue to pay Dalhousie $500 a year. The city did not do badly. The 1879 value of the Parade site was about $48,000; even after the legislation of 1883 Dalhousie still possessed a quarter of it, and the Dalhousie building had cost $52,000. The lot the city offered on the South Common was worth about $4,000.

The city took over the Dalhousie property as of 1 October 1886, Dalhousie leasing it for six months until April 1887. Once it got its hands on the property, the city set to work taking apart the old building. No sentiment stayed its hand; nor, it is fair to say, was there much public interest in saving the building. The students had mixed feelings. "Old Dalhousie has gone," said the *Dalhousie Gazette*, "and its site is occupied by a rising structure, which will tell a tale of Haligonian pride and magnificence ... Ugh! those old musty walls that left a stain on the clothes of the followers of Minerva! the strong savour of ancient days that pervaded the entire building!"

Yet students were not without their sentiments about the trying moment when old Dalhousie passed into the hands of the city. "Some of our happiest memories are associated with the whitewashed walls of the old gray stone building which has vanished from sight ... What though in the cheerless rooms, our books and manuscripts were the sport of winds from Aeolian caves." Progress was the watchword. A fine, spanking new city hall, with three storeys, a high mansard roof, and a tower would be a fitting mark of the progress and development of the city in the 1880s, rather than the old, modest, one-and-a-half storey, ironstone Dalhousie. That old stone was still good; the city hall contractors used it in the foundations of the new building. The new outside foundation stones were granite, but the inside was the old Dalhousie ironstone of 1820–1. On 18 April 1887 the workmen took out the cornerstone, and the tin box that had been there for fifty-seven years was opened the next day. It contained a brown pulpy mass, the remnants of the papers put there in 1820; but the original brass plate marking the occasion in 1820, and four George III coins were still in good condition.[40]

Nine days later, on 27 April, the cornerstone of the new Dalhousie was laid. The board had been busy. In May 1886 it issued a set of instructions for architects interested in submitting plans. The new building was to be of brick, the exterior of the best face-brick, with terracotta or stone trimmings. There were to be three storeys, with parts of the building running to four. There was to be a good basement, with the foundation walls tied with iron. The inside partitions of the basement and first storey were to be of brick. The first storey was to be five feet above the outside grade. There was to be an arts library of 1,400 square feet and a museum of the same size; both should be designed so as to be reused as classrooms. There was to be "a spacious Lobby" of 700 square feet from which the main staircase would ascend. The registrar's room was to be "a small office" near the main entrance. The whole building, read the instructions, was "to be capable of great extension." Finished, and with heating installed, it was to cost no more than $50,000.[41]

Those were the requirements, and architects were asked to conform, but of course submit their own designs since the board was "desirous of obtaining the best." Designs were to be submitted by 30 June 1886, and a prize of $150 was offered for the best. The winning architect was J.C.P. Dumaresq, who donated 1 per cent of his commission to Dalhousie. Tenders were called for and opened in October. The highest tender was $73,850 from S.M. Brookfield of Halifax. They were good builders; they had built Fort Massey Church in 1871 and two major sugar refineries in the 1880s. But Dalhousie stuck to the lowest tender, which was from E.A. Milliken of Moncton, at $53,846. They were also the low bidders in the contract for building the new city hall. The Milliken tender was accepted, and the building to be ready by 15 September 1887. Thus did it come to the laying of the cornerstone. The day before the weather was stormy, auguring ill for an outdoor ceremony, but the 27th was as lovely an April day as Nova Scotia was likely to produce. Large crowds came out; by two in the afternoon there were two thousand people on the field at Morris and Robie. Sir William Young, showing all his years, duly laid the granite stone. His speech was read for him by President Forrest. Among the crowd were three men, G.G. Gray, Garrett Miller, and W.H. Keating, who had all been present at the 1820 laying of the cornerstone by Lord Dalhousie.[42]

It was Sir William Young's last public appearance. He died ten days later. He had chaired the Dalhousie Board from 1848 to 1884, through many vicissitudes. He and Joseph Howe, united about Dalhousie and politics, enjoyed only a modicum of cordiality between them. Howe thought of Young as timid and unenterprising, except where money was concerned. It was Howe who was mainly instrumental in reviving Dalhousie in 1863, not the chief justice and chairman of the Dalhousie Board. Young was generous with his money, but liked people to know it. He left half of the residue of his estate to Dalhousie, and an endowment for the Sir William Young Gold Medal

Sir William Young, *c.* 1880, from a contemporary engraving. "He was generous with his money and liked people to know it."

to the undergraduate with the highest standing in Mathematics. That was a touch from Dalhousie traditions.

At the time of Young's death the old Dalhousie on the Parade was slowly coming down. The mortar was hard and the stone still good, and it was not easy going. The contractor underestimated his costs and the whole contract had to be re-tendered for in 1888. The old Dalhousie was thus going, but in many ways it had symbolized the Dalhousian. Those bare, unadorned walls and corridors, the rugged benches and desks seamed with initials, impressed the student that Dalhousie meant work, not buildings, still less comfort. The Dalhousie student's athletic opportunities had been limited, his social instincts underdeveloped, the cultivation of his aesthetic tastes negligible: but there were great professors and they mattered. It was their ability as teachers and scholars that was so impressive. Marks were low, honours were hard to come by, whatever a student got he certainly earned. As one put it, "Flowery sentences, rhetorical commonplaces, and windy words wilted or collapsed in the northern atmosphere of old Dalhousie. What the student said he was supposed to have thought out. Precision and reality were supreme academic virtues."[43]

It was a good legacy to bequeath to the big new brick Dalhousie now going up on the five acres out at the corner of Robie and Morris streets.

·7·

A Maturing Confidence
1887–1901

The new brick Dalhousie. Changes in Halifax. Archibald MacMechan. Difficulties of finance. Halifax Medical College and Dalhousie. The Law School's peculiar year. Shifts in curriculum. Student life and Senate discipline. Dances. Death of Charles Macdonald, 1901.

One of the first signs of Halifax visible to a ship coming to harbour from seaward after August 1887 was the tall brick tower of Dalhousie, 145 feet high. It was just ten feet short of the Citadel's height and stood a few degrees to the west. Closer up, the spacious new brick building on the South Common looked rather gaunt and puritan. "Externally," said the *Presbyterian Witness*, "it is not an imposing structure, but it impresses the spectator with the conviction that use rather than ornament has been the controlling idea." Utilitarian it was; its three-plus storeys of red brick on a foundation of grey-white granite were saved from being positively ugly by an engaging balance between horizontal and vertical lines, the former emphasized by stone trim, the latter by the tall tower above the main entrance. But on a rainy morning it was not inviting, as one young woman remembered: "After a dismal walk through rain and fog you arrived at a bleak building of red brick, which reared itself out of the mist, tall and lanky wearing the look of a child who has grown too fast."

The building was ready to be inhabited by mid-September of 1887. It was only the first half of a building eventually supposed to be double the size. The present one was big enough, said President Forrest, for a good many years to come. He bravely claimed that the building would be the equal of other such buildings in Canada, though, he noted, the University of Toronto buildings, built by the Ontario government, were costly and ornate. "But we have no money to lay out for expensive adornments, or costly architectural designs." Dalhousie was built from the city's $25,000 payment for the Grand Parade, from

Sir William's gift, and from whatever private money the Board of Governors could scrounge from a Halifax world not replete with millionaires. And even wealthy Haligonians had a tradition of being close-fisted with their money.[1]

The grounds showed the penury. There had been no landscaping, no trees; the ground was mere cinders, stones and dirt. The yard was enclosed with a large fence, with breaches soon made in it by impatient students. The cinder yard could yield up the odd empty tomato can, decayed orange, or dead cat. It was the wet and the mud that created the problems, "this yellow, yielding, yeasty campus mud," as the *Gazette* put it. Mud-scrapers were positioned on either side of the main door; their foundations are still there, anchored in the granite. One streaming day, while water was sluicing down Morris Street, President Forrest stood for an hour in the wet cautioning students not to use the usual route if he or she wanted dry feet.[2]

Once inside the building, the students enjoyed the space, the first in years. After having been "mewed up" as the *Witness* put it, in the old building, the wide corridors and staircases gave a new sense of amplitude. Enrolment in 1887–8 was 191; in arts (that included science) there were eighty-eight regular undergraduates and fifty-six general students; in law there were thirty-eight undergraduates and nine general students. Halifax was well represented. Of one hundred undergraduates in arts in 1889–90, twenty were from Halifax.[3]

If the curious undergraduate went up to the third floor, and climbed to the tower, he could see Mauger's Beach lighthouse and the surf at Thrumcap Shoal. The foreground would be occupied by Gorsebrook golf course, with Collins hill, used then, as now, for sleigh-riding and tobogganing. The Dalhousie tower was one of the best vantage points around. Private estates such as Oaklands had lots of trees, but a visitor from the 1990s to the Halifax of the 1890s would be struck by the absence of trees on city streets. The city had begun to plant saplings on the North and South Common in the 1880s; but planting trees between the sidewalk and the street was still unfamiliar. It was being urged in October 1900 as a new civic improvement. The Halifax streets were not the shady avenues they are now.[4]

Another difference would be the sidewalks. Downtown there were brick sidewalks, occasionally granite ones, and across the cinders, dust, and mud of the streets were stone or brick crossings. But the main staple for sidewalks was still the cinders and ashes from numerous fireplaces, stoves, and an increasing number of furnaces. Those sidewalks and street crossings were very hard on long skirts. Braid was often sewn around the bottom to help protect them against the mud and dirt. One whimsical letter of 1893 from "A. Skirt" complained, "un-

Entrance Hall, Dalhousie College, 1896.

Dalhousie Library, 1896. Note the paucity of books and working space.

luckily for myself as I am worn rather long just now, I cannot help gathering superfluous mud around me. Yours muckily." An 1893 poetic summary of the complaints of Halifax streets begins:

> No dust blows through the streets to make you blink,
> (At least not after thirty hours hard rain);
> No pitfalls in the pavements cause you pain;
> The lights about the streets number quite twenty
> You'll all agree with me that that is plenty.

As to lighting, Halifax was better than that, for there were eighty gas lamps, on tall cast-iron standards made in Glasgow. In the outlying parts of the city, and that meant Dalhousie, coal-oil lamps were common. In 1886 conversion to electric street lighting began, but it was far from perfect. One sarcastic description of electric light was "electric dark." It was 1890 before the system could be fairly trusted.[5]

The other impressive change of the 1880s was the beginning of Canada's long love affair with the telephone. The Nova Scotia Telephone Company was chartered in 1887; by that time Halifax had four hundred telephones, mostly in offices and businesses. Students at Dalhousie started asking for one in 1889, since there were so many part-time law teachers who were not always able to give their lectures owing to commitments in court. Dalhousie did not have money for such frills. There was still no telephone in 1893; Dalhousie appears in the Halifax telephone book of May 1900, the number, 1092.[6]

The other invention that obtruded itself into the university world of the 1880s and 1890s was the typewriter. At first the name applied to the women (and earlier, the men) who did the typing; more than one MP in Ottawa or MLA in Halifax liked having an attractive typewriter in his office. Machines were not considered proper for personal correspondence then, or for a long time to come. Sir John A. Macdonald never signed a typewritten letter; his secretaries wrote his letters by hand, keeping copies in great books of flimsies called letterbooks. President Forrest conducted Dalhousie's business correspondence, such as it was, in his own hand. It is difficult to believe he did not have an official letterbook, but since he did not have an official secretary, perhaps it should not be surprising. His methods of dealing with Dalhousie business were, to say the least, casual. It used to be said that at registration he would put the arts money in one trousers pocket, the law money in another, and the medical money in his waistcoat. One former Dalhousie secretary, Lola Henry, recalled that it was said the records of Dalhousie business were in pencil on the starched cuffs of President Forrest's shirts. Whether for these reasons, very little of

President Forrest's correspondence has survived, and what there is is mostly in the papers of others. Dalhousie seems to have bought its first typewriter in 1907 and its typewritten records start to appear after 1911, after Forrest stepped down as president.[7]

Dalhousie Staff

By the end of the 1880s Dalhousie had a staff almost double that of 1863. By now there were ten full-time professors, five George Munro ones, three McLeod, plus the two Presbyterian professors, Lyall and Macdonald. Ross, the third Presbyterian professor, retired in 1885, and the Presbyterian Church preferred to put its education money into Pine Hill Divinity College. Dalhousie was now on its feet. There were also two George Munro tutors, much needed in the basic subjects: in classics, Howard Murray, and in mathematics A.S. MacKenzie. Benjamin Russell was half-time professor in law, besides of course Dean Weldon. That was the teaching staff for Dalhousie's two hundred or so students, of whom 70 per cent were degree students in arts and law.

Dalhousie's choices for professor were too good; it could not always hold them. J.G. Schurman, who was Munro professor of philosophy, had written *Kantian Ethics and the Ethics of Evolution* in 1881. He was popular with students and much appreciated in Halifax as an evening lecturer. All the while he was working on a second major book, *The Ethical Import of Darwinism*, published in London in 1888, where he sought to distinguish between the animal and human contexts of evolution, between biology and morals. The *Dalhousie Gazette* claimed in 1886 that Dalhousie seniors were striking examples of the survival of the fittest, being evolved from freshmen over an eon of 1,400 days, during which "all the imperfect specimens drop out of sight." The conflict between science and revelation worried writers in the *Gazette*; they went mostly on hope that Darwin and Genesis would some day, somehow, be reconciled: "though we see a current in one direction, and a counter-current in another, we have yet scarcely found out in what direction the whole mass is drifting, yet we know the course is ever onward." Perhaps that was the reason why Darwinism was taught at Dalhousie in philosophy classes; biology did not come as a subject until the eve of the First World War. Schurman was invited in 1886 to take the Sage chair of philosophy at Cornell, an invitation he found impossible to resist. Within six years he would be president of Cornell, at the age of thirty-eight.[8]

Schurman was replaced by James Seth, a twenty-nine-year-old Edinburgh scholar, educated there and in Germany. His specialty, too, was ethics. He liked Dalhousie students for what he called their "fine earnestness of purpose." There is a charming description of young Seth and old William Lyall, thin and bent by then, on a sunny October afternoon in 1889 along Young Avenue. The two philosophers were walking towards what Halifax children called "the Golden Gates" of Point Pleasant Park, talking together, threading, as MacMechan put it "some Socratic dream." Lyall, still at seventy-eight professor of logic and metaphysics, was cautious and moderate, and if not enthusiastic about Charles Darwin (and still less about Herbert Spencer), that was, as the *Gazette* pointed out, the defect of virtues. Lyall taught philosophy as if it were "the one thing needful for the life that now is and for that which is yet to come." His *Intellect, and Emotions, and the Moral Nature*, a majestic book published in Edinburgh in 1855, was written in Halifax when he was teacher at the Free Church College. Lyall used it as his textbook in logic and psychology, metaphysics and esthetics, his courses at Dalhousie, and it was used in several other Canadian universities. It is a period piece; philosophy and psychology, poetry and piety, are put together, with metaphysics visible always on the horizon. Lyall was an acute observer of human nature; his theory of knowledge scorned the speculations of David Hume, and remained faithful to Scottish ideas of common sense. Lyall died in January 1890. James Seth went to Brown in 1892, then to Cornell to Schurman's chair. Seth moved partly for reasons of money, going from $2,000 at Dalhousie to $3,000 at Brown, to $3,500 at Cornell. He would end up back in Edinburgh in 1898, still grateful to Dalhousie and Dalhousie colleagues whom he remembered with considerable affection.[9]

W.J. Alexander, the Munro professor of English, went to the University of Toronto in 1889. He had formally applied for the Toronto chair in November 1888. Following the custom, he had printed a short pamphlet with a brief curriculum vitae and containing testimonials, not excluding those from Dalhousie colleagues, perhaps the most important of all. President Forrest hated to see Alexander leave and said so. "I regret very much that I am called upon to discharge a duty which, while pleasant in itself is yet ominous of evil to our institution." Forrest praised Alexander's teaching and scholarship, then concluded, "Justice to Dr. Alexander compels me to give this certificate; but I hope that Toronto University may find a suitable professor of English in some other quarter."[10]

Toronto did not so find, though it was not until May 1889 that Alexander actually resigned. The search for a new man had already started. George Munro's opinion was solicited, and in New York he interviewed one promising candidate, Archibald McKellar MacMechan. Forrest's brother wrote from Toronto, that the more he'd looked at MacMechan the better he got. "He stood a fair chance of obtaining the chair to which Professor Alexander has been called to Toronto, but was thought to be too young." Forrest's first choice among all the candidates was MacMechan. The difficulty was, he told MacMechan, "You are, as yet an untried man." There was nothing in Dalhousie rules indicating how long a professor could hold office, "but the practice has always been that the tenure of office is as long as the Professor wishes to stay." That was the difficulty; some governors worried that it was a great risk to appoint someone so young and inexperienced to so permanent a post. Forrest suggested the following to the twenty-seven-year-old MacMechan:

Now what I would like you to do is this. To authorise me to state that if after two or three years work you are not able to satisfy the Governors that you have the necessary qualifications for the position you will quietly withdraw. Now I ask this not because I have any misgivings myself. I fully believe you have the scholarship and the ability to fill the position with entire satisfaction to us all. You will get every encouragement, and every one will hope for and rejoice in your success. No public reference whatever will be made to this understanding ... My only object in getting it from you is to be able to meet possible objections to your inexperience. I think if I have that I will have no difficulty in securing your appointment.

MacMechan accepted this gentlemen's agreement, and as things turned out, it never needed to be invoked. MacMechan's is the only appointment for which there is evidence of Forrest's style and mode of working. The men he chose are the best illustration of his judgment. It is not clear that he had actually met MacMechan before he hired him; if he had not, his judgment is all the more remarkable. Walter Murray, later president of the University of Saskatchewan from 1908 to 1937, wrote of Forrest that when unfettered in his selection he never made a mistake. In Murray's opinion, Forrest's greatest gift to Dalhousie was his unerring sense for what was good in a professor.[11]

MacMechan was a golden choice. An Ontarian, born in Berlin (now Kitchener), Ontario, he received his BA from the University of Toronto in 1884. After two years of high school teaching he went to Johns Hopkins in Baltimore where he had fellowships in German. In 1889 MacMechan was awarded his PH.D. on *The Relation of Hans Sachs to the Decameron*, published in Halifax in 1889, probably at MacMechan's expense. The subject is remarkable enough, and it illustrates the wide range of MacMechan's intellect. Not only was he fluent in German and French, and of course Latin, but also Italian. He was thoroughly at home in Dante and the early Renaissance Italian writers. About middle height, with a trim torpedo beard, MacMechan was well-turned out, fastidious, and, although lame, played tennis and golf. He knew enough about rugby to coach a school team in Ontario and at critical moments to encourage the Dalhousie team.[12]

He fell in love with Halifax, and so did his new Ontario wife. "Something tells me," he said in 1893, "I shall live and die in Halifax and I have never been deceived in these premonitions. It would not be a sorry fate, I love the place: it made Edith and home and the dear children possible. I should be ungrateful not to love it. Dirty disreputable old wooden town…" He loved its seasons, for the autumn especially after the brilliant leaves had gone and the underbrush turned scarlet and the larch flamed yellow, and for the spring just before the leaves came out when the countryside for a week looked like an Impressionist painting. He loved Halifax for its history, its quiet hospitality, for the sea that surrounded it and the lakes that inhabited its very suburbs, for its ships and their mysteries. Something of MacMechan's style and his passion for his new home comes through in "A City by the Sea," an article he published in January 1890 in *The Week*, then Canada's only national literary weekly:

It is a city of strange sights, especially so to an eye bred inland. The most engaging of these owe their charm to the presence of the sea. At every turn, you are reminded of the ocean and the traffic in deep waters…

The sea itself is never far off. It closes the vista of the short streets, one after one, with a band of blue beside the black wharves. It bounds the prospect wherever you look over the dun roofs, with their clusters of chimney-pots and dormer windows … It is ever the same and ever changing glittering in the sunshine, dull under the broad, grey clouds; flecked with sails or smooth and featureless as a mill-pond. Half way down the bay, you catch a glimpse of a white line, the reef with its breakers. Here stands the little lighthouse, which, at the fall of darkness shows its light like a candle set in a lonely cottage window…

The houses are of wood, very plain without as a general thing, but pretty and comfortable within. They are all of the same pattern, painted a dull drab or grey which is soon further toned down by the action of the coal smoke. The English chimney-pot abounds, and the dormer windows on the roof. This last always prevents a house from being utterly ugly and some of the sloping streets where roof rises above roof, and the outlines are still further broken by these quaint devices half window, half room, are quite worthy of the study of the etcher.[13]

He turned out to be a delightful, though hardly flamboyant, lecturer. He had little of the flash and edge that made Charles Macdonald's lectures so memorable. His were more studied and deliberate. He dressed

Archibald MacMechan, Munro Professor of English, 1889–1931. "He loved Halifax for its history, its quiet hospitality, for the sea that surrounded it and the lakes that inhabited its very suburbs."

for the part, carefully, always with a gown. He expected students to dress as befitted gentlemen and ladies even if of limited means. Archie, as he was soon known by the students, read poetry – he read aloud a good deal – in a style more finished than dramatic. He was apt to shy away from the rougher scenes in Shakespeare or Fielding; the first scene in *King Lear* made him uneasy. His was a delicate, careful taste; his world reminded one of Watteau, not of Rubens. Among the greats of English literature his particular favourites were Kipling, Tennyson, and Carlyle – the Victorians, of which, it is right to say, he was one.

His public lectures in Halifax, on Shakespeare, Browning, and other literary figures, were soon well attended. He gave whole courses of lectures, a dozen or so on a theme over the winter. As he grew older his publications multiplied. He feared not working. He feared the weakness he said his father had, a lack of energy and application, and he fought it all his life, and with singular success.[14]

This was the young professor who started at Dalhousie in the fall of 1889, and made his whole life here. He would retire from Dalhousie only in 1931, and he was then much the same as he had always been, in style and manner. For the reputation of Dalhousie, in Canada and abroad, no professor, not even the great Charles Macdonald, matched Archibald MacMechan. He celebrated Nova Scotia's history and its ships and he loved its values, its independence, its hatred of sham.

Dalhousie Finances

One of the first things that MacMechan encountered at Dalhousie was the ongoing difficulties of Dalhousie's finances. He had already had to agree not to accept student fees. A new departure, beginning with MacMechan, Dalhousie asked all professors, as they were appointed, to renounce fees. The university would keep them.[15] This was only one aspect of a larger problem. The board informed Senate in March 1890 that for some years past there had been a deficit on current account, owing to the gradual shrinkage in interest rates, mortgage income, and rents, from which Dalhousie got its current funds. The aggregate debt had become, so the board said, "seriously embarrassing." It had had to borrow money on the personal security of some of its members. The board conceded that salaries were none too high. Would the university professors consider giving up, as new ones were doing, the fees they traditionally collected? Senate was not enthusiastic. They considered fees part of existing contractual arrangements. They proposed other options. One was to ask the Presbyterian Church to continue to contribute to the chair of logic and psychology now made vacant by the sudden death of William Lyall in January 1890. That hope proved illusory. The Presbyterian Church wished to put more money into theology at Pine Hill, and it now gave up the second professorship with which Dalhousie had been restarted in 1863. That left only one professor, Charles Macdonald, supported by the Presbyterian Church.[16]

The Munro professorships continued to be highly sought after, however. Walter Murray, a New Brunswicker (UNB '86), after graduate work in Edinburgh and Berlin, returned to his alma mater as professor of philosophy in 1891. Dalhousie was able to appoint him in 1892 as George Munro professor of philosophy, replacing James Seth, at double Murray's UNB salary. But then the Munro professorships were exceptional.

The new building had made Dalhousie's finances no easier. Sir William Young's promised $20,000 to the building fund had not yet been received; Milliken the contractor was paid by going to the Bank of Nova Scotia and getting an overdraft. That stood at $21,357.09 in June 1888. There were also a couple of Mechanics' liens out against the building, though they were eventually sorted out. The bank was willing to wait until money from the Young estate arrived, but the situation was sufficiently parlous that in the summer of 1888 the board struck a finance committee to report on the state of the Dalhousie endowment and current finances.[17]

The Dalhousie endowment in December 1888, with Munro and McLeod money added to the original Castine fund ($51,067 in 1863) now totalled $331,522, of which 55 per cent was Munro promissory notes. The rest was invested variously: 12 per cent in local mortgages, another 10 per cent in Canadian and American stocks; the McLeod properties on Hollis and Granville streets accounted for 17 per cent. That endowment did not mean Dalhousie was wealthy; it meant it was rich in tied money.

Its cash income was rather thin. The five Munro professors cost $10,000 per annum, paid by Munro in quarterly instalments. The other professors cost $6,900, which with maintenance and other expenses came to $10,500 per year. Income, outside of Munro, came to $7,000, making an annual deficit on current account of $3,500. In June 1890 some of the Granville Street property was mortgaged. Perhaps more important, a conference was held with Alumni to discuss Dalhousie's financial position. The Alumni urged the governors and the Senate to follow the example of Johns Hopkins and other American universities – that is, give a complete statement of the university's financial position to the public. Dalhousie governors had a Scottish reluctance to do quite that; what they did was to show that Dalhousie had an annual deficit of some $3,000 on current account, and why. A plan of campaign was approved; important Maritime towns were to be canvassed, the aim being to raise $50,000. By 1892

$7,000 had been subscribed. One alumnus thought that was not good enough; if the Board of Governors and the president were not dead, they were certainly asleep, and the main responsibility for this lassitude lay with President Forrest. Another alumnus remarked that he had met Forrest time and again and "he has not asked me for a V." (Many banknotes used "V" on their $5 bills.) What George Grant had done for Queen's, what Schurman was doing for Cornell, should be done by Forrest. There was no need to take an apologetic line; that never worked anyway. Take the public into your confidence, "give them facts and figures to dissipate the fiction that Dalhousie is rich, and the independent, if not the sectarian, public will substantially acknowledge her claims." Above all, said the alumnus, avoid the impression that Dalhousie had collected $7,000 under false pretences.

There was much good sense in that. It was true that President Forrest's talents did not include success at badgering the public for money. But, as another alumnus pointed out three weeks later, Forrest had done more for Dalhousie financially than any other president by a long chalk: the Munro, McLeod, and Young legacies were all owing to Forrest. If one took away those gifts, what with the government abandoning all college support after 1881, and the Presbyterians giving up two-thirds of their funding, where would Dalhousie have been without Forrest?

Dalhousie's finances slowly improved. By 1900 its annual income totalled $22,800 with expenditure only $500 more. That was manageable, though the arithmetic was narrow enough. By 1900 the total endowment was $343,000. Munro had died in 1896, and the Munro endowment came in between 1897 and 1900.[18]

Affiliation of the Halifax Medical College

The other change that came in 1889 was the reordering of arrangements with the Halifax Medical College. Since 1875 the college had gone its own way; it had put up a wooden three-storey building at the corner of College and Carleton streets, with a substantial mortgage. But as an institution it had rather marked time. Student numbers did not grow much. The college survived on student fees and a small government grant of $800 a year; its professors were local doctors who had their own practices to run. Facilities in the Halifax Medical College were very modest, really inadequate, and they were slowly losing staff. The best surgeon in Halifax, Dr John Stewart, who had been Joseph Lister's house physician at Edinburgh, resolutely refused to have anything to do with the Halifax Medical College. This may have been due as much to pique and personality as to professional dislike. There were good doctors in the college; but not all the doctors were good, and some very good ones were not there at all. At a large meeting at the Nova Scotia Hospital in Dartmouth in May 1884, Dr J.F. Black proposed the Halifax Medical College be discontinued. After much debate – it can be imagined! – that decision was put off. One more term would be tried, in 1884–5. For that session there were twenty-five regular medical students.[19]

Over the winter of 1884–5 negotiations about affiliation proceeded with Dalhousie, and these had almost come to fruition when the "Great Row" erupted. It was over the running of the City and Provincial Hospital, the principal teaching hospital of the Halifax Medical College.

The City and Provincial Hospital was under the direction of the provincial commissioners of public charities. Their view of the world gave higher allegiance to politics than to medicine. In May 1885 the commissioners appointed a recent McGill graduate, Dr A.C. Hawkins, as house surgeon at the hospital. The other candidate was Dr Goodwin of Saint John, a graduate of the Halifax Medical School. Both doctors wrote a special examination and both passed. Goodwin had much higher marks, but Hawkins was Haligonian Liberal and that mattered. Hawkins's appointment certainly put the fat in the fire. The doctors were revolted by this crass demonstration of political patronage. How could a medical question be decided by a political judgment? That was the issue. Resignations *en masse* from the Medical Board of the hospital followed. The debate waged hot and heavy all that summer of 1885, with political heavyweights, the *Morning Herald* and the *Morning Chronicle*, weighing in on opposite sides. For a time even the Saskatchewan Rebellion had to share the pages of Halifax newspapers with the hospital affair.[20]

In 1886 a committee of the legislature was struck to investigate the hospital. It produced bitter and violent testimony. In 1887 the Fielding government put the hospital wholly under provincial control, and it was now named, in honour of the Queen's golden jubilee, the Victoria General, and its administration put under the commissioner of public works and mines. In effect and intention it became a provincial hospital. Expansion followed, with new hospital wings added in 1888 and 1889, and with a School of Nursing established in 1891. The Nursing School was so successful that by 1896 there was a two-year waiting list for admission.[21]

With no hospital available for clinical use, Halifax Medical College had been forced to close down by August 1885. Dr A.W.H. Lindsay, the registrar, took pity on the students and solicited the nearest medical school, McGill, for moral and material support: would McGill recognize the Medical College's matriculation and preliminary MDCM examinations? Could they receive any Halifax college's medical students who might come, without additional fee? McGill Medical School rallied round nobly and accepted at once.[22]

A year later, in August 1886, the Medical College was forced to stay closed for the coming session, and it now began to look as if permanent closing of the school would follow. When the Halifax Medical College did open, a year later, for the session of 1887–8, it had four students. With a new Dalhousie building on the drawing board, and so close to the Medical College, Dr Lindsay speculated that the college might be revived as Dalhousie's Medical Faculty.

Affiliation discussions with Dalhousie were renewed in the autumn of 1887, the Board of Governors constituting the Medical Faculty on 13 December. It was the familiar arm's length affiliation that was being put in place. Halifax Medical College nominated, and Dalhousie would appoint, examiners in the Medical Faculty.[23] The Medical College then approached the government to renew the legislative grant, suspended since 1885. But the canny premier and provincial secretary, W.S. Fielding, was not going to have another college row on his hands if he could avoid it. Fielding had been at Dalhousie as a general student in 1873–4, was Halifax born and bred, and did not want to appear to be favouring Dalhousie; he insisted that the other colleges, including Mount Allison in New Brunswick, should approve any legislative grant to a Halifax Medical College affiliated with Dalhousie. Most of the colleges seemed to have had no objections; but there was one whose objections were both decided and effective: Acadia College. Acadia's position seemed to be that since no college got any money from the government, why should Dalhousie get its hands on $800 a year by this Trojan horse of HMC affiliation? It did not matter that the Medical College grant of $800 was for chemicals, upkeep, and mortgage. Dalhousie should not get near any of it.

Halifax Medical College had thus to turn, in the autumn of 1888, to Acadia's president, the Reverend Dr A.W. Sawyer. Dr Lindsay tried to explain that the Medical College had "an existence entirely distinct from the Board of Governors of Dalhousie." Its students were not Dalhousie students, nor did the Dalhousie Senate have any control over the Medical College. Dr Sawyer replied sharply that current Dalhousie calendars seemed to support quite another interpretation. Dr Lindsay returned a seven-page letter trying to dispel Acadia's apprehensions. He added that if Acadia were to continue to block the legislative grant to the college, two things might happen, neither of them desirable from Acadia's viewpoint: it might kill the Halifax Medical College completely, or "bring about the actual union with Dalhousie, supplying it with a teaching faculty instead of the present faculty of examiners." This argument seems to have carried little weight with the Acadia board; by the end of February 1889, Halifax Medical College reported to Dalhousie that Acadia was still opposed, and that the government still refused to make any grant to the Medical College so long as it remained affiliated with Dalhousie. The affiliation moves of a year earlier would have to be abandoned. There were hints that if Dalhousie itself could come up with $800 a year, disaffiliation would be unnecessary, but that was quite beyond Dalhousie's resources.

By the end of March 1889 Dr Lindsay informed Premier Fielding that the Halifax Medical College's affiliation with Dalhousie was at an end. And, "being now absolutely free from any connection with Dalhousie I am further directed to solicit a renewal of the grant previously allowed to the Medical College." In due course, the college got its $800 a year.[24]

As Acadia College may well have suspected, it was rather a trick of mirrors. The Medical College and Dalhousie changed their status vis-à-vis each other only a little. What made the claim of Halifax Medical College to be independent of Dalhousie legitimate was that it continued to hold its right to grant medical degrees. Its students could, if they chose, opt for a Halifax Medical College degree. Few did. As Dr Lindsay put it, "I presume everyone would prefer a degree from the University."[25] That was the nice point on which affiliation, or not, turned. Dalhousie got its Medical Faculty by calling the Medical College's professor-doctors Dalhousie University examiners.

The Halifax Medical College had a slow recovery from the disasters of the mid-1880s. There was only one graduate in 1890 and two in 1891, so much had the crisis weakened it. Even in 1895 there were only three, though by then total numbers were clearly on the rise. The largest entering class so far was in 1899, and while that meant something, many of the 1898 students had subsequently gone to McGill, Harvard or elsewhere. In 1905 fifteen doctors graduated, of whom four were women. It is useful to point out here that the college had never excluded women; in 1885 Dr Lindsay noted that "there are no restrictions preventing the attendance of female medical students at this college."[26]

The growth of numbers after 1895 did not mean that the arrangements with Dalhousie had produced a good medical school. The *Dalhousie Gazette* commented that that needed three things: a good general hospital with ample clinical possibilities; a sufficient number of general practitioners and specialists from which to select professors; and "energy, enterprise and enthusiasm" on the part of those teaching. It was the last that was lacking. And of course, Dalhousie had no control over the Medical College. The principal academic connection was the fact that the Dalhousie McLeod professor of chemistry, George Lawson, taught all the chemistry and botany in the college. He died in harness in November 1895, and his replacement, a first-class professor, Eben MacKay (Dal '86), took over Lawson's role. By 1905 there were some twenty-three doctors teaching in the Halifax Medical College, mostly for no remuneration. Some of them were not worth much more. There was some factional bitterness from the 1880s; after 1900 dissension and drink had played havoc with whatever *esprit de corps* the institution had possessed. Dr H.B. Atlee recalled that he and his class lost three-quarters of their lectures in medicine (that is, diagnosis, prognosis, treatment of diseases – fairly fundamental one must admit) because the professor, an able teacher when sober, was not so when drunk. In obstetrics, remarked Atlee, the professor was a dear old Victorian who felt it a mortal sin to expose the female perineum to the light of day; Atlee's two deliveries with him were conducted under a blanket. That may have been owing as much to manners and customs as to old-fashioned obstetrics; when Atlee went briefly into practice at Joggins he was compelled to do the same thing. In any case, 99 per cent of deliveries took place at home, and clinical opportunities were limited. Atlee described the surgeons as emotionally immature, by which he meant they were vain, greedy, and peremptory. One good surgeon, Dr Murdock Chisholm, had to do most of the surgical teaching. Besides, there was no physiology laboratory, no real one in pathology, and no money to build them. It was a devastating indictment. Yet good doctors did come out of the system. In 1911, of the fifteen students who graduated, there were at least three outstanding men, not least Atlee himself.[27]

Faculty of Law
The Faculty of Law, directly under the control of Dalhousie, had a better run of it. Eighteen eighty-seven marked a distinct departure, however, in the organization of its academic year. In February 1887 Dean Weldon was elected to the House of Commons for Albert County, New Brunswick, as a Conservative. As he saw his role and his duty, he was not doing anything unusual; still, how could he go to Ottawa and still attend sessions of the Law School and Parliament? The 1886 session of Parliament was over three months long, that of 1887 over two months, in 1888 three months.

Weldon put his position plainly to the Board of Governors and the Senate when he first accepted the nomination to stand in January 1887. Senate agreed that the Law Faculty could start at the end of the legal vacation, the last week of August, and run the usual length of twenty-three weeks, bringing it to an end in late February. This peculiar school year was thus established to accommodate Weldon's duties as MP, and when he was re-elected in the 1891 election the arrangement continued. In the 1896 election Weldon was defeated in Albert County; but Halifax, a two-member constituency, elected two exceptionally able lawyers on opposite sides of politics, R.L. Borden for the Conservatives and Professor Benjamin Russell of Dalhousie for the Liberals. So the school year continued as before. In 1900 Russell was re-elected for Hants and in 1904 was appointed to the Supreme Court of Nova Scotia. By natural academic or legal inertia the peculiar arrangement stood until 1911. The students did not seem to mind; they got an early start on the summer's work. R.B. Bennett, for example, was working in L.J. Tweedie's law office in Chatham, New Brunswick, by the end of February. More particularly, the law students had the rare advantage of having from 1887 to 1896 a dean who was an MP, and from 1896 to 1904 having a professor of contracts who was.[28]

The Law School moved out of Halliburton House in the summer of 1887, but its new quarters in the Dalhousie building were not yet ready, so for the first few weeks it used the virtually empty rooms of the Halifax Medical College building just across the street. It was November when the Law School moved to the first and second floors of the north wing. It would be its home for the next sixty-five years.

Its curriculum, once established, remained virtually the same until the First World War. It struck a balance between a liberal education and professional training. In both the first and second years, two of the seven hours a week of lectures were devoted to constitutional history; in the third year two of the seven hours were devoted to quasi-cultural subjects – international law and the conflict of laws. It was a curriculum sufficiently impressive that E.D. Armour, editor of the *Canadian Law Times* of Toronto, criticizing legal education in Ontario, pointed out in 1888 that Dalhousie's Law School was "as far ahead of Ontario in the practical education of its lawyers, as the Province of Ontario is ahead of Nova Scotia in vanity and self-adulation." There would come a time when Dalhousie's Law School was itself not devoid of that, but in the 1890s it set about its task of imbuing its students with the idea of duty to the public and the state with becoming modesty. Not least among its graduates were Richard McBride ('90), the first student from British Columbia, who would become the province's premier from 1903 to 1915, and R.B. Bennett ('93) of New Brunswick. When James Lougheed of Calgary, who had taken his law in Ontario, sought a new man for his Calgary law office, he consulted his friend and colleague Dean Weldon of Dalhousie, who recommended Bennett. Bennett would end up as prime minister of Canada in 1930.[29]

Bennett was an exceptional student, but his experience at Dalhousie from 1890 to 1893 was familiar: his boarding house on South Street, three blocks or so away from Dalhousie; his life – "talk, walk and work." Bennett even helped canvass Albert County, New Brunswick, for Weldon for his re-election to Parliament in February 1891. Meetings of Dalhousie's Mock Parliament was something the dean set great store by and which he regularly attended. Bennett was "prime minister" in the Dalhousie Mock Parliament in the autumn of 1892, when his "government" succeeded in passing resolutions uniting the three Maritime provinces, and incorporating Newfoundland into Canada. He and his government were defeated, however, when they proposed to give full voting rights to unmarried women and widows! Bennett was still better in Moot Court than in Mock Parliament, where his thoroughness at case preparation, and his power of argument, made him a formidable adversary.

The Dalhousie Constituency

By 1893 Dalhousie was starting to draw in students from other provinces, notably New Brunswick and Prince Edward Island. Of forty-four regular LL.B. students registered in 1893–4, six were from New Brunswick. A decade later there were more Prince Edward Islanders than New Brunswickers, owing probably to the establishment in 1892 of a law school in Saint John, tied to King's College, Windsor.

As for Dalhousie as a whole, of the 107 arts and science undergraduates in 1893–4, twelve were from Prince Edward Island, three from New Brunswick, and one each from Newfoundland, Trinidad, and California. Of the eighty-four Nova Scotian undergraduates, twenty-one were from Pictou County, seventeen from Halifax, and four from Cape Breton. Of the forty-two students registered in medicine 1893–4, ten were from Pictou County, ten from Halifax, three from Cape Breton, and two from Prince Edward Island. Besides the regular undergraduates in law, arts, and medicine, there were a number of general students, taking classes for the sheer interest of it, who had not matriculated into the university: sixty-five in arts, ten in science, ten in law, and four in medicine. Altogether in 1893–4 there were two hundred students in degree programs and eighty-nine general students. This compared to sixty-five regular undergraduates at Mount Allison at the same time. The University of New Brunswick passed the one-hundred mark in 1900–1.[30] The effect of numbers would show in the changing traditions of Dalhousie students. By 1895 enrolment had doubled from a decade earlier, and by 1905 it would virtually double again. This linear growth sometimes necessitated changes more of a geometric order.

Senior class, 1889–90. The lady student is Maria Freeman Saunders of Halifax.

One change initiated by the board and President Forrest had little to do with student numbers: the extension of the university year. The old system had been to start in late October and end in late April, examinations and convocation included. George Munro in 1886 suggested that it be lengthened by two months, by moving the opening date from late October to early September. Senate was willing to accept some increase, but resisted the idea of the American academic year. The board, with some sternness, pointed out that

a period of eight months, which is the shortest term in the leading universities of the United States and Canada is not too long for Nova Scotia. They do not see that there is anything exceptional in our circumstances to render it necessary to abridge the period adopted in these countries, and sanctioned by long experience. They wish therefore that the Senate should reconsider the question, and, in any case, if they do not see their way to the adoption of the Term suggested, that they will kindly favour the Board with a statement of the grounds on which they base their objection.

The Senate, mainly its arts members, finally bent to the eight-month idea, even though law, for reasons mentioned earlier, continued to retain the shorter year. At this point the students had something to say. They were unhappy with an eight-month university year, and for mainly material reasons. The average cost to a student of room and board in Halifax was about $33 a month, or $200 per six-month session. Another two months would add $65 to that bill. What could the student turn to that would earn him $265 in the now truncated four-month summer that remained to him? In April 1888, eighty-four students (of eighty-eight undergraduates in arts) submitted a memorial to the Board of Governors arguing against change. The board created a committee to investigate and report. The record is not clear, but what seems to have emerged was a compromise between what Munro, Forrest, and the board wanted – namely, the eight-month year – and the existing six-month one. That was a new seven-month regime that began in 1888–9, with the university year starting in late September and ending in late April. That regime would last until the 1960s.[31]

One consequence of the lengthened autumn term was Christmas examinations. That began in arts at Christmas 1890. The results were considered analogous to the Black Death of the fourteenth century; but the *Gazette* considered that the devastation was owing to the novelty of having examinations in mid-year. Certainly they would continue.

The curriculum had shifted too. In the early years of Dalhousie, two years of Greek was required along with four years of Latin and four of mathematics, and with very few options. That was changing in the mid-1880s. The *Gazette* in November 1888 asked for amelioration in the compulsory four years of Latin. It was notorious, it said, that too many students in those compulsory subjects aimed merely at a pass. That was not an argument that especially recommended itself to Senate, but by 1890 Latin was compulsory only for three years, mathematics for two years, with Greek now left as an option. An undergraduate in the bachelor of letters program could escape Latin altogether by choosing German. But few took that; Latin was still the important core subject of the curriculum. The *Gazette* had some useful suggestions for the many students struggling with writing in Latin:

> If you are wishful to be put in
> The curious art of writing Latin,
> 'Tis a good plan by heart to know
> Some Livy and much Cicero;
> Nor Caesar slight, for he is free
> From turgid phraseology:
> But, Oh! beware, 'tis dangerous
> To imitate terse Tacitus...
> Remember that Latinity
> Is very fond of brevity,
> Is studious of simplicity,
> Disgusted with redundancy...
> The Latin tongue, of this be sure
> In verbs is rich, in nouns is poor...[32]

Modern languages were now required for the BA, at least two years of French or German. English was required for two years. Chemistry was required in the first year, philosophy or physics in the second, with history a required subject in the third. In the fourth year a plethora of options opened up, any five of some eighteen possibilities.

When Professor Charles Macdonald, still going strong at sixty-four, was invited to address Dalhousie's fall convocation of 1892, he dealt with the cluster of issues around the curriculum. With forty years of translucent teaching of mathematics behind him, Macdonald had some wise things to say about education. "You cannot improve your teachers by lecturing them on *How to Teach*; at least to any important extent. You may furnish them with some general principles, or rules, or hints – these can be soon told ... Whom nature and education have fitted to teach, they will teach best in their own unrestricted style." Teachers' colleges were in Macdonald's view dangerous, at best fitting in a fashion the unfit.

Macdonald also deplored too much choice. If a person wished to attend university to acquire information as a general student, by all means encourage him; but if a student takes a degree, the university certifies that he is in possession of a definite minimum of mental training. Most students, he averred, if left to themselves, will, like all moving bodies in physics, choose the path of least resistance, the soft subjects rather than the hard ones. Nevertheless, he said, the hard ones were of fundamental importance. And there was rarely such a thing as inaptitude for certain subjects. He had never encountered a good classical scholar who could not pass muster either in mathematics or in metaphysics.

It is one of the best preparations for practical life to discipline ourselves to overcome dislikes. To learn to endure and do what we had rather not do, and to do it fairly well because duty bids; what better outcome of education is there than this? Or do you expect that in your future life duty will never point one way, while inclination invites you another?

His concluding point to the students of 1892 was not to let themselves be misled "by the vulgar cry of 'practical knowledge' as opposed to that which is useless, as if any kind of knowledge could be truly useless. Life is thought even more than it is action. Whatever enlarges your thinking powers, enlarges your life." The 1890s, with its increasing emphasis on material things, may make that a counsel difficult to follow, but give yourself generously to your work. "A great king said that every new language learned is like the gift of a new sense."[33]

Macdonald was probably right that whatever enlarged one's capacity to think, enlarged life. But it was a position that as time went on would be increasingly difficult to hold against student instincts for something that grappled more decidedly with current realities. At heart they probably preferred an easier subject: which they justified with the argument of relevance. Nevertheless, Dalhousie would hold to Macdonald's assertion, giving only a little ground; sixty years later a year of university Latin (or Greek) was still required for the BA.

Students could be irreverent about work put in those high-minded terms. As a UNB poem of 1900 about Latin had it:

> All the people dead who wrote it,
> All the people dead who spoke it,
> All the people die who learn it,
> Blessed death, they surely earn it.

Student high spirits were hard to contain. That Senate and students were not always at one about discipline in the university goes without saying. Still, at the time of the University of Toronto student strike of 1895, the *Gazette* said that real differences between students and Senate at Dalhousie were almost unknown. The main ones involved sheer boisterousness and the strong, inter-year rivalries reflected in the *Gazette*'s game with Shakespeare plays:

> Freshman – Comedy of Errors
> Sophomore – Much Ado about Nothing
> Junior – As you Like It
> Senior – All's Well That Ends Well.

Scrimmaging had moved up from the Parade, and students clung to their "right of scrimmaging" in the five minutes between classes, or in the late afternoon. Attempts to control the practice were resisted. Why should students "in the best days of their life be made to move around noiselessly and with bated breadth?" Thraldom, surely![34]

Nevertheless, Senate sought valiantly to keep control. But with the increasing number of freshmen outweighing the sophomores, the habit waned. The *Gazette* in 1895 said the scrimmage was dead. No longer were the yells of contending factions echoing through the halls, no longer was some unlucky freshman thrown ten feet in the air by brawny sophomores. The two classes were said to be going around like brothers. It was horrible. Senate's fines and suspensions may also have had some effect. Thus the satire:

> In College Hall the din and roar
> Of scrimmaging is heard no more,
> The art is number'd with the dead.
> A fine of forty cents per head
> Can bring the valiant, dauntless Sophs
> Upon their knees before the profs.
> And one may read in freshman's eye
> The consciousness of Sovereignty
> He owns the College and the Town;
> The Juniors crouch beneath his frown,
> 'Tis true he sometimes does consent
> To recognize the President.

There is no doubt that seniors, juniors, and sophormores alike were anxious to entrench status, that Dalhousie scrimmages, especially between freshmen and sophomores, were based on pride of status and the desire to maintain it. It was also mixed up with sophomoric foolishness, some sadism, as well as vicarious amusement. Portentous explanations were always possible and have been essayed; students at Dalhousie claimed that initiations and scrimmages helped to create college spirit, that any suppression of the former was certain indication of the decline of the latter.[35]

The attempts to control scrimmaging in college halls sent some of it occasionally into streets and public places. The *Gazette* complained of exaggeration of student adventures in the local papers; yellow journalism, the *Gazette* called it, accepted too readily by the public. The *Gazette* accused the *Acadian Recorder* particularly of running down Dalhousie and its students. The *Recorder*'s social editor, "Lady Jane," was bitterly critical of the behaviour of Dalhousie students at a play in late October 1893 at the Academy of Music. Lady Jane was in the balcony that night and was outraged by student conduct. She said she was thoroughly frightened and would have gone home if she could, but she dared not pass through "such a band of – well, WHAT were they?" she asked. Gentlemen, she feared, they were not. The *Gazette* came to the students' defence. All they did that night was to sing a few songs, give the college cheer,

I–2–3
Upidee
Dalhousie!

and all of it before the curtain went up. "We can assure Lady Jane," said the *Gazette*, "that it is quite as safe, though not half as nice, to pass through a crowd of students as it is through a crowd of 'deah offisahs'." The dear officers, British army and navy, were perhaps more Lady Jane's style.[36] There may also have been a few students like the Pictonian who, left alone on Thanksgiving Day – in the 1890s it was at a bleaker time than now, the first Thursday in November – decided it was an exceptional day for getting drunk. He went into town in the morning, and by four in the afternoon a police officer found him against a lamp post, his legs braced as if ready to sprint. The student told the policeman, "Dash all right, officer, please don't disturb me, – houses all goin' past. Want t'catch m'own when it comes 'long." About 1895 a group of students led, it was rumoured, by Murray Macneill ('96 and later Dalhousie's registrar) managed to get a cow inside President Forrest's none-too-large office. The cow was bewildered but unhurt: the condition of the office was not so good. The culprits were apparently never found, but the story circulated for many years afterwards.[37]

The staff of the *Dalhousie Gazette*, 1894.

Internal discipline of the university was of course the Senate's responsibility. In 1889 it had visited responsibility for minor infractions upon the president and appointed a student committee. In 1893 Senate set up a code of student discipline, defining disorderly conduct as "participation in 'scrimmages' or in 'bouncing', obstruction of doorways or passages, interference in any way with the work of classes." Convocations, especially the spring one, were apt to be disorderly, when students after the tension of examinations were released like springs. Dalhousie April convocations were not unlike the proceedings at the University of Edinburgh where speakers, graduates, and honoured guests were all subject to calls from the audience or the din of musical instruments from the balcony. At Dalhousie, as at Edinburgh, peas and pea-shooters were sometimes in evidence. The convocation of 1898 was sufficiently bad for the Senate to resolve that unless the students agreed to prevent such disorder, "no more public convocations [will] be held." After a major eruption in 1904 the threat would be carried out in 1905.[38]

Thus, as the university got bigger so inevitably did its problems with discipline. In 1899 the large college bell was carried off by N.G. Murray ('01) who was duly suspended until the bell, or its replacement, was restored. A more ingenious endeavour came the following year by sophomores aiming to harass freshmen meeting in the Munro Room. A large firecracker was surreptitiously lowered through the ceiling by sophomores hiding in the attic above. It was successfully exploded. No real damage was done, but the noise was huge, and there were fragments of the firecracker everywhere, and some burn marks from the exploding gunpowder. Several students were suspended, including the ringleader, F.A. Morrison; he was suspended indefinitely until Senate should reinstate him. He petitioned a year later, was readmitted, and duly got his degree.[39]

In late October of 1901, President Forrest was phoned at his house on Tobin Street by George Price, the janitor, and informed that there would be an attempt during the evening of Friday, 1 November, to make off with the college cannon. The cannon was French, originally taken from Louisbourg harbour and given to Dalhousie in April 1901 by Charles Archibald. The president went to the college and waited in the darkened front hall. Suddenly after 10 PM some thirty students materialized, pulling the cannon by a rope, one of their number pushing from behind, towards the Medical College. The president rushed out and grabbed the first student he could get and "persuaded" him to come back to the college. F.W. Day of the Medical College was given two months' suspension. He does not appear to have graduated, though probably not for that reason.[40]

As a result of these several events, the Senate decided that the control of misdemeanours should no longer be left up to the president, in order to spare Lord John these brisk, effective but dangerous pursuits. Forrest was in good health but getting on for sixty years of age. In November 1901 they appointed a dean of the college to keep an eye on such adventures. He was Howard Murray, professor of classics. Murray was made McLeod professor in 1894 after the retirement that year of John Johnson. He was Pictou County and Dalhousie, and in 1881 took the Gilchrist scholarship that admitted him to a BA at the University of London. He came back as Munro tutor in classics in 1887. Howard Murray was big and benign, and was jocular with the students about his new role. He could not explain why Senate had conferred on him such a high distinction unless "it might have been his avoirdupois that had turned the scale in his favour ... Perhaps they [the Senate] had formed the opinion that he possessed a disposition so serene and seraphic as to be able to remain calm and unruffled under any circumstances no matter how trying." He hoped the college treasury would not be greatly enriched by student fines.[41]

George Price, the janitor whose timely warning had saved the cannon from being stolen, was a rare character whom students liked to visit. They gave him a honorary "doctorate" in 1894-5. He'd had a curious life. Born near Birmingham, England, in 1837, the only son in a family of four daughters, he went to work at the age of eleven in the coal mines. After three years of that he joined a cavalry regiment as bugler, got to the Crimea, and ended up in India at the relief of Lucknow in November 1857. He blew the call to advance when Sir Colin Campbell entered Lucknow. Discharged, he came to Boston where he married a Cape Breton girl, came to Halifax and became janitor, running Dalhousie's furnace and lots more. One rainy day a student went down to the basement armed with a bottle, which the "Doctor" hid in the coal, and over that they sat and talked most of the afternoon and evening.

We skirted the Mediterranean in short order, turning aside for a passing comparison of Italian with Spanish girls; and had sighted the trenches of Sebastopol at supper hour. The doctor was even more mellow after supper, and before I left we were safe inside Lucknow.

Price's child had died from croup eleven years before. "Ain't nothin' harder 'an to lose a little youngster," he offered; the worst part was, you kept on losing him, year after year. Price himself died after a fall, still in Dalhousie's service, on 16 June 1902.[42]

The boisterous vigour among male students, of which Price had seen so much, helps to explain the vigorous debate in the *Gazette* in 1903 about Dalhousie culture. Frank Baird, a UNB graduate now at Dalhousie for his MA, asked the question, was Dalhousie a place that only tested and rewarded learning, an institution where one had to strive for high marks and honours? Was there to be no cultivation of good taste and manners? Perhaps it was true as Ovid said, that the liberal arts civilized character, but at Dalhousie there was not much evidence of it. Was not technical education, now being added in the form of the new mining engineering degree, symptomatic of a German-American attempt to wrench the university's direction to technical business? Dalhousie men strained after high standing and little else. Between high-minded but ill-mannered scholarship men, and grubby commercial mining engineers, where was civilization and culture? "The Dalhousie graduate was the worst-mannered graduate in Canada." He did not know enough to rise when ladies entered a room; he was devoid of table manners. Who's to blame? Don't blame faculty, said Baird; don't put all the blame, either, on Prince Edward Island, Cape Breton, or Pictou County. Blame the students themselves.

This provoked a vigorous response from Kenneth Ferns MacKenzie of Pictou County, then at Harvard. He claimed there were far worse graduates than Dalhousians,

and when you said that at Dalhousie life is a thing of marks, that culture counts for nothing, then in the names of the friends I have made, in the name of whatever appreciation and inspiration and purpose for life I have gained, knowing that many others have realized these things more fully than I have, I protest!

Both sides of that argument bespeak the nature of Dalhousie's students. The UNB man was of more conventional middle-class background, perhaps like his urban counterparts in Halifax. The lack of polish Baird objected to was to be found in the sons (perhaps the daughters?) of rural Nova Scotia and Prince Edward Island. They too were middle class, not in terms of what they or their families possessed but in the aspirations of themselves and their parents. They were middle class in the goals they set themselves, in perceptions of hard work, in their striving. Dalhousie students were often ministers' sons and daughters, not at all wealthy, best described as worthy. Norman A.M. (Larry) MacKenzie was a good example; he was a Presbyterian minister's son out of Pictou County, whose father, James Arthur MacKenzie, graduated from Dalhousie in 1878. Neither father nor son had money. Both had to work to go to Dalhousie at all, the father teaching school, the son helping his brothers on a Saskatchewan farm.

James Arthur MacKenzie was twenty-six years old when he graduated from Dalhousie, his son the same. Their manners may indeed have needed cultivating, but their minds were as strong as their backs. They could tolerate a great deal of work and fun. Country Nova Scotia and Prince Edward Island students were good quality; if they needed a deal of polishing, that was to be expected. It was easier to acquire manners than to retrieve corrupted morals.[43]

That certain roughness of edge, among Dalhousie male students particularly, suggests the good sense in the customs that surrounded women students. By 1900 25 per cent of the total Dalhousie enrolment in arts and science were women. In some special classes such as MacMechan's afternoon class in Shakespeare, 80 per cent of the students were women, half of them married. Regular women undergraduates generally found the preponderance of male students disconcerting. Could the halls be less crowded between classes? asked one female student in 1898. "It is most trying to be compelled to run the gauntlet of a hundred pairs of eyes when passing to and from our waiting room ... being stared at by a crowd of hungry-eyed youths." It was a tradition since 1881 that no male student spoke to a woman student in the halls. This tradition probably lasted until the First World War, but elements of it lingered on. When the Macdonald Library was opened in 1915, its main reading room was segregated, men at the east end, women at the west, until after the Second World War. Women students were surrounded by protective, unseen, but very real conventions. In the mathematics class, and doubtless others, the women students waited until the male students were inside, and then trooped in together to take the exact number of places reserved for them in the front row. When the class was over, the men waited until the women had left, were safely in their waiting room, and then dispersed.[44]

The Dalhousie women students delighted the professors with their ability and sprightliness of mind. Of the hundred or so who had graduated by 1900, those who did not take bursaries or other honours were the exception. While from a number of college societies women were excluded, by habit and tradition mostly, there were clubs where women members were essential, such as the Dalhousie Amateur Dramatic Club; in the Glee Club one-third of the officers in 1903 were women. Delta Gamma met twice a month, and the YWCA met every week. There was little or no evidence of male prejudice. There were no women in law, for example, not because law specifically excluded them but because it had not been settled if they could be admitted to the bar of Nova Scotia. That was for the Barristers' Society. The first test of that would be in 1915.

The single most common occupation of the fathers of Dalhousie women students, from 1881 to 1901, was that of clergyman. Many daughters of Halifax's wealthier families did not expect to earn their own living; marriage or family inheritance would solve that. Like the men, women students were from a range of society best described as lower middle class – that is middle class from aspirations and ideals rather than from a comfortable status quo. Almost by definition, they had the ambition of changing if not society (though that was often a hope too), at least their personal place and function in it. Many of the women students who attended Dalhousie looked to their own future independence; and some came after they had put themselves through normal school and taught several years, using their savings and scholarships to embark on a university education. They were not there for pleasure or husbands but for careers. What strikes one about the women Judith Fingard described is their determination to succeed. Of 392 women who attended Dalhousie in the twenty years from 1881 to 1901, at least 41 per cent needed their Dalhousie education to develop their career. Of the 174 known to have married, sixty-three married Dalhousie husbands. Women migrated, nearly as much as men, with probably 60 per cent ending up living outside Nova Scotia. Two-thirds of the Dalhousie women were from Halifax, whose fathers were either clergymen, or local businessmen from shopkeepers to bankers. There were also a number of women, daughters or matrons from the wealthier part of Halifax society, who did not seek a degree, but came to public lectures and treated Dalhousie rather like a club or a library.[45]

Thus the male boisterousness of the old Munro Day celebrations was giving way to other forms of amusement. The bachelor sleigh-ride to Bedford of a decade before was being replaced by a new fashion, perhaps suggested by the women students or faculty wives: the "At Home." Dalhousie had one on the evening of 13 January 1891, when the whole building was thrown open to some seven hundred guests. There was a formal receiving line, guests were duly announced as they arrived and were presented to President and Mrs Forrest and to Dr and Mrs Reid of the Halifax Medical College. The whole building was decorated with black and yellow bunting, evergreen boughs and flags. Dr Lawson in chemistry and Dr MacGregor in physics conducted experiments. The students gave a concert in the law library. The whole evening was pronounced a great success, and the local papers rather outdid themselves in its praise.[46]

The growing popularity of dancing made itself felt as well. In October 1893 the law students wanted to have an At Home, with dancing. In the Senate Walter Murray and J.G. MacGregor supported

Dalhousie Drama Club, 1908–9, the cast of *The President's Daughter*.

the application; but the Senate split, and President Forrest cast the deciding vote against dancing. In 1896 the ladies in the faculty, including the faculty wives, had a reception for all the male students of the junior and senior years. It was a great success, greater than the men anticipated. It moved the *Gazette* to quote Schiller:

> Ehret die Frauen! Sie flechten und weben
> Himmlische Rosen ins irdische Leben...
> (Honour the women, they plait and they weave
> The heavenly roses in earthly life we receive.)[47]

The first proper ball Dalhousie gave seems to have been Friday, 2 February 1900, the men in white tie and tails, with white kid gloves, the young women in dresses as elegant as possible, escorted by their brothers or their fathers, or in a few cases by husbands. A program exists for a similar occasion six years later. It began with a concert in the arts library at 9:30 PM. Then followed the dancing. There were sixteen dances: eight waltzes, a Lancers, and others; four different rendezvous points were arranged, where prospective partners would meet and sign up ahead of time for the dances, each on their own program. It was a system which would last into the 1930s. The last dance was a waltz. A popular waltz at the turn of the century was "Save the Last Dance for Me."[48]

The ball of February 1900 seems to have marked the shift of sentiment in Halifax towards Dalhousie; even the *Acadian Recorder* praised it. In the 1870s and 1880s there was some enmity between town and gown, surfacing at the football games between Dalhousie and the Wanderers. The problem may have been that Lady Jane was partly right, reflecting an inability of country boys to accommodate themselves to the style and manners of Halifax, or their sheer awkwardness in Halifax drawing rooms. A corner had perhaps been turned by 1900. By that time some 25 per cent of arts and science and law students were from the Halifax-Dartmouth area, though only 12 per cent of medical students were. Women students at Dalhousie did much to help cement local ties.

A number of Dalhousie professors were popular in Halifax. Young Archibald MacMechan was certainly one; old Charles Macdonald had long been another. Macdonald gave fascinating public lectures on astronomy or on psychological themes in the guise of fantasy. A local favourite that combined both was his "Visit to the Jovians," the inhabitants of Jupiter, a whimsical study of the effect on conduct of being able to read the thoughts of others. Macdonald continued to teach,

A Lismer sketch of Dalhousie College as it looked in 1900. Note the growth of trees since 1887.

and teach brilliantly. He converted many students who did not like mathematics into loving it. One student found that the elegance of Macdonald's explanation of repeating decimals changed a meaningless rule into something intelligible and beautiful. His honours men made an impression wherever they went, and as many ended up in physics as in mathematics. It would always please him to discover how, in postgraduate seminars elsewhere, a stiff question would be going the rounds of a mathematics or physics seminar, unanswered until the professor encountered one of Macdonald's honours men. The students loved Macdonald to the end; he was always Charlie to them.

In 1882, at the age of fifty-four, Macdonald married Maryanne Stairs, daughter of W.J. Stairs and Susan Morrow. Sadly, Maryanne died in 1883 after giving birth to a son; Macdonald never remarried. He lived in his house on Carleton Street, close beside the new Dalhousie, and somehow brought up his infant son, who in due time became his fishing companion. Early in March 1901, when he was seventy-two, he caught a severe cold. He continued to walk over to Dalhousie to teach; but it got worse and developed into pneumonia. He died in his sleep, early on Monday morning, 11 March. Dalhousie was devastated. The college stopped. His funeral two days later was a Dalhousie state affair, the main hall draped in black, Macdonald in an open coffin placed on a bier at the foot of the main stairway. Above on the stairs were president, Senate, and members of the Board of Governors. There was an honour guard of twelve students, all in black gowns, around the coffin. The funeral service was held there. President John Forrest, quite broken, had to struggle to give the eulogy to this last and greatest of the original six professors of 1863. Dr Allan Pollok, president of Pine Hill and an old friend, gave a short eulogy. Then six strong students shouldered the heavy coffin along Carleton Street, past Macdonald's house, over to Camp Hill cemetery. "He was a great an' good man," said George Price the janitor, "an' a big heart he had too, an' it's me that knows it."[49]

Macdonald came to Dalhousie in 1863 expecting rapid development of the college; had he foreseen how slow it would be he might not have stayed. He hoped to see established a great Nova Scotian university; the University of Halifax was not it, and he sternly opposed it as pretentious and overwrought. Dalhousie became the focus of his energy and spirit, and abundantly and fruitfully did he reward his colleagues and his students.

In his will, with uncanny prescience, Macdonald hit upon the greatest weakness in his university: its library. He left $2,000 to buy books, chiefly in English literature. In the decade of the 1890s the Dalhousie board had scarcely given 2000 cents to the library. Around

Macdonald's gift there would coalesce a great alumni movement, nourished by memories of the magic of his teaching, to build a real library in his honour.

· 8 ·

Expanding: A Quest for Space
1901–1914

Proposals for union with King's. Engineering and the Nova
Scotia Technical College. The Dalhousie Library. Problems of
campus space. The history and purchase of Studley. The
Flexner Report and the Medical College. President Forrest is
succeeded by A.S. MacKenzie, 1911. Designing the Studley
campus, 1911–13. Changes in Halifax by 1914.

Shortly after the death of Charles Macdonald, J.G. MacGregor,
Munro professor of physics since 1879, was invited to take the chair
of natural philosophy at the University of Edinburgh. Losing good
professors to universities with greater funds and fame Dalhousie met,
then and later, by making a virtue of it. It recognized the implied com-
pliment of losing Schurman to Cornell in 1886, Alexander to Toronto
in 1889, Seth to Brown in 1892. MacGregor found it impossible to resist Edinburgh's better salary, enormous prestige, superior equipment,
and good pension. Still, he was fond of his Dalhousie colleagues, especially MacMechan, and hated leaving them. He wrote MacMechan a
sad letter from King's Cross, London, on his way north to Edinburgh,
on 9 September 1901:

There are some things a man can't say to a man face to face. But now that [?]
the ocean is between us I feel impelled to tell you how deeply I regret that this
translation to Edinburgh must separate us – & how much your friendship
meant to me in the years we have had together. I always expected you to leave
me in Dalhousie ... Don't let the pessimists dishearten you. The day of better
things must come.

MacGregor was forty-nine years old. Slight but well proportioned,
with aquiline features, he radiated intense energy. His favourite position was astride a chair, his arms resting on the back. Despite a bad
heart, he was a great walker; he and W.J. Alexander climbed Mount

James G. MacGregor, *c.* 1896. Dalhousie's first Munro Professor of Physics, 1879–1901. "A radical in spirit, disliking rules and regulations almost on principle ... Students should have enough room to allow them to 'play the fool'."

Washington one summer holiday in the later 1880s. He never spared himself, summer or winter. Sometimes his physics laboratory was so cold that he had to work in an overcoat. MacGregor was a radical in spirit, disliking rules and regulations almost on principle. After he became Munro professor in 1879, he led the movement in Senate to broaden the tight Dalhousie curriculum and make it more flexible. He hated sham and humbug; that comprehended petty university regulations, so he was often on the students' side when their several misdemeanours came up in Senate. He thought they should be given enough room to allow them to "play the fool." Of course, if they broke rules, they must pay for their fun; but MacGregor believed there should be few rules. Students were men and women, not boys and girls.

He was much concerned about education in his native province. He opposed the University of Halifax, and he was one of the principal initiators for union with King's in 1884–5. His great passion was, indeed, university consolidation. He did not care what such a university was called, but government support was imperatively needed. When he heard about the new movement for King's-Dalhousie union in December 1901, he was enthusiastic. Their union would begin a nucleus, and it would give the government the justification it needed to step in and endow science. And, he told MacMechan, "Don't let our people haggle about terms, names &c. Offer liberal conditions."

That was, it is fair to say, President Forrest's attitude throughout. Like MacGregor, Forrest wanted university consolidation. The government of Nova Scotia should indeed fund science, but on the condition that there be one institution, strong enough to compete with McGill. He told President Alexander Thompson of St Francis Xavier that for the Nova Scotia government to spend money for technical and scientific education by "a renewal of the old system of giving small grants to five or six colleges" would be a great mistake.[1]

The first step was some form of university federation. The 1901 initiative came from King's, when Anglican Bishop Courtney called on President Forrest. Notwithstanding King's rejection of Dalhousie in 1885, would Dalhousie still consider that arrangement? Forrest said he would welcome such a union, again without specifying terms or conditions. Two large committees were formed, fourteen members each, from Dalhousie and from King's, and they agreed in December 1901 to a proposed union. Nor was it to be confined to the two colleges. As it developed, it envisioned a federation of all the Maritime province colleges, including UNB. There went to all of them a joint resolution of the committees that modern education "favours united work in a large university rather than divided efforts in scattered colleges." Public opinion in all three provinces tended the same way; the time was "ripe for promoting the federation of the higher education institutions of the Maritime Provinces."

Mount Allison's Board of Regents deemed the proposal inexpedient; the "proposed act of incorporation appeared to"touch but remotely the interests of this University."Acadia replied that the proposal would be referred to the next Baptist convention, where it got short shrift. None of the other colleges were interested. King's sent the proposed act to the different deaneries, from where in 1903 King's Alumni got to work and forced King's to back off. By 1905 a disagreement with King's about engineering extinguished any immediate possibility of renewal.[2]

Engineering and the Origins
of the Nova Scotia Technical College

In 1902 Dalhousie had decided to establish a program of mining engineering. Concerns about costs drove Senate to strike a committee to meet with George Murray, premier from 1896 to 1923, about overall funding for technical education. Murray's response was ambivalent: interest and helplessness. The Nova Scotia government could not afford politically to give any commitment to develop engineering at Dalhousie, however desirable in practice the idea might be. "Then I'll do it myself," said the little Red Hen, as Archie MacMechan put it. President Forrest and J.F. Stairs (chairman of the board) proceeded to do it themselves, put their own campaign together, collected $60,000, and had a School of Mining Engineering started by the fall of 1902. The Dalhousie Senate explained the background in appealing to the Carnegie Corporation of New York for funds in November 1902:

...an unfortunate system of denominational colleges paralyzes Government action. For the last four or six years every argument has been brought to bear upon the Government to induce it to provide a satisfactory system of technical education. The Government profess themselves willing to do so but assert that if they attempt to build up a School of Technology in connection with any one of the existing colleges, the other colleges will demand as much or turn them out of office.

At four different times the Governors of Dalhousie have made strong attempts to bring about a union of the different colleges on a non-sectarian basis, but without success.[3]

That appeal turned out to have a somewhat different outcome, but in the meantime mining engineering went ahead under Dalhousie's own funding, with civil engineering offered two years later. In January 1903 the Senate agreed that Eben Mackay of chemistry would give a science summer school in Sydney, with a mining school added by means of evening classes. By 1905 there were plans for extension work along similar lines at Sydney Mines, Stellarton, and Springhill. King's, however, had also done exploratory work in Cape Breton, and objected to Dalhousie's being there. It is difficult to know the rights and wrongs of the case; certainly the historian of King's was exercised on the subject. From the Dalhousie records, the only problem seems to have been an overlapping of schedules of two extension programs. By that time talk of union was very dead, and an engineering turf war was in the ascendant. [4]

Acadia and Mount Allison gave the first two years of a four-year engineering program, leading to two final years at McGill. Engineering was growing in popularity with the public and with business, but it was expensive to operate. The Nova Scotia universities rarely agreed about anything; but as a result of Dalhousie's 1902 initiative and needled by the Halifax Board of Trade and the Mining Society of Nova Scotia, King's, Acadia, Mount Allison, and Dalhousie arranged to meet in Halifax in April 1906. They agreed, King's more reluctantly than the others, that engineering education in Nova Scotia ought to be taken over by the government. It was too expensive and now, early in the twentieth century, too important, to be left to four competing colleges, all with limited funds. Civil, electrical, mechanical, and mining engineering degrees should all be given by a government institution, with the colleges offering the first two years. Thus, with four colleges supporting the idea, the government of George Murray acted, and decisively. The next year Murray brought forward the Technical Education Act. It had support on both sides of the House. R.M. McGregor, the MLA for Pictou and a recent graduate of Dalhousie, admitted there had been serious difficulties:

This province had long been suffering on account of the multiplicity of our colleges. It was too late now to discuss the question of university consolidation in Nova Scotia. Owing, perhaps, to the narrow-mindedness of our ancestors, we had today in this province four, five, or six colleges doing university work where we had only room for one. The sins of the fathers were being visited upon the children...

There was some opposition, he intimated, to the Nova Scotia Technical College being in Halifax, but it was the only place for it. The act passed with only minor debate.

The government asked for, and got, from Ottawa a site on Spring Garden Road, the old drill shed property that had once belonged to the British army. The cornerstone was laid in August 1908 and the

Technical College opened on 28 September 1909. The principal was
F.H. Sexton, Dalhousie's professor of mining and metallurgy, who had
been hired in 1905.[5]

Dalhousie also took the lead in expanding the terms of the Rhodes
scholarships. The South Africa that produced the Boer War also produced the wealth that had helped to cause it. Cecil Rhodes made his
fortune in diamonds and gold, and died in Cape Town just as the war
was drawing to an end. His will of 1899, carefully drafted and often
revised, left the bulk of his vast fortune for scholarships to Oxford. It
was his own hope for immortality, unbeliever that he was. His provisions were for scholarships from the British colonies, the United States,
and Germany. The German candidates were selected by the Kaiser; the
American states each had their own selection committees. Rhodes's arrangements for Canada were peculiar, betraying lack of knowledge of
at least one major portion of the British Empire, since only scholarships for Ontario and Quebec were included. The Dalhousie Senate
prepared a draft memorial, sent to the presidents of Acadia, Mount
Allison, King's, St Francis Xavier and UNB, pointing out the inadequacies in the Rhodes provisions, and sent it forward to the Rhodes
trustees.

The trustees took cognizance of Dalhousie's and other colonial objections, and they had enough discretionary power to establish a working system that included all the Canadian provinces. Dalhousie's first
nominee, and the first Rhodes scholar from Nova Scotia, named in
1904, was Gilbert S. Stairs (BA '03).

Oxford University was horrified at the prospect of being swamped
every year by a hundred colonials and a hundred Americans, to say
nothing of Germans. Not a few Americans came from states whose educational standards were, to say the least, elementary. By a considerable majority the Oxford Union passed a motion condemning the
Rhodes scheme. One safety barrier for Oxford was, however, the
Responsions – not exactly an entrance examination, but close enough;
among other things, it demanded simple competence in Latin or in
Greek. For the first fourteen years of the Rhodes scholarships, half the
American nominees failed Responsions, lacking sufficient Latin or
Greek. Dalhousie's long insistence on classics avoided that embarrassment! In the end, the Responsions requirement was abolished in 1919.
As for the Rhodes scholars themselves, they turned out to be not all
that bad. Not many got firsts, but North American committees put
some emphasis on intellectual ability and that helped. Rhodes had
emphasized moral character and athletic abilities. Had the North
American Rhodes committees taken this literally, they could have pop-
ulated Oxford with, as Professor John Flint graphically put it, "some

two hundred athletic duffers of sound moral character." That would have been disastrous.[6]

A Dalhousie Library

The Dalhousie curriculum, centred as it had been on mathematics and classics, had required in its original form much work but few books. Teachers, and Latin or Greek texts, were the main requirements. Textbooks were listed regularly in Dalhousie calendars. Science was different; it required modern, up-to-date information. The first letter addressed to the governors from the faculty, on 11 May 1839, was on the subject of the needs of science:

The Colleges where is usually appended a Library, containing books upon the various branches of science, which Professors may occasionally consult, and which the improvement of the students requires them to peruse: and in Dalhousie College, in order that the Lectures may keep pace with the progress of science, such an appendage is particularly requisite; because in this province, neither Professors nor students can conveniently supply themselves with the extensive means of information, which an academical course of studies requires.

There were libraries in Halifax: the Garrison library, founded at Lord Dalhousie's initiative in 1817; the law courts library; the legislative library, dating from 1819; and the Mechanics Institute library, installed in Dalhousie College from 1831. Perhaps for these reasons the Dalhousie governors were not especially concerned about a Dalhousie library. But one member of the board, G.M. Grant, in April 1867 pointed out the need for a college library. He had been promised $200 toward one, whereupon another $1,000 was at once subscribed.[7] The next question was where to put the books. In 1868 the Mechanics Institute space was taken back by the governors. An annual printed catalogue of books emerged.

None of this was very satisfactory, however. Students complained in 1881 that when a book was wanted, it couldn't be found. Mathematics books tended to disappear at the beginning of the session and reappear only at the end. And it was quite wrong to ask one overworked professor to be the librarian. If something wasn't soon done, the *Gazette* said, all that would be left in the library would be the government's *Sessional Papers*, the *Canada Gazette*, and some German treatises on physics. In 1882 the students presented the library with a card catalogue and annual lists of books ended. Nevertheless, J.T. Bulmer, who was law librarian in 1883–4, claimed the Dalhousie library lagged behind all the other college libraries in Nova Scotia. In

1897 the Senate passed a resolution, proposed by MacMechan, that equipment in both laboratories and libraries had not kept pace with the rapid increase in students, and the efficiency of the university was seriously impaired.[8] Moreover, access to the library had been very limited; in the mid-1870s it was an hour a week. By 1905, however, Dalhousie was proud to boast its library was open five days a week, from 10 AM to 1 PM, and 3 to 5 PM, and that it had twelve thousand volumes and three thousand pamphlets in the main library and seven thousand volumes in the law library.[9]

Charles Macdonald's gift of 1901 has to be read in this context. The Macdonald Memorial Library Fund had by 1905 reached $25,000 in pledges and $8,622 in cash. The Board of Governors promised in 1903 that they would supply additional money to start building the new library as soon as $25,000 was pledged, and $8,000 cash was on hand. The problem was, where? The passage of time had made this decision no easier. Dalhousie's growth had made the 1887 building very congested. There was also a sense, expressed in the *Gazette* in 1903, that Dalhousie now deserved to be housed in buildings a little less repellent than the once spacious, but still very plain, brick building. A Macdonald Library, light, airy, dignified, where a hundred students might read together in some comfort, would be a wonderful metamorphosis from the present, "grim, gaunt, puritan Dalhousie." There was sense in the *Gazette*'s remarks in 1910:

Dalhousie College has had a great past. Though her brick walls and her unfenced and neglected lawns, where a stray cow often pastured at ease, offered little that was pleasing to the eye, yet it was only such strict economy which enabled her to pay the Professors' salaries even then insufficient, and keep the laboratories and libraries abreast with the times. And the results have justified the means...

But there comes a time when old methods must give place to new ones ... Dalhousie must expand and at once if she is to do her duty to Nova Scotia and to her Alumni.

But Dalhousie had no land to expand into. She had the 450-foot by 400-foot piece of the South Common, all of 4.1 acres. Even that had an 80-foot strip on the south side – on Morris Street – reserved by the city for a future boulevard. To talk of new buildings meant in effect to talk about new space.[10]

The Search for Space

Dalhousie had a new and able businessman on the Board of Governors appointed after J.F. Stairs died of a heart attack in September 1904.

Stairs's sudden death at the age of only fifty-six had been a shock to the board, as it was to the whole business community of Halifax, not least to his knowledgeable and still young apprentice in business, Max Aitken. The Dalhousie board found itself rather bereft of leadership. Into this hiatus came George S. Campbell in 1905. He was the son of Duncan Campbell, historian and journalist, who had come to Nova Scotia from Scotland in 1866. George, born in Edinburgh in 1851, was brought up in Halifax and went into shipping. Success came late to him, but when it came, it did so with a vengeance. He was president of the Halifax Board of Trade in 1901 and 1902, and had a share in the movement for the Nova Scotia Technical College. He threw himself into work for Dalhousie with enthusiasm and in March 1908 was elected chairman of the board. He would remain there for nearly twenty years, probably the most able and devoted chairman Dalhousie ever had. He took the lead in improving Dalhousie's contacts within the city, and it was Campbell, perhaps more than anyone else, who would contribute most to making Dalhousie part of Halifax's life.[11]

He, too, was concerned about space. He wrote Enos Collins's son Brenton, about Gorsebrook. Brenton Collins was then living in Tunbridge Wells, and pronounced himself tired of being solicited by people wanting Gorsebrook for Dalhousie. Gorsebrook was not for sale, nor would it be until after his death. Had he been approached twenty or thirty years ago, it might have been different, but now, in 1906, he thought "it would be well to exercise a little patience." Dalhousie's next move was to confer with the city to see if they would give a piece of vacant land in front of the Dalhousie building. Then, in February 1909, Dartmouth offered a site to Dalhousie. Perhaps it was that Dartmouth offer, rejected in the end, that persuaded the City of Halifax to offer Dalhousie, free, the next block eastward along Morris Street. That offer, made by City Council in May 1909, was accepted by Dalhousie. The block was not as large as Dalhousie's existing four acres, being only about three, but it was valuable enough, being set down in 1912 as worth $30,000.

That did not end Dalhousie's search, of course. The new addition on Morris Street was not nearly sufficient for what Dalhousie now had in mind. In the summer of 1910 there were talks with the city about the poorhouse property at South Street and Robie. There were sketches made of possible alterations to the building to make it suitable. That acquisition would have the advantage of placing Dalhousie adjacent to Gorsebrook. In August 1910 the City Council offered to sell the poorhouse property, plus some other small lots between Summer Street and the new Anglican Cathedral, along Morris Street. The Board of Governors authorized its committee to offer $50,000 for all of it. Then

George S. Campbell, chairman of the Board of Governors, 1908–27, from a Lismer sketch. More than anyone else, he was responsible for the purchase of Studley.

a hitch occurred. One of City Council's devices for taking back an earlier decision was a motion for reconsideration; it did that with the
poorhouse offer, and then sent it to the Board of Works for a report.[13]
The *Dalhousie Gazette* made sport of this hitch in delicious doggerel,
"The Council and the College":

> Of all the farces I have seen
>   Or e'er came to my knowledge,
> There's none to beat the comedy
>   Of the Council and the College.
>
> The Council ups and says, says they,
>   "You offer us a price
> For this here Poor-House-City-Home,
>   You'll find it cheap and nice."
>
> The Governors considered well,
>   And took advice of Roper;
> They looked the Poor House inside-out,
>   As was both fit and proper.
>
> "Now fifty thousand dollars fair
>   For this Poor House we'll give,
> It is the kind of place in which
>   Professors ought to live.
>
> 'Twill cost us fifty thousand more
>   To make it fit to live in,
> But don't you mind, if you're inclined,
>   That is the price we're givin'."
>
> The Council, they debated sore,
>   And then they up and voted
> To take the money offered them,
>   With one exception noted.
>
> This was the valiant alderman,
>   Whose name was Mr. Hubley
> He moved to think it all over again,
>   When everything looked lubbly.
>
> This noble Council now declares, –
>   "We do not care to sell."

> If I was Dalhousie's Governors,
> I'd tell em to go to – Rockhead.[14]

That was, in effect, what happened. Out of the blue came an offer, through Eastern Trust, to sell the whole Studley estate, forty-three ample acres on the hill above the Arm, between Coburg Road and South Street, Oxford and LeMarchant streets, for $50,000.

The estate at Studley was a hundred years old and had a curious history. It was bought and put together by Alexander Croke, the vice-admiralty judge in Halifax. He called it after his own place in Oxfordshire, Studley Priory. Eight of his eleven children were born in the house on the hill. When Croke returned to England, Studley was sold to a Halifax merchant, Mathew Richardson. Then a fire destroyed the house and Richardson rebuilt, about 1832. He died in 1860, his widow in 1867, after which Studley came up for sale again. This time it was bought by a wealthy spinster, Antoinette Nordbeck. She eventually offered to share her home with the Reverend Robert Murray, editor of the *Presbyterian Witness*, his wife and family. Miss Nordbeck died in 1898 and left her whole property to the Murrays. That included the 1832 homestead, a bit run-down, but still a handsome, two-storeyed frame building that faced east towards Halifax town. There were two carriage drives, one straight in from Coburg Road, where the present road is; the other was more dramatic, starting at Coburg and LeMarchant, crossing a brook at the bottom of the shallow valley, through a few willows and oaks, to the homestead on the hill amid pines and maples.[15]

Robert Murray resigned from the Dalhousie board in August 1910. He was seventy-five years old and had given good service since the day he was appointed in 1884. He had also served the *Presbyterian Witness* for fifty-five years as a sympathetic and knowledgeable editor. He was a delightful writer; his readers claimed they could see the trees and hear the birds of Studley in Murray's luminous prose. He was also a poet; the hymn, "From Ocean unto Ocean," often to be heard in later years at Dalhousie gatherings, was his, though the tune was imported. He loved Studley, and he died peacefully there in December 1910. President Forrest wrote an elegant eulogy; they had known each other since the 1850s. A fortnight or so after Murray's death, the board were suddenly notified that Studley was for sale, and that Dalhousie could buy it for $50,000, exactly the price that Dalhousie was offering the city for the poorhouse property.

It was not the first time Dalhousie had been thinking of Studley. It made an offer in 1908 to Eastern Trust and was refused. In March 1909 Robert Murray offered Studley for $60,000 to George

Watercolour of the Murray Homestead. The house was built in 1836, demolished in 1949.

Campbell, the new chairman of the board. Murray was sure the price was too high for the governors to accept and expected it to be turned down; he would then put up lots for sale on the south side of Coburg Road, "as originally intended." Whatever he intended, no lots were sold. Thus $50,000 was a good price, but even so it was a great deal of money.[16] The board had a long discussion, and agreed that in view of the importance of the offer, and of the competing question of the poorhouse property, still in limbo at City Council, the whole question ought to be reviewed by a joint meeting with the Senate and representatives of the Alumni Association. That was held on 17 January 1911. There was considerable weight of opinion on the board in favour of Studley, and virtual unanimity among Senate and Alumni. The board had for some time held the view that expansion on the present campus was fundamentally undesirable, not only because of the small size but also because, although the title to the land was Dalhousie's, it was only for so long as the land was used for educational purposes. It could not be sold or leased, for it would then revert to the city. The board decided to revoke its offer for the poorhouse land, and to buy Studley. They counter-offered Murray's widow $45,000 – rather a petty lawyer's gesture, that – but $50,000 was the price and Dalhousie finally paid it. Dalhousie got one of the best large pieces of unoccupied land in the whole Halifax peninsula. The board would need to find the money, but students, staff and alumni were enthusiastic. G.S. Campbell explained in the *Gazette*:

For years we have been confronted by a very difficult problem. More classrooms have been urgently required, and yet we did not feel justified in erecting new buildings on our present contracted campus. We felt that it would be a grave mistake to anchor ourselves permanently on a site that gave no adequate room for future expansion.

In order to pay for the property and to erect essential buildings, the governors agreed to launch the Dalhousie Forward Movement, an appeal for $300,000. The basic plan, not yet fully matured, was first to build two structures, a science building for chemistry and physics, and the Macdonald Memorial Library. Law and arts would stay on the old campus until Dalhousie could afford to move them to new quarters at Studley. When that was accomplished, the big brick building would be devoted to medicine and dentistry, an ideal location for the purpose.[17]

In February 1912 the Alumnae Association (organized in 1909) got tentative permission to use the Murray homestead as a residence until Dalhousie needed it. Dalhousie was disconcerted to find the late owners still using it for occasional visits, and furthermore, it was in no shape for a ladies' residence. G.S. Campbell was much disappointed in its condition; it needed substantial repairs and a whole range of new plumbing.[18]

The Flexner Report and Its Effects

More was needed to fix the Halifax Medical School. With no full-time teachers in the essential pre-clinical sciences, one miserable laboratory, no money to build any, it now survived on the devotion of local practitioners. It drew a little strength from its affiliation with Dalhousie but certainly gave none. Its students took Dalhousie degrees, but its professors went their own way. In September 1909 a letter from President Henry Pritchett, of the Carnegie Foundation for the Advancement of Teaching (founded in 1905) indicated a visit to Halifax was in prospect. A small team would look at the Medical School. Two gentlemen, Abraham Flexner of the Foundation and Dr N.P. Colwell of the American Medical Association gave thirty hours' notice. They arrived late on a Friday night in early October and spent Saturday morning with the president and Dr A.W.H. Lindsay, secretary of the faculty; they visited the Halifax Medical College, Dalhousie, and the Victoria General Hospital, and left by the afternoon train that same day. In a few months there came a blistering draft report, asking Dalhousie and the Medical College for comment. It roused the ire and the sensibilities of the Medical College. Many condemned the draft report out of hand, as grossly superficial and misleading, and with several mistakes. The college made stiff representations, and although obvious mistakes were corrected in the final printed version, the basic condemnation was not altered.[19]

Abraham Flexner was not a doctor but a classicist, educated at Johns Hopkins, who was hired in 1908 by the Carnegie Foundation to survey the medical schools in the United States and Canada. He began in January 1909 with Tulane University in New Orleans, determined to cover a great deal of ground as expeditiously as possible. He soon knew his way around many of the medical schools and their tricks. His basic position, and the Foundation's, was that the problems of medical education in North America were not so much medical as educational. The decisive points Flexner sought were:

1 What were the entrance requirements? Were they enforced?
2 The size and training of the faculty.
3 What money was there from endowment and fees? How was it spent?
4 Quality of the laboratories and of work in the pre-clinical years.
5 Relations between the medical school and hospitals.

Flexner claimed that with half an hour in the dean's office, a few hours elsewhere, a few pertinent questions in the right places, he could obtain a reliable judgment. As one colleague of his remarked, "You don't need to eat the whole sheep to know it's tainted." The Halifax Medical College complained that Flexner and Colwell had spent less than twenty-four hours in Halifax. The two had also spent the same amount of time at the Maine Medical School in Portland; one doctor there said afterward, "That is where we were lucky!"[20]

The effect of the Flexner report was devastating. Of the 155 medical schools in the United States and Canada (there were eight in Canada), nearly half of them were forced to close down, although none in Canada. In many others, including Western Ontario and Dalhousie, serious modifications were undertaken. For the report was close to being right. Wrong in some details it may indeed have been – Dr D.A. Campbell, in his July 1910 address to the Nova Scotia Medical Society, concentrated on those – but the thrust of the report was so close to the truth as to be intimidating. As Dr H.B. Atlee observed, "we didn't have a chance. What saved us was geography. We were the only medical school in the east of Canada. There simply had to be a school in this region."[21]

The report had not been particularly flattering to Dalhousie either, suggesting that it had been giving medical degrees to students trained under wholly inadequate facilities. Atlee had things to say about that; Dalhousie "had been run by a dear old be-whiskered Presbyterian minister, and a moribund board of governors." But in 1910 Dalhousie had George Campbell as chairman of the board; both Dalhousie and Halifax Medical College acted. In March 1910 the Senate struck a committee to investigate, and it met jointly with one from the Halifax Medical College. There was frankness on both sides, but little bitterness. Dalhousie would simply *have* to take over the Medical School. That was a resolution passed without a dissenting voice by the Dalhousie Medical Faculty on 9 May and on the following day by Halifax Medical College, that "the best interests of Medical education can only be attained by a complete fusion of the Medical School with the University."

The Dalhousie Board of Governors took all that on manfully. It would require the appointment of at least three full-time professors in anatomy, pathology, and physiology. Dalhousie would have to buy out the Halifax Medical College, its building and equipment. They would have to find the money for it. Nevertheless, a Medical Faculty was duly created in 1911, with a minor row developing with certain doctors who refused to be called lecturers. (They wanted to be professors.) The Medical Faculty would be represented on Senate by its secretary, ex-officio, and two others chosen by ballot. The law to tidy this up went through the legislature in 1912. Thus did the Halifax Medical College come to an end.[22]

The End of Lord John's Regime

The Studley purchase in hand, the Halifax Medical College taken over, President Forrest decided it was time for him to step down. In June 1910 he had intimated that he would like to resign but gave the board the option of whether they would act on it. The board was not anxious to do that, but once the Studley decision was made, Forrest set 31 August 1911 as the date of his retirement. At the age of sixty-eight it was time to let younger men take over.

Forrest's great concern had always been the quality of Dalhousie's professors and the welfare of its students. He went regularly to student games and urged the players on. At a football game a couple of Dalhousie men were hurt and a call was raised for a doctor. "I am two or three doctors!" cried Dr Forrest, and he ran onto the field to care for the injured. With student misdemeanours he was a firm disciplinarian. The students used to sing a song about him, especially when they knew he was within earshot:

> When the great Lord John goes down below,
> He'll ride in a fiery chariot,
> And dine in state
> On a red-hot plate,
> 'Twixt the Devil and Judas Iscariot.

G.R. McKean ('06) was fined for something he had done. Lord John said to him, "I am sorry to have to take this from you..." McKean replied, "I am equally sorry to have to give it to you, Sir." The flippancy nettled Lord John, and he flashed back, "If this happens again you can pack your trunk and go home." He was not always so hard. Students on one occasion painted the Louisbourg cannon with yellow stripes. The leader was fined $10. He could not pay it, and his parents wouldn't or couldn't. The student would have to leave. The public reproof over, the student found a $10 bill slipped into his hand by the president.[23]

Forrest asked the board to make application to the Carnegie Foundation for a retiring allowance. This was a new system that Forrest had accepted in 1906. The Carnegie Foundation for the Advancement of Teaching was established during Andrew Carnegie's lifetime in 1905, and offered pensions to certain colleges for retiring professors. Some forty-six colleges in the United States and two in

Dalhousie debating team, 1910

Canada, McGill and Dalhousie, qualified as "accepted institutions" for this purpose – that is, they had no formal religious affiliations and were not supported by government, state, province, or municipality. One of the first Dalhousie professors to benefit was one of the oldest, James Liechti, who retired to Lunenburg in 1906 on a pension of $1,260 per annum. He was pleased, as well he might be, for it was fully half salary.[24]

When Forrest stepped down in August 1911, there was not so much regret for his going as appreciation of what he had accomplished. Forrest had never been one to stick at trifles. When King's wanted to join Dalhousie in 1885, and again in 1901, it received generous and open treatment from Forrest. He was anything but a rock-ribbed Presbyterian bigot: generous, flexible, he brought Halifax Medical College to Dalhousie in 1889, brought in the dentists on the same principles in 1908, opened the School of Mines. He tried to make Dalhousie accommodate the diversities around it, while still holding to standards. His years from 1885 to 1911 were ones of such development that every Dalhousian could be proud of him, and of the university.

MacMechan's essays, *The Life of a Little College*, written in the last years of Forrest's regime, were his homage to the Dalhousie of those years. He praised its modesty, its tradition of hard work, and not least did he praise its students. He liked their substance and their background. One freshman of MacMechan's was born in his father's ship off Bombay; one quiet girl's earliest recollection was of being taken ashore at Valparaiso during a "Norther." Another student had seen knife fights at Rio. His students had, in short, known perils of ocean, forest, and mine; they had worked for their living, often on farms. Not a few of them, he said, had "already taken degrees in that rugged school of privation" and were at Dalhousie only through their own powers of self-denial.

As much as MacMechan admired male students, he could be enchanted by women students. He sketched them with their quiet eyes and unobtrusive determination: Alicia, with her "strength to endure, an unvarying sweet patience, the scholar's modest ambition and enthusiasm, a richness of gentle affection that radiates warmth on all about her ... If only the jewel had not so frail a casket!" Or Honour, the best listener he ever had, "frank, proud, sensitive, alert, open as the day." Perhaps MacMechan may be allowed to record a moment of that Dalhousie world at Christmas Eve, 1909:

The night is windless and still. Some snow has fallen and covers the frozen ground with the thinnest of veils. A new, slim moon, with a single, blazing star, is low down in the west above the roofs. The traffic is hushed. The lights in the college window tell of boys and girls there dancing and making merry, but the music is too far away for me to hear. The wonderful hush of the silent streets is almost overpowering. It is as if the Earth were listening, waiting...

There was truth in the 1911 summation of the *Presbyterian Witness*:

Dalhousie has gone on her way unostentatiously, without waving of flags, or blowing of trumpets, depending for her ultimate success and recognition upon the thoroughness of her work ... Her growth within the last quarter century has been very remarkable ... until her very growth has become her greatest embarrassment.

It would be the task of Forrest's successor to provide the focus and find the funds that would convert embarrassment into asset.[25]

The choice of Forrest's successor offered no great difficulty. The board produced three names, all of them professors, two at Dalhousie: Howard Murray, McLeod professor of classics and dean of the college; Robert Magill, professor of philosophy; and A.S. MacKenzie, former professor of physics, and since August 1910 in New Jersey at the Stevens Institute of Technology. On motion of J.A. Chisholm (later Chief Justice Sir Joseph) then mayor of Halifax, the board accepted the recommendation that the presidency be offered to A.S. MacKenzie, at $3,600 a year. He was the unanimous choice. MacKenzie was pleased and proud, his delight "sadly tempered," as he put it, "by the knowledge of the responsibility to be assumed." He accepted but ventured one condition: that in all appointments to Dalhousie staff, the board would give consideration only to those nominated by the president. Here MacKenzie was probably thinking of the three professors of 1863 nominated by the Presbyterians, and the Munro professors who in the first instance had been nominated by Munro himself. Principal Ross seems to have had little say in selecting MacGregor, Schurman, Forrest, Weldon, or Alexander. When Forrest became president in 1885 he took a more specific interest in the Munro and other chairs, evidenced by MacMechan's appointment in 1889. As to later appointments, Forrest seems to have listened to his colleagues in the discipline and then recommended to the board. In 1908 C.D. Howe was appointed to engineering that way out of MIT, Boston. The board's 1911 reply to MacKenzie was polite but firm: "the Board is of opinion that it ought not to surrender its power of appointment to the respective chairs though the Board recognizes that the utmost deference should as in the past be paid to the recommendations of the President." A.S. MacKenzie came anyway.[26]

Arthur Stanley MacKenzie was the fourth successive Dalhousie president from Pictou County. Born in 1865, he came to Dalhousie from New Glasgow with a Munro bursary in 1881. He undertook the classic Dalhousie regimen: Latin with Johnson, mathematics with Macdonald, philosophy with Schurman, chemistry with Lawson, and physics with MacGregor – all of them courses where the standard of teaching was high, examinations severe, where accuracy, thoroughness, and hard work were essential. MacKenzie took honours in mathematics and physics and the Sir William Young Gold Medal in 1885, taught in Yarmouth for two years, then returned to Dalhousie as tutor in both his subjects in 1887-9. He was much intrigued with MacGregor's physics and his style of scientific research, acquired in London and in Germany. MacKenzie went to do his own PH.D. at Johns Hopkins. By 1894 he was associate professor of physics at Bryn Mawr, a women's college established by the Quakers nine years before. There he met and married Mary Lewis Taylor of Indianapolis in 1895. It was a sad story. She died a year later having given birth to a daughter. He buried her near her home in Indianapolis, taking the baby girl back with him to Bryn Mawr, bringing her up as best he could. Charles Macdonald wrote him in 1899 to come to see him, for "in the sorrows incident to this little life of ours, we have so much in common." MacKenzie, like Macdonald, made a gallant effort to keep his sorrow in the background, and make his child's life as happy as possible. Marjorie MacKenzie was brought up to go fishing with her father, much as Charles Macdonald's son was.[27]

When J.G. MacGregor, Dalhousie's professor of physics, was invited to take the Edinburgh professorship in 1901, he very much wanted MacKenzie to succeed him. Even in Edinburgh, MacGregor kept urging MacKenzie back to Dalhousie. The truth was, MacGregor missed Dalhousie and Halifax; he missed the freedom to set and run his own courses; at Edinburgh there was too much routine. He was made doubly regretful after the Carnegie pensions were introduced in 1905. Had they been in place in 1901, MacGregor said, he would never have thought of leaving Dalhousie, even for the University of Edinburgh. Dalhousie wanted MacKenzie in 1904, but he loved his research and needed a year to work at the Cavendish Laboratory in Cambridge, England. MacKenzie's special interest was in particle physics, especially the alpha rays of radium on which he published an important paper in 1905. Hence the poem, made into a song of course, from the *Post-Prandial Proceedings of the Cavendish Laboratory*:

> Oh I am a radium atom
> In pitchblende I first saw the day,

> But soon I shall turn into helium
>> My energy's wasting away

> Electrometers got in a frenzy
>> When quietly by them I lay
> So they send me downstairs with MacKenzie
>> Who's wanting my last alpha ray.

In 1905, after a tug-of-war with Bryn Mawr, MacKenzie accepted Dalhousie's offer to be George Munro professor of physics. President Forrest welcomed him with a kindly note about Dalhousie and its prospects:

I think you will find the Dalhousie Senate a happy family. If there is one thing that Dalhousie has had to be proud of it is the character of its teaching staff. Every man is a teacher ... Then they are all self-sacrificing good fellows with whom it is a pleasure to live and work. You know most of them ... and we all feel as if it will be just another member of the family coming home ... Of course the weak part is the library and laboratory. We are of course a little better off than when MacGregor was here. Still we are weak...

MacKenzie himself was a characteristic product of Nova Scotia, of that old Nova Scotia diet, as he put it, "of religion, politics and porridge." But he wore it all gracefully. Tall, sporty, with a lively sense of humour and a good game of golf, he was also a gifted teacher of physics. He loved research even more. That was the rub; there was not enough money, equipment, or time available to him at Dalhousie, and when in 1910 the Stevens Technical Institute in New Jersey offered him a research position, MacKenzie weighed it all up and made up his mind to go. The Dalhousie community was desolated, students not least. Archie MacMechan, who loved him, sounded the lament at the farewell dinner at the Halifax Club on 31 August 1910:

> Farewell to MacKenzie! farewell to A. Stan!
>> Farewell to six foot of good, muscular man!
> He is leaving us now for a far Yankee shore –
>> Maybe to return to Dalhousie no more!...

> Farewell to Mackenzie, farewell to the Prof.,
>> Who can mingle his Physics and fishing and Goff
> With a drop of the liquid that betters the score,
>> And we hope he'll return to Our City once more.[28]

MacKenzie did return, to everyone's delight. He himself could not give a reason why he did, for he had never been attracted by administrative work. Perhaps it was the fact that Hoboken, New Jersey, across the river from New York, was not Nova Scotia. Archie MacMechan had spent more than one summer teaching at Columbia to help support his family; he knew the heat and aggravations of "tawdry, garish, gaudy, noisy, man-eating New York," as he called it in 1910. The most critical factor in pulling MacKenzie back to Halifax was the January 1911 purchase of Studley; "it brought a cheer from every one of us," said he a few months later, "for we felt that at last the long-delayed marching orders had arrived."

Whatever MacKenzie did, his was going to be a different presidency from John Forrest's. Forrest was a Presbyterian cleric, not called Lord John for nothing. MacKenzie was neither Presbyterian nor cleric. He was Pictou County Anglican, a rare breed. There was much more of a free and easy air about him; he mixed easily on fishing trips and at the golf club. He liked a drink of Scotch at the nineteenth hole. But he had determination and toughness. What he said he would do, he did. He had also an agreeable touch of diffidence, enough to appreciate Archie MacMechan's praise in 1912:

I know too well my own limitations to have that exuberant confidence which so makes for success in this world. My main support in this business is the knowledge that I am doing the best I can, and the further one that when I perceive that that won't make the old machine go smoothly I'll retire with more equanimity than I entered.

MacKenzie had common sense and he had patience. He rarely dealt with issues when they were hot; he liked to have them, and himself, cool. The board early came to rely on him; they gave him a great deal of room, and he used it wisely.[29]

MacKenzie Tackles Dalhousie Problems

MacKenzie was thrown at once into a range of problems, so many, so pressing, that he told an old friend at Cornell that there was no time even to worry about having an inauguration: the new campaign for money, planning the new campus, supervising the architects, to say nothing of making some sort of organization of the president's office. It had hitherto been almost wholly devoid of any. "The whole machinery of the College," he said, "was either nonexistent or completely run down, and out of order – and I could continue the list." He obtained a much needed secretary, who became also the bursar, Miss H. Joyce Harris. She asserted, many years later, that when MacKenzie came in 1911 there were no papers, no correspondence, nothing that could be

A. Stanley MacKenzie, president, 1911–31.
A Lismer sketch done from life in 1919.

handed over to him. Anything in the Dalhousie files before 1911, she said, was picked up from among the books and pamphlets in the attic of the Dalhousie building. The presidential correspondence that MacKenzie started in 1911 comprehended whole new ranges of information about the inner workings of the president's office at the very time when its ramifications were expanding.[30]

The Dalhousie Forward Movement, a major fund-raising enterprise, was launched in November 1911, and continued to June 1912. It was given a considerable fillip at the start by James Hamet Dunn's gift of $25,000, sent from London and announced in November 1911. This was followed by a carefully orchestrated run of articles in the *Herald*, the *Chronicle* and elsewhere about Dalhousie and its history, published at close intervals in November and December. President MacKenzie made many speeches in Halifax and elsewhere. His Ottawa one on 13 April 1912 on "Science and the State" stressed the need for the powerful cooperation of governments at both levels, provincial and dominion, in helping universities create the cadres of scientific experts to meet the new demands of governments. Scientific research was needed to discover, for example, what had recently devastated oyster beds in Prince Edward Island. Casual "Walrus and the Carpenter" techniques were of little use in meeting such modern problems. The impact of MacKenzie's speeches that weekend was partly lost in the flaming headlines of the Monday and Tuesday: the *Titanic* sank at two in the morning of 15 April. The dead were being buried in Halifax's Fairview cemetery as he returned.[31]

In May 1912 MacKenzie headed west to meet Dalhousie alumni, beginning with Saskatoon where his old Dalhousie colleague, Walter Murray, was now president of the University of Saskatchewan. There is no evidence that MacKenzie crossed the Rockies to Vancouver, however. It might have been better if he had. Edwin B. Ross reported that it was difficult to pump much enthusiasm into British Columbia Dalhousians for they heard little of what was going on, receiving neither reports, calendars, nor the *Dalhousie Gazette*. President MacKenzie conceded that Dalhousie was having great difficulty keeping the addresses of some two thousand alumni up to date. The Halifax part of the campaign, however, went very much better. It began in June 1912 with ten canvassers. The total amount subscribed from Halifax, MacKenzie reported, was $213,349. W.H. Chase of Wolfville offered 10 per cent of whatever Halifax gave. Lord Strathcona, with pressure from George Campbell, sent $15,000. By October 1912 the overall total, given and promised, was $444,891. Of that, $150,000 would be reserved for endowment, with the rest used for building.[32]

Most of this was comprehensively reported by MacKenzie in

Dalhousie's first printed annual report of 1911–12, with statistics, pictures, and prospects. The student body, he reported, totalled 411 in all faculties, of whom 287 were in arts and science. This was an overall increase from 1891 of 60 per cent. The most striking increase was in arts and science which went up by 75 per cent, suggesting to MacKenzie that more students were taking arts and science before going on to professional programs. Thirty-one per cent of all students were from Halifax and vicinity, 11 per cent from Pictou County, both figures only slightly changed from twenty years earlier. Cape Breton students increased from 11 per cent in 1891 to 17 per cent in 1911.

Women students were 28 per cent of arts and science students, an increase from 23 per cent in 1891, and half of them were from Halifax. Some 30 per cent or more of women students were daughters of business and professional men; the predominance of clergyman fathers, now only about 18 per cent, had clearly passed. Farmer fathers were 6 per cent, manual workers 6 per cent. About 30 per cent of the fathers, occupations were not given. By the end of the First World War about 10 per cent of Dalhousie women students, perhaps more, came from homes where the father was dead. Scottish Presbyterian traditions were still strong.

One problem for women students was the lack of Dalhousie residences. They had to board in town or find space, as they frequently did, at the Halifax Ladies College on Barrington Street. Landladies as a rule preferred male students; they created less problems, they did not always want to make tea, coffee, do laundry – or so at least it was reported at the University of Toronto. At Dalhousie the problem was eased a little in September 1912 when the Alumnae rented a house on South Park Street, which they called Forrest Hall. It accommodated eleven students and two maids. The board appointed Dr Eliza Ritchie as warden. The youngest daughter of Justice J.W. Ritchie, she graduated from Dalhousie in 1887, taking her PH.D. at Cornell in 1889. She taught philosophy at Wellesley College from 1890 to 1900. She then returned to Halifax, where she promoted the advancement of women, not least Dalhousie women. Dr Ritchie pointed out to the Board of Governors that Forrest Hall was inadequate, and emphasized the benefits from having lady students supervised as they would have been at home. The board was sympathetic, but pointed out that the money in sight at the moment had to be kept for the new Science Building and the Macdonald Memorial Library. They promised that when the Alumnae had raised one-third of the cost of a suitable building, the board would try to find the rest.[33]

Within a week of the purchase of Studley at the end of January 1911, George Campbell telegraphed Frank Darling, one of the leading architects in Canada, to do a survey of the new campus. Dalhousie was clearly anxious to get cracking, though the architect wondered how much would be gained by such a survey in the depths of winter. Frank Darling of Darling and Pearson, Toronto, was the architect for the University of Toronto and the firm had designed buildings in most major cities of Canada. Elected to the Royal Canadian Academy in 1886, Darling was ingenious, flexible, sensitive to local conditions, and best of all, willing to listen to suggestions. That at least would turn out to be Dalhousie's experience. Darling came to be responsible either directly or indirectly for all the major buildings on the Dalhousie campus before 1923, taking on, at Dalhousie's suggestion, a young and able local architect, Andrew Randall Cobb, in June 1912.

Darling duly came to Halifax, taking a week to look over the ground, liking very much both the site and the Dalhousie men – so much so that he offered his landscape advice free in return for out-of-pocket expenses. He thought that such a large site should be surveyed by a proper landscape architect, and at the end of November 1911 Professor Mawson of the University of Liverpool came and was given a tour of the campus by President MacKenzie and George Campbell. Mawson was as enthusiastic as Darling. He declared Studley the finest college site that he had seen in Canada and worthy of the best scheme that could be devised.

Mawson liked the idea of making Morris Street the main entrance to Studley. That solution was ingenious and has largely survived, though it depended on Dalhousie's making arrangements with the city to extend Morris Street and its proposed boulevard through to the Studley campus, breaking through from Seymour to LeMarchant Street. That arrangement was accomplished in 1913; Dalhousie would give a strip five to eight feet wide along Coburg Road to the city to enlarge that street and would give the eighty-foot-wide strip that the city had reserved along Morris Street. In return, the city would give Dalhousie right-of-way to Studley by expropriating the properties between Seymour and LeMarchant. Dalhousie would allow public access to any roads that might be made through Studley.[34]

In March 1912 Darling sent four different proposals, three with Professor Mawson's input and a fourth with his own. The British ones were in general very expensive, calling for an elaborate system of terraces, perhaps not sufficiently taking into account how close Halifax ironstone lay beneath the surface of much of Studley, and how close were Dalhousie's finances. The British plans seem also to have envisaged a substantial attack on Studley trees, particularly the white pines on the south-west. Darling observed, sensibly enough,

Frank Darling, of Toronto, the architect of the Studley campus, 1911–23, "ingenious, flexible, sensitive to local conditions."

It appears to me that we should strive to place the buildings in such a way as to call for the spending of as little money as possible on landscape effect, depending almost entirely for the present on what nature has done for the property ...

I feel confident that the eastern treeless portion of the property is quite sufficient for the number of buildings you would want for years to come. To destroy the wood in any way at all would be a serious mistake. The trees are indigenous to the soil and I should imagine that new ones likely to attain to any size would be very difficult to cultivate on such land.

As to the architecture, Darling liked the public buildings already in Halifax, Government House and Province House especially, and he wanted "Georgian architecture, built of some native rock in rough random rubble with grey slate roof, with whatever woodwork there might be, painted white – it would follow the general style of the best architectural work in Halifax." [35]

President MacKenzie and his young professor of engineering, C.D. Howe, went to work on the suggestions Darling had made. Howe made a new and accurate two-foot contour map of Studley, marking in all the trees. MacKenzie and Howe devised an overall campus plan, using suggestions from Darling, that kept in the forefront Dalhousie's main requirements. Economy was one, changing the existing grades as little as possible, and using existing roads as much as possible. MacKenzie and Howe deliberately left the crown of the hill untouched, keeping it for "a great auditorium" sometime in the future. They wanted the approach from Morris Street to end in a large grass courtyard, up the gentle slope that led to the Murray homestead. There would be approaches also from South Street and from Coburg Road. The athletic field they put closer to South Street than had Darling, to avoid any more levelling than necessary. They reserved the whole of the Coburg Road and Oxford Street sides for possible future colleges or dormitories. The area along South Street, downhill from the South Street entrance, they reserved for women's residences. Darling was delighted and congratulated MacKenzie and Howe, that new firm of landscape architects, on what they had done. They had so much improved his suggestions that between the three of them they had reached a pretty satisfactory solution. But it had all proved "very much more difficult" than Darling had first thought it would be. Still, it is astonishing how much of the present campus still retains the stamp of that Darling, MacKenzie, and Howe design. [36]

Campbell and MacKenzie decided that their first building would be for science. That priority dated from before 1902, along with the Macdonald Memorial Library. The $200,000 request to Carnegie in

1902 for endowing a School of Mines had by 1906 become a more modest one for $50,000 for science. Carnegie in 1907 offered $40,000 on the condition that Dalhousie itself first raise $40,000 in endowment to erect and maintain a science building. With this backing, Dalhousie decided to go ahead. Before plans were quite ready, the cornerstone of the Science Building was laid on 15 August 1912 by the governor general, the Duke of Connaught. It was a state occasion, with the high commissioner for Australia, the governor of Newfoundland, and the premiers of Quebec and Nova Scotia on the platform. The duke well and truly laid the block of Wallace freestone that would mark the corner of the Science Building on the Studley campus.[37] Detailed plans were worked out by close consultation between the two science professors – Eben Mackay of chemistry and MacKenzie's replacement in physics, Howard Bronson – and Andrew Cobb, the local architect.

Andrew Randall Cobb was then regarded, and still is, as the best all-round architect in Halifax. He was hired in June 1912 by George Campbell to prepare the plans for the new Science Building. Cobb needed to be good, for he had to handle plumbing, heating, ventilation, and electricity, all in great detail. Cobb's suggestions and plans would then go forward to Frank Darling in Toronto for approval or revision.

Darling and MacKenzie had liked one another from the start. One of Darling's early suggestions to MacKenzie was that he was to criticize regardless of consequences. That MacKenzie did; Darling's revisions to Dalhousie's plans of the Science Building were substantial and would be expensive. The plans represented, said MacKenzie, two years' hard work by two professors, with later input from Cobb and MacKenzie. There were specific reasons for the peculiar design of the Science Building, reasons that Darling seemed quite to ignore. MacKenzie reminded him that the Science Building was really two buildings deliberately put together to look like one, for chemistry and for physics. As Dalhousie grew larger that double building would become a single one for chemistry. Physics would then get its own building. The Science Building had thus to have two sections, functioning separately, because fumes from all the chemical work had to be kept away absolutely from physics. Darling's revisions were also far too heedless of increased cost. Darling listened. In late November 1912 MacKenzie and Cobb went to Toronto and spent a full day going over revised plans. Final drawings were ready from Cobb by the end of January 1913. Darling thought them first class.[38]

The Science Building was built with ironstone from the old Queen's quarry across the Arm at Purcell's Cove. It was hard stone. One contractor suggested to Andrew Cobb it was a bad choice, that mortar would not long adhere to it. But there are different kinds of mortar. Representations were made that cement from Sydney ought to be used, since Sydney had given such liberal support to Dalhousie. That sort of argument got short shrift from C.D. Howe. He insisted on Portland cement.* Cobb backed Howe.[39]

The Macdonald Memorial Library cornerstone was laid in 1914. John Johnson, professor emeritus of classics, Macdonald's old colleague, was asked to come down from Quebec and lay it. Johnson was seventy-nine and unwell, and deeply saddened that he could not come. So it was laid by another old friend of Macdonald's, even older than Johnson, Allan Pollok of Pine Hill. He was a stately Auld Kirk Scot, who would still walk to the Bedford Road on fine days, and stop there for bread and cheese and ale. The day, 29 April 1914, was fine but with a stiff cold wind, and it shortened the speeches. MacKenzie's was from his own memories. Macdonald was himself a foundation stone of Dalhousie, he said; every student for thirty-eight years of its life after 1863 went out into the world with Macdonald's stamp on him. In truth, "Macdonald the mathematician was lost in Macdonald the man."[40]

Halifax had changed a good deal since Macdonald's death in 1901. The population had jumped 14 per cent to nearly 47,000 in the census of 1911. The appearance of the city had also changed somewhat. The British army had gone at the end of 1906; the constant presence of soldiers on Halifax streets, at Halifax parties, was no more. The port had changed too. Many of the new ocean liners were so big that there was not a wharf in Halifax where they could tie up. In 1913 the Borden government announced major wharf and railway reconstruction for Halifax. New wharves capable of handling the big new ships would be built along the harbour southward from South Street toward Point Pleasant. To do that they would need abundant rock fill. That would come from a new railway line that would be cut through the ironstone of the Halifax peninsula, along the North-West Arm. Blasting for that huge work was already in progress by 1914.

Halifax now had a movie theatre or two, not replacing stage shows yet, but threatening to do so. Automobiles were seen on the still unpaved streets. Aeroplanes were not unheard of and were sometimes seen at the Exhibition Grounds, as for example in 1913 when an enterprising American successfully demonstrated parachute jumping.

---

* Portland cement is a specific preparation of lime, very strong, and which, when dry, resembles the whitish colour of Portland stone. That was the limestone from the Portland peninsula, off the south coast of Dorset, used for St Paul's Cathedral.

The Science Building, the first building built on the
Studley campus. The cornerstone was laid in August 1912.

The newspapers reflected this slightly different society. The *Daily Echo* by 1914 carried comic strips, one of them the familiar "Mutt and Jeff." There were advertisements for vacuum cleaners, for washing machines, even for Victrolas – the hand-wound gramophones.

Social conventions sometimes had difficulty adjusting to the effects of such new inventions. Perhaps that was why, over the winter of 1913–14, there was a great debate between Senate and students over dancing at Dalhousie. In 1909 it had been agreed that there would be permitted eight "At Homes" during the academic year, three before Christmas, the rest in the spring. Since the beginning of the 1912–13 session, Dalhousie students had been operating under a student council. It took on responsibility for the supervision of student societies, and it was entrusted by Senate with student discipline. Senate would impose specific penalties recommended by the student council. Senate kept ultimate authority, the right to withdraw powers so delegated.

These arrangements were tested in the hazing season of 1912, but they had worked well enough. Dancing, however, was a more difficult and touchy subject. In the autumn of 1913 Senate learned, rather to its surprise, that at the meetings of the Dramatic Club, dancing was indulged in at rehearsals, presumably to someone's gramophone. Senate disapproved. The students claimed that dancing relieved the monotony of continual drama rehearsals and was a perfectly harmless indulgence. The student council president, J. McGregor Stewart, however, was against it, as were some other students. There was a mass meeting to insist on a conference with Senate. Senate did not find dealing with dancing very easy. Two younger professors, Bronson of physics and Todd of history, moved the question be given to a committee to study all student extra-curricular activities. When the report came, the extent of student activities took Senate by surprise. In the end, dancing was permitted at Drama Club rehearsals (for no more than thirty minutes), in exchange for giving up two of the less frequented "At Homes." But the issue occupied Senate most of the winter of 1913–14.[41]

Senate feared that there might be creeping influences baneful enough to weaken the stern imperatives in the Dalhousie motto, "Work and Pray." The poetry in the *Gazette* of June 1912 was not reassuring:

> Myself when young did eagerly frequent
>   Tutor and Prof. and heard great Argument
> Of Latin and of Greek; but all I heard
>   Came out by the same Ear wherein it went.
>
> Some for the Glory of High Firsts; and some
>   Sigh for the Pleasure of Rink Night to come.

Ah, take your skates and let your Latin go –
   Hark the glad Music of the Band and Drum!

Why if a Chap can fling his books aside,
   And o'er the Ice with Her for eight Bands glide,
Were't not a Shame – Were't not a *Shame* for him
   In some dark Attic cramming to abide?

And if the Puck you chase, the Hand you press,
   End in a Pluck in every Subject, – yes,
Think then you know Today what Yesterday
   You knew – Tomorrow you cannot know Less![42]

But there was more constructiveness in the students than that might suggest. In 1914 Stewart devised with his council the Students' Forward Movement. It would imitate, with equal success it was hoped, the Dalhousie Forward Movement of 1911–12. It was announced in April 1914, publicity to begin on 1 May, with an active canvass to begin on 1 July. The program was distinctly ambitious: the students aimed to raise $50,000 to put up a student union building on the new Studley campus. They hoped to be able to break ground in September 1914 and have the building ready by January 1915. The project had the backing of President MacKenzie; there was a place chosen for it, across from the library. Drawings were made; it would have a gymnasium and a "swimming tank" among other facilities. It was breathtaking and was announced with full detail in the *Daily Echo* on 29 June, with pictures and sketches on the following day.

   But on the same front page that day, in rather bolder print, was European news: the assassination on Sunday, 28 June of the heir to the Austrian throne, the Archduke Ferdinand and his wife Sophie, at Sarajevo, in Austrian-occupied Bosnia. The assassin was a young Serb, Gavrilo Princip. Pictures followed of that too. Within five weeks the fall-out from those assassinations had quite extinguished any immediate possibility of a student union building. Indeed, Dalhousie students would now be called upon to assume far more serious responsibilities. As of 4 August 1914, Britain and Canada were at war with Germany.

· 9 ·

The Great War and After
1914–1922

The Canadian militia and Dalhousie. A Dalhousie soldier. Dalhousie's Stationary Hospital No. 7. Moving onto the Studley campus. The Law School revised. The 1917 explosion. Mrs Eddy and Shirreff Hall. Carnegie, Rockefeller, and new medical buildings. Postwar students and the Student Christian Movement. Deaths of Eben Mackay and John Forrest. Changing Dalhousie traditions.

War in 1914 was still glorious. Haligonians remembered the sailing of Canadian contingents to South Africa just fifteen years before, and there was a bright flame of glory even about that war. There were few photographs of actual battlefield conditions; war was illustrated by splendid paintings that glorified the smoke, the fury, the wounding, and the dying. War was adventure; there were risks, as in all adventure, but risks were good for the maturing of young men. They toughened moral fibre, gave men the grit that society, increasingly civilized, was failing to give. Men, and women, needed some stress. Women got it naturally from child-bearing; men got it from fisticuffs and fighting – and war.

That hardships were good for you was the philosophy prevailing in the Canadian militia and there was no better publicist for it than Colonel Sir Sam Hughes, Robert Borden's mercurial and headstrong minister of militia. Hughes extolled the virtues of the volunteer militia in whirlwind trips across Canada, often in colonel's uniform. He promoted its moral character and discipline, the stern virtues, even in peacetime, of military training. The three main centres of Canadian morality were, in Hughes's mind, the school, the church, and the militia. The militia was a panacea for the ills of modern society, instilling into young men, as Hughes put it, "the spirit of obedience, discipline, patriotism, veneration and love for principle."[1]

Hughes knew full well the art of managing newspapermen, having been one. He was able to establish the impression of himself as a dynamic man, with superabundant energy applied to original ideas. He succeeded in doubling the militia budget, and in 1912 and 1913 began building drill halls and local armouries. By 1914 some fifty had been established across Canada. (Halifax's had been erected in 1899 at the time of the Boer War.) Dalhousie was looking for a combined drill hall and gymnasium before the 1914 war; Hughes had promised President MacKenzie as much. But he was hard to pin down, and his military estimates were by the spring of 1914 meeting more resistance from his colleagues.[2]

The last major war, the Russo-Japanese War of 1904–5, was effectively over in fifteen months, and there was uncertainty, not to say unease, that the War of 1914 might be over before young Canadians could have a fair crack at it. One French general assured the press that the war would not be over until 1917 and that the British need not refrain from joining up because of the mistaken belief that it would soon end.

The war had overwhelming popular support in English Canada and propaganda about bleeding Belgium and the demon Hun augmented it, and soon compromised civilized behaviour. Concerts began to avoid including works by Beethoven, Brahms, and especially Wagner. German teaching dried up. Berlin, Ontario, an essentially German-speaking community, decided to change its name to Kitchener.

The *Dalhousie Gazette* at first tried to present something of both sides. An article on 4 November 1914, "The Apathetic Man," criticized the war. Suppose, said its author, Frank Graham, that France had crashed into Belgium on its way to attack Germany. Would we, the British and the Canadians, rush to help the Germans against the French? Not at all. "We wage a jealous war. We care not a jot for principle. Neutrality is a word. Expediency is our God ... We saw a chance to smash [Germany] and we leapt at it. Accident made us appear to act with honour ... In our day we have broken our national word of honour many times – we have been perfidious Albion. It happens to suit us to keep our word now."

That fairly put the cat among the pigeons. And while Graham's remarks were mainly directed against the formation of the Dalhousie Canadian Officer Training Corps (COTC), the local papers could not resist taking it up. The *Acadian Recorder* said that Graham's "sophomoric but offensive effusion" could only be published under the aegis of the British freedom of expression. The *Herald* did not even accept that. It sternly recommended that Dalhousie, governors, Senate, and students alike, should repudiate the article. The Dalhousie Senate did not do that. It agreed in private that Graham's was a "most unpatriotic" article, that it "had given rise to a strong feeling of indignation in the community," but all it would say in public was that, as in most universities, Senate exercised no supervision over the student paper. It authorized President MacKenzie to write the Halifax newspapers to that effect. Nor did the *Dalhousie Gazette* have much sympathy for Frank Graham's views. There was much correspondence about it, though the *Gazette* thought that the *Herald* was being needlessly critical. The *Herald's* propaganda began in September 1914, and continued to the end of the war. A sample:

> Why do they call, sonny, why do they call
>   For men who are brave and strong?
> Is it naught to you if your country fall,
>   And Right is smashed by Wrong?
> Is it football still and the picture show,
>   The pub and the betting odds,
> When your brothers stand to the tyrant's blow
>   And the Empire's call is God's?[3]

In fact, propaganda was not much needed. The Dalhousie COTC had a good deal of student support and it was a movement that preceded the outbreak of war. It had been devised by Sam Hughes and in 1912 the Department of Militia and Defence offered university students the opportunity to acquire elementary military training. The control of each unit was left to a local military committee composed of student representatives, a member of the Dalhousie staff, and a representative of the army. Drill was required: twenty-five parades of at least forty-five minutes each. In return students got the free issue of uniform and accoutrements from militia funds. By June 1914 some 59,000 men, in universities and outside, were undergoing military training. By November Dalhousie had eight companies in training, each afternoon and evening, company by company, in the South End Rink.[4]

Within a year of the outbreak of war some 165 Dalhousie graduates and staff had enlisted and eighty-three undergraduates. By October 1916 President MacKenzie told the chief Halifax recruiting officer that while he would duly post up the recruiting notice just received, the fact was that in arts and science at Dalhousie there were only sixty-eight male students altogether, of whom only forty-five were over eighteen years of age. Of those forty-five, many were foreign, or lame, or had already been turned down on medical grounds. In the third and fourth years, the classes of 1918 and 1917 respectively, there were only ten male students altogether. "I fear," said MacKenzie, "that there are not many recruitable men left..." By this time 60 per cent of Dalhousie arts and science students were women, a figure that rose to 63 per cent in 1917–18.[5]

The career of one Dalhousie COTC student may illustrate something of the lives of the 567 Dalhousie graduates and undergraduates who enlisted. Larry MacKenzie was from Pictou County and Pictou Academy, the son of a Presbyterian minister, and the grandson of another. He would later become president of the University of New Brunswick from 1940 to 1944 and the president of the University of British Columbia from 1944 to 1962. He had come to Dalhousie in 1913, at the age of nineteen, having left home four years before to work with his brothers on a homestead in Saskatchewan. He did very well the first year, with firsts in mathematics and English. Into his second year, 1914–15, he joined the Dalhousie COTC but found prospects too slow and shifted in December 1914 to the 6th Canadian Mounted Rifles. He officially left Dalhousie on 10 February 1915 and would, like other students in similar circumstances, be given his year. He went overseas with his regiment at the end of July 1915 and duly arrived in Flanders.

By that time, the western front was at a stalemate from the English Channel to the borders of Switzerland. It was the reverse of a war of movement; the technology had become heavily defensive, with men living for months in trenches guarded by heavy machine guns and barbed wire. Indeed, you could smell the front lines before you ever got to them – the stench of mud, decay, and death. Horses were needed to haul even machine guns. At the Battle of Sanctuary Wood on 2 June 1916, Larry MacKenzie was lucky: he was hauling supplies. Of Larry's battalion 90 per cent were wounded or killed. During the Battle of the Somme, a couple of months later, the horse he was riding was killed by shrapnel. Invalided to England with pneumonia, his papers got lost and by the end of 1917 he was with the 85th Battalion, Nova Scotia Highlanders. He won the Military Medal at Amiens in August 1918, and had a bar added to it a few weeks later, when the Canadian Corps became the main striking force of the British army's final offensive.[6]

That he survived all of that without a scratch was blind luck. Larry would send reports back to the *Dalhousie Gazette;* one, in September 1918, tells his story well enough:

Have just come through another "over the top" stunt without a scratch, though how I did it I don't know, for they [my fellow soldiers] were falling all around me. Of course we got what we were after, but we certainly paid for it. Personally I don't think the whole of France is worth the boys I helped to carry out, but then it isn't land we are fighting for but liberty ... The more I think over this miserable business the worse I feel about it, I think of thousands of fine young chaps like him [John O. MacLeod, on his first foray] going under.

That was what Larry and many other Dalhousie soldiers could never quite get over. It was not so much the Germans – though it took Larry a long time before he could view them with equanimity – it was the slaughter of his pals, as he called them. For them he would always be, as he told Archie MacMechan later, "boiling over." The camaraderie of his old soldiers was for Larry something profound, and to the end of his life he never forgot his pals of the 85th. "Lest we forget" for Larry meant the living as well as the dead.[7]

One major Dalhousie contribution was the creation of a stationary hospital, using the Medical School professors, senior students, and nurses as staff. In the British army (and Canadian hospitals were under its administration) a stationary hospital was the stage between a field hospital and one back in Britain or in Canada. A wounded soldier was taken by stretcher-bearers to battalion headquarters, looked at, then sent via field hospital and clearing station to a stationary hospital. The stationary hospital was what it said it was – a building adapted as far as possible to being like a civilian hospital where the full range of operations and surgery was performed.

Over the winter of 1914–15 similar units were being organized at Toronto, Queen's, and McGill. The idea was that graduating medical students would receive degrees before sailing from Canada and would be given commissions as captains in the army. Nurses would receive commissions as lieutenants. The British government was by no means ready to accept these Canadian offers. It was only in September 1915 that the War Office cabled that they would be glad to accept Dalhousie's offer of doctors, nurses, orderlies, to staff a four-hundred-bed hospital. The equipment would be provided by the Canadian government. Dalhousie's Stationary Hospital No. 7 was finally mobilized on 9 November 1915, in the old Halifax Medical College building. It sailed from Saint John, New Brunswick, on 31 December in the *Metagama*. The Dalhousie unit included 162 staff: twelve doctors, one dentist, twenty-seven nursing sisters, two administrative officers, and the rest orderlies, typists, and cooks. Most were Dalhousie professors or students, but there were also men from Acadia and Mount Allison.

They arrived in Plymouth after an uneventful passage, and ended up in Shorncliffe Hospital, just west of Folkestone on the Channel in Kent. They dealt mainly with Canadian wounded, who would arrive in groups of ten to forty on hospital ships from France. As Dr John Stewart, head of the hospital, described it to President MacKenzie, "Our surgical cases are chiefly bone and joint injuries, operations for the removal of dead bone, pieces of shrapnel & various deformities ... some, poor fellows, armless or legless or minus an eye or with heart or lungs damaged, but almost invariably cheerful, are discharged to go home to Canada."

The Dalhousie hospital unit was anxious to go to France, and to their great relief were embarked from Southampton, on 18 June 1916. They took over a British stationary hospital in Le Havre, in an old hotel. Sanitary arrangements were primitive. After the Battle of the Somme started on 1 July 1916, there was a flood of wounded – twelve to sixteen train-loads every twenty-four hours – with three or four hospital ships constantly being used to transfer cases to England. The scene at the railway station in Le Havre is described by Dr Stewart: "The stretcher cases lay in hundreds on the railway platforms so close together that there was barely room for the orderlies to pass among them with tea and other refreshments or to arrange bandages and dressings. Some lay quietly, too ill, or suffering too much to talk or to move."

Eventually, in June 1917, Stationary Hospital No. 7 was moved to an old chateau close enough to the front lines for the staff to see and hear the artillery at night. They were near Armentières; after the Battle of Messines nearby, 7 to 11 June 1917, they found themselves treating not only Canadian wounded, but Germans as well. The German prisoners were both surprised and grateful for the treatment they received.[8]

Moving to the Studley Campus

Dalhousie was now fairly established on its new campus. The new Macdonald Memorial Library was finished in the autumn of 1915, and Dalhousie began to move into it that summer. They moved at the same time into the Science Building. It cost $144,000, of which $40,000 was met by the Carnegie Foundation. The library cost $90,000, without the five-storey book stack at the back, added in 1921. The library was placed in between the big Science Building to the east and the Murray homestead to the west; the narrow space allotted for it was rather a measure of the function of a university library in 1912. Darling, and even more Cobb, were ingenious in devising a handsome building in the space restricted as much by money as design. Moreover, it was clear by 1913 that the Macdonald Library would have to be not only a library building but would also house a couple of arts classrooms thrown in for good measure.

In the big red brick building on the Carleton campus, renamed the Forrest Building by the board in 1919, books had suffered from want of space, from dust, and from the omnipresent threat of fire and water.

When the dentists moved into the Forrest Building in September 1908, one of the rooms they took over had been used for storing un-catalogued books. Some five thousand books had to be reshelved, some in the faculty room (a small room on the north side), the others in the attic.

The move to the Macdonald Memorial Library took place while the carpenters were still working. The books were placed in the handsome main reading room. Even so there was not enough space. Chemistry, physics, and geology got departmental libraries, while other books judged less needful were put in the new attic. The best part of the transfer was that the new librarian, Frances Jean Lindsay, persuaded MacMechan, the university librarian, and MacKenzie, to adopt the new Library of Congress system for cataloguing the books. No other university library in Canada, except the embryonic one at University of British Columbia, used it.[9]

The move to Studley had one effect not altogether anticipated: it split the campus. True, the split was only half a kilometre, four city blocks wide, but there it was. It was true also that even in the Forrest Building, arts, medicine, dentistry, and law did not mix very much, having little in common but the Dalhousie name and government. Nevertheless, the separation that began in 1915–16 made the two campuses seem like separate worlds. The remedy suggested by the *Dalhousie Gazette* was to form a student union, and still better, to get rid of the Forrest campus altogether. The first was a dream for the future, the latter an illusion in the present. The capacious thirty-year-old Forrest Building could not be given up; the land on which it stood was essentially without value, for the city possessed the reversion to it.

The Law School Revised

Richard Weldon, dean of law since 1883, retired in 1914. He had created almost singlehandedly the Dalhousie Law School over the past thirty years. He and Benjamin Russell, the half-time professor, *were* the law school. The rest were downtown lecturers; some were good, but they were an uncertain lot, not always arriving to give their scheduled lectures, and when they did, sometimes ill-prepared. By 1914 student criticism of the Law School was mainly directed at three things. There were too few lectures compared to other law schools, only six to seven hours a week. The standard of admission was too low; in other words, there was no standard, other than ordinary matriculation into the university, and no arts classes were required. The students' main complaint, however, was that the curriculum was not sufficiently practical. They wanted to have international law struck out, constitutional history shortened, and more mundane subjects, such as proce-

The Macdonald Memorial Library, a Lismer sketch of 1919

The interior of the Macdonald Memorial Library, looking west

dure and agency, chosen. Weldon and Russell resisted, for it struck at the public law curriculum that made the Dalhousie Law School so distinctive. Nevertheless the poem in the *Gazette* in January 1914, had relevance:

...A BA and an LL.B. – both from Dalhousie College,
He seemed to have strangle-hold on all the useful knowledge;
He knew it all from Alpha to Omega, but the fact is,
The things he'd learned at law school didn't cover all his practice...

He'd achieved a signal victory in appeals in two Moot Courts
For he'd won a case in shipping and another one in torts;
The Dean had listened to his plea with one eye almost open,
As he waltzed through his citations like a melody from Chopin...

In his office, newly painted, where he'd sat a week or more,
With his shingle swinging gaily to the breeze outside the door,
And his LL.B. diploma in a brand new varnished frame,
These sombre meditations to the young attorney came: –

"I'm familiar with the judgements of all the higher courts,
From the Fourteenth Century Year-Books to Dominion Law Reports;
In general jurisprudence I can give full satisfaction,
But – I don't know what is proper for the conduct of an action." [10]

In the two or three years prior to 1914 Dean Weldon had been obviously failing. Russell rather than Weldon seemed to be in charge, and he was only half-time. President MacKenzie happened to be in Weldon's office one day early in September 1913, supervising the cleaners – one of the president's multifarious duties? – and found on Weldon's desk a large number of unopened letters, many of which had been lying there for eight or nine weeks. MacKenzie's letter about this to Weldon is instructive, for he was gentle with the old dean, the criticism more implied that stated. "I am afraid some people will feel badly neglected, as the post mark on some of the letters is as early as June ... I presume the janitor must have thought you were coming over [from Dartmouth], once in a while to look over your mail." [11]

MacKenzie had already acted to remedy one of the Law School's most notorious deficiencies, its teaching period of only twenty-one weeks. This anomaly he swept away and by 1912–13 the school's year was the same as the rest of Dalhousie's. As to admission standards, pressure came from the council of the Nova Scotia Barristers' Society; they decided that at least one year should be added to the law student's education before he went into law. The Law Faculty fell into line and went one better: the student now had to spend at least one year in an arts program, pass five classes, of which four had to be Latin, mathematics, French or German, and English. The meeting that decided this, on 5 April 1914, was the last faculty meeting that Weldon attended.

The Barristers' council did more than that. They were concerned about other inadequacies in the preparation of Nova Scotia lawyers. There emerged from their disquiet in 1914 a *modus vivendi*, between Dalhousie's right to say what, and how, law should be taught, and the Barristers' Society's duty to see that poorly trained lawyers were not let loose on the Nova Scotian public. This consisted of joint examinations. The Barristers' Society did not really exercise any great control but joint examinations offered a common ground between lawyers too busy to teach and teachers too busy, or out of touch, with legal practice.[12]

President MacKenzie wanted a new law dean whose whole energy would be given to the Law School, not an aging one whose work was being dissipated in a retreat in Dartmouth. He wanted to put, as he said, "life and energy and snap and go into it which it does not now possess." Finding such a dean was not easy. First-class lawyers at the top of their profession were not to be hired at $3,000 – Weldon's salary after twenty-one years of teaching. What MacKenzie was looking for and, surprisingly, got was an educated, mature, and civilized lawyer who had a yen to teach. He got Donald Alexander MacRae.[13]

MacRae, though a junior lawyer in a Toronto firm, was forty-two years old. He was born in Prince Edward Island, worked in a clothing store for seven years, then came to Dalhousie at the age of twenty-two with an entrance scholarship. He swept the board in classics, taking the University Medal in 1898. MacRae spent six years at Cornell getting a PH.D. and instructing in Greek, ending up at Princeton as an assistant professor of classics. He may have found teaching Greek a harder road than learning it; at the age of thirty-seven he turned suddenly to law, at Osgoode Hall, Toronto. He was low man on the roster at a Toronto law firm when MacKenzie found him.

MacRae liked Dalhousie and had no particular brief for big universities as such. His view in 1900 was that the size and facilities of a university did not make all that much difference. What mattered was the capacity of the student. Having more courses to choose from, as at Cornell, was a mixed blessing. University life was what the student made it.

Nevertheless, MacRae produced a decidedly revised curriculum over the session of 1914–15, implemented in 1915, and it came to be a model for other common-law law schools in Canada. It was designed to fill the gap in practical classes without quite giving up Dalhousie's old allegiance to cultural ones. But definitely the old slant was shifted. International law was in abeyance for a decade after 1915, and in that time constitutional history would disappear. Something of the old character still held. A later dean, Sidney Smith (LL.B. '20), put it in 1933 to a new professor, "Sink a shaft and sink it deep, don't bother over much about coverage."

As Dalhousie stiffened its law curriculum in 1915, there were new pressures that sought to expand the reach of its arts and science. Mount St Vincent Academy was a Roman Catholic boarding school for girls, run by the Sisters of Charity who had come to Halifax in 1849. They bought a handsome property at Rockingham on Bedford Basin, and had fought off control by the Archbishop of Halifax. As it developed, the Mount acquired ambitions to educate its Roman Catholic girls beyond matriculation. They wanted a charter as a college, but the government, perhaps prompted by a disapproving frown from the archbishop or perhaps conscious of the existence already of five degree-granting institutions in the province, refused. The sisters then appealed to Dalhousie, saying that since Dalhousie was virtually a provincial university, Dalhousie should find some way to accommodate their wish to have their first-year college classes recognized. The stumbling block was Dalhousie's uncertainty over the quality of that first-year work, and particularly of the sisters teaching such classes. The Mount was willing to send two or three of its best to the United States to be trained, so that it could, with a PH.D. or two, eventually take on even second-year work. The sister's idea was that Dalhousie professors could teach the third and fourth years at the Mount, and they would pay Dalhousie a proportion of the professors' salaries. The same examinations would apply to third and fourth year classes at both the Mount and Dalhousie. Transportation was a problem, though the proposal itself was made viable by the existence of automobiles.

Senate approved the scheme, in principle, on 9 April 1914. The war set Dalhousie's own plans awry, the Board of Governors being unwilling, as MacKenzie put it to the sisters, to "undertake any new matter of policy or to enter on any new avenues of college activity." Another difficulty for Dalhousie was the very small number of students – less than five – that would benefit from the arrangement. The only reason Dalhousie was willing to discuss it was because "we have felt it our duty to meet what seems a real need and hardship." By September 1916 the board were willing to put it into operation on a year-by-year basis. Mount St Vincent gave ten classes of the first two years, given by sisters who had a PH.D., examinations to be set and marked by

Dalhousie. The Mount would pay Dalhousie $2,500 a year for giving the ten classes of the final two years. This agreement held until 1925, when it came abruptly to an end with the sudden, and to Dalhousie inexplicable, incorporation of Mount St Vincent as a college.[14]

St Mary's too had ambitions. In October 1916 it asked if its first year could be accepted for admission to Dalhousie Law School. It submitted examination papers to indicate its standards. These were duly reported on to the Senate by Dalhousie professors. Some reports were favourable, but in the key subjects of mathematics and English, they were not. For the time being St Mary's request was refused. Meetings were held to help bring their work into line with Dalhousie, and by 1916 MacMechan was ready to accept St Mary's first-year work in English. But the issue then lapsed, revived in 1919 and again in 1921, the main problem being whether St Mary's could satisfy the Senate's conditions.[15]

St Mary's wanted its students educated under a curriculum that it could control – one that was Catholic in moral and intellectual emphasis – and it did not feel Dalhousie should deny it access to Dalhousie's professional schools merely because St Mary's intellectual purposes were different. The Dalhousie Senate felt, and would continue to do so for a long time, that what St Mary's was asking for was, in effect, an end run around Dalhousie standards. Dalhousie students had to meet certain criteria for admission to the Law School, and it seemed reasonable to the Senate that an outside institution should at least meet those standards. The Mount was willing to meet Dalhousie's criteria and St Mary's seemed to be able to find reasons to avoid doing so. So the issue remained in limbo for some time yet.

The Effects of the War on Dalhousie

The war made none of this any easier, with student numbers down, half the medical faculty overseas, and other staff depleted. Research in the sciences almost stopped, so much had the energies of the remaining staff been dissipated by war work of various kinds. The worst of it was that Dalhousie was thrown backward financially. The university was kept running, but each year saw the deficit on current account getting worse. By the end of 1916 arts and law were only 40 per cent of prewar enrolment, and fees were the main source of Dalhousie's income. Medicine and dentistry were the only faculties that were near normal; there the demand was so great that the government asked Dalhousie to keep running continuously even in summer. Students by this time were as much concerned with casualty lists as with pass lists. Then in December 1916 the Military Hospitals Commission in Ottawa under Sir James Lougheed urgently asked the Dalhousie board to give up the Forrest Building for use as a military hospital. Dalhousie had the only building in Halifax, so they said, suitable for use as a convalescent hospital. The board replied that to give up the Forrest Building would completely disrupt medicine, law, dentistry, and pharmacy, but if the matter were very urgent, someone should be sent down at once to discuss it. Eleven days later Captain W.L. Symons, military architect, arrived and with other officers met with the board. It was more than urgent: it was desperate. The consequences of the Somme offensive were now, literally, coming home. Canadians had moved into the Somme line in September 1916, and were in a series of battles until the heavy rains of November stopped the offensive. Their casualties were over twenty-four thousand. The Military Hospitals men pleaded with the board, as MacKenzie remarked, "almost with tears in their eyes and begged us to let them have that building as otherwise they could not be ready." The pressure they put on Dalhousie was so great that simply for the sake of humanity, as MacKenzie put it, Dalhousie agreed to offer the Forrest Building rent-free. There was only one condition: that Military Hospitals agree to fix up and substantially extend the old Halifax Medical College building at Carleton and College, so Dalhousie could use that.

Captain Symons had adapted Grant Hall at Queen's for hospital use. Although college buildings looked as if they were well suited to hospital needs, they required substantial and costly changes in structure and in plumbing. That Dalhousie dithered, as one historian suggested, is improbable, that being unlike either George Campbell or President MacKenzie; what probably happened was a decision based upon costs and time. The Hospitals Commission started its own hospital, Camp Hill, in the spring of 1917 and had it finished by the autumn, a light, two-storey affair but a triumph of new, quick-construction techniques. Camp Hill became the inspiration for analogous hospitals at Montreal, Whitby, and Vancouver, all of them with the same character: ugly, functional, and inexpensive. In Halifax, Camp Hill Hospital was just in time, and for reasons of rather grim physics.[16]

Dalhousie and the Halifax Explosion

Dalhousie's George Munro professor of physics was Howard Bronson. He had come in 1910, replacing A.S. MacKenzie, who had departed for New York and New Jersey. Bronson was an American who had gone to McGill and worked with Ernest Rutherford, perhaps the greatest physicist of his day. Rutherford exemplified research, not teaching. When Yale wanted Rutherford to head their physics department, Rutherford said to Bronson, impatiently, "Why should I go there?

Damage to windows on the east end of the Science Building by the 1917 explosion

They act as though the university was made for the students." There spoke the research man. Bronson was much influenced by Rutherford, but at thirty-two years of age he had published much of his output in physics. He seems to have chosen Dalhousie deliberately, knowing its weakness in equipment, but knowing also its students were good. Bronson was now turning towards teaching. His research would slowly die, like Rutherford's and MacKenzie's alpha rays.

On Thursday morning, 6 December 1917, Bronson was at work in his physics laboratory on the second floor at the east end of the new Science Building. Suddenly, at 9:05 AM, the whole building shook, as if there had been a heavy blast in the new railway cutting, half a mile distant, though it seemed to come from directly underneath the building. Bronson thought the boiler might have blown up and started towards the door. He hadn't gone thirty feet across the laboratory when the full air compression of explosion hit. It destroyed the windows on three sides of the Science Building and much more, including nearly all of north-end Halifax beyond North Street. It was the *Mont Blanc* blowing up.

She was a small French freighter of 3,100 tons with a valuable and dangerous cargo, 2,500 tons of picric acid and TNT plus thirty-five tons of monochlorobenzine stowed in steel drums on the open deck. *Mont Blanc* had come up the harbour that morning and near the narrows collided with a larger Norwegian vessel, the *Imo*, on her way out to sea and going too fast. That occurred at 8:45 AM. On board *Mont Blanc* the monochlorobenzine caught fire almost at once. The crew fled to the Dartmouth shore and headed for the woods as fast as possible. Twenty minutes later the *Mont Blanc* exploded. The total energy was $10^{11} \times 8.7$ kg.-metres, as Bronson later calculated. All buildings within three thousand feet were destroyed, and those within a mile and a quarter rendered largely uninhabitable. All sections of Halifax beyond that radius had serious damage to windows, doors, and plaster. There was damage at Sackville, nine miles away, and at Truro, sixty-two miles distant, the shock was heavy enough to jar buildings and knock things off shelves.[17]

The disaster was so universal in Halifax that no one section could think of the other; all thought they were in exactly the same kind of trouble. As President MacKenzie remarked, "If we at the south end had known that north-enders were buried under their houses and being burned to death," more might have been done, though it is difficult to imagine what that might have been.

The toll on Halifax's people was frightful; sixteen hundred people were killed outright and another six hundred died later of injuries. Several thousand were scarred or maimed for life. The worst was the glass: every window instantly became shrapnel; windows shot shards of glass across rooms with a force that buried them in plaster or in people. The effect on faces and eyes was horrifying. Hundreds of people lost an eye, at least fifty were completely blinded, and the fear then was that the latter figure would double. A call for volunteers went out. Dalhousie medical students of all levels went to the Victoria General or to the new veterans' hospital, Camp Hill. Many of the young medical students worked without sleep for thirty hours or more. Dalhousie's women students, wrote K.A. Baird in the *Gazette*, were angels of mercy, going quietly to work, helping in dressing wounds, comforting patients, "amid scenes of agony and death to which they were absolutely unaccustomed and which are known to have shocked the nerves of even those accustomed to surgical work." Those scenes beggared description. Sometimes one could not distinguish the living from the dead. Volunteers were needed sometimes to help hold down patients being operated on without anaesthetic, for by the end of that awful Thursday the hospitals had run out of anaesthetic and, later, sutures. Mercifully, help for these shortages was not far away, nor long in coming.[18]

Dalhousie casualties were comparatively light. One student lost an eye, and another was badly wounded in face and hands. Several occupants of the law library got cut. Edith Clarke, the assistant registrar, by one of those miracles not uncommon, was sitting beside a window when it blew in. She was not even scratched. But the new Science Building and library suffered badly. MacMechan hurried over to Dalhousie and found the tall Palladian windows of the library blown in, glass everywhere. The big globes for reading light had fallen and smashed. He and others set to work with brooms and dustpans, sweeping up the broken glass and in three hours had it cleaned up. The books were moved from under the gaping, empty window spaces to far corners where rain and snow couldn't reach them. Windows would be covered in somehow by boards. He walked down to President MacKenzie's house on Hollis Street to find out what was to be done next. At an emergency meeting at MacKenzie's house that afternoon, the Senate decided that in view of the damage to university buildings, all classes would have to be stopped until after the Christmas holidays.[19]

As the Senate was breaking up that Thursday evening, the east wind had already started, presaging one of the worst gales to hit Halifax in years. By morning a savage south-easter had set in, with blowing wet snow, that lasted into the Friday night. By Saturday it had abated and a few flickers of sunshine came through. On Sunday a thaw set in, turning the sixteen inches of snow into slush. It was only a brief pause:

the next day another snowstorm came on, this time followed by a pattern every Dalhousian would recognize – a biting north-west wind, with everything frozen bone hard, slush and all. Dalhousie, its windows and woodwork heavily damaged, with the help of professors, staff, and janitors, managed to stop up the gaping holes that once were windows, and most of all, to keep the furnaces going. Thus the basic interior functioning of the buildings survived. Had the heating, and thus the plumbing, gone, Dalhousie would have had to close, not just for the Christmas holidays but for all of 1918. As it was, Dalhousie reopened at the usual time, if not in quite the usual form, in January 1918.

Five days after the explosion MacKenzie telegraphed the Carnegie Corporation asking if they would consider helping out with repairs to the new Science Building, for there was extensive damage to windows, doors, roofs. The Carnegie replied that they would "consider it a privilege to pay for repairing the damage to [all] Dalhousie University buildings by the explosion." MacKenzie estimated $4,000 for the Science Building alone, $10,000 for all of them. But the repairs came to double that, as on closer inspection the damage was much greater than first thought, and the costs of material and labour had risen steeply. Carnegie still paid.

Return from Overseas

MacKenzie pushed hard to get his Medical Faculty back home after the armistice on 11 November 1918. He and George Campbell were joined by Hector McInnes, a well-established Halifax lawyer, who had been on the board since 1892. The three went to Ottawa in December 1918 to press for the return of the staff of Stationary Hospital No. 7. There were five on the Dalhousie medical staff and three of those carried heavy teaching responsibilities. Sir Robert Borden was sympathetic, but the military had their own ways of doing things and resented personal appeals to politicians to jump the huge queue for transport back to Canada. Most of the staff had returned by May 1919 and Colonel Dr John Stewart arrived on the *Mauretania* on 6 June; by that autumn he had become Dalhousie's dean of medicine, and would so remain until 1932.[20]

The soldiers returned too. They were given what was called a War Service Gratuity, announced in December 1918. Three years or more overseas service entitled a soldier to six months' pay, at $70 a month for a single man, $100 for married men. Wounded soldiers received free hospital treatment, much of it of a high standard, with pensions depending on the severity of the wound. The universities, Dalhousie included, pressed for a more generous settlement in education. The

The Alumni procession of the centennial of 1919 forming up on the Grand Parade

Repatriation Committee of the Borden government asked the universities to meet in Ottawa in January 1919. The universities had agreed – Acadia apparently excepted – to urge the government to pay tuition of all men whose college program, current or prospective, "was broken into by their enlistment." The government agreed to do it for wounded soldiers; the universities wanted it for all. Although MacKenzie was sanguine, they did not get it. Borden said the credit of the country would not stand it. Dalhousie gave students in arts who had been delayed by anything more than a year the relief of one year's work. In law it applied only to the year of arts preliminary to law. Nothing was taken off in medicine.[21]

In the fall of 1919 Dalhousie had 622 students, the largest so far in its history, and double that of 1918–19. In 1920–1 it was still larger at 677, and in 1922–3 was 753. Of those 23 per cent were women.

After the war the most critical question facing the Board of Governors was housing for its women students. They were 31 per cent of the student body of 1918–19, and housing in Halifax was expensive and scarce. The board resolved to proceed with a women's residence on the Studley campus. Dalhousie then rented 121 South Park Street, a substantial brick house housing about twenty girls, and eventually bought it for $15,000. It was called Marlborough House, was administered by a committee of alumnae, and would remain a women's residence until 1924. In the meantime President MacKenzie set about visiting Canadian and American colleges to find out what were the basic requirements for a campus women's residence. Feeling was unanimous, he discovered, that each girl have her own room; prevailing views favoured ample public space, large enough for dancing, with lounge areas broken up into alcoves where young women could meet their callers. Dining rooms should not be barrack-like but should be broken up into semi-private sections. All of this MacKenzie duly reported to Frank Darling, the architect in Toronto.

From the beginning Darling took a distinct interest in Dalhousie's women's residence. He drafted floor plans and MacKenzie liked them. The problem was that what Darling proposed would cost $200,000, double what Dalhousie could afford. Moreover, MacKenzie wanted to build in stone, not brick, and problems were surfacing with the nearest and cheapest available stone, Halifax ironstone. It was a metamorphosed slate with iron in it, and in the building of the new Anglican cathedral in Halifax some problems were revealed, where the mortar would not bond properly with the stone. That rang alarms with MacKenzie and Dalhousie's professor of engineering, J.N. Finlayson. They inspected Dalhousie's ironstone on the Science Building and the Macdonald Library and found early evidence of similar problems.

MacKenzie was reluctant to use ironstone at all until more extensive tests had found a proper mortar. Then in the summer of 1919 they found a new stone, a handsome pink quartzite from New Minas that had been successfully used at Acadia.[22]

As soon as the frost was out of the ground in early April 1919, MacKenzie went over the south-west corner of Studley with Finlayson. They wanted to preserve as many of the white pines as possible, so the site was moved to within thirty feet of Oxford Street. Tests with a three-foot crowbar showed rock at only one point in the main part of the building site, though the kitchen would have to sit squarely on an outcrop.

The cornerstone was laid by the Prince of Wales at the beginning of his tour of Canada in August 1919. It was now an open secret that Dalhousie was looking for a donor; whoever that was would get their name attached to what might well be a handsome residence. One Dalhousie alumnus well aware of this need was R.B. Bennett. Dalhousie offered Bennett an LL.D. in 1919, at the celebration of Dalhousie's 1918 centennial. That had been put off until 1919 owing to the war. Bennett couldn't come because of his presidency of the Alberta Red Cross, but there were talks. Bennett said he knew a lady who might be interested in putting up the money for Dalhousie's women's residence and would discuss it with her. He was, as usual, as good as his word. The lady was Jennie Shirreff Eddy.[23]

Bennett had known her when he worked as apprentice lawyer in Chatham, New Brunswick. She was born there in 1864, trained in Boston as a nurse, and in 1894 married E.B. Eddy, in Halifax. He died in 1906 leaving her with control of Eddy's, holding 51 per cent of the stock. She was thus very wealthy indeed, with a current income of about $250,000 per annum (roughly $2.5 million in 1992 terms). She was Presbyterian, and lived in excessive modesty at the Russell House, Ottawa, a long-established watering hole of parliamentarians which in 1919 had distinctly seen better days. Bennett knew her well, having helped her in the manifold problems of running Eddy's. He told her she should take the Dalhousie residence idea in hand and give it her family name, Shirreff Hall. He strongly suggested to MacKenzie that he go to Ottawa to see her. MacKenzie had had private opinions that Mrs Eddy was eccentric and difficult and when he was teased about the prospects of meeting her, he protested that Dalhousie would be "perfectly safe to allow me to go up and see her without fear of any entangling alliances."[24]

So MacKenzie travelled to Ottawa in March 1920. Because she was incapacitated with the 'flu, MacKenzie explained what he had in mind in letters back and forth between the Russell House and the Chateau

The Prince of Wales, later Edward VIII, laying the cornerstone of the women's residence in August 1919. By the following year it would be named Shirreff Hall. The somewhat irascible-looking gentleman on the left is MacCallum Grant, lieutenant-governor of Nova Scotia, 1916–25.

Shirreff Hall during construction. Note the white pines still standing: both President MacKenzie and Frank Darling were insistent upon retaining as many of them as possible.

Shirreff Hall, the dining room. Mrs Jennie Shirreff Eddy wanted
to avoid a barracks-like appearance, hence the alcoves.

Shirreff Hall, the Library and study room.
This was another of Mrs Eddy's decisions.

Laurier, and doubtless by telephone. On 20 May 1920 Mrs Eddy offered Dalhousie $300,000 for its women's residence. There were certain terms: the residence would be called Shirreff Hall; it would be non-denominational; she would want to approve the architect's plans. Construction should be started as soon as practicable and payment would be made $100,000 annually, beginning by 1 July 1921. MacKenzie and Dalhousie accepted with enthusiasm the largest single gift Dalhousie had ever received and the largest in Canada ever given by a woman. They used the gift as their launch for Dalhousie's Million Dollar Campaign on 1 June 1920.[25]

Jennie Shirreff Eddy was anything but a retiring widow who just paid the bills. She had certain standards for Dalhousie's young women that she wanted reflected in the residence. She wanted the dining room and servants' quarters built at once. She was dissatisfied with Darling's design for the library. She wanted fireplaces, "having regard for the climatic conditions of Halifax," which she knew well. Excavations were even halted while this impasse, in August 1920, was negotiated by MacKenzie going to Ottawa and discussing plans with Mrs Eddy and R.B. Bennett. She got her way; the library was made bigger and brighter. She suggested that there should be study rooms on the first and second floors, something quite overlooked by the men. She came to Halifax in October 1920, met the women students at MacKenzie's house, and went from there to throw a hugely successful theatre party for the students at the Majestic. She was formally thanked by the president of the Dalhousie student council between acts two and three of a production of *The Cave Girl*. She gave a speech. Canada needed educated women, she said. How they were to be educated was for Dalhousie and other universities to say. She wanted to provide a residence with some semblance to the life the girls might have had at home, not spartan but comfortable, spacious, and civilized, to round out the training the university offered. It all gave her tremendous satisfaction. Owing to illness of Halifax relatives, she was kept in Halifax several weeks longer than Dalhousie found altogether convenient; nevertheless, said MacKenzie, "I found she had very good ideas about most things and found her reasonable in all things."[26]

Construction started in the spring of 1921 as soon as the frost was gone. By that time Mrs Eddy was ill; she died on 9 August at her home in Aylmer, Quebec. The funeral was in Chatham; Bennett came from Ottawa, and Dalhousie sent its president and chairman of the Board of Governors. The will made over the balance of the $300,000 to Dalhousie, but there was more than that, given in the form of trusts. Her sister was given the income of $350,000 during her lifetime but the capital was to come to Dalhousie on her death. Shirreff Hall would open in 1923, with eighty-six girls in residence, some twenty more than expected.

Supporting the Faculty of Medicine

As Shirreff Hall was going forward, MacKenzie had on his plate a more difficult problem to resolve: the proper support and development of the Faculty of Medicine. As MacKenzie pointed out to the Carnegie Foundation, Abraham Flexner had done medical education in the Maritime provinces a great service in 1910, by exposing the considerable deficiencies of the old Halifax Medical College. But the effect was to throw a tremendous burden on Dalhousie that it was ill equipped, financially, to bear. It would have been difficult at any time to bring the Medical School up to standard; the war made it impossible, and for two reasons that pulled in opposite directions. Dalhousie's income had shrunk owing to a fall in enrolment; at the same time there were great improvements in medical techniques and practice. Dalhousie had three chairs in medicine, only one of which was endowed, and that recently, by Dr D.G. Campbell, in anatomy. It needed two additional ones, in hygiene and pharmacology, and, if possible, to get endowed the two chairs yet unfunded in physiology and pathology. The clinical facilities in Halifax were good, MacKenzie said, except in obstetrics where a maternity hospital was badly needed.[27]

Dalhousie stood in high regard at the Carnegie Foundation. They liked MacKenzie and the men they had seen of the Dalhousie board. The Scottish ambience sat well in New York. There was a disposition to believe that Dalhousie might become the Johns Hopkins of Eastern Canada, closely knit, modest in claims, good in substance. Halifax had a good nucleus, and if a medical school was needed for Canada's eastern provinces, then Halifax and Dalhousie was where it ought to be. MacKenzie went to New York in March 1918, and with Dr D.G. MacDougall again in May 1919, seeking money for the medical school. Dr H.S. Pritchett, president of the Carnegie Foundation, said he would lay the Dalhousie proposal before his own board; but there would be conditions. Dalhousie should have sufficient control over hospitals so that there would be proper access for students, and there would have to be out-patient arrangements. These did not yet exist in Halifax. Pritchett would arrange a visitation to see matters on the spot. It looked hopeful, so much so that MacDougall could scarcely contain himself until the two were outside the building. MacKenzie was more cautious and rightly so. The Carnegie trustees took no immediate action, and while there was decided sympathy, they evinced a disposition to find out if there were the elements of support for the Dalhousie Medical School in the Nova Scotia government, the Victoria General Hospital, and even among the people of Halifax.

The hospital arrangements between Dalhousie and the Victoria General had long been loose and informal. Dalhousie needed control over appointments to hospital medical staff. And then there were the students. The superintendent of the Victoria General was Wallace W. Kenney, an able layman who was a good administrator but who was averse to having medical students in his hospital. Medical students were worse than a nuisance; they were against the best interests of the hospital. In short, the Dalhousie Medical School had concessions in the Victoria General rather than rights.

Armed with this information, and with a letter from the Carnegie Foundation of 2 June 1919, MacKenzie went to Premier George Murray and laid the whole question in front of him. He listened, and gave it over to the Board of Hospital Commissioners with the intimation that he would approve whatever they would recommend. The result was a reorganization of the appointment of Dalhousie's clinical staff, passed unanimously by the Board of Hospital Commissioners on 18 October 1919: all clinical appointments would be made on the recommendation of a Dalhousie committee, consisting of the chairman of the board, the president, and the dean of medicine. Although the appointments themselves would be made by the hospital board, that was really window-dressing. In effect Dalhousie got the power it wanted over clinical appointments, and it got its medical students accepted. There would be periodic tiffs in the future, as when Dalhousie recommended a brilliant young gynaecologist, H.B. Atlee, in 1922, or when the medical students stole parts of a hospital skeleton in 1923. Dalhousie stood its ground on the first and gave way with an apology and offer to pay on the second.[28]

At Christmas 1919 the Rockefeller Foundation of New York announced it had $50 million for the improvement of medical education, Canada included. In January 1920 Campbell and MacKenzie called at New York. Two months later two Rockefeller senior officials, Dr Richard Pearce and Dr George Vincent, visited Halifax for two days to review the whole medical scene. MacKenzie wined and dined them at the Halifax Club with thirty-nine selected guests. In a day and a half they talked to the legislature, dined at Government House, gave a public lecture at a packed Strand Theatre on public health, then departed. President MacKenzie was a wreck.

Pearce and Vincent were the most reticent pair he had ever met. They offered no plans of their own; they brought forward nothing. MacKenzie, brilliantly, devised the right stance: he never mentioned money. The word "dollars" never passed his lips. He took the view that they wanted to see what Dalhousie and Halifax could do for medical education. Taciturn as the visitors were, Dr Vincent's speech on public health was brilliant. MacKenzie said he had never heard a witty and amusing speech on such a subject freighting so much information, and making the time seem like five minutes. The Rockefeller doctors left without the slightest intimation of what they might do.[29] They were, of course, experienced and knowledgeable in the ways of state governments and medical groups in the United States. They had some idea of what to expect. What they were looking for was confirmation on the ground of conclusions already tentatively reached.

Their report to the Rockefeller Foundation on 6 April 1920 was based upon what was practicable in Halifax. The Rockefeller doctors understood well enough that there was no use hoping for a Nova Scotia government grant to Dalhousie Medical School; the other colleges would oppose it unless they received something commensurate. The government could not even build an out-patient department; the country MLAs would say it was purely for Halifax's benefit and Halifax got too much from the government as it was. Based on this report, the final overall arrangements were complex but sensible and had been worked out, doubtless with suggestions from Dalhousie, between the two foundations in New York. Carnegie would give $500,000 as endowment to support chairs in Dalhousie's Faculty of Medicine, conditional on Rockefeller giving the same amount. The Rockefeller half million would be for buildings: the Public Health Centre, $200,000; Medical Sciences Building, $150,000; equipment and remodelling, $50,000; an endowment for maintenance, $100,000. Both the Carnegie and Rockefeller grants were built upon an agreement with the Nova Scotia government that it would make extensions to the Victoria General and the Pathology Building totalling $675,000.[30]

That was not the end of medical improvements. The most critical need in medical teaching in Halifax, to say nothing of the well-being of the province, was a maternity hospital. Dalhousie stepped in there as well. Learning that the Salvation Army was interested in building one, President MacKenzie and George Campbell went to New York in the spring of 1920 to ask Carnegie and Rockefeller to contribute. Neither foundation could make a contribution to the Salvation Army directly – that precedent was impossible – but both promised help indirectly through the Dalhousie Medical School. They each offered $50,000 to Dalhousie, on condition that at least $100,000 would be found by the Salvation Army. Medical students were to be allowed in the hospital on maternity cases and in the care of newborn children. Dalhousie deeded the Salvation Army a piece of land along Morris

Street west from Summer Street (in effect half of the city lot given in 1909) between Morris and College streets.

As the building of the Grace Maternity Hospital began the contractors ran into underground water and costs rose rapidly from that and other causes; before the building was half finished the Salvation Army used up all the money and had to borrow. The two foundations' money was not paid over until there was clear evidence the building was finished and furnished. That done, the money was duly paid and the Grace opened early in 1922.[31]

Premier Murray laid the cornerstone of the Public Health Clinic on 9 November 1922. The existing hospitals in Halifax had one major shortcoming: none had out-patient departments. These contributed much to the training of students in illnesses and injuries that did not need hospital treatment. President MacKenzie's speech that day reminded everyone, the premier included, how Dalhousie had been compelled to take on, and pay for, the Medical School out of its own money, hoping that eventually private help and, even more important, the government would relieve Dalhousie of the burden. That was not in sight yet. Dalhousie was still a private institution, privately endowed, beholden to no government for its funds, and rather wishing it were. It had to find its own money. Dalhousie had greatly improved the Medical School after taking it over from the old Halifax Medical College but, MacKenzie admitted, Dalhousie did all this "at the expense of the Arts and Science Faculty from the funds of which came the money to make up the relatively large annual deficit of the Medical School."[32]

Dalhousie needed a men's residence as well as a women's. Many Dalhousie students boarded at Pine Hill, which had space and not enough divinity students, but the growth of students in 1919 and 1920 forced the board's hand. The same time as the Million Dollar Campaign was launched in 1920, the board bought the Birchdale Hotel for $160,000. It was a handsome old property; the hotel itself was no longer much patronized but it was right on the North-West Arm at the foot of Coburg Road. It had 6.83 acres with a frontage along the Arm itself, and it would accommodate about forty-five students.

Dalhousie's other immediate need was for an arts building. None of the arts staff had even a room of their own, where they could work or consult with students. All they had in the Forrest Building was one small common room. The administrative offices, such as they were, had become awkward and crowded. By 1919 academic needs had become as important as dormitory needs. The decision was made at the end of 1919 to construct a building for arts that would in due course

The Studley campus, *c.* 1924. Note the elms and maples on this angled approach road to Dalhousie from Coburg Road.

revert to law, when arts got its own building sometime in the future. Hence the peculiar title, the Arts (Temporary) Building. It was anything but temporary in appearance. It was placed opposite the Macdonald Library, designed in Darling's and Cobb's best colonial style, to cost about $100,000. The cornerstone was laid by G.S. Campbell in April 1921, a well-deserved honour. And it would, many years later, become the Law School. It is now Dalhousie's University Club.

Postwar Dalhousie and the Student Christian Movement

The Law Faculty added two full-time professors, John Read ('09 and Rhodes scholar) in 1920, and Sidney Smith ('20) in 1921. In history J.E. Todd had gone overseas in 1916, ending up in India, and there were temporary replacements, one of them an Oregon Rhodes scholar. MacKenzie assumed Todd was returning, and so did Todd. He was finally demobilized after recovering from malaria in June 1919. He hoped there would be an increase in salary, for he and his family were poor, the result of two transatlantic moves. MacKenzie offered the maximum $2,500, plus 10 per cent and $500 in travel expenses, and a further vote of $1,000 to get Todd's housekeeping started again in Halifax. That was generous. Then a chair of history at Belfast opened, with more money and no perennial worry about the children's education in North America. But, Todd added, even if he did go to Belfast, "I want you to know that I shall never again enjoy such freedom & independence in my Department, such good fellowship with my colleagues, and such generous appreciation both from students & from a wider public as were mine when I lectured at Dalhousie." A month and half later Todd cabled that he had been appointed to Belfast.[33]

The board would have liked to appoint D.C. Harvey ('10 and Rhodes scholar) but Harvey was now at Wesley College, Winnipeg, and unavailable. Dalhousie were now a bit desperate, the measure of their desperation being a telegram to Harvard on 16 September 1919, the day the cable arrived from Todd. Harvard recommended George E. Wilson. He was on a Harvard fellowship, and it took an appeal to Dean Haskins and the offer of $2,500 to bring Wilson, reluctantly, off his fellowship. He walked up to Dalhousie on a fine morning at the end of September 1919; he was to stay for half a century.[34]

The Dalhousie Wilson came to was replete with war veterans, many of whom had returned from overseas with very different ideas than when they had started. Some simply wanted to get on with their lives and careers; but there were others among the veterans who now abhorred war and everything connected with war, who believed in international law and arbitration of disputes. Some had also developed some ideas about what Canadian society should be, and put emphasis on what can be called Christian socialism – the belief that Christianity, shorn of arid theological disputes, had a great message for postwar mankind: the principles of the Sermon on the Mount. Wealth represented wickedness. To be a true Christian one probably had to be a socialist. These views came to be incorporated in a group called the Student Christian Movement. It was born in 1920, out of the war and much else, and its ideas were articulated and developed by Dr Henry B. Sharman as a comprehensive, dutiful, even exacting Christianity. It was based on two questions, "Who is Jesus?" and "What is he saying?" The answers shaped one's moral code.[35]

The contrast between this new form of Christianity and the old Presbyterian one could be illustrated by old Dr Forrest at the funeral of Professor Eben Mackay, the greatly loved professor of chemistry, who died in January 1920. Much of Dalhousie crowded into St Matthew's Church for that funeral. Forrest in his eulogy pointed to Mackay's coffin and cried out, "And what is the message to you, young men, that comes from him now in that coffin? It is a clear and unmistakable one. Be ye also ready; be faithful in whatever is entrusted to you, if need be, like he was, faithful unto death." It was characteristic of the cohesion and sentiment of Dalhousie board and Senate that at the funeral the wife of the chairman of the board, Mrs George Campbell, sang a Gaelic lament.

Out of Pictou County, Mackay had taken the gold medal in chemistry at Dalhousie in 1886 and came back with a PH.D. from Johns Hopkins in 1896 as George Munro professor. He was a first-class teacher; he gave so much time to his teaching that it could be said his own work was subsumed in that of his students. And his own money as well. When Dalhousie could not afford the journals in chemistry he thought essential, such as *Zeitschrift für physikalische Chemie*, he bought them and had them bound at his own expense so that they would be available to students. "Oh well, we *had* to have them," is all he would say. He read his subject, and he imbued students with the sheer excitement of research. Mackay's was a sunny and cheerful nature; he seemed not to know envy and jealousy. He was like malleable iron, mild and strong: no one ever saw him angry. MacKenzie's private tribute was to reflect

how much of his thought he gave to the problems of the University in general, and how valuable was his counsel and judgment in all matters. I never felt that I had seen and thought of all sides of a question until I had asked Eben what he thought of it ... His was always a thought-out judgement and he was never carried away by incipient enthusiasms or chilled by difficulties and doubts.[36]

Three months after Eben Mackay's death, John Forrest himself died at the age of seventy-eight. Forrest was a man of transparent sincerity and kindliness. But he was also, as the Scots say, "a bonnie fechter," a ready and hardy fighter, but of the sort who left few antagonisms. As MacKenzie said, one never fought Forrest personally, only on ideas. He took risks. It required moral courage of a high order to throw in his lot, as he did in 1878, with Dalhousie when it seemed to be sinking. He saw the need for money and found it. Forrest chose staff brilliantly. He saw the need for law and engineering, and one may add, the need for union with King's and other colleges. When he came Dalhousie was "a neglected starveling and [he] left it a university, a source of pride to the citizens." So said MacKenzie.[37]

MacKenzie had had a strenuous several years. At one point in March 1920, he had on his plate the visit of Drs Vincent and Pearce from Rockefeller about the Medical School Buildings, having newly returned from negotiations with Mrs Eddy about Shirreff Hall; the new Arts (Temporary) Building; the need for a men's residence, and, as if that were not enough, the fallout after the King's College fire at Windsor on 3 February 1920. As he wrote to George Campbell, "Things have followed each other in such rapid succession ... that I have almost lost track of the time..." At the end of 1920 he came down with severe influenza and tired out after three years filled with problems, he could not shake the illness off. The doctors ordered a complete rest, and in January 1921 shipped him off to Florida for a month.[38]

In the autumn of 1921 Dalhousie's enrolment stood at 712 in all faculties. The big increases that began in 1919 were in fact permanent. The little college of MacMechan's youth had doubled, and as with all such linear increases, carried with it geometric consequences. Dalhousie's charm and cohesiveness of staff still survived, but new strains and new staff would make the old ways difficult to hold. There was an interesting illustration in 1916. Dr D. Fraser Harris, professor of physiology, had come in 1911 from England with fine recommendations. He was an excellent lecturer and it showed. "Physiology," he used to say, "was romance, glorious romance." But he could be a difficult colleague. In 1916 the professor of clinical medicine, Dr K.A. MacKenzie, was taken ill and Harris had to do his lectures for him. Harris asked to be paid for these extra lectures. President MacKenzie wrote back, politely enough, reading Harris a lesson in Dalhousie traditions:

It has been the permanent policy of the University so long as I have known anything about it [i.e. 35 years] to consider that the salary of a full-time mem-

Eben Mackay, McLeod Professor of Chemistry, 1896–1920.
"He was like malleable iron, mild and strong."

ber of the University covered the pay for any duty he might assume ... so that if a member of the staff undertook new work on account of stress of circumstances, like the sickness of a colleague, etc., or stayed in the city during the summer to do some special service for the University, it has always been considered that he did it to serve the University and the question of remuneration has never arisen.

Indeed, perhaps the success of this little University is in no small measure due to the spirit of that kind which has animated its staff from the very beginning of things in 1863. If we did not have this general principle I think that there would be eternal trouble and envyings and jealousies ... a thing which we have never had to contend with in my knowledge of the whole place ... Next year, as part of what I consider my war duty, I have promised Professor Bronson to take some of the work of his assistant, whom we cannot afford to pay next year.

It says much about MacKenzie's style, and charm, that notwithstanding all of that, he asked that Harris be paid the extra honorarium for the work he had done.[39]

The deaths of Forrest and Mackay marked the passing of part of an older Dalhousie. There was in both of them a surrender of ego, an ascetic contentment in work as a pleasure in itself, that was part of the old Presbyterian tradition of Dalhousie. It still retained the belief that the university's duty was to produce an aristocracy of learning, refinement, and sensibility, that a student should graduate with mind and manners civilized. Ovid was quoted from time to time, "fideliter artes emollit mores et nec sinit esse feros" (A faithful study of the liberal arts humanizes character and prevents it from being savage). In other words, Dalhousie aimed to create an intellectual elite, and it should if possible be a moral elite as well.

But less austere modes of thought and conduct were creeping in. A student from western Nova Scotia recounted in the *Gazette* how in his town anyone that went to university, went to Acadia. Dalhousie was a place for doctors, dentists, lawyers, and Presbyterians. Moreover, people said, it was "a d—ed hard place to get through," a man might have to sacrifice sport to study, unless he were really good. But Dalhousie itself could not avoid such student attitudes. One writer in the *Gazette* complained in 1921, that "where a competitive examination is the basis of judging students it is always a case of the survival of the fittest. But where is this getting us? Every year we lose some of our best athletes. We know a college is not an athletic institution, but other colleges give attendance for varsity games." A student asked to try out for the debating team said there was not enough in it for him at Dalhousie, that in this respect St Francis Xavier or some other col-

Dalhousie Student Council, 1922–3. The president was Larry MacKenzie, Pictou County, second row, third from left, later president of the University of British Columbia. Back row, extreme right, is Donald McInnes, later chairman of the Board of Governors.

lege was more generous. The *Dalhousie Gazette* observed, a little archly, in February 1923, that "following lines of least resistance makes rivers and men [run] crooked."[40]

Sports at Dalhousie had developed on sufferance. Dalhousie was a city university and in sports it showed. Neither the Parade campus nor the Forrest one, academically or physically, had much space for sports. In both there was a sort of basement room, ill-equipped, that might euphemistically be called a gymnasium. There was no university playing field at all. A form of rugby practice could be managed in space along College Street, fifty yards or so wide; but a rugby field is 75 yards wide and 110 yards long, with another 25 yards at each end. That was some 3.3 acres, equal to three-quarters of the whole area of the Forrest campus. In the 1880s and after, the Dalhousie Athletic Club rented time at the Wanderers grounds. Rugby was the game that mainly interested Dalhousie students until after the turn of the century. Hockey started in the 1890s, Dalhousie sending its seven-man team (seven until 1911) to Mount Allison in 1897, where it won, seven to four. Basketball was invented in 1891 by Dr James Naismith, a Canadian, and became popular after the turn of the century. Hockey and basketball teams at Dalhousie scrounged whatever facilities they could.[41]

Even after Studley was acquired, it took another decade, what with war and finances, to get a playing field available. There was no proper gymnasium until the late 1920s. A proposal to build a War Memorial Gymnasium was announced at the Alumni reunion of August, 1924, and it would take another few years before it was built and functioning.

Probably MacKenzie realized that the development of Studley would bring changes in its train; good administrator that he was, he anticipated some of them. Others came from forces outside Dalhousie that stirred hopes and ambitions within. The most far-reaching was the movement for university federation, by 1922 well under way.

Girls' basketball team, 1922.

· IO ·

Towards University Federation
1921–1925

The 1920 King's fire. The 1921 Carnegie report on Maritime education. A Maritime federated university. First federation meetings, July 1922. The October 1922 conference. Acadia withdraws, February 1923. King's joins Dalhousie, 1 September 1923. Mount Allison postpones federation. Central Advisory Committee and Memorial College, Newfoundland, 1924–5. Carnegie grant to Dalhousie, 1925. Some concluding reflections.

Arthur Stanley MacKenzie, Dalhousie's widower president, had two great loves: his daughter and his university. Marjorie, a graduate of Bryn Mawr, was twenty-six years old in 1922 and occasionally acted as unofficial Dalhousie hostess. MacKenzie had never returned to active physics research after 1911; Dalhousie was too poor to afford much equipment, and his replacement in physics, Howard Bronson, had come to Dalhousie knowing that, and had become a teacher more than a researcher. MacKenzie could have escaped Dalhousie gracefully; in October 1920 the National Research Council invited him to be its chairman. But he was not much drawn to the offer; the question with MacKenzie was whether his going was good or bad for Dalhousie. Dalhousie was at a stage where he seemed to be the only one who saw its final shape, and the stages by which that could be reached. So he stayed.[1]

By 1922 MacKenzie's desk was laden with serious questions; knowing that, Archie MacMechan sent the following:

> Methusaleh ate what he found on his plate,
>   And never, as people do now,
> Did he note the amount of the calorie count,
>   He ate it because it was chow.
> He was never disturbed, when at dinner he sat,

Destroying a roast or a pie,
  By the thought it was lacking in granular fat,
    Or a couple of vitamins shy.
He cheerfully chewed every species of food,
    Untroubled by worries or fears
  Lest his health should be hurt by some fancy dessert,
    And he lived over nine hundred years.[2]

MacKenzie could use that light-hearted counsel. It was not just Dalhousie; the campus was busier and more filled with students than ever, and those big new numbers produced problems. But it was university federation that had come to preoccupy him.

University consolidation, union, federation – it had names as varied as its several forms – had long been a question not far from the centre of Dalhousie's *raison d'être*. Lord Dalhousie had founded his non-denominational college in 1818 intending it as the provincial university. King's College was for Nova Scotia's Anglicans, at that time 20 per cent of the population but gradually shrinking. In 1823 union of King's and Dalhousie was proposed and accepted by both institutions, only to be blocked by the Archbishop of Canterbury. The one-college idea of the 1840s failed. The University of Halifax movement of the 1870s was an attempt, abortive in the end, to bring the Nova Scotian colleges together within a comprehensive system. There were movements for the union of King's and Dalhousie in 1884–5 and again in 1901–2. Both failed.

Some children playing with matches changed all that. They started a fire in the upper floor of the steward's quarters at King's on 5 February 1920; it caught the wallpaper and then spread via the tar roofing to other sections. The fire hydrant outside was frozen up, and by the time it was got working, the whole wooden building was in flames. By the next morning all that stood amid smoking ruins were four chimneys and the stone walls that divided the bays, along with the stone chapel. Few were yet ready to concede what the Halifax *Herald* said that day, "it remains true – and the churchmen feel it with a sense of chill – that old King's has passed away."[3] King's struggled manfully to keep going, using whatever was left and leasing Windsor houses for residences. There was talk of rebuilding, even talk of an appeal to the Carnegie Foundation.

Having for the past ten years received applications for money from Maritime province colleges for every kind of project the ingenuity of administrators could devise, the Carnegie Foundation of New York in 1921 decided to make a general inquiry as to the state of higher education in the Maritime provinces. It would suggest directions for a constructive overall policy. Dr William S. Learned of the Carnegie Foundation staff, and Kenneth C.M. Sills, president of Bowdoin College in Maine, were asked to undertake it, and they visited the provinces and colleges in October and November of 1921.

The study that emerged over that winter concentrated more upon Nova Scotia than the other provinces; that was where most of the colleges were and most of the requests originated. It was a cool, dispassionate, and judicious report. Learned and Sills praised much. They appreciated the quality of the Maritime people and their traditions, they admired unreservedly the best in the public school system, especially the high schools at Truro and Halifax where the senior mathematics was better than in most American schools. The same was true of Latin grammar. Nonetheless, Nova Scotia public schools were weak in science and social science. Maritimers, especially Nova Scotians, excused weaknesses on the ground that obstacles were not a bad thing for students to learn to surmount; there was virtue in being challenged and in meeting challenges. On the other hand, Learned and Sills believed not enough thought was given to the obligation of provincial educational systems to fit a student to handle his "duties as an intelligent citizen."[4]

The Nova Scotian colleges all admitted students with incomplete matriculation, some with as many as three subjects lacking, on condition that they finish them before the BA was awarded. Most of this incomplete work was in mathematics and Latin. Dalhousie offered a class in elementary Latin to help remedy weaknesses, which met for four hours a week. In 1922–3 it had sixty students.

Learned and Sills gave high marks to Dalhousie. They pointed out that Dalhousie's religious orientations still followed Lord Dalhousie's liberal principle: President MacKenzie was Anglican; of the thirty-four professors only thirteen were Presbyterians, nine were Anglicans. Half the student body were Presbyterians, 14 per cent Anglican, 13 per cent Roman Catholic, 9 per cent Baptist.* Acadia had a better library than Dalhousie, which had only 32,000 volumes and no permanent profes-

* The religious specificity of the other colleges in 1922–3 was:

Mount Allison	238 students	62.6%	Methodist
Acadia	278	75.9%	Baptist
King's	83	77.1%	Anglican
St Francis Xavier	201	95.5%	Roman Catholic

The University of New Brunswick, with 138 students, had the most even religious distribution among the Maritime colleges: Anglicans 28%, Baptists 24%, Presbyterians 21%, Methodists 14% and Roman Catholics 13%. (See DUA, POC, A-706; A-195, C.C. Jones to ASM, 22 Feb. 1923.)

sional librarian. Learned and Sills were severe on all the colleges for lack of libraries and of science equipment and, not least, for low academic salaries. What had been a Munro professor's substantial salary in 1885, $2,500 a year, had ceased to be so by 1921. Although some salary increases had been given, the endowment for them did not yet exist. The maximum salary level for good senior men should be, they said, close to $6,000 per annum. With existing endowment there was no prospect of affording able new men. The Nova Scotian colleges, Dalhousie not excluded, were coasting on the loyalties of old and faithful staff, some of whom were worth retaining, some not. Thus, underfunded, undermanned, under-equipped, with no money at all from the Nova Scotian government, Nova Scotia's colleges were fundamentally in parlous condition, struggling not so much to meet national standards as to survive. They were unable to compete with other Canadian universities; even Dalhousie, weighed down by the heavy costs of medical education, was in some difficulty. Thus, said Learned and Sills, "to seek to perpetuate present arrangements ... is foregone defeat." They recommended a scheme they called Confederation of the Colleges, using funds not to extinguish colleges but to bring them onto one campus where their best teachers could collectively be brought to bear on one group of students. For a long time past, said the report,

Dalhousie has figured as the prospective host, and has offered such generous terms of participation that, as was discovered by repeated interviews, the college has actually educated her alumni and friends to the unselfish and far-sighted view that Dalhousie would undergo almost any sacrifice of prestige, control, and even of name, if thereby the educational facilities of the province could be placed upon a permanently satisfactory and well-ordered foundation.[5]

Each constituent college, once moved to the Halifax campus, would keep its name but would hold in abeyance its degree-granting powers, except in theology. A new Board of Governors would be chosen, to which Dalhousie would relinquish all her buildings and endowments, retaining only Shirreff Hall and University Hall as its own college residences. The Arts Faculty of this new Maritime university would be bifocal, as at the University of Toronto: certain subjects would be taught and supported by the university, and others offered within the federating colleges. Subjects such as languages or history would be college subjects, science would be a university field. Thus the scheme would establish a Halifax university of several colleges, each of which would retain its original denominational base; perhaps even a Presbyterian college could be created from Dalhousie and Pine Hill. The best professors would be retained, ineffective ones gradually retired. The new Maritime university so created might begin to rival McGill or Toronto in quality, if not in numbers.

President MacKenzie saw the Carnegie report in February 1922 as a confidential draft and liked it very much. He thought that a federation scheme equitable to each college would not be difficult to produce; the question was mainly one of will. If the denominational colleges did not want it, there was nothing Carnegie or Dalhousie could do.

One point MacKenzie made to Learned was that Dalhousie's experience suggested that wealthy men and women preferred to give their money to a larger institution rather than a small denominational one. Two of Dalhousie's largest Nova Scotia donations in recent years were from Senator Dennis, a Baptist ($100,000 for a chair in political science and government), and W.A. Black, a Methodist ($60,000 for a chair in commerce). Mrs Eddy's $700,000 came from her Presbyterian background.[6]

For Dalhousie loyalists, however, the college federation scheme posed difficulties. Looked at critically, it boiled down to this: the central Maritime university, in which Dalhousie would be only one of several on a central Board of Governors, would be an institution to which Dalhousie would give everything it had – grounds, buildings, endowment, equipment – and into which the other colleges would put nothing. They would keep their names and their endowments for themselves. Even the cost of moving to Halifax and putting up new buildings there would, it was presumed, be subsidized. Seen that way, college federation looked to many Dalhousians, old and new, as unreasonable, giving far too much and getting far too little. R.B. Bennett warned that the Dalhousie alumni he had talked to in Ottawa and the West had "a very great opposition to the blotting out of the name 'Dalhousie'." That was the most disheartening element, the loss of the old Dalhousie name, traditions, and educational ideals for which they had all struggled for so long. Dalhousie had to hold its alumni; that could not be done if it were to make all the sacrifices, while the only sacrifice the other colleges had to make – a big one, perhaps – was one of location. Could the name Dalhousie be kept, perhaps, and given to the new overall Maritime university? The colleges could retain their names, and the arts college to be created from Dalhousie's Arts Faculty could be called University College, rather like the one at the University of Toronto. Dalhousie University could thus be the umbrella name. Suggestions to this effect were made by MacKenzie to President Robert Falconer of the University of Toronto, an old friend, on the basis of the confidential draft of the Carnegie report. Would Falconer write the

Carnegie people with those considerations in mind?[7] When the report finally appeared in May 1922, that part dealing with Dalhousie's name and its preservation was probably the result of those MacKenzie-Falconer representations. Thus the *quid pro quo* for Dalhousie's giving up its grounds, buildings, and financial resources to a wholly reconstituted university was that the new university would be called Dalhousie. As Learned and Sills put it, "it would be a well-deserved tribute if the distinctive university structure that may be created should bear the Dalhousie name, representing as it would that common service to all for which in principle Dalhousie College was originally established."[8]

Implied rather than stated in the whole endeavour was the most important consideration of all: once federation of the Maritime colleges was achieved, it could be confidently predicted that at last the Nova Scotian government would be brought into the funding of college education. Medicine and science, which cost Dalhousie so much, would at last be subsidized, not by the ignominious process of scrounging private money to sustain them, but by the only body capable of doing it properly. As MacKenzie put it to Dalhousie students at New Year's, 1923, Dalhousie favoured "some scheme of [college] confederation because she sees that would bring state aid."[9]

Learned and Sills estimated that such an institution as the new Maritime university, whatever it was called, would need some $4.5 million in endowment. Half of that was already on hand, that is, the $2.5 million in the endowments of the five colleges. The report said nothing of what the Carnegie Foundation itself had in mind, should the scheme be accepted. But President MacKenzie knew roughly how the land lay. The Carnegie idea was to give each college (Acadia, King's, Mount Allison, and St Francis Xavier, and it was presumed Dalhousie too), a grant of $500,000, of which $200,000 would be used for putting up a new building on or near the Dalhousie campus. It was a big scheme, and two new aspects made it more cogent than ever before: outside money to the tune of about $2.5 million would be put into it; and, as MacKenzie put it to Falconer, "the approaching, if not present dissolution of King's."[10]

After the 1920 fire King's was having a difficult time. It asked for and got an informal meeting in February 1920 with Dalhousie, kept as quiet as possible at King's request. Negotiations then broke off, perhaps owing to Carnegie's provision of an emergency grant of $20,000 for 1921. In February 1922, as Dalhousie was beginning to assess the draft Carnegie report, the King's board officially requested formation of committees to discuss federation with Dalhousie. The Carnegie Corporation thought this might be a useful beginning, a nucleus that would attract others. It did not seem so to MacKenzie. He told Carnegie on 20 February that while his board members seemed able to contemplate the big federation scheme and even "the passing practically away of the name of 'Dalhousie'" with a surprising degree of equanimity, there was no enthusiasm for the same sort of sacrifice in a federation with King's alone. There seemed to be no point in an expensive central superstructure if only King's was to be added. Dalhousians, as MacKenzie put it, "cannot see that the addition of a weak sister like King's was sufficient reason for trying to merge the two into a new institution." Moreover, King's had so little money that in Halifax it could not support more than divinity and build its classrooms. If King's were to insist upon Dalhousie and King's going into a new central university, the discussions would not, in MacKenzie's opinion, go very far.

On the other hand, Dalhousie did not wish to undercut in any way the larger federation movement: "We are going into the whole question with purely one aim in mind, viz.: – to better the higher educational position in these Maritime Provinces, and anything that really looks as if it would solve that situation we will go into with full heart." In the meantime, whatever Dalhousie and King's did, they would notify the other colleges what was afoot. Dalhousie had to avoid at all cost anything that was not above board. The colleges were very touchy, MacKenzie told Learned, their presidents especially, and he had had some recent experiences of it.[11]

Learned in New York accepted MacKenzie's reasoning. It seemed sensible, therefore, that while Dalhousie should not reject King's initiative, it should treat it in the context of the wider scheme of federation. The wisdom of this proceeding was illustrated when Dr Tompkins, vice-president of St Francis Xavier, and Dr Cutten of Acadia were in town, and when told of the meeting with King's, seemed keenly to regret it, as prejudicing the larger scheme. MacKenzie was away, but G.F. Pearson, vice-chairman of the Dalhousie board, was able to quiet such fears. After that, MacKenzie wrote all the presidents personally explaining what Dalhousie was doing in discussions with King's.[12]

These took place in March. Not much was accomplished from Dalhousie's point of view. King's brought a plan for federation with Dalhousie: after Dalhousie gave them a site, they would come to Halifax with whatever they had, dividing power equally, in policy and administration, over a new central university. To MacKenzie it seemed that King's did not understand their relative positions at all. In any case, it was agreed that further talks be postponed until after the Carnegie report was actually released and the general federation discussed. Privately MacKenzie told the Carnegie Corporation that the

King's proposals had been "unreasonable," almost foolish. Dalhousie did not want to tell King's that directly, but since Carnegie were subsidizing King's to the tune of $20,000 a year just to keep it going, they could tell King's how unreasonable their proposals were.[13]

Four college presidents (St Francis Xavier, uncertain and divided, did not attend) met on 22 March to exchange information over what confederation would mean to each. Most felt they should know what the financial inducements from Carnegie might be. Pursuant to the need for more information, Learned called a meeting in New York for 13 April. G.F. Pearson warned MacKenzie that he should not assume that the other colleges were "meet for repentance." They might enjoy "picking the carcase of Dalhousie, but they fear the old bird might in some manner come to life again and gobble them all up." There were also some points that MacKenzie should make privately to the Carnegie people ahead of time. An important one was that Dalhousie could not be a Presbyterian college in the new central university, as hinted in the Learned-Sills report. If it were to have a college at all, it would have to be a non-sectarian one. Moreover, before much more time was spent on federation, King's, Acadia, and Mount Allison should get their governing bodies to accept the basic principle of college federation. Pearson claimed that Dr Cutten of Acadia had a scheme up his sleeve for a three-college Protestant federation based at Wolfville. Pearson put it to MacKenzie, "If Dalhousie is to be sunk 'without a trace' we must at least ensure that the entity which takes her place shall have a Board of Governors chosen irrespective of the religious affiliations of its members and solely on merit."[14]

The discussions at the Carnegie Corporation took the whole day. Carnegie took the position that small grants had been useless, that big money was needed to effect big changes. That was, indeed, why the Maritime situation appealed to them.

MacKenzie was then asked to state Dalhousie's position. He said that Dalhousie's charter of 1863 contemplated just such a union as the Carnegie report had suggested, and current conditions enjoined it more than ever, with university costs rising so rapidly. One point he did emphasize: that Dalhousie's commitment to university federation was predicated on the central Board of Governors being absolutely non-sectarian. Dr Borden of Mount Allison then bluntly asked how much money the Carnegie Corporation was willing to provide to effect so desirable a change. Carnegie refused to be specific about that, saying only they would give generous support. The next move was up to the colleges.

The first meeting between King's, Acadia, Mount Allison, and Dalhousie was called for 7 July 1922. King's brought a long document they wished to discuss clause by clause, but MacKenzie thought they should deal instead with general principles, and he got his way. As to the basic principle of college federation, Mount Allison expressed the hope that it could be put through. Acadia refused to be drawn out as to its general position. St Francis Xavier was not present, owing to the antagonism of President MacPherson to federation. His vice-president, J.J. Tompkins, however, was favourable. So were Halifax Catholics. Pine Hill, the Presbyterian theological college, was not invited. MacKenzie believed this was a mistake and said so. At that G.B. Cutten of Acadia remarked that if they would also invite the Masons and the Oddfellows, he would accept the presence of Pine Hill. King's also objected to Pine Hill. Nevertheless, the invitation to Pine Hill was eventually accepted.[15]

The group then appointed two committees, one to study a constitution for a federated university, the other the financial implications. MacKenzie was on the constitutional committee, which met at his house on 17 July with three other university presidents – Boyle of King's, Borden of Mount Allison, and Cutten of Acadia, along with Dr Kent of Pine Hill. The University of New Brunswick was not represented.

By this time the Carnegie suggestion that the name of the proposed central university be Dalhousie was public knowledge. This did not seem to create a problem, nor did the principle of selecting its new Board of Governors on the basis of merit. The split came over the inclusion of a non-denominational college within the federated university. Dr Cutten said no one would come to such a college, to which Dr Boyle added, "Except atheists." The problem really was Dalhousie's desire for its own college. It was one thing for Dalhousie to go out of business completely leaving only her name behind, like the Cheshire cat's smile, as the mark of its contribution to Nova Scotia's higher education; that is what the Carnegie federation plan envisaged, what MacKenzie and the Dalhousie Board had accepted, and what the other colleges expected. It was rather another to have a University College that reproduced Dalhousie's principles, perhaps even ambience, under a new name. Such a possibility has been alluded to in the Learned-Sills report, but in the form of a Presbyterian college with Pine Hill participating. Two things made a Presbyterian college impossible. One was the proposal, already in train, of union between the Presbyterian and Methodist churches as the United Church of Canada. In that case Mount Allison might well take up Dalhousie's Presbyterian constituency. The second was Dalhousie's long and honourable non-sectarian tradition that it had fought (and bled) for since 1818. Dalhousie was,

University federation meeting at Dalhousie, July 1922. President MacKenzie is standing in front of the pillar to the left of the door. On his right is Dean Howard Murray. G.F. Pearson is front row, extreme left. G.S. Campbell is just to the left of the pillar to the right of the door. President Borden of Mount Allison is last row, extreme right. President Cutten of Acadia is third row from the front, extreme right. President Boyle of King's is front row, third from right. The lady in the second row is Eliza Ritchie.

after all, only 50 per cent Presbyterian, and it had always stood to its founding principles.

But to some others it seemed that Dalhousie was having it both ways – its name on the central university, and a non-denominational college to help perpetuate its principles. In that context Cutten's position at the constitutional committee meeting is partly understandable, if his rudeness was not. His attitude was, according to Pearson, one of "carping criticism approaching nastiness." He accused Dalhousie of selfishness and of plotting to bring the whole federation movement to naught; under the guise of self-sacrifice, Dalhousie was giving up nothing and really gobbling up the other colleges. Cutten kept interrupting MacKenzie's exposition of the confederation proposal and at the end of it half rose, buttoned his coat, and said if that was Dalhousie's proposal, he was going home to Acadia. Much as MacKenzie "felt like allowing him to go, and even supplying any necessary additional momentum," to do so would have been playing Cutten's game. The other presidents made no move to follow Cutten, and he stayed. If college federation in Halifax failed, with King's on the verge of collapse, and Mount Allison's financial position desperate, it was possible that Acadia could become the major Protestant college. Mount Allison shared some of Cutten's suspicions of having Dalhousie coming at them from two positions, at the top with the name and the site, and at the bottom as University College, the latter bringing with it all of Dalhousie's non-denominational traditions. In Cutten's and Borden's view, there might well be too much Dalhousie.[16]

There is not a scrap of evidence to support such a distorted interpretation, and it seems far from the spirit that animated MacKenzie and Pearson. But as Learned conceded, it was a possible gloss on Dalhousie's strong support for college federation. By the autumn of 1922, however, Cutten was appointed president of Colgate University, a Baptist institution in Hamilton, in upstate New York, and Pearson was hopeful his replacement would prove less querulous. Learned made the point privately to Pearson that to an outsider all the results Carnegie wished for could be achieved simply by adding outside colleges to Dalhousie as it stood. That was precisely the suspicion in Cutten's mind. It was, of course, impossible politically. Learned also felt that Dalhousie exaggerated its need for a non-denominational college. All the colleges accepted students regardless of religious affiliation. What made the non-denominational college important with the Carnegie officers was the hope of including the University of New Brunswick.

President C.C. Jones of UNB thought the Learned-Sills report had been too critical of New Brunswick education, though in fact Nova

Scotia fared rather worse. In any case, the circumstances of UNB fitted none of the others since it was provincially supported and the others were not. Still, money talked, even in New Brunswick, and if the participation of UNB were contingent upon the establishment of a non-denominational college in Halifax, then so be it. "I would go far to make it possible," Learned said. And don't rush things, he told Pearson. If you go slowly enough, the Catholics may come on side, and perhaps Acadia, with its new president, will be more favourably disposed. The Carnegie Corporation was really tempted by this great opportunity: "After surveying so attractive a possibility as this, I am sure the Corporation would be sorry to pass it by and leave these six struggling institutions to continue in their present helpless straits."[17]

By October 1922 Dalhousie had worked out what it would surrender in buildings and endowment to the central university. With buildings it was virtually the whole campus, for Dalhousie would give those that were related to the central university's future functions – that is, Science, Medicine, Law, and Dentistry. On the Forrest campus Dalhousie would surrender the Forrest Building, and the new Medical Sciences Building and the Public Health Clinic, both as yet unfinished; on the Studley campus, the Science Building, the Law (temporary Arts) Building, and the Macdonald Memorial Library. Dalhousie's endowment would be split. Science, medicine, and law endowments, about $800,000, would be given to the central university. The rest, about $700,000, the endowment used for arts, would be reserved for the non-denominational college. It was that proposal, and the Carnegie grant to go with it, that was tempting UNB.

By the time of the next full meeting, the importance of college federation had broadened. It was a big conference of some fifty delegates that met in Province House on 24 October 1922. Newfoundland sent three representatives, including its minister of education. New Brunswick was represented by its premier, W.E. Foster, Nova Scotia by its premier, E.H. Armstrong, a cabinet minister, R.M. Macgregor, together with Dr F.H. Sexton, head of the Nova Scotia Technical College, and Dr Melville Cumming, principal of the Nova Scotia Agricultural College. Prince Edward Island sent a representative. Then there were the colleges: Acadia with its acting president, Dr F.E. Wheelock, and three others; King's with R.E. Harris, chairman of the board and chief justice of Nova Scotia, who chaired the meeting, with Archbishop Worrell, President Boyle and five others. Mount Allison was represented by President Borden and five others; UNB by President C.C. Jones and one colleague; Pine Hill by Dr Clarence Mackinnon and four others. St Dunstan's of Prince Edward Island sent a representative. Nor was this the end, for the archdioceses of Halifax and

Newfoundland between them sent six representatives. Only St Francis Xavier was missing.

The constitutional committee duly reported, recommending the principle of a federation of colleges at Halifax under the name Dalhousie University, with a non-denominational college included in the federation. Much of that day, however, was spent in discussing that terrifying Dalhousie name. As W.W. Judd of King's remarked, the debate over "what the name of this [central] University should be, epitomizes the whole situation." MacKenzie and Pearson were furious with King's and Acadia, for both colleges had agreed in committee to accept the Dalhousie name, and then in full conference went against it. Privately MacKenzie told Robert Falconer afterward, "You see what a breed of cattle we were dealing with, really not gentlemen and Christians, but slippery and hypocritical tricksters. We had to keep our tempers and patience during the conference, but we were driven to the very limit of endurance in doing it." [18] What MacKenzie said in conference was much milder: that it would be advisable to wait until the baby were born before trying to name it; that if a satisfactory college federation could be evolved, if everyone went into it, and if Nova Scotian government support were assured, Dalhousie would not ruin such a fair prospect by cavilling at the name. On the other hand, neither would the Dalhousie representatives commit themselves to giving it up. The names of the university, and of the non-denominational college, were in the end left to a future meeting. Pearson pointed out that the six colleges – UNB, St Francis Xavier, Acadia, Mount Allison, King's, and Dalhousie had 1,759 students between them, of which 40.5 per cent were at Dalhousie. The total endowment of all six colleges was about $3,350,000. That was the same as the endowment of Bowdoin College in Maine, which had only five hundred students.

The conference had its difficulties. There was a great need to bring all the delegates' information to the same level; politicians were fearful of saying too much. Nevertheless, by the time of the evening meeting of that long day, there were hopeful signs. The University of New Brunswick declared that it was not impossible that part of its work, in senior years especially, might conceivably be moved to Halifax; the Catholics of the Halifax archdiocese and of Newfoundland declared positively they wished to have a constituent college; the Newfoundland government delegates promised to recommend a government grant for the central university. Prince Edward Island remained mute, but it was apparent that St Dunstan's were thinking along the same lines as the delegates from Newfoundland. John Bell, the premier of Prince Edward Island, was soon in touch with President MacKenzie for details. [19]

The two committees on constitution and finance were now merged, and the new committee met on 22 and 23 November in Halifax. As Pearson had earlier pointed out, for each college there was "an infinitude of detail which every College is entitled to be consulted about." Nevertheless, considerable headway was now made, and a scheme of college federation unanimously adopted and presented to another full conference held on 12 December. A small group went to New York to meet with the officers of the Carnegie Corporation on 21 December. Three weeks later, on 12 January 1923, the executive of the Corporation agreed to give $3 million to the project, provided all colleges joined. The boards of King's and Mount Allison ratified the arrangement, as did Dalhousie's board on 29 January. Dalhousie added a note of gratitude "to the impartial, helpful and sympathetic attitude of the officers of the Carnegie Corporation."

Dalhousie's position in this considerable enterprise was one of enlightened interest in developing Maritime higher education; but there was more to it than that. What was driving MacKenzie and Pearson was the distinct realization that Dalhousie was simply out-running its resources; that the $2.5 million it had acquired by luck and a good reputation in the 1920 campaign had been valuable in meeting the doubling of its students, but even with that it was increasingly difficult to consolidate these gains. None of the changes, said President MacKenzie, had had much effect in improving the education the university was offering. If student numbers had doubled, costs had quadrupled; furthermore, the

breadth and scholariness of the training we are giving has not greatly improved ... With all we can reasonably hope for from our friends in the future, we cannot see how we can do more than hold our own. And it is not good enough. Do the officials of other colleges see better things in their cases? ... Confederation would first of all make for economy, and secondly it would force adequate state aid. Hence its necessity.

Some, MacKenzie said, raised the bogey of the big college and praised the virtues of small ones. Smallness alone was not a virtue, and the Maritime population was hardly large enough to sustain a big college. It is often pointed out, he said, how well Maritime students do when they have gone abroad to other universities. It was, indeed, "astonishing what we have accomplished in the past with so little. It was more due, however, to the students than to the Colleges ... I do not for a moment contend that what we did was not good; but it was *not good enough*." And the opportunity now presented for Maritime higher education would not come again.[20]

The whole outcome, however, hinged upon Acadia. The Acadia board met on 16 February 1923 and declared that "it was in the interests of Higher Education that Acadia should continue to carry on her work in Wolfville, as in the past, and not enter the proposed Federation." On the 19th, the Halifax *Chronicle* came out with a blistering editorial against the Acadia board. Its actions would not, said the *Chronicle*, "be supported by any substantial body of informed opinion." No one could deny the right of the Acadia board to say no to federation, but to base that refusal on the grounds of the best interest of higher education was absurd. No responsible university president could say that university federation was not in the best interest of higher education in the Maritimes. That was G.F. Pearson speaking, no doubt, but there were certainly important Baptist laymen in Halifax who opposed the action of the Acadia board. Their pressure could well be felt when the Baptist conference met to ratify the Acadia decision. On the other hand, there was much talk in Baptist circles of the spiritual values of higher education whose roots, it was believed, were in the soil of Wolfville, and Wolfville alone, and which could never grow in Halifax. That sentiment was the one that prevailed at the Baptist conference at Moncton in April. It declared that it was not in the interest of Baptist ideals that Acadia join university federation.[21]

Federation was now fairly halted. The University of New Brunswick had indicated in January that it would not join, as had St Francis Xavier. But those defections, although unfortunate, were not crucial. New Brunswick had always been doubtful. As for St Francis Xavier, if the Halifax archdiocese were in favour, federation could survive uncertainty in Antigonish. But Acadia's withdrawal, while it did not sink the project, left it without momentum, awash in the slow, receding swells of a project long laboured over and now perhaps moribund. MacKenzie was puzzled as to what his next move should be. President Borden of Mount Allison and his board still supported the idea; even with Acadia out, the Methodist Board of Education believed that King's, Mount Allison, and Dalhousie could still join. Hopes were not at an end, but they sagged in the absence of drive from any quarter. Dalhousie wanted it, but she was thought to be *parti pris*. President Borden would not, perhaps could not, move actively.

King's parlous circumstances now enjoined action. It sent a delegation to New York in April 1923 to tell Carnegie that something had to be done at once. What emerged in New York was an interim plan of union between King's and Dalhousie, to be effective within a few months, but not precluding King's joining a college federation should that eventually be resuscitated. But the Carnegie Corporation were not going to give any more money to keep King's alive at Windsor, as they had been doing to the tune of $20,000 a year since 1921. If King's wanted Carnegie money to continue, they would have to move to Halifax. MacKenzie, in New York just before the King's delegation arrived, suggested ameliorations of the proposed Carnegie terms. Carnegie were going to offer King's $600,000 as endowment on condition the college would find another $600,000. MacKenzie suggested King's would have difficulty raising that much and recommended the smaller sum of $400,000. And there was another Carnegie condition that MacKenzie succeeded in having eased. Carnegie wanted to insist that King's be not allowed to give separate classes to its own students but that all classes be held in common to students of both Dalhousie and King's. MacKenzie suggested that King's be allowed to offer separate freshman classes; that would allow their student body to acquire some solidarity and their staff to become acquainted with King's students.[22]

Neither MacKenzie's interventions nor his familiarity with the Carnegie terms was known to King's officials. On their return from New York, they asked for a conference with Dalhousie, to meet on 16 May 1923. Before that happened, however, the Anglican archbishop published in *Church Work* the minatory suggestion that if "Dalhousie is determined to take advantage of the present economic weakness of King's and push it to the wall crushing out all that King's holds dear," then the King's alumni, and the Anglicans of Nova Scotia, would have to rise, rally round and defend the integrity of the old college. But Dalhousie had not even approached King's on any ground other than to offer temporary help in 1920 after the fire; MacKenzie found Archbishop Worrell's message incomprehensible, not to say querulous. President Boyle of King's explained that the archbishop was trying to patch things up within King's Anglican constituency, fractured as it was. But he admitted the archbishop's language was unfortunate; in particular the verb should have been in the subjunctive, not the indicative mood, and should have read, "if Dalhousie *were* determined..." So said Boyle. But that minor, though significant, rendering of the verb left "a feeling of intense indignation among the friends and supporters of Dalhousie."[23]

Dalhousie insisted that Mount Allison attend the King's-Dalhousie meeting on 16 May so that they could keep in touch with developments. When the two committees, King's and Dalhousie, met that day, to Dalhousie's great surprise King's laid out a new and quite preposterous scheme of federation, with a central university and two colleges, one that in no way resembled the Carnegie scheme that King's had already accepted in New York. That presentation taxed MacKenzie's patience to the limit. King's had to be brought down to earth. He asked if this strange scheme was King's understanding of what they had already agreed to in New York. There was a gasp from the King's committee. "Do you *know* those terms?" they asked. There could in fact be no federated university between Dalhousie and King's. There would have to be some sort of union, and it would have to be on terms that King's divided counsels found difficult to accept. What they had agreed to in New York did not sit well in Windsor.[24]

Thus negotiation of the terms of association between Dalhousie and King's went through a number of vicissitudes. King's wanted to keep its teaching of history, psychology, and philosophy independent, supposing that Dalhousie's instruction in those disciplines to be unorthodox. Dalhousie held to the Carnegie principle of a curriculum common to all students. Another wrinkle King's had in mind was to permit the whole Dalhousie-King's affiliation to be cancelled by either party on a year's notice. MacKenzie wasn't having that. "I hope," he said, "we have not been spending all the time and thought and energy which we have given to this matter to make a temporary arrangement which may be upset at any time on a year's notice. Our Board would not have anything to do with this scheme of affiliation unless it were a permanent one until the larger and much-desired federation can be brought about."[25]

King's found all this trying and difficult. Finally the board met on 27 July 1923 and agreed to affiliation with Dalhousie. Although the *Chronicle* said it was unanimous, President Boyle remarked to MacKenzie, a little sadly, that it was very far from unanimous. The divisions on the King's board did not inspire him as president with any enthusiasm for the work that now devolved upon him. Nor would he stay. He had come to King's in 1916, and would resign in 1924. MacKenzie was not without sympathy for King's reluctance to give up a style and way of life that had endured, somehow, for well over a hundred years. He knew well enough, as he told the *King's College Record*,

the strength of the associations which bind one to the old walls, the old spot, the old ideas and the old ways. I can well remember the keen regret with which we who had been students in the original Dalhousie College on the Parade saw it removed to Carleton Street. We learned later to look upon it as a blessing. But I still cannot forgive the act of vandalism of those who tore down that beautiful old building to make way for the present City Hall.[26]

The Agreement of Association negotiated between Dalhousie University and the University of King's College became effective on 1 Sep-

tember 1923. King's was to move to Halifax and locate on or near
the Dalhousie campus. If King's wished it, Dalhousie would provide,
within three years, a piece of the Studley campus, up to five acres.
King's could erect whatever buildings it thought desirable, using an architectural style in keeping with Dalhousie's. Plans of King's buildings
were to be approved by Dalhousie's consulting architect, Andrew
Cobb. King's would hold in abeyance its power of granting degrees,
except in divinity, which it retained. It would continue to hold its own
funds and endowments. The new Carnegie money, $600,000, would
not go to King's directly but to a trustee, since the capital, ultimately,
would be for the joint benefit of both Dalhousie and King's. All appointments to the King's teaching staff would require Dalhousie's
prior approval; the departments to which they would be appointed
would be governed by the needs of both Dalhousie and King's. The
curriculum was to be the same at both institutions, as were salaries.
King's staff would have the same rights to membership on the
Dalhousie Senate as Dalhousie professors. King's name would appear
on the BA and B.SC. Dalhousie degrees that King's students were
awarded. All students, except those in divinity, would register with
Dalhousie and pay Dalhousie fees. Dalhousie would in turn pay those
fees to King's, retaining fees paid for Dalhousie science classes and $25
per student for the use of Dalhousie facilities by King's students. King's
would transfer its library to Dalhousie, the books being marked as
King's property. Dalhousie would give King's two vacancies on its
Board of Governors. King's Law School at Saint John would be discontinued as soon as the students enrolled finished their courses.
King's would retain the right to enter the college federation scheme, if
and when it were revived, as a corporate and sovereign entity. In that
case its affiliation with Dalhousie would cease.

Behind King's reluctant move to Halifax lay stark necessity. King's
Anglican constituency simply was not strong enough to keep it going
once the main buildings had been lost by fire. Carnegie offered
$600,000 as new endowment on condition that King's find an addi-
tional $400,000 from Anglicans. That was not easy; it would take un-
til the end of 1927, and it was a near thing. In the meantime, Carnegie
agreed to pay King's the interest on that sum per annum, $30,000, as
salaries for professors to keep King's going. In July 1923 King's asked
for a lease on Birchdale, the Dalhousie men's residence. Dalhousie was
loath to give up Birchdale, its only men's residence and only direct access to the North-West Arm; the fact that there was really nowhere
else for King's to go settled the matter. King's got an initial two-year
lease on Birchdale at $6,000 a year, but it would hold Birchdale until

October 1930. That was when the new King's buildings, on the five-acre piece of land on the north-west part of Studley, were finally opened.[27]

The arrangements with Dalhousie were not all sweetness and comfort to King's. It chafed under its new regime – in effect, a condition of quasi-tutelage – and it found old habits difficult to shake, for it had long been able to decide things for itself. Now it would search for (and find) chinks and holes in the affiliation agreement by which its own life could be expanded and nourished, something of its old independence recovered. It was not easy for either King's or Dalhousie. For the affiliation was not, it could not be, a union of equals. In September 1923 King's had, to MacKenzie's surprise, only fifty-one students. They could fill Birchdale, their new home, but Dalhousie counted over twelve times that many. For its part, Dalhousie found King's new president, Dr A.H. Moore of Montreal, rather less tractable than President Boyle had been.

Seven weeks after King's affiliation with Dalhousie took effect, Mount Allison's Board of Regents announced that they would take no further action on university federation until a decision was made about the union of the Presbyterian and Methodist churches. This led to the union of Mount Allison's Methodist theological faculty with the Presbyterian one at Pine Hill in Halifax. Mount Allison's postponement of federation did not mean rejection, as Dr J.C. Webster, on the Mount Allison board, pointed out to MacKenzie in October 1923. Two years later, in June 1925, church union took place, and in December Pine Hill became the theological college of the United Church of Canada in the Maritimes, with Mount Allison as its arts and science college.[28]

Dalhousie's gloss on these later events was that Mount Allison was having it both ways: staying where it was in Sackville, New Brunswick, and getting (or trying to get) Dalhousie's Presbyterian students. Dr Webster believed that it was a sordid and unworthy attempt by Mount Allison's new president, G.J. Trueman, to use church union to keep Mount Allison exactly where it was. By that time, Mount Allison was sliding away from its commitment to federation; though not yet public knowledge, those on the inside knew. Slowly, with painful reluctance, officials at the Carnegie Corporation watched the project for which they had given so much energy, had promised so much treasure, cloud over with Maritime sectarianism. College federation by 1925 was dying.[29]

But it left a bantling behind. Out of the three years of resolutions, talk, and treachery, there came something less grandiose than federation, but something that worked. Its cumbersome name was the Central Advisory Committee on Education in the Maritime Provinces and Newfoundland, and it reported to the Carnegie Corporation. It would bring into being the Memorial College of Newfoundland.

In December 1923 the Carnegie Corporation received a request from Newfoundland about funding a junior college at St John's. Newfoundland had tried it in 1917 and in 1919 without success, but its needs had been mentioned briefly in the 1922 Learned and Sills report. Just before Christmas of 1923 the premier of Newfoundland, William Warren, an old friend of G.F. Pearson, was visiting in Halifax. He was taken around Dalhousie and was much impressed. "This is the place for our Newfoundland boys," he told Pearson. Dalhousie heartily approved of a junior college in St John's and embraced the further Carnegie idea that current discussions on federation could be used to generate a Maritime province committee that could advise the Carnegie Corporation on educational requests from all four Atlantic provinces. As G.F. Pearson wrote to F.P. Keppel, "We sadly need in these Provinces some body or group thoroughly representative of all interests which could discuss and come to agreement upon our problems of higher education and bring harmony and co-operation where distrust and competition now prevails."[30]

There were meetings in New York in January 1924 about forming such a committee. But dangerous Dalhousie could not take such an initiative. Nor should the Carnegie Corporation. In March 1924 the presidents of Dalhousie, Mount Allison, and Acadia met on neutral ground in Truro. Neither Trueman of Mount Allison, nor F.W. Patterson, the new president of Acadia, liked the idea of a committee of that kind; there was too strong a whiff of federation about it. In the meantime, however, the Carnegie Corporation had decided, in principle, to give the Newfoundland Council for Higher Education $15,000 a year for five years to establish a junior college, and needed a Maritime province committee to decide on conditions and the appropriateness of such a grant. After much discussion of ways and means, the Central Advisory Committee came to be a committee of presidents, MacKenzie going to some trouble to get Acadia to agree to serve on it. Patterson thought that the Carnegie Corporation was giving Newfoundland too much money, and MacKenzie was concerned about political conditions in Newfoundland. As he put it to Keppel in New York, "The lack of responsibility, not to use a stronger word, which the men in political life in Newfoundland have shown for some years makes it necessary ... that there should be no chance for the frittering away of the Corporation's money or the utilization of it for other purposes." The Carnegie Corporation took the loftier, if less realistic, view that it was unwise to appear to distrust those to whom the money was being given, once it was allocated.[31]

These preliminaries were the background to the first official meeting of the Central Advisory Committee, which was held at Dalhousie on 28 October 1924. There was still uneasiness about federation, as if, like a spectre, it threatened to exude from those sinister Dalhousie walls! But the meeting went well. Father Vincent Burke, the deputy minister of education of Newfoundland, and the moving spirit in St John's behind the push for a junior college, came to Halifax to answer questions. The presidents of UNB and Nova Scotia Technical College moved that the committee recommend to Carnegie that $15,000 a year be given for five years towards the establishment of a junior college at St John's. It passed unanimously and was, of course, accepted in New York. It was a very important gift. The Carnegie grant for the next five years would represent 40 per cent of Memorial's annual income.[32]

The next determination of the Central Advisory Committee that day was also dramatic. For the past four years, while federation and King's amalgamation was afoot, Dalhousie had forsworn any further financial campaigns. And Dalhousie had been running into difficulty, from the usual, and still often unexpected, result of growth. The university was falling steadily behind on current account. Law and dentistry deficits were $2,000 a year each, and while the deficits in medicine were being covered by income from Rockefeller and Carnegie money, that situation could not continue. New members of staff and the full expenses of running the two new medical buildings would bring Dalhousie's deficit for 1924–5 to $19,000. Patterson of Acadia moved that the Central Advisory Committee recommend that the Carnegie Corporation wipe out Dalhousie's accumulated deficit and give it an annual grant of $20,000 for the next five years. It was open, generous, and it delighted MacKenzie. Said Patterson (via MacKenzie's paraphrase),

Dalhousie was carrying a burden of education which was really a state duty, and the least the rest of the colleges could do was to aid us [Dalhousie] in every way to get help in carrying this burden, because it was for the good of every college, of every denomination and of every part of the Maritime Provinces.

That motion was approved by every member of the committee. MacKenzie positively beamed at the good will evinced around the table that day in the Dalhousie board room. He explained to Keppel,

"I think it marks a turning point in the relations of our various institutions. They have in this manner proved that they can throw petty jealousies aside in the interests of higher education."

MacKenzie hoped the resolution would have effects in New York. It did. Within a week came a telegram from Keppel offering Dalhousie $90,000 for the past deficits and $20,000 a year for five years for the future ones. MacKenzie wired Pearson in Montreal the news, adding, "Bring wherewithal for celebration." Pearson wired back at once, "Hurrah! Leaving tonight to join in..." Thus Pearson arrived at the president's old house on Hollis Street bearing his Montreal liquor. The Carnegie offer would be effective in just over seven weeks, at the beginning of the new year.[33]

There was more to come. In November 1929 Carnegie told MacKenzie that, as of 1 July 1930, Dalhousie would be given $400,000. It was the capitalization, calculated from 5 per cent, of the $20,000 per year that Dalhousie had been receiving since 1925. R.M. Lester, of the Carnegie Corporation, wrote in 1930 that sending that money gave him "almost as much pleasure as to sit out on Square Lake with you, Hughie [a guide?], and the obliging fishes." MacKenzie was touched by the spirit that animated Lester's letter, and replied how typical it had been of Dalhousie's happy experience with everyone at Carnegie.[34]

As to college federation, in July 1929 the Carnegie Corporation's offer of $3 million to fund university federation in the Maritime provinces finally lapsed. College federation was dead. Probably the Carnegie Corporation underestimated the depth and intensity of Maritime sectarianism and the devotion of religious constituencies to the colleges for which they had made such sacrifices. Acadia went along with the movement towards federation because it was sponsored by a powerful and rich American foundation whom it would be unwise to offend by outright refusal. But, as Joseph Howe remarked a little ruefully in 1849, "You may withdraw your public money, but there will be more socks and mittins [sic] knit in the hills of Wilmot – more tubs of butter made – more fat calves killed – and more missionary travellers sent through the country – and Acadia college will stand on the hillside in spite of withdrawal of our [Government] grant."[35] President George Cutten's defence of Acadia, querulous as it often seemed to others, had the virtue of a strong perception of those Baptist realities which were, in their own way, as admirable as they were sometimes restrictive.

If naïveté were to be attributed, Dalhousie might not be exempt. Perhaps Dalhousie's necessities, the desperate need to bring government funding to bear, with Carnegie's willingness and generosity, drove Pearson and MacKenzie to nourish the hope that even should Acadia refuse federation, provided Mount Allison and the Halifax Roman Catholics accepted it, Acadia might be forced eventually to come in. As it turned out, Acadia, like the others, was left to stand on its own on the hillside at Wolfville, its back to Halifax, facing Blomidon and the great valley over which it was still academic master.

University federation was shown to be unrealizable, and perhaps for a long time. King's move to the Dalhousie campus was not the nucleus of federation. It brought an accretion of needed academic strength to Dalhousie in arts, but King's also created difficulties of its own over points in the 1923 agreement. Dalhousie now gathered itself together and began to address its own concerns, its own neglected constituency.

Conclusion

Dalhousie was proud of what it had accomplished since 1863; Dalhousians could see whence their university had come. But they found it less easy to perceive the distance Dalhousie still had to go. A visitor from a European university coming to Dalhousie in the 1920s would not have been impressed. The raw North American environment, its society commercial to the core, made North American universities, especially Canadian ones, training grounds more for the professions and the job market than places for the development of the mind, or the enlargement of the soul. Too much of North American, and Dalhousie's, education was forced feeding. For seven months a year students were driven by lectures, tests, examinations; once released from university exigences in April, they tended to revert to their primordial state. Their summers were usually lost, academically speaking, to other pursuits, often in finding enough money to finance their next year. That in itself was not without concomitant virtues. But it was taken up as if the worth of a summer's reading had not been grasped, nor that longer perspective, the cost of losing it, ever fairly weighed.

The European system took the long view. Examinations were at the end of three or four years' work, when the students thought they were ready; in Britain examinations were usually both written and oral; on the Continent they were often just oral, the questions drawn from a hat, the candidate dressed with whatever formality she or he could muster, and in full public view of students, family, friends. If candidates survived that ordeal, intellectually and psychologically, it could be reasonably concluded that they had the strength to serve the state, embassy, or civil service, fit eventually to help run an empire, domestic or abroad.[36]

Henry James felt the gap between North America and Europe as few other North American writers and he measured it ceaselessly. An example of reverse shock is in President MacKenzie's contemporary, Principal William Hamilton Fyfe of Queen's University, appointed in 1930. Fyfe came from England; he found Queen's students dreadful and the professors almost as bad. Fyfe believed university education was for an aristocracy of mind and spirit that loved learning and scorned utility. Queen's students, probably not unlike Dalhousie's, he found inactive physically, spoon-fed intellectually, confusing memorizing with knowing, rejoicing mainly in gladiatorial spectacles like football games. Lowering the academic ladder to help such students was for Fyfe a betrayal of what a university stood for. Queen's was, declared Fyfe, a place where false pearls were thrown before real swine.[37]

The answer to such views was the vast difference between Canada and Europe. In English Canada there was little social foundation for the type of student Principal Fyfe sought at Queen's, or that MacKenzie might have liked at Dalhousie. The difference between Fyfe and MacKenzie was that Fyfe was a British intellectual who after six years at Kingston was glad to return to Britain as principal of the University of Aberdeen; MacKenzie had grown up in Nova Scotia with Canadian realities. He and others worked to raise Dalhousie to levels of learning and aspiration recognizably international. The academically gifted of Dalhousie's students would have cherished such ideals; certainly MacKenzie never really despaired of the hope that enough learning, and even more the love of it, would develop in students to justify, perhaps even occasionally to glorify, the name of Dalhousie University.

Appendices

APPENDIX I

THE DALHOUSIE ACT OF 1863

*26 Victoria, chap. 24, 1863. An Act for the regulation
and support of Dalhousie College.*

Whereas it is expedient to extend the basis on which the said College is established, and to alter the constitution thereof, so as the benefits that may be fairly expected from its invested capital, and its central position may, if possible, be realized, and the design of its original founders as nearly as may be carried out.

Be it enacted by the Governor, Council, and Assembly, as follows:

1. The Board of Governors now appointed, consisting of the Honorable William Young, the Honorable Joseph Howe, Charles Tupper, S. Leonard Shannon, John W. Ritchie, and James F. Avery, Esquires, shall be a body politic and corporate, by the name and style of the Governors of Dalhousie College at Halifax, and shall have and exercise all usual powers and authorities as such, and have the title, control and disposition of the building on the Parade at Halifax and of the property and funds belonging to the said College, and held for the use thereof by the present Governors; and all vacancies at the Board shall be filled up on recommendation of the remaining members thereof by the Governor in Council, and any of the Governors shall be removable by the Governor in Council, at the instance of the Board of Governors.

2. Whenever any body of Christians of any religious persuasion whatsoever shall satisfy the board that they are in a condition to endow and support one or more chairs or professorships in the said College, for any branch of literature or science, approved of by the Board, such body in making such endowment to the extent of twelve hundred dollars a year, shall have a right from time to time, for every chair endowed, to nominate a Governor to take his seat at the Board, with the approval of the Board of Governors and of the Governor in Council, and shall also have a right, from time to time, to nominate a Professor for such chair, subject to the approval of the Board of Governors; and in the event of the death, removal or resignation of any person nominated under this section, the body nominating shall have power to supply the vacancy thus created.

3. The same right of nominating a Professor from time to time shall belong to any individual or number of individuals who shall endow to the same extent and support

a chair or professorship, and to the nominee of any testator by whose will a chair or professorship may be so endowed.

4. The Governors shall have power to appoint and to determine the duties and salaries of the President, Professors, Lecturers, Tutors and other officers of the College, and from time to time to make statutes and bye-laws for the regulation and management thereof, and shall assemble together as often as they shall think fit, and upon such notice as to them shall seem meet for the execution of the trust hereby reposed in them.

5. The said College shall be deemed and taken to be a University, with all the usual and necessary privileges of such institutions; and shall have liberty within themselves of performing all scholastic exercises for the conferring of such degrees, and in such manner as shall be directed by the statutes and bye-laws.

6. No religious tests or subscriptions shall be required of the professors, scholars, graduates, students, or officers of the College.

7. The internal regulation of the said College shall be committed to the Senatus Academicus formed by the respective chairs or professorships thereof, subject in all cases to the approval of the Governors.

8. The legislature shall have power from time to time to modify and control the powers conferred by this act.

9. The acts heretofore passed in relation to Dalhousie College are hereby repealed, except the act passed in the fourth year of his late Majesty King George the Fourth, entitled, "An Act authorizing the lending a sum of money to the Governors of Dalhousie College, and for securing the repayment thereof."

APPENDIX 2

AGREEMENT OF ASSOCIATION BETWEEN

DALHOUSIE UNIVERSITY AND KING'S COLLEGE

1 SEPTEMBER 1923

This agreement made this first day of September, in the Year of Our Lord One Thousand Nine Hundred and twenty-three.

Between the Governors of King's College, Windsor, a body corporate under the provisions of Chapter 66 of the Acts of the Legislature of Nova Scotia for the year 1853, (hereinafter referred to as "King's College" or King's)

of the One Part

And the Governors of Dalhousie College, Halifax, a body corporate under the provisions of Chapter 24 of the Acts of the Legislature of Nova Scotia for the year 1863, (hereinafter referred to as "Dalhousie")

of the Other Part

Whereas, the University of King's College located at Windsor in the Province of Nova Scotia was founded in the year 1789 and in the year 1802 was, by Royal Charter, endowed with university powers and has since the said date to the present time functioned as a university granting degrees in Arts, Science, Law and Theology, and by said Chapter 66 was incorporated as aforesaid as a body politic and corporate having a common seal and succession forever under the name of "Governors of King's College, Windsor", and so incorporated was granted all the usual privileges of a university with the powers of administration necessary for the management of its affairs and executing the purposes of its foundation;

And whereas Dalhousie University was, in the year 1818 at the instance of Lord Dalhousie, then Governor of the Province of Nova Scotia, established in the City of Halifax in said Province where it has since exercised the usual powers and privileges of a university for the study of Arts and Science, as well as giving instruction in the professional courses of Law, Medicine, and Dentistry, and by Chapter 24 of the Acts of the Legislature of the Province of Nova Scotia for the year 1863, the Board of Governors of the said University were created a body corporate under the name and style of the "Governors of Dalhousie College, Halifax," with the powers necessary for the conduct of the affairs of the said University and the carrying out of the objects of its foundation;

And whereas there are in the Maritime Provinces of Canada other institutions of learning having and exercising university powers and privileges in addition to the institutions of learning above named;

And whereas it has for a long time been thought by many interested in liberal and professional education in the said Maritime Provinces that the circumstances existing in such Provinces render it expedient that some method be adopted by which such educational work might be carried on with greater efficiency than is possible under present conditions;

And whereas it is thought by the parties to These Presents that the cause of higher education in the Maritime Provinces would be much advanced by the adoption of a scheme of federation in which the resources of the various existing institutions of learning may be so combined that the duplication of effort incident to the maintenance of a number of colleges and universities might be avoided and an institution established capable of supplying the requirements of the people and at the same time preserving, so far as possible, the traditions of the constituent colleges;

And whereas commissioners appointed by the Carnegie Corporation of New York to investigate and report upon the educational resources and needs of the institutions of higher learning in the Maritime Provinces of Canada in a report to the said Carnegie Corporation recommended the federation at Halifax aforesaid of the said institutions of higher learning;

And whereas from time to time various efforts have been made to promote some scheme of federation, and particularly at a conference of the representatives of the various institutions held at Halifax, December 12th, A.D. 1922, at which a plan of federation was unanimously agreed to contingent upon the acceptance of the same by the authorities of the various institutions having power in that behalf and the obtaining of adequate government or other financial assistance;

And whereas it is found to be at present not practicable to bring about a complete federation of all the said institutions as proposed in said plan contingently agreed upon as aforesaid;

Now therefore the parties to this Agreement having in view the considerations above set out and desiring to promote, and as a step toward, such federation and in the hope that the same many ultimately be established, have agreed upon the terms of association following, the same to be binding on the parties hereto until the consummation of a further federation of the existing colleges, institutions and universities upon the basis proposed by the representatives at the conference above referred to or upon some other basis of union or confederation which may be hereafter agreed to.

1. King's shall remove from Windsor to Halifax, and locate on the Dalhousie campus, or on a site adjacent and convenient thereto.

2. King's shall erect whatever buildings it considers desirable or necessary for the housing of the students enrolled with it, for the teaching of Divinity and such first year Arts classes as are referred to in Section 18, and for devotional and recreational purposes. The general architectural features (type of architecture, materials, etc.) if erected on the Dalhousie campus, shall be in keeping with the buildings already erected at Studley, and meet with the approval of the consulting architects of Dalhousie University.

3. Nothing in these Terms of Association shall affect the right of King's to the absolute control or disposal of its present buildings and grounds at Windsor.

4. King's shall transfer to Dalhousie its library collections other than those in Divinity, except such as may be set apart by the Dalhousie University Librarian for the library of the residence of King's. All books retained in the University Library shall be catalogued and marked as the property of King's.

5. King's shall transfer to Dalhousie all its scientific apparatus and collections, with an inventory thereof.

6. King's shall hold and administer all its present funds and endowments and any additions which may be made thereto.

7. The Carnegie Corporation shall be asked to transfer to a trustee to be mutually agreed upon by King's and Dalhousie, any moneys which it may give to King's for the joint benefit of King's and Dalhousie. The form of the Deed of Trust shall meet with the approval of the Governing Boards of King's and Dalhousie. Such Deed of Trust shall contain the provision that should King's cease involuntarily to function continuously according to these proposed Terms of Association such trust fund is to become the absolute property of Dalhousie.

8. King's shall apply the income from all funds it may receive in the future for endowment of instruction in other than Divinity for the joint benefit of Dalhousie and King's.

9. King's shall have absolute control over the appointment and payment of its administrative and executive officers, its staff in Divinity and all necessary employees for the maintenance of its buildings and grounds.

10. King's shall retain its corporate entity with its desired form of government and its name.

11. King's shall hold in abeyance its power of granting degrees except in Divinity.

12. King's shall hold its present funds and endowment intact and expend only the income arising therefrom.

13. King's may use all or part of the income arising from its present funds and endowment, not now expended for the teaching of Divinity, for administrative and maintenance purposes, or for further teaching in Divinity.

14. King's shall use the income from the funds it may receive from the Carnegie Corporation, as under Section 7, and until such funds are received the amount given

by the Corporation as an annual equivalent for the payment of professors or instructors in Arts (as opposed to Science) subjects.

15. No appointment of any professor or instructor, except in Divinity on the foundation of King's shall be made by King's until the approval of the Board of Governors of Dalhousie University of the proposed appointee shall have first been secured.

16. The departments in which such professors or instructors may be appointed shall be determined, firstly, by the need for enlargement of the staff of the present departments of Dalhousie University to take care of the combined student body of Dalhousie and King's, and, secondly, by the provision of departments not now existing, or inadequately existing, therein. The following are the most needed appointments based on these criteria at the present time, (1) Classics, (2) Moderns, (3) English and Rhetoric, (4) English Language and Literature, (5) Mathematics, (6) History, (7) Economics (and Sociology), (8) Applied Economics, (9) Mathematical Physics, (10) Psychology, (11) Pedagogy, (12) Librarian, (13) Sociology, (14) Accounting, (15) Commerce (Law), (16) Romance Languages, (17) Canadian History, (18) Philosophy.

17. The same scale of salaries as may from time to time prevail in Dalhousie University shall be adopted by King's for all appointees on the Foundation of King's, except in Divinity.

18. All the classes in the Faculty of Arts and Science given by the staff of Dalhousie University and all the classes given by the staff on the foundation of King's except in Divinity, shall be open on equal terms to the Students of Dalhousie and King's, except that the Arts staff supported on the foundation of King's may give instruction to the first year students of King's only in Latin, French, English, Mathematics, and History to the exclusion of other students.

19. The curriculum and academic regulations of the Faculty of Arts and Science of Dalhousie University shall govern the work given by the staff on the foundation of King's, except in Divinity, and the first year work referred to the Section 18 shall be identical in the two institutions.

20. Scholarships, prizes, etc., now awardable by King's in Arts subjects shall not be affected by these Terms of Association.

21. The name of King's College may appear on the BA or B.SC. Diploma granted by Dalhousie University when the recipient has been a student enrolled in Arts at King's during his course.

22. Undergraduate, but not Special, students registered in Arts or Science at King's previously to May 1st, 1923, shall be at liberty to proceed to their degrees under the regulations now in force in King's and receive their degrees from King's. If such undergraduate students elect to proceed to their degrees in Dalhousie University they shall receive *pro tanto* standing in Dalhousie for work already done in King's.

23. Graduates in Arts or Science of King's shall be eligible to proceed to the corresponding Master's degree in Dalhousie University on the same conditions as graduates of Dalhousie.

Those graduates in Arts or Science of King's who have already received approval of their candidature for the M.A. or M.SC. degree at King's shall be at liberty to proceed to those degrees and receive their degrees from King's.

24. Dalhousie University shall conduct all matriculation and other examinations in Arts and Science for the students of both institutions, but King's shall have the right

to conduct matriculation examinations in June, 1924, unless Dalhousie University shall make provision for such examinations.

25. (a) Dalhousie, if so desired by King's within three years from date, shall convey to King's a portion of the present "Studley" campus, not exceeding five acres, for the purpose of King's establishing itself thereon, on the express condition that, should King's cease involuntarily to function continuously according to these proposed Terms of Association such ground and the buildings thereon shall revert to Dalhousie University, and Dalhousie shall, if so desired by King's, pay King's as compensation for the buildings a sum of money to be fixed, in default of agreement by arbitration, on the basis of their then value to Dalhousie for University purposes. King's shall not place any mortgage or other encumbrance on such ground or on the buildings thereon.

(b) In the event of King's taking part in a Confederation such as that embodied in the report of the Conference of Universities on December 12th, 1922, the fore-going provisions shall apply *mutatis mutandis* to King's in its then relationship to the Central University.

26. Dalhousie University shall find means to make two vacancies in the Board of Governors and nominate to the Governor-in-Council persons to fill such vacancies after consultation and agreement with a committee of three appointed for such purpose by the Governor Board of King's, and their successors shall be appointed in the same manner.

27. The staff appointed on the foundation of King's, except in Divinity, shall have the same rights to membership on the Senate and Faculty of Arts and Science of Dalhousie as members of the staff of that university.

28. All Students, except Divinity Students, shall register in Dalhousie University, and pay to that University the Registration fee.

29. Arts and Science students of King's shall enroll in King's but no charge therefor shall be made.

30. Male Students of Dalhousie University in any faculty, may, at the discretion of King's, enroll in King's for residential purposes only, and in such case shall be subject to the discipline of that institution.

31. King's shall be responsible for the discipline of all students enrolled therein, except in such matters as, in the opinion of the Senate, affect the general good of the University (which shall be under the Senate) and may require all such students to attend College Chapel or other religious excercises.

32. King's shall fix its own charges for board and lodging in the residences conducted by it.

33. The Bursar of Dalhousie University shall collect all tuition fees, except in Divinity, from all students on the basis of the regulations of Dalhousie University. He shall pay over to King's the fees paid by those students enrolled in Arts and Science in King's except as follows:

(a) He shall retain the fees paid for all Sciences classes, also

(b) A sum of $ 25.00 for each such student enrolled in King's to cover use in common of University Buildings, campus, libraries, and general University expenses and incidentals. This amount shall be subject to change as experience and equity warrant.

Note: With regard to (a) it is to be understood that this statement of the amount to be retained for science classes holds only for the year 1923–24. On account of the high cost of giving instruction in Science as compared with Arts, the amount retained by Dalhousie for each Science class must be re-adjusted as an investigation of the account books of the University warrant as equitable. King's must contemplate sharing equitably with Dalhousie the augmented cost for staff, apparatus and buildings made necessary by the addition of King's students to those of Dalhousie.

34. As soon as the present students enrolled in King's School of Law at St. John, N.B., shall have completed their courses, such School shall be discontinued by King's.

35. Nothing in these Terms of Association shall compromise the right of King's to take part as a separate and sovereign entity in negotiations to enter a federation along the lines embodied in the report of the conference of December 12th, 1922, as soon as such federation is feasible through adequate financial support from governmental or other agency.

36. This Association shall begin September 1st, 1923.

37. This Agreement of Association shall terminate only in the case of the federation referred to in Section 35 coming into existence or in the event of King's ceasing involuntarily to function continuously according to these proposed Terms of Association.

38. These Terms of Association may be altered at any time by mutual consent.

In witness whereof The Board of Governors of Dalhousie University have caused the corporate seal of said University to be hereunto affixed and these Presents executed on its behalf by George S. Campbell, Chairman, and Colonel W. Ernest Thompson, Secretary, of said Board of Governors; and the Board of Governors of King's University have caused the corporate seal of said University to be hereunto affixed and these presents executed on its behalf by the Most Reverend Clare L. Worrell, Archbishop of Nova Scotia, Chairman, and Reverend Dr. Voorhees E. Harris, Secretary of said Board of Governors, the day and year first hereinbefore mentioned.

Signed Sealed and Delivered in the presence of	The Board of Governors of Dalhousie College
(Signed) Evan P. Wainwright	(Signed) G. S. Campbell, Chairman
	(Signed) W. Ernest Thompson, Secretary
	(Signed) Clare L. Worrell Archbishop of Nova Scotia Chairman Board of Governors, King's College
	(Signed) Voorhees E. Harris Secretary of the Board of Governors of King's College

APPENDIX 3

ENROLMENT, 1863–4 TO 1924–5

From 1863–4 to 1898–9 Dalhousie grouped its student lists into Undergraduates, those proceeding to a degree, and General, those not doing so. During this period non-degree students were roughly half of the regular undergraduates. In this list, however, no distinction is made between the two types of students. Enrolment in special afternoon and evening classes, laid on for the Halifax public, has not been included.

The distinction between regular Undergraduates and General students continued in law and medicine, although by the 1920s the latter's numbers were much reduced and they were then called Special students.

	Arts and Science	Law	Medicine	Engin.	Dentistry	King's	Total
1863–4	26						26
1864–5	40						40
1865–6	56						56
1866–7	54						54
1867–8	53						53
1868–9	58		21				79
1869–70	64		24				88
1870–1	61		26				87
1871–2	72		26				98
1872–3	73		26				99
1873–4	78		29				107
1874–5	87		35				122
1875–6	98						98
1876–7	100						100
1877–8	93						93
1878–9	91						91
1879–80	90						90
1880–1	87						87
1881–2	116						116
1882–3	140						140
1883–4	140	55					195
1884–5	141	57					198
1885–6	114	50					164
1886–7	128	46					174
1887–8	144	47					191
1888–9	151	57					208
1889–90	137	67	25				229
1890–1	163	67	41				271
1891–2	170	66	38				274
1892–3	155	60	38				253
1893–4	156	59	38				253

	Arts and Science	Law	Medicine	Engin.	Dentistry	King's	Total
1894–5	217	53	46				316
1895–6	216	60	50				326
1896–7	222	67	65				354
1897–8	242	54	77				373
1898–9	228	46	76				350
1899–00	198	36	67				301
1900–01	212	46	106				364
1901–02	231	42	92				365
1902–03	231	57	81				369
1903–04	252	66	58				376
1904–05	256	59	46				361
1905–06	193	68	44	60			365
1906–07	213	50	42	58			363
1907–08	235	72	67	61			435
1908–09	260	67	69	63	5		464
1909–10	299	73	60		6		438
1910–11	262	68	71		11		412
1911–12	294	60	72		17		443
1912–13	269	60	78		13		420
1913–14	279	72	72		13		436
1914–15	260	78	70		17		425
1915–16	228	39	72		18		357
1916–17	170	27	71		18		286
1917–18	176	19	79		22		296
1918–19	186	22	94		27		329
1919–20	391	72	142		53		658
1920–1	407	86	165		56		714
1921–2	417	92	175		64		748
1922–3	443	79	201		67		790
1923–4	482	68	159		50	51	810
1924–5	516	58	166		34	43	817

Sources: Dalhousie *Calendars*, 1864–5 to 1925–6; *Presidents' Reports*, 1911–12 to 1922.

APPENDIX 4

ORIGINS OF DALHOUSIE STUDENTS

AVERAGE PERCENTAGE BY DECADE

	1863–70	1871–80	1881–90	'91–1900	1901–10	1911–20	1921–30
	%	%	%	%	%	%	%
Annapolis	2.4	0.8	1.6	1.6	0.4	1.6	0.8
Antigonish	1.6	0.8	0.8	1.6	0.8	0.4	–
Cape Breton	2.0	3.6	4.4	2.8	5.2	11.6	11.2
Colchester	13.6	12.2	8.4	9.2	8.4	3.2	8.0
Cumberland	1.6	2.0	2.4	4.4	2.0	4.0	3.6
Digby	–	1.2	–	1.2	1.2	0.8	0.8
Guysborough	0.4	0.4	2.0	0.8	2.0	0.4	–
Metro Halifax	28.0	32.8	30.0	32.4	35.2	33.2	33.2
Halifax Co.	2.4	0.8	1.6	2.4	3.2	1.6	2.8
Hants	1.2	3.2	4.8	2.8	2.0	2.4	2.4
Inverness	4.0	1.6	2.4	2.4	1.2	3.6	0.8
Kings	3.6	3.6	3.2	2.4	3.2	2.0	0.4
Lunenburg	0.8	0.8	2.4	0.8	2.4	4.0	2.4
Pictou	22.8	17.8	15.2	8.0	10.4	6.8	7.6
Queens	–	1.2	0.8	0.4	1.2	0.4	–
Richmond	1.2	–	2.0	2.4	1.2	0.8	–
Shelburne	–	1.2	2.0	1.2	0.4	0.8	0.4
Victoria	–	1.2	2.0	1.6	2.4	2.4	0.8
Yarmouth	0.4	0.8	1.6	1.6	–	2.4	1.6
Sub-Total							
Nova Scotia	86.0	86.0	87.6	80.0	82.8	82.4	76.8
New Brunswick	2.8	5.6	6.0	6.0	6.4	5.6	8.0
PEI	7.2	6.4	4.4	5.6	3.2	2.0	4.4
Newfoundland	0.8	–	–	1.2	0.8	3.6	2.8
Sub-Total							
Atlantic Prov.	96.8	98.0	98.0	92.8	93.2	93.6	92.0
Other Prov.	0.8	0.8	1.2	0.4	1.2	2.0	3.2
USA	0.4	0.8	–	1.2	0.8	1.6	2.0
BW Indies	0.8	–	0.8	0.8	–	2.0	2.8
Other	1.2	0.4	–	4.8	4.8	0.8	–
TOTAL	100.0	100.0	100.0	100.0	100.0	100.0	100.0

Sources: Dalhousie *Calendars*, 1864–5 to 1925–6; *President's Reports*, 1911–12 to 1924–5; David Andrews, "Trends in the Enrollment of Dalhousie University, 1863–1962," unpublished paper for History 327 in 1970, PBW Archive.

APPENDIX 5

TWO DALHOUSIE STUDENT SONGS

In cold print, without music or a properly raucous setting, student songs can look silly. "There's not a flaw, flaw, flaw/ In the boys in Law, Law, Law..." Still, one ought not to underestimate old memories, old loyalties. When R.B. Bennett visited Dalhousie in 1934, forty-one years after his graduation, to the parting cheers of the students, the prime minister replied, with a smile,

> One, two, three,
> Up-i-dee,
> Dalhousie!

Two songs from around 1906 can stand on their own legs, even without the music:

ENGINEERS' SONG

> Transits, levels, tapes and chains,
> Engineers!
> Dynamos, bridges, turbines, cranes,
> Engineers!
> Who was it drained away the flood –
> Engineers!
> Dammed the Nile to save the mud –
> Engineers of Dalhousie.
>
> Who build walls to balk the sea –
> Who drink their fill of T.N.T.
> Who pulled Jonah out of the whale
> Built the ark that Noah sailed –
> Engineers of Dalhousie.
> Who really love the girls the most –
> Engineers!
> Men who do and never boast –
> Engineers –
> Who was it put the heat in H ——
> Slammed the door and rang the bell –
> Engineers!
>
> Who'll go to Heaven when they die –
> Engineers!
> Who'll grow wings and learn to fly –
> Engineers!
> Who will keep the Golden Gate,
> And swear at those who come in late –
> Engineers!

Y.M.C.A.

I'm a meek and humble Freshman,
From a Cape Breton home I steer.
I've always thought it a dreadful sin
To look at a glass of beer.
But now I'm down at Dalhousie,
My life's both bold and gay,
For I've joined the gang of terrible toughs,
  Dalhousie's Y.M.C.A.

Yes, now I am the gayest sport
That ever walked the town.
It takes a mighty cantankerous Prof. to
  dare to call me down.
And I drink my glass, and I hug my lass,
And I turn night into day,
When I'm off with the gang of pirates
  known as Dalhousie's Y.M.C.A.

Now if I had a barrel of rum
And sugar three hundred pound,
With the college bell to mix it in,
And the clapper to stir it round,
I'd stand on the top of the Citadel
And loudly I would say,
Come, drink to President Forrest and
  Dalhousie's Y.M.C.A.

Bibliographic Essay

This essay is an introduction to the sources for Dalhousie's history. Many of these are cited in detail in the notes. Primary sources, of course, comprehend Dalhousie's official records, the minutes of the Board of Governors from 1818 onward, and the minutes of Senate from 1863. These are by no means as complete as one might wish; university bodies are adept at concealing, or even omitting, real difficulties. They usually offer bland versions instead. Other than those, the university kept no official records until 1911, deeming board and Senate minutes sufficient. Hence the *Dalhousie Gazette*, started by students in 1869, is of fundamental importance, especially so prior to the establishment of the President's Office Correspondence (POC) in 1911. That was begun by President A.S. MacKenzie and is now housed in some forty-three large boxes in the Dalhousie University Archives (DUA). It is the single most important source for Dalhousie's history from 1911 to 1963.

Lord Dalhousie's papers, at the Scottish Record Office in Edinburgh, are considerable. He was Lieutenant-Governor of Nova Scotia from 1816 to 1820, and Governor General of Canada from 1820 to 1828; his papers are valuable not only for Dalhousie's and Nova Scotia's history but Canada's as well. Especially interesting are the three volumes of *Dalhousie Journals*, edited by Marjory Whitelaw. The first one is devoted to Nova Scotia (Toronto: Oberon Press 1978). The whole of Lord Dalhousie's Canadian correspondence has been microfilmed in fifteen reels by the National Archives of Canada (NA). The personal papers of Thomas McCulloch at the Public Archives of Nova Scotia (PANS), Joseph Howe (NA), and Charles Tupper (NA) are referred to in the notes.

Of Dalhousie presidents before A.S. MacKenzie, only Thomas McCulloch left papers; MacKenzie's are by no means ample. The most comprehensive set of private papers are those of Professor Archibald MacMechan, Munro Professor of English, at DUA. MacMechan's own essays about Nova Scotian and Dalhousie history are labours of love, wrought with care by a consummate stylist: *The Life of a Little College and Other Papers* (Boston: Houghton Mifflin 1914); *Old Province Tales* (Toronto: McClelland and Stewart 1924); *The Book of Ultima Thule* (Toronto: McClelland and Stewart 1927); *There Go the Ships* (Toronto: McClelland and Stewart 1928). They may now seem a little old-fashioned; Victorian is what they were and what MacMechan was too.

Dalhousie is frequently mentioned in Halifax newspapers. The newspapers are very extensive, and no historian, or two historians, could search them through from 1818 to 1925. The best that can be done, at least in this book, is give an irregular and uneven sampling, when men and issues appeared to warrant it.

Secondary sources have served Dalhousie and its history well, though not sufficiently comprehensively. Two good ones, George Patterson's *A History of Dalhousie College and University* (Halifax: Herald Printing 1887), and D.C. Harvey's *An Introduction to the History of Dalhousie University* (Halifax: McCurdy Printing 1938), are both by Dalhousie graduates, 1882 and 1910 respectively. Both do not go beyond the 1880s. Harvey's is done with diligence and scholarship, written in an elegant, succinct style. Not for nothing was he Dalhousie's Rhodes scholar in 1910. Patterson's was written at an earlier stage in life, but has details found nowhere else. John Willis wrote *A History of Dalhousie Law School* (Toronto: University of Toronto Press 1979), a delicious mixture of shrewdness and sentiment, showing at every stage Willis's Oxford first. Patricia Monk has recently published a fine biography of Dalhousie's first professor of history, James De Mille, *The Gilded Beaver: an Introduction to the Life and Work of James De Mille* (Toronto: ECW Press 1991). Articles about Dalhousie's history are mentioned in the notes, but one deserves notice here – Judith Fingard's "College, Career, and Community: Dalhousie Coeds, 1881–1921" in Paul Axelrod and John Reid, eds., *Youth, University and Canadian Society: Essays in the Social History of Higher Education* (Kingston and Montreal: McGill-Queen's University Press 1989), pp. 26–50.

Dalhousie's history is also subsumed within the political, social, and educational history of Nova Scotia, especially for Dalhousie's first half-century. Here Murray Beck is essential: first, his two-volume biography of Joseph Howe, *Joseph Howe: Volume I: Conservative Reformer, 1804–1848*, and *Volume II, The Briton Becomes Canadian, 1848–1873* (Kingston and Montreal: McGill-Queen's University Press 1982 and 1983). Not less important is Beck's *The Politics of Nova Scotia*, Volume I: *1710–1896*, and Volume II: *1896–1988* (Tantallon: Four East Publications 1985 and 1988).

From the beginning, Dalhousie's history is tied to that of Halifax. One history of Halifax must be mentioned, Thomas H. Raddall, *Halifax, Warden of the North* (Toronto: McClelland and Stewart 1948). It is a survey covering the two hundred years since 1749. It has the once-over-lightly feel of such books, but try to write one like it! With its faults, it is a great achievement, and there is no other to match it. Raddall was a boy of fourteen at the time of the Halifax Explosion of 1917, and describes it vividly in *In My Time: A Memoir* (Toronto: McClelland and Stewart 1976), pp. 30–41.

Perhaps the most useful secondary sources are the short essays, some of them masterpieces of compression and research, in the *Dictionary of Canadian Biography*, especially volumes VII (1836–1850) to XII (1891–1900). Volume XIII (1901–1910) is expected to be published in 1994. One could mention here Peter Burroughs's "George Ramsay, ninth Earl of Dalhousie" and Susan Buggey and Gwendolyn Davies's "Thomas McCulloch" in volume VII, Allan Dunlop's "James Ross" in volume X, Murray Beck's "William Young" in volume XI, and Judith Fingard's "George Munro" in volume XII.

Numerous alumnae and alumni, and Dalhousie professors, have taken the trouble to write or talk about aspects of Dalhousie history. Many of their contributions are mentioned in the notes; my records of these conversations, and the correspondence, will be given to DUA.

Notes

I   A BRAVE BEGINNING

1 The history of the Dalhousie Castle and the Ramsay family is contained in a pamphlet available at the Castle. It strikes one as accurate, but it is the only authority that I have for the Duke of Wellington's remark about Lord Dalhousie at the Battle of Waterloo. See also Elizabeth Longford, *Wellington: The Years of the Sword* (London 1969), pp. 383–6; and Peter Burroughs, "George Ramsay," *Dictionary of Canadian Biography (DCB)*, VII: 722–33.

2 There is a brief but interesting description of this trip in NAC, Lord Dalhousie Papers, vol. 2, letter to the Duke of Buccleuch, 2 Dec. 1816, from Halifax. The most accessible source for Dalhousie's journals is Marjory Whitelaw, ed., *The Dalhousie Journals* ([Toronto] 1978). This is an edited version of an extensive journal that Lord Dalhousie kept from 1800 onward, which is in the Earl of Dalhousie Papers, in the Scottish Record Office, Edinburgh. These papers are extensive, and the British North American section of them has been microfilmed by the National Archives of Canada in fifteen reels. In 1938 the same organization published a catalogue with brief annotations of the letters. There are volumes of typed transcripts of these letters from the 1938 catalogue.

3 Brian Cuthbertson, *The Old Attorney General* (Halifax [1980]), p. 70.

4 Lord Dalhousie Papers, vol. 2, Dalhousie to Sir John Sherbrooke, 15 June 1818, private, from Halifax.

5 Thomas Chandler Haliburton, *The Clockmaker or The Sayings and Doings of Samuel Slick of Slickville*, New Canadian Library edition (Toronto 1958), pp. 46–7.

6 The original watercolour is in the J. Ross Robertson Collection in the Toronto Central Library, and is the frontispiece in vol. 2 of T.C. Haliburton's *An Historical and Statistical Account of Nova-Scotia* (Halifax 1829), published by Joseph Howe. For the Duke of Kent, see W.S. MacNutt, "Edward Augustus, Duke of Kent and Strathearn," *DCB*, V: 297–8; also Cecil Woodham-Smith, *Queen Victoria: From her Birth to the Death of the Prince Consort* (New York 1972), pp. 10–11. For the history of the Citadel, see John Joseph Greenough, *The Halifax Citadel, 1826–60: A Narrative and Structural History*, Occasional Papers in Archaeology and History, no. 17 (Ottawa 1977).

7 See Nova Scotia, *Statutes at Large, 1817–1826* (Halifax 1827). The 1817 act on the Halifax Water Company is 57 Geo. III, cap. 15; that for the Halifax Watch is

58 Geo. III, cap. 13; the "Act to prevent disorderly Riding, and driving of Carriages" is 3 Geo. IV, cap. 23.

8 Whitelaw, ed., *Dalhousie Journals*, 11 Nov. 1816, pp. 21–2. Alexander Croke's satire is called "The Inquisition," and is in PANS, MG1, 239C, reprinted in the *Dalhousie Review* 53, no. 3 (Autumn 1973), pp. 404–30. The quotation is from canto 4, lines 89–95.

9 See Thomas H. Raddall, *Halifax: Warden of the North* (Toronto 1948), pp. 108–9, for the raffish life led by garrison officers in Halifax. For drinking in rural Nova Scotia, see Whitelaw, ed., *Dalhousie Journals*, 10 Aug. 1817, p. 45.

10 Cuthbertson, *Old Attorney General*, pp. 76–7.

11 For the full story of this action see H.F. Pullen, *The Shannon and the Chesapeake* (Toronto 1970), pp. 52ff.

12 Peter Burroughs, "Sir John Coape Sherbrooke," *DCB*, V: 713.

13 Lord Dalhousie Papers, vol. 2, Dalhousie to Sherbrooke, 17 Jan. 1817, from Halifax.

14 Archibald MacMechan, *Late Harvest* (Toronto 1934), pp. 49–50. It was composed as a song, to be sung to the tune of "The Laird of Cockpen." MacMechan was professor of English at Dalhousie University from 1889 to 1931.

15 Lord Dalhousie put a summary of Sherbrooke's suggestions before his council. See PANS, RG1, vol. 193, Nova Scotia, Executive Council, Minutes, 11 Dec. 1817, pp. 195–8. Although the reference here is to the Executive Council, in fact the Council, as it was called, combined legislative and executive functions and there would have been no Executive Council as such. In 1838 when they were officially separated the designations Executive Council and Legislative Council begin.

16 Lord Dalhousie Papers, vol. 4, "Daily Memoranda of Business." These are brief notes by Lord Dalhousie on what went on in council, and cover the years 1816 to 1820. See 31 Oct., and 6 Nov. 1816.

17 Ibid., 20 Feb. 1817. Lord Dalhousie noted that Council's suggestions were so various that he set them down without approving any one of them. This clutch of important, long-serving, powerful, and sometimes greedy men can be best studied in *DCB*, VI and VII.

18 Lord Dalhousie Papers, microfilm A525, Dalhousie to Bathurst, 15 May 1817. These papers include an outgoing correspondence book in which despatches were copied.

19 Whitelaw, ed., *Dalhousie Journals*, 24 Sept. 1817, pp. 62–3. For a more benign and perhaps bowdlerized account of King's at this time, see F.W. Vroom, *King's College: A Chronicle, 1789–1939; Collections and Recollections* (Halifax 1941), pp. 50–2. For a general perspective on King's within the setting of the Anglican Church establishment, see Judith Fingard, *The Anglican Design in Loyalist Nova Scotia 1783–1816* (London 1972), especially pp. 152–4.

The story of the docking of the Bishop's horses comes from Thomas McCulloch, a dozen years later. See PANS, Thomas McCulloch Papers, vol. 553, McCulloch to James Mitchell of Glasgow, 4 Sept. 1829, from Pictou.

20 For McCulloch, see the essay by Susan Buggey and Gwendolyn Davies in *DCB*, VII: 529–41, with a comprehensive bibliography. Marjory Whitelaw has published a

useful booklet with the Nova Scotia Museum, *Thomas McCulloch: His Life and Times* (Halifax 1985).

21 From a letter to Edward Mortimer by Lord Dalhousie, 12 Mar. 1819, published in the *Pictou Observer and Eastern Advertiser*, 11 Sept. 1838. See also Whitelaw, ed., *Dalhousie Journals*, 10–15 Sept. 1817, pp. 53–8.

22 There is an extensive literature on the history of the Presbyterian Church. One of the best is J.A.S. Burleigh, *A Church History of Scotland* (London 1960). There is a useful chart at the back that shows the history of the splits and subsequent reunions in the Scottish church.

23 A good description of the Pictou County feuds is in W.L. Grant and F. Hamilton, *Principal Grant* (Toronto 1904), pp. 14–18. See also George Patterson, *The History of Dalhousie College and University* (Halifax 1887), p. 8.

24 PANS, Thomas McCulloch Papers, vol. 553, McCulloch to James Mitchell of Glasgow, 6 Nov. 1834, from Pictou.

25 Ibid., McCulloch to James Mitchell, 4 Sept. 1829, from Pictou.

26 PANS, RG1, vol. 193, Nova Scotia, Executive Council, Minutes, 11 Dec. 1817, pp. 195–8.

27 This despatch and the reply to it Lord Dalhousie presented to the legislature on 17 Feb. 1819, asking for support. The despatches appeared in print, however, only in 1836. See Nova Scotia Assembly, *Journals 1836*, Appendix 58, pp. 125–6.

28 Lord Dalhousie Papers, vol. 2, Dalhousie to Sherbrooke, 29 Dec. 1817; ibid., Sherbrooke to Dalhousie, 4 Feb. 1818, from Quebec.

29 PANS, RG1, vol. 193, Nova Scotia, Executive Council, Minutes, 6 June 1818, pp. 240–1; ibid., 18 Dec. 1818, p. 272.

30 See George Shepperson, "Andrew Brown," *DCB*, VI: 87–9.

31 Both letters are in Lord Dalhousie Papers, microfilm A525, 20 May 1818, from Halifax. They are also in Dalhousie University Archives (hereafter DUA), MS-I-I B1, Board of Governors Correspondence.

32 Almost any edition of Robert Burns will have "A Man's a Man for a' that" and "The Cottar's Saturday Night." The only point to be made here is that the last line, in quotation marks, is from Alexander Pope's *Essay on Man* (1733). The previous line, "Princes and lords are but the breath of kings" is from Oliver Goldsmith's "The Deserted Village," put in more succinct form. Burns was well read in the English poets of his time.

33 Elie Halevy has a good short description of Scottish education in *England in 1815: A History of the English People in the Nineteenth Century* (New York 1949), pp. 540–1.

34 G.E. Davie, *The Democratic Intellect: Scotland and her Universities in the Nineteenth Century* (Edinburgh 1961), pp. 11–13.

35 DUA, Board of Governors Correspondence, George H. Baird and Andrew Brown to Earl of Dalhousie, 1 Aug. 1818, from the College, Edinburgh.

36 Ibid., George H. Baird to Lord Dalhousie, 4 Aug. 1818, from Edinburgh.

37 Lord Dalhousie Papers, vol. 2, A. Brown to Lord Dalhousie, 3 Aug. 1818, from Larkfield, near Edinburgh.

38 Nova Scotia, Executive Council, Minutes, 18 Dec. 1818, p. 272.

39 Nova Scotia Assembly, *Journals 1819*, 11 Feb. 1819, pp. 6–7.

40 Ibid., 14 Apr. 1819, p. 113.

41 See David Sutherland, "Michael Wallace," *DCB*, VI: 798–801.

42 DUA, Board of Governors Correspondence, Minutes of the Trustees of the College, Halifax, 12 Mar. 1819. See also Whitelaw, ed., *Dalhousie Journals*, 12 May 1819, p. 110.

43 DUA, Board of Governors Correspondence, Trustees to Earl of Bathurst, 3 Dec. 1819; ibid., Nathaniel Atcheson to Lord Dalhousie, 6 Jan. 1820, from London; ibid., Bishop Robert Stanser to Lord Dalhousie, 8 Jan. 1820, from London.

44 Ibid., Lord Dalhousie to Bathurst, 15 May 1820. For King's Royal Charter, see Vroom, *King's College*, pp. 34–5; Fingard, *Anglican Design*, pp. 151–2.

45 DUA, Board of Governors Correspondence, Board of Trustees to Professor James H. Monk, 15 May 1820.

46 Lord Dalhousie Papers, A525, Lord Dalhousie to Bathurst, 20 May 1818, private, from Halifax; Whitelaw, ed., *Dalhousie Journals*, 2 Aug. 1819, p. 153.

47 Ibid., 22 Nov. 1819, p. 173.

48 Nova Scotia, Assembly, *Journals 1820*, 3 Apr. 1820, p. 246.

49 Lord Dalhousie Papers, vol. 12, Inglis to Kempt, 12 Sept. 1823, from Halifax; Whitelaw, ed., *Dalhousie Journals*, 23 May 1820, p. 195; Judith Fingard, "John Inglis," *DCB*, VII: p. 433.

50 This speech was reported by the *Royal Gazette*, 24 May 1820 and reprinted in the *Acadian Recorder*, 27 May 1820. A partial version of it is in Whitelaw, ed., *Dalhousie Journals*, 23 May 1820, pp. 195–6.

2 NEW BUILDING, SILENT ROOMS

1 See Peter Burroughs, "Sir James Kempt," *DCB*, VIII: 458–65.

2 NA, Lord Dalhousie Papers, Microfilm A527, Dalhousie to Kempt, 16 Oct. 1820, confidential, from Quebec.

3 Ibid., Wallace to Kempt, 6 Nov. 1820; Kempt to Dalhousie, 6 Nov. 1820.

4 Ibid., Kempt to Dalhousie, 15 Jan. 1821, confidential, from Halifax.

5 Ibid., vol. 7, Dalhousie to Blowers, 26 Feb. 1821.

6 Ibid., A527, Kempt to Dalhousie, 30 Jan. 1821; *Acadian Recorder*, 27 Jan. 1821.

7 Lord Dalhousie Papers, A527, Dalhousie to Kempt, 10 June 1820, confidential, from on board HMS *Newcastle*; also Whitelaw, ed., *Dalhousie Journals*, 14 Apr. 1820, p. 191; Lord Dalhousie Papers, A527, Kempt to Dalhousie, 10 Feb., 6 Mar. 1821; Nova Scotia Assembly, *Journals 1821*, 21–23 Feb., pp. 91–103; Lord Dalhousie Papers, A527, Kempt to Dalhousie, 4 June 1821.

8 Lord Dalhousie Papers, A527, Dalhousie to Kempt, 29 Oct. 1821. A Mr Temple had written Lord Dalhousie to say, "I am sorry to find greater difficulty in providing a president for Halifax College than I first anticipated – the great hindrance to our success Mr. Monk tells me is this, clever men can always make so much more at home than this situation holds out."

9 Ibid., vol. 11, Kempt to Dalhousie, 21 Jan. 1823, private and confidential.

10 Ibid., vol. 11, Dalhousie to Kempt, 12 Mar. 1823, from Quebec.

11 Nova Scotia Assembly, *Journals 1823*, 25 Mar., p. 275.

12 Lord Dalhousie Papers, vol. 11, Kempt to Dalhousie, 26 Mar. 1823.

13 Nova Scotia Assembly, *Journals 1823*, 25 Mar.-4 Apr., pp. 275–94.

14 Lord Dalhousie Papers, vol. 14, Kempt to Dalhousie, 21 Jan. 1824. The letter from McCulloch that Kempt quotes is written to Inglis, from Pictou, 26 May 1823.

15 Ibid., vol. 12, John Inglis to Kempt, 12 Sept. 1823; Nova Scotia Assembly, *Journals 1836*, Appendix 58, sec. 2, on King's.

16 Ibid., vol. 12, Dalhousie to Kempt, 26 Oct. 1823, from Trois-Rivières; vol. 14, Dalhousie to Kempt, 13 Mar. 1824.

17 Nova Scotia Assembly, *Journals 1836*, Appendix 58, sec. 2. Blowers had a list of fourteen objections to the union. This quotation is from no. 5. See also G.G. Patterson, *The History of Dalhousie College and University* (Halifax 1887), p. 19.

18 Lord Dalhousie Papers, vol. 14, Dalhousie to Kempt, 13 Mar. 1824. Dalhousie was also commenting on objections from Vice-President Cochran of King's.

19 Ibid., vol. 14, Michael Wallace to Dalhousie, 10 May 1824. See Carol Anne Janzen, "Sir Alexander Croke," *DCB*, VII: 216–19.

20 DUA, MS 1–1, Dalhousie Board of Governors, Minutes (hereafter BOG Minutes), 13 Jan. 1823; Nova Scotia Assembly, *Journals 1836*, Appendix 58, p. 135. The Halifax figures are in Halifax currency, where £1 equalled $4.

21 An estimate like this makes huge assumptions of what £1 Halifax currency would buy in the 1820s and what its equivalent would purchase in 1990s. Convert to dollars by multiplying by four; then comes a huge leap of faith, *viz.* multiply by forty. The net effect is to give a very good salary of the 1820s, say £400 per annum, a modern equivalent of $64,000. It is a question of whether such a calculation is worth doing at all; on balance I think some rough contemporary equivalent is more useful than not.

22 Lord Dalhousie Papers, A527, Kempt to Dalhousie, 6 July 1825, from London; for Michael Wallace, see D.A. Sutherland's article in *DCB*, VI: 800.

23 PANS, MG1, vol. 553, Thomas McCulloch Papers, 151, McCulloch to Lord Dalhousie, n.d., probably 25 Sept. 1823. DUA, MS 1–1, B1, Dalhousie Board of Governors, Correspondence, Lord Dalhousie to McCulloch, 4 Nov. 1823, from Quebec. This letter has a hole through it, and some words are missing, but it is clearly in reply to McCulloch's letter above.

24 D.C. Harvey, *An Introduction to the History of Dalhousie University* (Halifax 1938), p. 32; Patterson, *Dalhousie*, p. 17.

25 Harvey, *Dalhousie*, p. 9.

26 See Nova Scotia Assembly, *Journals 1832*, Appendix 41, p. 54, statement signed by Michael Wallace and his son Charles W. Wallace.

27 J. Murray Beck, *The Government of Nova Scotia* (Toronto 1957), p. 21, and Appendix C, p. 349.

28 See Phyllis Blakeley, "Sir Brenton Halliburton," *DCB*, VIII: 354.

29 Howe's speech at the "One College" meeting at Mason's Hall, 25 Sept. 1843, reported in *Novascotian* (Halifax), 9 Oct. 1843.

30 Nova Scotia Assembly, *Journals 1829*, 7 Apr., pp. 537–8.

31 DUA, hereafter BOG Minutes, 26 May, 4 Oct. 1829.

32 Nova Scotia Assembly, *Journals 1830*, 27 Feb.-2 Mar., pp. 610–20.

33 DUA, Board of Governors (BOG Minutes, 26 May 1829, 6 Mar. 1829, 6 Dec. 1831; Harvey, *Dalhousie*, p. 37, citing correspondance of Jotham Blanchard of Pictou,

from Glasgow, 12 Oct. 1831. See also Patterson, *Dalhousie*, p. 21, quoting the *Pictou Observer*, 23 Nov. 1831.

34 Sir George Murray to Sir Peregrine Maitland, 31 Aug. 1829, in Nova Scotia Assembly, *Journals 1836*, Appendix 58, p. 104.

35 Goderich's despatch is described in detail in Patterson, *Dalhousie*, p. 22; DUA, BOG Minutes, 13 July 1832. Archibald's protest is dated 6 Jan. 1832. He was also warning the joint meeting not even to bother drafting a bill for the union, "as the Assembly would be more influenced by the general wishes of the country than by any opinion intimated by the Governors."

36 Colonial Office despatches on microfilm, at NAC and PANS. See CO 217/154, Maitland to Goderich, 19 Mar. 1832. Maitland's opinion on the general attitudes in British North America is worth noting; he had been lieutenant-governor of Upper Canada from 1818 to 1828 prior to coming to Nova Scotia.

37 Glenelg to Campbell, 30 Apr. 1835, in Nova Scotia Assembly, *Journals, 1836*, Appendix 58, pp. 105–7.

38 Ibid., p. 121; Patterson, *Dalhousie*, p. 24.

39 *Acadian Recorder*, 30 Aug. 1834 to 27 Sept. 1834.

40 3 Feb. 1836, quoted in J. Murray Beck, *Joseph Howe: Conservative Reformer 1804–1848* (Kingston and Montreal 1982), p. 152.

41 D.A. Sutherland, "Michael Wallace," *DCB*, VI: 800–1; Susan Buggey and Gwendolyn Davies, "Thomas McCulloch," *DCB*, VII: 535; Beck, *Joseph Howe*, pp. 77–8.

42 The Pictou Academy Act is 2 Wm. IV, cap. 5, given royal assent 30 Mar. 1832; Thomas McCulloch gives useful details; see PANS, Thomas McCulloch Papers, vol. 553, no. 62, McCulloch to James Mitchell of Glasgow, 6 Nov. 1834, from Pictou.

43 Nova Scotia Assembly, *Journals 1835*, 4 Feb., p. 833. The story is a little more complicated than the text suggests. The first part of O'Brien's resolution, that the House require repayment of the £5,000, was passed, twenty-two to sixteen. The second part of it, that the attorney general take immediate steps to get the money, passed twenty to sixteen.

44 Nova Scotia Assembly, *Journals 1836*, 21 Jan., p. 883; 7 Mar., pp. 1004–5; 23 Mar., pp. 1049–50; 4 Apr., p. 1090.

45 Two useful works on this complex period of Nova Scotian politics and education are W.B. Hamilton, "Education, Politics, and Reform in Nova Scotia, 1800–1848" (PH.D. thesis, University of Western Ontario 1970), and Susan Buggey, "Churchmen and Dissenters: Religious Toleration in Nova Scotia, 1758–1835" (MA thesis, Dalhousie University, 1981).

3 ONE COLLEGE OR SEVERAL?

1 J. Murray Beck, *Politics of Nova Scotia, Vol. 1, 1710–1896* (Tantallon 1985), p. 103: J. Murray Beck, *Joseph Howe: Conservative Reformer 1804–1848* (Kingston and Montreal 1982), pp. 102–3; D.C. Harvey, "The Intellectual Awakening of Nova Scotia," *Dalhousie Review* 13, no. 1 (April 1933), pp. 1–22.

2 See J. Murray Beck, "S.G.W. Archibald," *DCB*, VII: 21–5.

3 PANS, MG1, Thomas McCulloch Papers, vol. 553, McCulloch to Mitchell, 6 Nov. 1834, from Pictou, and 23 Nov. 1835; McCulloch to John Mitchell (the father of James) June 1838, from Pictou.

4 Ibid., C.D. Archibald to McCulloch, 18 Nov. 1837, from Halifax.

5 Ibid., vol. 554, C.D. Archibald to McCulloch, 21 Mar. 1838, private, from Halifax.

6 Nova Scotia Assembly, *Journals 1838*, 16 Mar., p. 350; Thomas McCulloch Papers, vol. 553, no. 141, Dickson to McCulloch, 5 Apr. 1838, from Halifax. Dickson was the brother-in-law of S.G.W. Archibald. See Allan C. Dunlop, "Thomas Dickson," *DCB*, VIII: 222.

7 Thomas McCulloch Papers, vol. 553, no. 140, Charles Archibald to McCulloch, 28 Mar., 10 Apr. 1838, from Halifax; *Novascotian*, 12 Apr. 1838, reporting on the Legislative Council for 27 Mar.

8 Thomas McCulloch Papers, vol. 554, E.A. Crawley, "An Outline suggesting some principles and regulations for putting Dalhousie College into active operation," n.d. [*c.* 20 Apr. 1838]. The date is made clear from McCulloch's letter to Charles Archibald of 24 Apr. 1838. See also Barry Moody, "Edmund Ahern Crawley," *DCB* XI: 214–15; Thomas McCulloch Papers, vol. 554, Charles Archibald to McCulloch, 21 Mar. 1838. Crawley's discussion with Charles Wallace is referred to in Crawley's interview before the Assembly, 13 Feb. 1839, in the debates for that day, reported in *Novascotian*, 21 Mar. 1839.

9 Thomas McCulloch Papers, vol. 554, McCulloch to Charles Archibald, 24 Apr. 1838, from Pictou.

10 On McCulloch's appointment there is a singular touch of animus in the board minutes. Deleted at the request of the lieutenant-governor was the statement that "the Revd. Thomas MacCulloch ... is hereby appointed President." Substituted was "the Revd. Dr. T. MacCulloch who for the present is appointed President." See DUA, BOG Minutes, 9 Mar., 6 Aug., 15 Sept. 1838; McCulloch Papers, vol. 553, no. 140, Charles Archibald to McCulloch, 10 Apr. 1838.

11 Ibid., vol. 550, Memorial of Synod of Nova Scotia, 11 Aug. 1838. The *Pictou Observer and Eastern Advertiser*, 11 Sept. 1838, a Kirk supporter, had a strong anti-McCulloch editorial; DUA, BOG Minutes, 15 Sept. 1838.

12 *Novascotian*, 27 Sept. 1838, "Dalhousie College – No. 1." There followed three others, one a week, up to 18 Oct. 1838.

13 Thomas McCulloch Papers, vol. 553, McCulloch to John Mitchell, 26 May 1839, from Halifax.

14 The source of this and the preceding paragraph is G.G. Patterson, *The History of Dalhousie College and University* (Halifax 1887), pp. 32–6. The writer he quotes from was "an old Dalhousian"; and Patterson's father, the Reverend George Patterson fits perfectly, being both at Pictou Academy and Dalhousie College in exactly those years. After the *History* came out, some further reflections occurred to George Patterson, Sr., and these were duly published in the *Dalhousie Gazette*, 2 Dec. 1887, pp. 32–3, as a letter from the son. See also Allan Dunlop, "George Patterson," *DCB*, XII: 828–9.

15 See W.B. Hamilton, "Education, Politics and Reform in Nova Scotia 1800–1848" (PH.D. thesis, University of Western Ontario 1970), pp. 265–6.

16 *Novascotian*, 31 Jan. 1839, reporting Assembly debates for 18 Jan. 1839.

17 Ibid., 21 Mar. 1839, reporting debates for 13 Feb.; also DUA, BOG Minutes, 15 Sept. 1838. Details are set out in Appendix 30, Nova Scotia, Assembly, *Journals 1839*, pp. 55ff.

18 *Novascotian*, 21 Mar. 1839, reporting debates for 13, 14, and 20 Feb. 1839.

19 Nova Scotia Assembly, *Journals 1839*, 8 Mar., pp. 561–2.

20 Nova Scotia Statutes, 3 Vic. cap. 7.

21 *Novascotian*, 19 Mar. 1840, reporting Assembly debates for 14 Feb. See also Beck, *Howe: Conservative Reformer*, p. 204.

22 Nova Scotia Legislative Council, *Journals 1840*, 15 Feb., pp. 43–4.

23 *Novascotian*, 16 Apr. 1849, reporting Assembly debates for 26 Feb. The account in the Halifax *British Colonist* suggests that Huntingdon was in a furious rage: "He doubled his fist, and shook it, at his arm's length, in the direction where the Gentlemen he alluded to [Crawley] stood among the spectators below the bar." *British Colonist*, 3 Mar. 1849 reporting debates of 26 Feb. Huntingdon had also a falling out with Howe that same session. See A.A. MacKenzie, "Herbert Huntingdon," *DCB*, VIII: 415–18.

24 This story can be traced in Nova Scotia Assembly, *Journals 1842*, 5–8 Mar., pp. 300–12; Howe comments on it later in the *Novascotian*, 24 Nov. 1842. See Beck, *Howe: Conservative Reformer*, pp. 249–50.

25 This is from G.W. McLelan's apeech in Mason Hall, Halifax, 25 Sept. 1843, reported in the *Novascotian*, 16 Oct. 1843.

26 *Novascotian*, 20 Feb. 1843.

27 Nova Scotia Assembly, *Journals 1843*, 22 Feb. to 27 Mar., pp. 421–513. The debate of 20 Mar. is reported extensively (though even at that much condensed) in the *Novascotian*, 17 Apr. 1843.

28 *Novascotian*, 20 Mar. 1843, editorial; ibid., 17 Apr. 1843, reporting debates for 20 Mar.

29 *Novascotian*, 9 Oct. 1843.

30 Ibid., 2 Oct. 1843.

31 Ibid., 16 Oct. 1843, reporting the Onslow meeting; ibid., 6 Nov. 1843, reporting Stewiacke meeting.

32 *Christian Messenger* (Halifax), 21 July, 6 Oct. 1843; Beck, *Howe: Conservative Reformer*, pp. 259, 265. See also Beck's *Politics*, vol. I: 123.

33 DUA, BOG Minutes, 31 Dec. 1842, pp. 40–7.

34 Ibid., 12 Nov. 1842; the new board is listed in full in Patterson, *Dalhousie*, p. 38. It met for the first time on 5 July 1842.

35 DUA, BOG Minutes, 8 Mar., 28 Apr. 1843.

36 PANS, RG 41, vol. 19 (1843) no. 8, coroner's report is dated 23 Aug. 1843. This material has been brought to my attention by Professor John Barnstead, Department of Russian, Dalhousie University, to whom I am most grateful. DUA, MS-1–1 B1, BOG Correspondence, Lord Falkland to P. Rolandi, London, 29 Sept. 1843. Peter Rolandi was a foreign book specialist in London.

37 PANS, McCulloch Papers, vol. 553, McCulloch to Rev. John Campbell, at St Mary's, 4 July 1841. McCulloch was using the metaphor to apply to letter writing; I have extended the metaphor, I hope not unwisely.

38 William McCulloch, *The Life of Thomas McCulloch, D.D. Pictou* [ed. by T.W. and J.W. McCulloch] (Truro, NS 1920), pp. 192–3.

39 The student was George Patterson, in *A History of the County of Pictou, Nova Scotia* (Montreal 1877), pp. 330–1. The *Stepsure Letters* were first published in the *Acadian Recorder* in 1821–2, reprinted in 1862, and in more recent years by J.A. Irving and D.G. Lochhead ([Toronto] 1960).

40 DUA, BOG Minutes, 22 Sept., 30 Dec. 1843; 27 Mar. 1844.

41 Nova Scotia Assembly, *Journals 1845*, 31 Mar., 1 Apr., pp. 321–6.

42 Ibid., Appendix 12, pp. 43–6; DUA, BOG Minutes, 13 June 1845.

4 THROUGH THE SHALLOWS

1 *Novascotian*, 12 July 1838, written 16 May on board *Tyrian*; Phyllis Blakeley, "Sir Samuel Cunard," *DCB*, IX: 180.

2 Charles Dickens, *American Notes* (London n.d.), p. 39.

3 J. Murray Beck, *Joseph Howe: The Briton Becomes Canadian 1848–1873*, (Kingston and Montreal 1983), pp. 3, 9, 32, 42–3.

4 Hugo Reid, *Sketches in North America...* (London 1861), p. 299.

5 DUA, BOG Minutes, 2 Nov. 1848.

6 Ibid., 8 Nov. 1848.

7 Howe's speech is in the *Novascotian*, 2 Apr. 1849, reporting debates for 19 Feb.; Uniacke's in ibid., 9 Apr. 1849.

8 BOG Minutes, 8 Mar. 1848; 20 June 1849; 18 Mar. 1853; 15 July 1854; *British Colonist*, 24 June, 1 July 1856; Halifax *Morning Chronicle*, 3, 10 July 1856. See also John A. Bell, "Dalhousie College and University," 1887, typescript, DUA, MS-1, p. 30.

9 See C.B. Fergusson, "Hugo Reid," *DCB*, X: 611–12; *Morning Chronicle*, 24 Jan. 1856; *British Colonist*, 24 June 1856; DUA, BOG Correspondence, Hugo Reid to William Young, 27 Dec. 1856, the annual report for the year.

10 There is a long account of these discussions in the *Presbyterian Witness*, 9 and 16 Feb. 1856. For Ross, see Allan Dunlop, "James Ross," *DCB*, X: 772–3.

11 See Stanley Brice Frost, *McGill University: For the Advancement of Learning: Vol. 1, 1801–1895* (Montreal and Kingston 1980), pp. 172, 177–84; P.R. and J.S. Eakins, "Sir John William Dawson," *DCB*, XII: 230–7; John P. Vaillancourt, "John William Dawson, Education Missionary in Nova Scotia" (M. Ed. thesis, Dalhousie University 1973). For University of New Brunswick, see K.A. MacKirdy, "The Formation of the Modern University, 1859–1906" in A.G. Bailey, ed., *The University of New Brunswick, Memorial Volume* (Fredericton 1950), pp. 33–7.

12 PANS, MG100, vol. 133, no. 15: this is a small collection of letters between Dawson and Young, mostly in typed copies: Dawson to Young, 9 Dec. 1854, from Pictou; same, 22 and 28 Feb. 1856, from McGill College.

13 Ibid., Young to Dawson, 29 Apr. 1856; DUA, BOG Minutes, 11 and 18 Mar. 1856; *Presbyterian Witness*, 14 June 1856, letter from "A." See Judith Fingard, "George Munro," *DCB*, XII: 771–3.

14 See Grace McLeod Rogers, "The Story of a Nova Scotia College," *Dalhousie Review* 18 (1938–9), pp. 494–512.

15 DUA, BOG Minutes, 18 Mar., 17 and 21 July 1856.

16 Ibid., 13, 17 July 1857.

17 Ibid., 30 Oct. 1858; 31 Jan. 1859; 14 Feb. 1860. Count d'Utassy's subsequent career is curious. He joined a cavalry regiment on the Union side in the American Civil War and became a buyer of horses. Some very odd transactions developed and Count d'Utassy found himself transferred to prison. He objected strenuously to having to don a convict's uniform, he, *Count* d'Utassy, *and* a former university professor! See John A. Bell, "Dalhousie" typescript, p. 27, DUA.

18 See Bailey, ed., *The University of New Brunswick*, pp. 30–3.

19 Maritime Conference Archives (MCA), Pine Hill, Halifax, Joseph Howe Papers, F and I, box 149, no. 135, Howe to Rev. P.G. MacGregor, 23 June 1862, confidential, from Halifax. Mrs Carolyn Earle has kindly brought this correspondence to my attention.

20 *Christian Messenger*, 10 Sept. 1862. The *Christian Messenger* was the Baptist paper, the editor of which, Stephen Selden, was married to the daughter of Reverend J.M. Cramp, the president of Acadia College. *The Monthly Record of the Church of Scotland in Nova Scotia and the Adjoining Provinces* was first published in 1855, and was based in Pictou. George Grant's letter, "The Meeting of Synod," is in the August 1862 issue, pp. 175–6. The *Monthly Record* is in MCA.

21 The source for this is G.G. Patterson, which he said was inside knowledge, undoubtedly from his father. See Patterson, *Dalhousie*, pp. 64–5.

22 *Presbyterian Witness*, 5 July 1862; *Monthly Record*, Aug. 1862, pp. 175–6; *Colonial Standard* (Pictou), 1 July 1862.

23 Allan Dunlop, "George Patterson," DCB, XII: 828–30; also Patterson, *Dalhousie*, pp. 64–5.

24 *Presbyterian Witness*, 12 July, 16 Aug. 1862. The reference to the condition of the buildings is ibid., 13 Mar. 1862, letter by Candor.

25 *Monthly Record*, Aug. 1862, p. 176.

26 DUA, BOG Minutes, 30 July 1862; 31 Jan., 18 and 26 Mar. 1863.

27 *Christian Messenger*, 25 Mar. 1863; *Evening Express* (Halifax), 2 Sept. 1863.

28 Nova Scotia Assembly, *Journals 1863*, 10 Mar., 23 and 29 Apr., pp. 37, 101–2, 108–9, 112.

29 *Evening Express*, 5 Aug., 2 Sept. 1863; *Christian Messenger*, 25 Mar., 1 Apr. 1863; also *Provincial Wesleyan*, 25 Mar. 1863.

30 *Monthly Record*, Aug. 1863, "Appeal of the Educational Board of Synod, in favour of Dalhousie College," p. 181.

31 Ibid., p. 182. For the student figures see Nova Scotia Assembly, *Journals 1864*, Appendix 51. Figures given in the *Evening Express*, 2 Sept. 1863, are close to these. Neither group distinguishes between part-time and full-time students. In the case of St Mary's and St Francis Xavier, the figures given do not seem to distinguish between students in the college program and those in academy programs.

32 DUA, BOG Correspondence, Ross to James Thomson (board secretary), 21 Sept. 1863, from Truro; Ross to Thomson, same date [?], private and confidential. At the end of this second letter is a note, underlined twice, that it is to be destroyed.

33 Patterson in *Dalhousie*, p. 67, says that the Kirk Synod was unanimous in approving the Dalhousie move. If so, it was after Pollok and Grant had succeeded in

quieting opposition. Hence I have used the words, "without dissent."

34 *Evening Express*, 5 Aug. 1863.

35 The motion at the convention was moved by Dr Cramp, president of Acadia. See *Presbyterian Witness*, 5 Sept. 1863, "The Baptists on Education and Dalhousie College." Also *Christian Messenger*, 30 Sept., 7 Oct. 1863.

36 *Provincial Wesleyan*, 5 Aug., 18 Nov., 2 Dec. 1863. The last editorial is entitled "The Presbyterian College."

37 Nova Scotia Assembly, *Journals 1864*, 23 Mar., pp. 79–80; 29 Mar., pp. 88–90. For the debates, see *British Colonist*, 7 Apr. 1864, reporting debates for 23 Mar.; also *Presbyterian Witness*, 2 Apr. 1864.

38 *Presbyterian Witness*, 25 June 1864.

39 *Evening Express*, 22 July 1863.

5 GREAT TALENT, LITTLE MONEY

1 For the weather report, see *Morning Sun* (Halifax), 11 Nov. 1863, under "Almanac."

2 For a history of the later stages of the Halifax Citadel, see John Joseph Greenough, *The Halifax Citadel, 1825–1860: A Narrative and Structural History* (Ottawa 1977), Canadian Historic Sites Series No. 17, pp. 128–9.

3 Hugo Reid, *Sketches in North America* (London 1861), p. 296.

4 *Morning Sun*, 17 Apr. 1863; *Morning Chronicle*, 18 Apr. 1863; *Presbyterian Witness*, 18 Apr. 1863.

5 The quotation from Burke is from his *Reflections on the Revolution in France* (1790); *Presbyterian Witness*, 2 Feb. 1856, quoting the *Edinburgh Witness*; ibid., 9 Aug. 1856; *British Colonist*, 19 Aug. 1856; *Presbyterian Witness*, 23 Aug. 1856; *Provincial Wesleyan*, 9 Sept. 1863.

6 *Presbyterian Witness*, 6 Sept. 1856.

7 *Morning Sun*, 20 Apr. 1863. The Anglican journal is the Halifax *Church Record*, 2 Sept. 1863. For the chairman's remarks, see *Morning Chronicle*, 12 Nov. 1863. De Mille's remarks are made ten years later, in his inaugural address. See *Dalhousie Gazette*, 15 Nov. 1873.

8 *Morning Sun*, 11 Nov. 1863 (italics added). The French quotation means "to move back, the better to jump forward." The Latin means "I rise again with splendour augmented."

9 DUA, BOG Minutes, 6 Aug., 3 and 19 Oct. 1863; BOG Correspondence, James Thomson to McCulloch, 10 Aug. 1863; Thomson to George Lawson, 5 Oct. 1863. Perhaps it was as well that Pryor was not appointed. He got into trouble with his Granville Street congregation in 1867 over misapplication of church funds and impropriety with a woman of doubtful character, and was ousted from his church. A full account of this incident is given in Patricia Monk, *The Gilded Beaver: An Introduction to the Life and Work of James De Mille* (Toronto 1991), pp. 129–33. See also Barry M. Moody, "John Pryor," *DCB*, XII: 871–3.

10 DUA, BOG Correspondence, Thomson to Rev. C.M. McDonald, 29 Oct. [1863]: Charles Macdonald to Secretary of Dalhousie College, 14 Nov. 1863, from Aberdeen.

11 The account here and on the following pages is based largely on descriptive evidence. There is no plan of the old Dalhousie College building that I have seen. In 1871 Dr J.F. Avery tried to get "the original plan" of Dalhousie College to make some changes after the departure of the post office, but apparently none could be found (BOG Minutes, 25 May 1871). J.G. McGregor, professor of physics, had a sketch of some changes he would like made on the second floor in 1881 (BOG Correspondence, MacGregor to BOG, 3 Jan. 1881). There are a number of personal descriptions. The earliest is by Calor, *Dalhousie Gazette*, 19 Jan. 1871. The *Gazette* issued an important historical number, on 12 Jan. 1903, in which George Patterson has a useful essay on "The Old Building," pp. 111–19. There is also a photograph, probably taken in the early 1880s. D.C. Fraser reminisces about 1872 in ibid., 25 Jan. 1908, pp. 112–18. "M" writes of "Dalhousie in the 60s" in ibid., 20 Oct. 1908, as does Dr J. McG. Baxter, ibid., 30 Jan. 1919.

12 There is a picture of one, looking exactly like its name, in a photograph of one of the redan residences in the Citadel, taken *c.* 1890, in Greenough, *The Halifax Citadel*, p. 103.

13 D.C. Fraser, "Reminiscences of 1872," *Dalhousie Gazette*, 25 Jan. 1905, p. 117. There is a resolution in the Senate, 2 Feb. 1876: "Students must understand that any act, however trifling in itself, becomes serious when it tends to cause interruptions or distraction in a class, and that it then both necessitates and merits punishment." Senate let the group of students responsible for an incident off, after their apology, and one third-year student, John S. Murray, was given a warning, that it was hoped he would in future maintain behaviour "unobstrusive as respects his fellow students and, in every instance, respectful as regards his Professors."

14 Allan Dunlop, "James Ross," *DCB*, XI: 773. The Board of Governors registered a complaint against the boys of the National School for shouting and throwing of stones, "a most serious evil for some time past." The board was to ask the school to confine the boys to a line south of George Street. BOG Minutes, 12 Nov. 1875.

15 MCA, Thomas McCulloch Papers, box 22, McCulloch to Ross, 16 June 1835, from Pictou.

16 *Morning Herald* (Halifax), 16 Mar. 1886; E.D. Millar, "Rev. James Ross, D.D." in *Dalhousie Gazette*, Historical No. 1903, pp. 144–52; J. Macdonald Oxley, "Some Reminisences of the Men of '76," ibid., pp. 159–63; Benjamin Russell, *Autobiography* (Halifax 1932), pp. 48–9. There is a retrospective article on James Ross in the *Morning Chronicle*, 1 Jan. 1912, and a much better one in George Patterson, *Studies in Nova Scotian History* (Halifax 1940), "Dalhousie's Second Principal – an old boy's tribute," pp. 100–5.

17 The source for much of this paragraph and subsequent ones on Macdonald is the *Dalhousie Gazette*, Macdonald Memorial issue, Apr. 1901. See also J. Aubrey Lippincott, "Dalhousie College in the Sixties," *Dalhousie Review* 16, no. 3, (1936–37), p. 287. Dr Lippincott graduated in medicine in 1867.

18 *Dalhousie Gazette*, Historical No., 12 Jan. 1903, p. 161; Ibid., 7 May 1894.

19 Ibid., 30 Jan. 1890. See also William B. Hamilton, "William Lyall," *DCB*, XI: 534; and Lippincott, "Dalhousie College in the Sixties," p. 286.

20 *Dalhousie Gazette*, 17 Nov. 1877; Ibid., 22 Nov. 1895. See also Suzanne Zeller, "George Lawson," *DCB*, XII: 539–43.

21 DUA, Senate Minutes, 17 Mar. 1865.

22 BOG Minutes, 1 July, 11 Sept. 1865; BOG Correspondence, De Mille to BOG, 2 July 1865, from Chester; Thomson to De Mille, 12 Sept. 1865.

23 Patricia Monk, *The Gilded Beaver: An Introduction to the Life and work of James De Mille* (Toronto 1991), *passim*; George Patterson, *More Studies in Nova Scotian History* (Halifax 1941), "Concerning James De Mille," pp. 146–7; Lippincott, "Dalhousie College in the Sixties," p. 288.

24 I have not found the matriculation examinations for the 1870s. Doubtless they did not differ all that much from the ones given here for 1893–4.

25 See Calendar of Dalhousie College and University, Session 1872–1873, p. 20; Senate Minutes, 8 Feb. 1866; David Allison, *History of Nova Scotia*, 3 vols. (Halifax 1916), II: 840–1. Allison was however given an honorary LL.D. by Dalhousie in 1919.

26 *Dalhousie Gazette*, 29 Apr. 1876. This was in a parting address by the students graduating in 1876.

27 The Senate rule was laid down on 6 Feb. 1865, but it was not easy to enforce. When the Board of Governors raised the question, the Senate replied, that the existing rules could be "approximately enforced within the limits of the college and the Parade with the aid of a Janitor whose whole time were secured for duties connected with the College." But since he was not so available, "there is virtually no check upon the conduct of students or others outside the Class-Rooms." The Senate also noted that the mortar-board was not suitable for winter wear and ought to be modified. For Duncan Fraser's reminscences, see *Dalhousie Gazette*, 25 Jan. 1908, p. 116.

28 Ibid., 14 Dec. 1872, "Ragamuffins"; ibid., 25 Apr. 1870, p. 73.

29 The two Pictou County students are described in Kenneth F. Mackenzie, *Sabots and Slippers* (Toronto 1954), pp. 114–15. This reference has been brought to my attention by Allan Dunlop, to whom I am most grateful. An early rugby game was devised, twenty-five students a side, which was a mixture of rugby and soccer.

30 Colin D. Howell, *A Century of Care: A History of the Victoria General Hospital in Halifax 1887–1987* (Halifax 1988), pp. 1–34. See also C.B. Stewart's history of the Dalhousie Medical Faculty in *Mail-Star* (Halifax), 14 Sept. 1968.

31 BOG Minutes, 28 Nov. 1863; see also Howell, *Century of Care*, pp. 22–3, and *Acadian Recorder*, 11 Aug. 1875.

32 D.A. Campbell, "Medical Education in Nova Scotia," *Maritime Medical News*, July 1910, p. 13; and Colin D. Howell, "Medical Science and Social Criticism: Alexander Peter Reid and the Ideological Origins of the Welfare State in Canada" in C. David Naylor, ed., *Canadian Health Care and the State: a Century of Evolution* (Montreal and Kingston 1992), pp. 26–37. See also BOG Minutes, 12 Aug. 1870; 26 Jan., 6 Apr. 1872.

33 Much of the correspondence is in the BOG Minutes. See especially 19 Mar., 26 May, 2 June 1873; 9 July, 16 Sept. 1874.

34 Ibid., 5 Feb. 1875. It is signed by all nine members of the Dalhousie board: Sir William Young, Charles Tupper, J.W. Ritchie, S.L. Shannon, G.W. Hill, G.M. Grant, J.F. Avery, C. Robson, and Alexander Forrest.

35 *Halifax Evening Reporter*, 11 Mar. 1876; Nova Scotia, *Statutes 1876*, 39 Vic. cap.

28; Nova Scotia Assembly, *Journals 1876*, 10 Mar., pp. 52–3. See Denis Healy, "The University of Halifax, 1875–1881," *Dalhousie Review* 53, no. 1 (Spring 1973), pp. 39–56. Pictou *Colonial Standard*, quoted with approval in *Morning Chronicle*, 1 Apr. 1881. For Samuel Creelman, see Nova Scotia, *Debates and Proceedings of the Legislative Council, 1881*, 8 Apr., p. 69.

36 I have not found the origin of the delightful alliteration, "Church, Chance or Charity." It is in the *Halifax Evening Reporter* of 22 Feb. 1876, in the leading editorial, "The College Question," and is attributed to Dalhousie or the Presbyterians. *Dalhousie Gazette*, 31 May 1876, editorial entitled "The College War." For Lyall's address to convocation see ibid., 21 Nov. 1874. *Halifax Evening Reporter*, 2 Mar. 1876, letter from "One of the People." The *Reporter* gave general support to the Hill government.

37 *Dalhousie Gazette*, 1 Apr. 1876.

38 A Professor, *The University of Halifax Criticised in a Letter Addressed to the Chancellor* (Halifax 1877), pp. 3, 5, 6–8, 21. There is no external evidence that Charles Macdonald wrote this pamphlet, but the level of sophistication in both classics and mathematics displayed in the pamphlet strongly suggests his authorship.

39 For a fuller gist of MacGregor's letters, see Healey, *University of Halifax*, pp. 50–1. On the adventures of the Colleges bill see my *The Man from Halifax: Sir John Thompson, Prime Minister* (Toronto 1985), pp. 98–9.

40 The sources of financial information for the 1870s are not very satisfactory, for the BOG Minutes are sporadic with financial information. There are only occasional indications of where Dalhousie's capital (that produced the $3,000 from investments) actually was. Some $8,000 was put into Bank of Montreal stock in 1876. Most of the rest seems to have been in mortgages. The total capital was probably about $75,000. See BOG Minutes, 21 Apr. 1871; 26 Jan., 12 Mar. 1872; 3 Feb. 1876; 19 Mar. 1879. The *Morning Herald* of 23 Apr. 1896 has a long retrospective on Dalhousie, including some useful financial information, some of it written by Professor Archibald MacMechan. For the Dalhousie Alumni Association, see the pamphlet, *History of the Dalhousie Alumni Association* ([Halifax] 1937), with no author given.

41 BOG Minutes, 18 Sept. 1876; 21 Aug. 1879.

42 See Walter J. Chute, *Chemistry at Dalhousie* (Halifax 1986), p. 10; BOG Minutes, 14 Sept. 1877; BOG Correspondence, J.J. MacKenzie to Sir William Young, 6 Dec. 1877; 13 Apr., 23 June 1878; ibid., Young to Reverend C.B. Pitblado, 28 Sept. 1878, from Halifax; ibid., extract from Minutes, Board of Superintendence of Theological Hall, Pictou, 1 Oct. 1878, reported by P.G. MacGregor, secretary; *Dalhousie Gazette*, 8 Feb. 1879.

43 BOG, Correspondence, Young to Pitblado, 26 May 1879, from Halifax. W.L. Grant and F. Hamilton, *Principal Grant* (Toronto 1904), pp. 187–8. Hilda Neatby, *Queen's University: And Not to Yield: 1841–1917* (Kingston and Montreal 1978), pp. 151–3; *Dalhousie Gazette*, 14 Dec. 1877.

44 *Dalhousie Gazette*, 20 Dec. 1892, "President Forrest," p. 141; ibid., 19 Jan. 1893, letter from "Another Alumnus," pp. 164–5.

6 GEORGE MUNRO AND THE BIG CHANGE

1 See W.D. Forrest, "Our First Great Benefactor," in the *Dalhousie Alumni News*, October 1943, pp. 23–4. Reference to Munro's leaving Halifax is in *Presbyterian Witness*, 25 Oct. 1856.

2 See my *The Man from Halifax, Sir John Thompson, Prime Minister* (Toronto 1985), pp. 263–5, where I have essayed a short history of copyright, with particular reference to the United States and Canada.

3 For George Munro, see Judith Fingard, "George Munro," *DCB*, 12: 771–3; also A.J. Crockett, *George Munro, the Publisher* (Halifax 1957) which originally appeared as four articles in the *Dalhousie Review*, 1955–7; BOG Minutes, 21 Aug. 1879.

4 George Patterson, "Concerning James DeMille," in *More Studies in Nova Scotian History* (Halifax 1941), p. 145; Senate Minutes, 19 Feb. 1880.

5 BOG Minutes, 15 Oct. 1880; BOG Correspondence, Murray to Sir William Young, 28 Oct. 1880; ibid., Munro to Young, 27 Jan. 1881, from New York; Senate Minutes, 15 Mar. 1881.

6 *Dalhousie Alumni News*, Feb. 1939, "Lord John," by "G.F.," pp. 4–5. For Forrest and the gymnasium see *Dalhousie Gazette*, 29 Nov., 27 Dec. 1888; for his 1881 inaugural, see ibid., 11, 26 Nov. 1881. The doggerel is ibid., 14 Apr. 1920, by "Smoke '97"; *Morning Chronicle*, 27 Apr. 1911, as Forrest steps down as president.

7 PANS, MG17, vol. 58, Minutes of the Dalhousie Athletic Club. The club began 22 Apr. 1884, with Professor Forrest as honorary president. The account of the 15 Nov. 1884 game with Acadia is by the club secretary, A.S. MacKenzie, later president of Dalhousie. For the colours question, see meetings of 13 Dec. 1886; 20 Apr., 30 Oct. 1887.

8 BOG Correspondence, S.H. Holmes to James Ross, 28 Feb. 1881; J.W. Ketch to John Doull, 11 Mar. 1881; Senate Minutes, 10 Mar. 1881; BOG Minutes, 4 May 1882.

9 For Ross's speech see *British Colonist*, 3 Nov. 1870, reporting the opening of the Dalhousie session. For McGill, see Stanley Brice Frost, *McGill University: For the Advancement of Learning, 1801–1895* (Montreal 1980), pp. 251–5, 261.

10 *Halifax Evening Reporter*, 28 Feb. 1877; *Dalhousie Gazette*, 16 Nov. 1872.

11 BOG Correspondence, A. Alice Cameron to Macdonald, 22 Aug. 1881; Senate Minutes, 24, 30 Oct. 1881.

12 *Dalhousie Gazette*, 11 Nov. 1881.

13 The University of Aberdeen poem was recited by the sheriff of Edinburgh, Nigel Thomson, 8 May 1988, and recalled by Professor Henry Best, of Laurentian University; *Dalhousie Gazette*, 23 Nov. 1878; 17 Jan. 1880; 19 Dec. 1884.

14 *Morning Chronicle*, 23 Nov. 1911, "Women's Debt to Dalhousie." This was written at the time of a major Dalhousie campaign, and may have been a little *couleur de rose*. By this time she was Dr Eliza Ritchie, who took a PH.D. from Cornell and taught philosophy at Wellesley for ten years before returning to Halifax in 1899. For a more important perspective, see Paul Axelrod and John G. Reid, *Youth, Univeristy and Canadian Society. Essays in the Social History of Higher Education*

(Kingston and Montreal 1989), esp. Judith Fingard's essay, "College, Career and Community: Dalhousie Coeds, 1881–1921," pp. 26–50.

15 BOG Minutes, 31 Aug. 1880; 9 July 1881; 15 Oct. 1885. For the interview with Forrest, see *Dalhousie Gazette*, 15 Dec. 1886, p. 33.

16 The 1883 sleigh ride is in *Dalhousie Gazette*, 26 Jan. 1883. The 1885 one is ibid., 6 Feb. 1885. For the swan song, see ibid., 3 Dec. 1886.

17 See "Student Life in Halifax" by the "Freshmen," *Dalhousie Gazette*, 23 Feb. 1884, and its 1904 version, 21 Dec. 1904. The Dalhousie calendars list student societies and their times of meeting.

18 The letter is printed in *Dalhousie Gazette*, 21 Mar. 1884, with a minor error which I have corrected.

19 BOG Minutes, 22 Mar. 1883.

20 *Halifax Evening Reporter*, 26 Sept. 1876; see especially John Willis, *A History of Dalhousie Law School* (Toronto 1979), p. 23.

21 Ibid., p. 26; Charles Morse ('85), later editor of the *Canadian Bar Review*, has a description of Weldon in *CBR* 11 (1933), pp. 402–3. A.S. MacKenzie's tribute is in the *Dalhousie Alumni News*, December 1925.

22 Willis, *Dalhousie Law School*, p. 21.

23 Weldon's inaugural address of 30 Oct. 1883 is in *Dalhousie Gazette*, 10 Nov. 1883.

24 There is a full description of this effort, and of the shortcomings of the Dalhousie Library in other respects, by J.T. Bulmer, the law librarian, 1883–4, in *Dalhousie Gazette*, 7 Dec. 1883.

25 BOG Minutes, 3 July 1885; Willis, *Dalhousie Law School*, p. 38.

26 For an important light on the hiring of the Munro professors in the 1880s, see the letter from Judge Benjamin Russell, *Dalhousie Gazette*, 7 Nov. 1923. For the Munro endowment, see BOG Minutes, 11 Dec. 1896; 16 June 1897.

27 *Acadian Recorder*, 16, 18, 28 Jan. 1883; *Evening Mail*, 22 Jan. 1883; BOG Minutes, 22 Apr. 1884. See especially the unpublished paper by Michael C. Haynes, "The Alexander McLeod Endowment: an Investigation," 1 May 1992.

28 *Presbyterian Witness*, 13 Oct. 1883, reporting meeting of the Maritime Presbyterian Synod, 9 Oct. 1883; Senate Minutes, 1 Apr. 1886. For an account of Ross's life, see *Novascotian*, 20 Mar. 1886, and *Morning Herald*, 16 Mar. 1886. A more extended life is by G.G. Patterson, "Dalhousie's Second Principal – an Old Boy's Tribute" in Patterson's *Studies in Nova Scotian History* (Halifax 1940), pp. 100–5. The phrase is from Tacitus.

29 See John A. Bell, "Dalhousie College and University," DUA, MS., 1887, pp. 35–8. Bell was Dalhousie gold medallist in 1883. The City Council's view of the Parade question is set out in City of Halifax, *Annual Report*, 1877–8. There is a good account by Walter C. Murray, president of the University of Saskatchewan from 1908 to 1937, "The College and the Parade," *Dalhousie Gazette*, 28 Nov. 1902, partly based on the Bell manuscript.

30 *Halifax Evening Reporter*, 31 Jan. 1877; BOG Minutes, 4 Jan., 16 Feb. 1877.

31 *Presbyterian Witness*, 20 Nov. 1880; Murray, "The College and the Parade," p. 38.

32 BOG Minutes, 30 Sept., 9 Oct. 1884.

33 See F.W. Vroom, *King's College: A Chronicle, 1789–1939: Collections and Recollections* (Halifax 1941), p. 126; a modern and more searching perspective of King's is Henry Roper, "Aspects of the History of a Loyalist College: King's College, Windsor and Nova Scotian Higher Education in the Nineteenth Century" in *Anglican and Episcopal History* 61 (1991), pp. 443–59. See also BOG Minutes, 11 Mar., 2 Apr. 1885; *Morning Chronicle*, 26 June 1885.

34 Munro's Seaside Library was, indeed, cheap – that is, inexpensive. That it was not always wholesome depends upon one's view of Dickens, Thackeray, Reade, and Seaside No. 1000, a new text of the Bible.

35 *Morning Chronicle* and *Morning Herald*, 25, 26 June 1885.

36 BOG Minutes, 2, 17 Apr. 1885.

37 Ibid., 30 Nov. 1885.

38 Ibid., 24 Mar. 1886. There is reference on 6 Mar. to S.M. Brookfield having prepared an estimate for enlarging the existing Parade building, but no indication of what the estimate was, or what changes were proposed.

39 Ibid., 26 Mar., 15 Apr. 1886.

40 Ibid., 12 Oct. 1886; *Dalhousie Gazette*, 4 Nov. 1887, and 7 May 1888, valedictory address by David M. Soloan. For the 1820 cornerstone, see *Novascotian*, 23 Apr. 1887.

41 The printed set of instructions to prospective architects turns up at the back of BOG Correspondence.

42 BOG Minutes, 12, 18 Oct. 1886, give details about tenders. On laying the cornerstone, see *Morning Chronicle* and *Morning Herald*, 28 Apr. 1887.

43 *Dalhousian*, May 1914, in DUA, President's Office Correspondence, A-798.

7 A MATURING CONFIDENCE

1 There is an extensive description of the new Dalhousie building in both the *Morning Chronicle* and the *Halifax Herald*, 10 Sept. 1887. These references have been brought to my attention by Gary Shutlak of the Public Archives of Nova Scotia. For other details, see *Presbyterian Witness*, 10 Sept. 1887; *Dalhousie Gazette*, 30 Jan. 1906, "M.M. Experience Number 2"; ibid., 15 Dec. 1886, interview with President Forrest.

2 *Dalhousie Gazette*, 26 Mar. 1897; ibid., 2 Feb. 1901.

3 *Presbyterian Witness*, 10 Sept. 1887; *Dalhousie Gazette*, 20 Feb. 1890.

4 See G.G. Sedgwick, "A.M. [Archibald MacMechan]" in *Dalhousie Review* 13, no. 4 (1933–4), p. 452; Phyllis Blakeley, *Glimpses of Halifax* (Halifax 1949), p. 210.

5 *Acadian Recorder*, 21 Oct. 1893; Blakeley, *Glimpses of Halifax*, pp. 112–15.

6 *Dalhousie Gazette*, 28 Nov. 1889; ibid., 16 Oct. 1893. DUA, Nova Scotia Telephone Co. Directory, May 1900.

7 This is gossip, but is reported by an experienced and reliable president's secretary, Miss Lola Henry, secretary to two presidents, Carleton Stanley (1931–45) and A.E. Kerr (1945–63). Interview, 18 Apr. 1990.

8 For Schurman, see A.B. McKillop, *A Disciplined Intelligence: Critical Inquiry and Canadian Thought in the Victorian Era* (Montreal 1979), pp. 201–2, 270.

Schurman's frequent addresses are reported in the *Dalhousie Gazette*, 7 Apr., 11 Nov. 1882; 9 Feb. 1883; 16 Jan., 27 Mar. 1886; 17 Dec. 1887. For the satire on Darwin, see ibid., 15 Dec. 1886. Student opinions on the reconciliation of religion and Darwin are in ibid., Jan. 1879, "Science"; Apr. 1886, "Is a Belief in Darwinism Consistent with a Teleological View of the Natural World?"; Mar. 1886, "The Age and Its Tendencies," by J.E. Creighton. Creighton graduated in 1887 in honours philosophy, with the governor general's silver medal and became professor of logic and metaphysics at Cornell. See McKillop, *A Critical Intelligence*, pp. 139–40. The quotation is from Creighton. Darwin's *Origin of Species* appears in the curriculum for Philosophy 2, taught by Professor Walter Murray, in the calendar for 1904–5. Biology is in the calendar a decade later.

9 Seth's letters to Archibald MacMechan are fragmentary but interesting. DUA Archibald MacMechan Papers (hereafter AMM Papers) MS2, 82, C854, Seth to AMM, 26 Mar. 1896, from Providence; same, 15 June 1898, from Ithaca; same, 1 Aug. 1906, from Edinburgh. See Archibald MacMechan, "Memories of James Seth," *Dalhousie Review* 4 (1924–5), pp. 322–6. Seth died in 1924.

For Lyall, see McKillop, *A Disciplined Intelligence*, pp. 44–52. For Lyall's inaugural address, see *Halifax Witness*, 29 Oct. 1864; his obituary is in ibid., 25 Jan. 1890, and *Dalhousie Gazette*, 30 Jan. 1890.

10 The pamphlet is in the BOG Correspondence; Forrest's letter is on pp. 20–1.

11 Ibid., Munro to Forrest, 18 Mar. 1889, from New York; [James?] Forrest to John Forrest, 1 Mar. 1889. This is one page from a letter addressed to "My dear Brother." Forrest's letter to MacMechan is in AMM Papers, box 2, C230, 2 Apr. 1889, from Halifax. Murray's appreciation of Forrest is in the *Morning Chronicle*, 1 Jan. 1912.

12 See Sedgwick, "A.M." Also *Presbyterian Witness*, 25 May 1889.

13 AMM Papers, Private Journals, 28 June 1893; *The Week* (Toronto), 7, no. 5 (3 Jan. 1890). AMM was a good archivist of his own, as well as others' papers. He also kept twenty or so scrapbooks of his published writings, with the date of publication and sometimes with the amount of money he received for them. Scrapbook A covers 1883–91, and has this piece from *The Week*.

14 That success was not obvious to MacMechan at his thirty-first birthday in 1893. "I have done literally nothing: plenty of schemes and no energy to carry them out. I have had all my warnings. My father [was] really a failure from the same cause ... laziness. That is my rock ahead..." He held before himself however the Latin motto, "Justum ac tenacem propositi virum. The design of an upright and steadfast man." DUA, MacMechan Papers, Private Journals, 28 June 1893.

15 BOG Correspondence, Munro to Forrest, 18 Mar. 1889, from New York.

16 BOG Minutes, 6 Jan., 11 Apr. 1890; Senate Minutes, 17 Mar. 1890; *Dalhousie Gazette*, 3 Apr. 1890.

17 BOG Minutes, 7 Apr., 26 June 1888.

18 The lengthy report of the finance committee on Dalhousie's endowment fund is dated 27 Dec. 1888, and in BOG Minutes, 23 Jan. 1889. The committee noted that they had some difficulty preparing the report owing to the absence of any memorandum of investments before 1875, and that there was no account book prior to 1856. "A loose sheet of paper in the College box" gave a short financial historty

from 1819 to the 1830s. See also BOG Minutes, 11 Apr., 3 June 1890. For the correspondence in the *Dalhousie Gazette*, see 20 Dec. 1892, "That $50,000 Fund" signed "Alumnus," and 19 Jan. 1893, letter, signed "Another Alumnus." For the Munro estate, see BOG Minutes, 11 Dec. 1896; 16 June 1897. For 1900 finances, see ibid., 6 Feb. 1900.

19 PANS, RG83, vol. 2, no. 51, Letterbook of the Halifax Medical College 1875–93, Dr A.W.H. Lindsay, registrar, to A.G. Archibald, 7 Aug. 1885; H.L. Scammell, "The Great Row of '85," *Nova Scotia Medical Bulletin* 22 (1943), pp. 38–44. Additional details about this contretemps have been given to me by Dr T.J. Murray, dean of medicine from 1985 to 1992.

20 Letterbook of Halifax Medical College, Lindsay to registrar of McGill Medical Faculty, 14 Sept. 1885; H.L. Scammell, "The Halifax Medical College, 1875–1911," *Dalhousie Medical Journal* 11, no. 1 (1958), pp. 12–17.

21 Colin D. Howell, *A Century of Care: A History of the Victoria General Hospital in Halifax 1887–1987* (Halifax 1988), pp. 32–9.

22 Letterbook of Halifax Medical College, Lindsay to Dean, McGill Medical Faculty, 25 Sept. 1885.

23 Senate Minutes, 1 Nov. 1887; 22 Mar. 1888; letterbook of Halifax Medical College, Lindsay to Wm. M. Doull, secretary, Dalhousie BOG, 14 Dec. 1887, recommending four appointments, so the Medical Faculty could be organized as early as possible. See also Scammell, "The Great Row of '85," p. 42.

24 HMC Letterbook, Lindsay to A.W. Sawyer, 29 Oct., 20 Nov. 1888; BOG Minutes, 20 Dec. 1888; 16 Jan. 1889; 27 Feb. 1890; HMC Letterbook, Lindsay to W.S. Flielding, 27 Mar. 1889.

25 HMC Letterbook, Lindsay to H.V. Kent, Truro, 24 Apr. 1889.

26 *Dalhousie Gazette*, 25 Oct. 1889; HMC Letterbook, Lindsay to J.S. Calder, Bridgewater, 8 July 1885.

27 *Dalhousie Gazette*, 17 Oct. 1892; H.B. Atlee, "Dalhousie Medical School 1907–1957," *Dalhousie Medical Journal* 11 (1958), pp. 21–33; Atlee's statement about Joggins recalled by Dr S.C. Robinson, 21 Mar. 1992.

28 Senate Minutes, 4 Apr. 1887; see especially John Willis, *A History of Dalhousie Law School* (Toronto 1979), pp. 41–4.

29 *Canadian Law Times*, 71, quoted in Willis, *Dalhousie Law School*, pp. 44–5. For Bennett at Dalhousie Law School, see my Goodman Lectures, *The Loner: The Personal Life and Ideas of R.B. Bennett, 1870–1947* (Toronto 1992), pp. 18–22.

30 See John G. Reid, *Mount Allison University: Volume I, 1843–1914* (Toronto 1984), p. 364; A.G. Bailey, ed., *The University of New Brunswick* (Fredericton 1950), p. 44.

31 BOG Minutes, 20 May 1886; also Senate Minutes, 8 Feb. 1887; BOG Minutes, 12 Dec. 1887; *Dalhousie Gazette*, 24 Feb., 10 Mar. 1888.

32 *Dalhousie Gazette*, 26 Oct. 1898, written by a former professor of King's College, London, and published in the pages of the "Home University" in England.

33 Extensive extracts from Macdonald's convocation address are given in ibid., 17 Oct. 1892, pp. 5–19. See *Gazette*, 8 Nov. 1888 for editorial comment on too many required courses in classics.

34 Ibid., 13 Feb. 1895; 20 Dec. 1887.

35 Ibid., 20 Dec. 1893; 13 Feb. 1895. The literature on the subject of initiations and hazing is reviewed in Keith Walden's article, "Hazes, Hustles, Scraps, and Stunts: Initiations at the University of Toronto, 1880–1925" in Paul Axelrod and John G. Reig, eds., *Youth, University and Canadian Society: Essays in the Social History of Higher Education* (Kingston and Montreal 1989), pp. 94–121. Walden's article is a social history of the subject.

36 *Dalhousie Gazette*, 18 Nov. 1905; ibid., 3 Nov. 1893; *Acadian Recorder*, 28 Oct. 1893.

37 *Dalhousie Gazette*, 20 Dec. 1893, poem by "H.F." For the drunk from Pictou, see ibid., 20 Dec. 1894. The cow story is probably true, though I have not been able to pin it down. Macneill makes reference to it, along with other high jinks, in his "Recollections," p. 2, the typescript of which, dated 7 Nov. 1934, was made available to me through the kindness of Murray Macneill's daughter, Janet Macneill Piers, and is now in DUA.

38 Senate Minutes, 9 Dec. 1889; 2 Oct. 1893; 29 Apr. 1898; 29 Apr. 1904; 18 Apr. 1905.

39 Ibid., 5 May 1899; 14, 15 Mar. 1900; 9 Apr. 1901. The story about Morrison is confirmed by his son Hugh W. Morrison of Thornhill, Ontario. He pointed out that his father took his LL.B. first in 1897, and then went on to do English, graduating with a BA in 1901. There is a family story, told by Mrs F.A. Morrison, that President Forrest refused to allow Morrison to graduate with honours in English because of this incident. This is more doubtful; at least Senate does not seem to have recorded it. Telephone interview with Hugh W. Morrison, 4 June 1992.

40 Senate Minutes, 5, 7 Nov. 1901.

41 Ibid., 12 Nov. 1902; *Dalhousie Gazette*, 10 Dec. 1901; ibid., 9 Oct. 1931, letter from T.A. Goudge.

42 See *Dalhousie Gazette*, 1 July 1902; 24 Apr. 1903, "Recollections of the 'Doctor'," pp. 295–302.

43 Ibid., 13 Feb. 1903, "Dalhousie and Culture," by Frank Baird. K.F. MacKenzie's letter is in ibid., 4 Apr. 1903. MacKenzie was later the author of an intriguing little book about Nova Scotian history, *Sabots and Slippers* (1954). For James Arthur MacKenzie (no relation to the above) and his more famous son Larry, see my *Lord of Point Grey* (Vancouver 1987), pp. 1–13.

44 *Dalhousie Gazette*, 26 Jan. 1898, letter to editor from "Genevieve." There are very few accounts of everyday student customs and traditions. This one is by George Farquhar ('07), later a member of the Dalhousie Board of Governors. See *Dalhousie Alumni News*, January 1938, p. 12. There is also a survey in the *New York Sun*, 1 Jan. 1899, of women in eastern colleges, in which Dalhousie was included. The *Dalhousie Gazette*, 10 Feb. 1899 describes part of the survey.

45 This paragraph owes its substance to the article by Judith Fingard, "College, Career and Community: Dalhousie Coeds, 1881–1921" in Axelrod and Reid, eds. *Youth, University and Canadian Society*, pp. 26–33.

46 There is a compilation of extracts from the Halifax papers in *Dalhousie Gazette*, 28 Jan. 1891.

47 Senate Minutes, 22 Oct. 1893. The German lines were quoted in the *Gazette* of

11 Feb. 1896 without attribution. My colleague in the German Department, Professor Friedrich Gaede, at once said it was Schiller, and soon found the source. It is the first two lines of "Würde der Frauen" ("Dignity of Women").

48 There is an account of the Dalhousie Ball in the *Acadian Recorder*, 5 Feb. 1900. The 1906 dance program was given to me by A.O. Hebb, himself editor of the *Dalhousie Gazette* from 1926 to 1927, to whom I am most grateful.

49 *Morning Chronicle*, 12, 13, 14 Mar. 1901; *Dalhousie Gazette*, 23 Mar. 1901; Memorial Issue to Charles Macdonald, Apr. 1901. Price's recollection is in ibid., 24 Apr. 1903.

8 EXPANDING: A QUEST FOR SPACE

1 DUA, MacMechan Papers, box 3, J.G. MacGregor to MacMechan, 9 Sept. 1901, from King's Cross; same, 28 Dec. 1901, from Edinburgh. MacGregor died suddenly of a heart attack, on 21 May 1913. MacMechan published a brief and elegant tribute to him in *Dalhousie Gazette*, September 1913. See also "MacGregor: Personalia" in the same issue.

St Francis Xavier University Archives, RG5/8/333, President Thompson Papers, Forrest to Thompson, 26 Dec. 1900. Forrest is here replying to Thompson's request to support a proposal to the government, patently science grants to the Nova Scotia colleges. This letter has been brought to my attention by James D. Cameron of St Francis Xavier University, to whom I am most grateful.

2 BOG Minutes, 2 Jan. 1902; 14 Aug. 1903; *College Federation*, a pamphlet in PANS, vertical file v. 130, no. 16, includes a draft of the proposed bill. See also F.W. Vroom, *King's College: a Chronicle, 1789–1939* (Halifax 1941), 139–40.

3 MacMechan's story is in *Dalhousie Gazette*, 27 Oct. 1915. BOG Minutes, 28 May, 1 July 1902; Senate Minutes, 7 May 1902; DUA, President's Office Correspondence (hereafter POC), A-352, "Carnegie Corporation of New York, 1902–1915," Howard Murray, secretary of Senate to Carnegie, 26 Nov. 1902. There is a further appeal to Carnegie from President Forrest and J.F. Stairs, 24 Mar. 1902. Dalhousie was then asking for $200,000.

4 BOG Minutes, 8 Jan., 14 Aug. 1903; Senate Minutes, 28 July 1905. There is a calendar of the Sydney summer school for 1903, sponsored by the Dalhousie School of Mining and Metallurgy, in PANS, Gilpin Pamphlet Collection, nos. 29 and 30. Allan Dunlop kindly brought this to my attention. King's unhappiness is noted in Vroom, *King's*, pp. 141–2.

5 Nova Scotia Assembly, *Debates and Proceedings*, 2 Apr. 1907, pp. 264–5. A brief sketch of the early history of the Nova Scotia Technical College (now called the Technical University of Nova Scotia) is given in Jill and Lee Cameron, *The First 50 Years: Nova Scotia Tech* (Halifax 1959), pp. 7–10. Sexton was principal until he retired in 1947. Problems similar to Dalhousie's with engineering arose contemporaneously at Queen's, Toronto, and McGill. See Mario Creet, "Science and Engineering at McGill and Queen's Universities and the University of Toronto, 1880s to 1920s" (PH.D. thesis, Queen's University 1992).

6 Senate Minutes, 24 May 1902. For Rhodes, see John Flint, *Cecil Rhodes* (Boston 1974) especially p. 241 and note.

7 BOG Correspondence, faculty to BOG, 11 May 1839; Senate Minutes, 24 Apr. 1867. There is a comprehensive history of the whole Dalhousie library system, warts and all, by J.P. Wilkinson, "A History of the Dalhousie University Main Library, 1867–1931" (PH.D. thesis, University of Chicago 1966).

8 *Dalhousie Gazette*, 26 Feb. 1881; ibid., 7 Dec. 1883; Senate Minutes, 26 May 1897.

9 Dalhousie *Calendar*, 1904–5, pp. 111–16

10 *Dalhousie Gazette*, 4 Apr. 1903; 27 June 1910.

11 For George S. Campbell, see *Dalhousie Gazette*, 25 Nov. 1927.

12 BOG Correspondence, Brenton H. Collins to G.S. Campbell, addressed to Campbell in London, 6 June 1906, from Tunbridge Wells; BOG Minutes, 8 Mar. 1909, letter from the Dartmouth Board of Trade, 17 Feb. 1909. Dalhousie thanked Dartmouth for "their very generous offer," but found it impossible to move Dalhousie from Halifax. The offer from the City of Halifax was officially accepted by Dalhousie on 4 June 1909. Carleton Street itself was specifically excluded from the grant by subseequent decision (BOG Minutes, 3 Jan. 1912).

13 Ibid., 3 Feb., 4 July, 15 Aug. 1910.

14 *Dalhousie Gazette*, March 1911.

15 See Carol Anne Janzen, "Sir Alexander Croke," *DCB*, VII: 216–19. Jim Bennett has a lively article on the history of Studley, "Shades of Studley Past," in *Dalhousie Alumni Magazine* (Winter 1988), pp. 7–9. (The issue has a handsome watercolour of the Murray homestead on the cover.)

16 *Presbyterian Witness*, 17 Dec. 1910. Robert Murray was born at Earltown, Colchester County; he came to Halifax in the early 1850s to go to the Free Church College on Gerrish Street. He was soon editor of the *Presbyterian Witness*. For earlier offers of Studley, see POC, A-971, "Studley Campus, 1908–1963," Eastern Trust to Hector McInnes, 24 June 1908, to the effect that Dalhousie's offer was not accepted; R.H. Murray to G.S. Campbell, 31 Mar. 1909.

17 BOG Minutes, 18 Jan., 7 Feb., 5 May 1911; *Dalhousie Gazette*, Feb. 1911, "The Future of Dalhousie."

18 BOG Minutes, 6 Feb., 5 Mar. 1912; *Dalhousie Gazette*, January 1911; POC, A-325, "G.S. Campbell 1908–1927," Campbell to A.S. MacKenzie (hereafter ASM), 27 Mar. 1912, from New York. The board asked one of the Murray sons to occupy the building as caretaker rent free; POC, A-780, "Murray Homestead," W.E. Thompson (secretary of the board) to George T. Murray, 9 May 1912. Eventually in 1921 the building would become the temporary home of the Dalhousie YMCA.

19 Senate Minutes, 18 Mar. 1919. Abraham Flexner, *Medical Education in the United States and Canada* (New York 1910). D.A. Campbell, "Medical Education in Nova Scotia," *Maritime Medical News*, 1910. See also T.J. Murray, "The Visit of Abraham Flexner to the Halifax Medical College," *Nova Scotia Medical Bulletin* 64, no. 2 (February 1985), pp. 38–41.

20 [Abraham Flexner], *I Remember: The Autobiography of Abraham Flexner* (New York 1940) pp. 120–2.

21 H.B. Atlee, "Dalhousie Medical School, 1907–1957," *Dalhousie Medical Journal* 91, no. 1 (1958), p. 22.

22 Senate Minutes, 18 Mar., 9, 16 May 1910; BOG Minutes, 7 Feb., 5 May 1911; letter

from A.W.H. Lindsay, interim secretary, Provisional Medical Faculty, to G.S. Stairs, 13 June 1911; 7 Nov. 1911. There is an informative letter on the negotiations in POC, A-572, "Faculty of Medicine 1868–1912," A.W.H. Lindsay to [G.S.] Campbell, 11 May 1910.

23 G.R. McKean in *Dalhousie Alumni News* 1, no. 3 (June 1938); ibid., 2, no. 2 (February 1939), "Lord John," by G.F., pp. 4–5. There is reference to this song in *Dalhousie Alumni News* (April 1944), p. 15.

24 BOG Correspondence, Henry S. Pritchett, president of the Carnegie Corporation for the Advancement of Teaching, to John Forrest, 10 July 1906; BOG Minutes, 2 Aug. 1906.

25 *Dalhousie Gazette*, March 1911, has a good photograph of President Forrest; Archibald MacMechan, *The Life of a Little College and Other Papers* (Boston 1914), pp. 23, 47–9; for MacMechan's Christmas Eve, 1909, see MacMechan Papers, Scrapbook H, p. 112; *Presbyterian Witness*, 4 Feb. 1911.

26 BOG Minutes, 5 May, 28 June, 18 July 1911.

27 W.A. Craick, "How Personality Creates: The Task of President A. Stanley MacKenzie of Dalhousie University" in *Maclean's Magazine* (December 1913), pp. 21–24 is a good contemporary piece; Walter C. Murray, "Stanley MacKenzie of Dalhousie," *Dalhousie Review* 18 (1938–9), pp. 427–34 is by an old friend and colleague. There are brief accounts of his marriage and life in *Indianapolis Star*, 7 Oct. 1938, and *New York Times*, 3 Oct. 1938. For MacKenzie's correspondence, see DUA, MS2, 43, A.S. MacKenzie Papers, Charles Macdonald to ASM, 1 Sept. 1899, from Halifax.

28 ASM Papers, John Forrest to ASM, 2 June 1905, from New York; W.A. Craick, "MacKenzie," *passim*; for MacMechan's poem, see his *Late Harvest* (Toronto 1934), pp. 52–3.

29 DUA, MS2, 82, Archibald MacMechan Papers, Scrapbook H, 28 May 1910. For MacKenzie's "marching orders," see a circular letter addressed "To All Fellow Alumni" dated Halifax, 5 Dec. 1911, recounting the history of 1911 and the Dalhousie campaign for funds. This is in the Archibald MacMechan Papers, Dalhousie Campaign Scrapbook, p. 71. MacKenzie's letter is ibid., box 3, C655, MacKenzie to MacMechan, 30 Dec. 1912.

30 POC, A-566, "Faculty of Law," ASM to J.E. Creighton at Cornell, 10 Nov. 1911; A-509, "Eddy-Shirreff Foundation," H. Joyce Harris to Hector McInnes, chairman of the board, 19 Nov. 1934; interview with Lola Henry, 18 Apr. 1990.

31 BOG Minutes, 7 Nov. 1911, record James Hamet Dunn's gift. It is usually assumed James Dunn got his LL.B. in April 1898. For some reason he did not. Dunn wrote his final examinations in March 1898 but some academic rule got in the way, for it was only on 14 Sept. 1898 that Senate recommended him for LL.B. That was the day Dunn was admitted to the bar of Nova Scotia.

In November 1911 alone there were numerous articles in the *Herald* and the *Morning Chronicle*. For details of the June campaign, see *Morning Chronicle*, 31 May 1912. For MacKenzie's speeches, and the *Titanic*, see *Daily Echo* (Halifax) 15, 16 Apr. 1912.

32 See POC, A-260–A-268, "Campaigns, 1911–1912"; ibid., A-268, Edwin Ross to ASM, 22 Jan. 1914, from Vancouver; ASM to Ross, 2 Feb. 1914; ibid., A-264, ASM

to William H. Chase, Kentville, 19 Oct. 1912; ibid., A-268, Lord Strathcona to Campbell, 4 June, 23 Nov. 1912.

33 See Judith Fingard, "College, Career and Community: Dalhousie Coeds, 1881–1921" in Axelrod and Reid, eds., *Youth, University and Canadian Society: Essays in the Social History of Higher Education* (Kingston and Montreal 1989), pp. 33–35. Landladies preferring men students is in a clipping from an unknown Toronto newspaper, April 1920, in POC, A-508, "Mrs. E.B. Eddy, 1920." For the board's discussion with Dr Eliza Ritchie, see BOG Minutes, 28 Apr., 7 Nov. 1913.

34 POC, A-493, "Frank Darling, 1911–1920," Darling to Campbell, 6 Feb. 1911, telegram; Campbell to Darling, 29 Nov. 1911; BOG Minutes, 7 Nov. 1911; 9 Dec. 1912, letter to the city.

35 POC, A-493, Darling to Campbell, 4 Mar. 1912.

36 Ibid., ASM to Darling, 29 Mar. 1912; Darling to Campbell, 31 Mar. 1912; Darling to ASM, 4 Apr. 1912.

37 The Carnegie conditions are summarized by ASM in POC, A-352, ASM to James Bertram of the Carnegie Corporation, 13 Jan. 1912. As to the building itself, Campbell was anxious that a start should be made in 1912, but told MacKenzie that "it must not be a false start. Better to take the summer to mature our plans than begin wrong." POC, A-325, Campbell to ASM, 27 Mar. 1912; Campbell to Darling, 30 Apr. 1912. For the Duke of Connaught's visit to Halifax, *Daily Echo* (Halifax), 14, 15, 16 Aug. 1912.

38 POC, A-493, Darling to Cobb, 3 Feb. 1913, telegram.

39 Ibid., A-237 "Science Building, 1912–1932," Falconer and McDonald to Cobb, 14 June 1913; ibid., A-386 "A.R. Cobb, 1912–1932," H.C. Burchell to Cobb, 27 June 1913; C.D. Howe to Cobb, 25 June 1913; Cobb to ASM, 30 June 1913. Andrew Randall Cobb (1876–1943) was born in Brooklyn, New York, educated at Horton Academy and Acadia, and took degrees at MIT, Boston. He worked in Cleveland, studied at the École des Beaux Arts in Paris, and settled in Halifax in 1909. The Art Gallery of Nova Scotia had an exhibit of his work in 1990, and published a catalogue: *Rich in Interest and Charm: the Architecture of Andrew Randall Cobb, 1876–1943* (Halifax 1990). His drawing of the south elevation of the Science Building, March 1913, is illustrated on p. 23.

40 POC, A-216, "Macdonald Memorial Library," ASM to Johnson, 23 Mar. 1914; Johnson to ASM, 31 Mar. 1914. MacKenzie's notes for his speech are in this file. John Johnson's moving letter was read by MacKenzie and is in *Dalhousie Gazette*, 22 Jan. 1915. Johnson died in his house at Drummondville in December 1914. For Allan Pollok, see Archibald MacMechan Papers, Scrapbook Q. Pollok died in 1918.

41 Senate Minutes, 2 Oct. 1909; 14 Oct., 13, 20 Nov., 11 Dec. 1913; 12 Feb. 1914. It is also discussed in the *Dalhousie Gazette*, December 1913.

42 Ibid., June 1912, "Omar at College." The poem is a twisted version of the *Rubaiyat of Omar Khayyam*.

9 THE GREAT WAR AND AFTER

1 For Canada in the First World War, or the Great War, as contemporaries called it,

see G.W.L. Nicholson, *Canadian Expeditionary Force, 1914–1919* (Ottawa 1964), the official history. A more manageable volume is John Swettenham, *Canada and the First World War* (Toronto 1973). For Sam Hughes, see Ronald G. Haycock, *Sam Hughes, the Public Career of a Controversial Canadian, 1885–1916* (Toronto 1986), especially pp. 136–40.

2 POC, A-342, "Major R.W. Leonard, June-July 1914," ASM to Kenneth F. Mackenzie, Toronto, 5 June 1914.

3 *Acadian Recorder*, 11 Nov. 1914; President MacKenzie's letter is in *Herald*, 13 Nov. 1914, p. 10; Senate Minutes, 12 Nov. 1914. Changes in the management of the *Gazette* had been agreed to by the Senate on 9 Apr. 1914. It was to be published under the authority of the student council by a board of editors comprising an editor-in-chief, financial editor, an editor for each faculty, together with one each for alumni and alumnae, plus five additional editors. There were to be twenty issues per year.

The propaganda poem is probably imported, unacknowledged, from a British source, and is in *Herald*, 10 Nov. 1914, p. 5.

4 POC, A-343 "COTC, South End Skating Rink 1914–15," Henry Roper to ASM, 4 Nov. 1914; W.E. Thompson (secretary of the board and head of the Dalhousie COTC) to G.S. Campbell, 13 Nov. 1914.

5 *Dalhousie Gazette*, 4 Dec. 1915; POC, A-762, "Military Affairs, 1909–1919," ASM to Major W.B.A. Ritchie, 27 Oct. 1916.

6 University of British Columbia Archives, Norman A.M. MacKenzie Papers, "Memoirs," pp. 41–74.

7 *Dalhousie Gazette*, 5 Dec. 1918, letter from Sergeant Norman A. MacKenzie, C Company, 85th Battalion, dated 7 Sept. 1918. His letter to MacMechan is in DUA, Archibald MacMechan Papers, C 666, MacKenzie to MacMechan, 13 Nov. 1928, from Toronto.

8 POC, A-486, "Dalhousie Number Seven Stationary Hospital 1914–1917" has correspondence and memoranda. See especially ASM to Borden, 12 Oct. 1914, telegram, and 27 Nov. 1914, telegram; ASM to Mrs Harold Putname, president, Truro Red Cross, 6 Jan. 1916.

9 See J.P. Wilkinson, "A History of the Dalhousie University Main Library, 1967–1931" (PH.D. thesis, University of Chicago 1966), pp. 117–54; POC, A-215, "Macdonald Memorial Library, Construction and Equipment, 1914–1930."

10 For the split campus, see *Dalhousie Gazette*, 22 Feb. 1916. For student criticisms of the law curriculum, see John Willis, *A History of Dalhousie Law School* (Toronto 1979), pp. 59–61.

11 POC, A-560, "Faculty of Law 1907–1921," ASM to Weldon, 6 Sept. 1913.

12 Willis, *Dalhousie Law School*, pp. 72–4.

13 Ibid., pp. 69–71, citing ASM to Judge Benjamin Russell, 11 Sept. 1914.

14 POC, A-776, "Mount St. Vincent University," ASM to Sister M. DeSales, 6 May 1914; ASM to Sister Maura, 11 Aug. 1914; ASM to Sister M. DeChantal, 6 Aug. 1915; BOG Minutes, 21 Sept. 1916; Senate Minutes, 3 Oct. 1916.

15 Senate Minutes, 3 Oct., 9 Nov., 18 Dec. 1916; 2 Aug. 1919; especially 8 Apr. 1921.

16 For the effect of the war on Dalhousie research, see A-866, ASM to J. Patterson of

Toronto, 16 Dec. 1918; for negotiations re hospital, see BOG Minutes, 21 Dec. 1916, 2 Jan. 1917; for Camp Hill, see Desmond Morton and Glenn Wright, *Winning the Second Battle: Canadian Veterans and the Return to Civilian Life, 1915–1930* (Toronto 1987) p. 39.

17 The literature on the Halifax explosion grows. The most recent and most comprehensive work is Janet Kitz, *Shattered City: the Halifax Explosion and the Road to Recovery* (Halifax 1989), based on new research and many interviews with survivors. An older narrative is Michael Bird, *The Town that Died* (Toronto 1962). The best first-hand account is in Thomas H. Raddall, *In My Time: A Memoir* (Toronto 1976), pp. 30–41. Raddall was fourteen years old and at Chebucto Road School the morning of the explosion. Bronson's paper on the explosion was published in Royal Society of Canada, *Transactions*, section III, 1918. Useful selections are republished in Ernest Heighton, *Dr. Howard L. Bronson, Physicist* (Halifax 1990), pp. 130–5. Archibald MacMechan was made director of the Halifax Disaster Record Office, and wrote a manuscript about the explosion. See Archibald MacMechan Papers, MS2, 82, K15, C1, especially chapter 7 on the hospitals.

18 Kitz, *Shattered City*, 58–66; *Dalhousie Gazette*, 29 Jan. 1918. There is a good description on the effects of the explosion in a private letter by ASM, Staff files 509, ASM to Mrs J.E. Todd, 11 Jan. 1918.

19 MacMechan Papers, Private Journals, 6 Dec. 1917. There is a discrepancy over the timing of the Senate meeting. MacMechan says it was 10 AM on the Friday, at Studley. The Senate Minutes record the meeting as 5 PM at MacKenzie's house.

20 POC, A-353, "Carnegie Corporation of New York, 1918–1922," ASM to Carnegie Corporation, 11 Dec. 1917, 9 Jan. 1918; telegrams; James Bertram of Carnegie Corporation to ASM, 10 Jan. 1918.

For the correspondence re the return of No. 7 hospital staff, see POC, A-487, "#7 Hospital 1917–1936," especially ASM to Stewart, 16 Dec. 1918, 14 Feb. 1919; R.L. Borden to G.F. Pearson, 28 Dec. 1918.

21 See Morton and Wright, *Winning the Second Battle*, pp. 112–13; POC, A-941, "Soldiers (returned) Education of, 1919–20," ASM to B.C. Borden, president of Mount Allison, 9 Apr. 1919; ASM to Cecil Race, registrar, University of Alberta, 25 July 1919.

22 POC, A-752, "Marlborough House 1919–1924"; ibid., A-493, "Frank Darling 1911–1920," ASM to Darling, 13 Jan. 1919; Darling to ASM, 17 Feb. 1919; ASM to Darling 18 Feb., 1 Apr., 18 July 1919.

23 There is considerable correspondence with R.B. Bennett in the President's Office Correspondence, POC, A-148 to A-151, from 1912 to 1945. See A-148, R.B. Bennett to ASM, 4 Oct. 1919, from Calgary; same, 16 Feb. 1920, from Windsor Hotel, Montreal.

24 POC, A-508, "Mrs. Eddy, 1920," P.C. Stewart to Dugald Macgillivray, 23 Mar. 1920, confidential, from Canadian Bank of Commerce, Ottawa; ASM to Macgillivray, 3 Apr. 1920; ASM to Mrs Eddy, 6 Mar. 1920, from Chateau Laurier.

25 Ibid., Mrs Eddy to ASM, 20 May 1920, from Hull; W.E. Thompson, secretary of BOG, to Mrs Eddy, 1 June 1920.

26 Ibid., ASM to Darling, 16 June 1920; Mrs Eddy to ASM, 23 Aug. 1920; four tele-

grams back and forth, 30–31 Aug. 1920; ASM to Mrs Eddy, 18 Sept. 1920; ibid., A-494, ASM to Darling, 20 Nov. 1920; *Morning Chronicle*, 10 Aug. 1921.

27 POC, A-325, ASM to Dr H.S. Pritchett, 26 Jan. 1918; ASM to G.S. Campbell, 3 Apr. 1918.

28 Ibid., A-993, "Victoria General Hospital 1910–1929," W.W. Kenney to ASM, 31 Oct. 1919; ASM to W.W. Kenney, 23 Sept. 1923. For Atlee, see staff files 10, "H.B. Atlee," with a wealth of correspondence.

29 POC, A-325, ASM to G.S. Campbell, London, 23 Mar. 1920.

30 Ibid., A-353, "Carnegie Corporation of New York 1918–1922"; J. Bertram to ASM, 20 May 1920; ibid., A-874 "Rockefeller Foundation, 1919–1921"; Report on Dalhousie Medical School to Rockefeller Foundation, 6 Apr. 1920; Dr George Vincent to ASM, 9 Aug. 1920. The additions to the Victoria General were, by agreement, to be: a new private patient pavilion; doubling the size of the nurses' residence; and a $150,000 extension to the Pathology Building. When the money from Rockefeller and Carnegie actually came in September 1920, the premium on US funds was between 10 and 11 per cent. Rockefeller's cheque for $500,000 actually brought in $551,706.31 and Carnegie's, by bankers' auction, $555,000. See BOG Minutes, 11, 16 Sept. 1920.

31 POC, A-648, "Grace Maternity Hospital 1911–1939," G.S. Campbell to Brigadier Thompson Walton, Salvation Army, Halifax, 3 July 1921, confidential.

32 Ibid., A-353, ASM to Beardsley Ruml, assistant to president, Carnegie Corporation, 29 Nov. 1921; *Morning Chronicle*, 10 Nov. 1922; *Daily Echo*, 9 Nov. 1922.

33 DUA, staff files 509, "J.E. Todd," Todd to ASM, 5 Aug. 1919; ASM to Todd, 22 July 1919.

34 Ibid., 543, "George Earle Wilson," has the correspondence.

35 See Richard Allen, *The Social Passion: Religion and Social Reform in Canada, 1914–1928* (Toronto 1973), especially "The New Evangelism," pp. 219–30. For the history of the SCM at Dalhousie see my *Lord of Point Grey: Larry MacKenzie of UBC* (Vancouver 1987), pp. 31–4.

36 DUA, Staff files 298, "Ebenezer Mackay," ASM to Professor John Waddell of Queen's, 28 Jan. 1920.

37 DUA, staff files 138, "Rev. John Forrest," draft eulogy in ASM's handwriting for Forrest's funeral, 25 June 1920.

38 POC, A-325, ASM to G.S. Campbell, 23 Mar. 1920; A-494, "Frank Darling 1920–1923," Joyce Harris to Darling, 3 Feb. 1921.

39 The reference to physiology as romance was given to me by Dr T.J. Murray, from Harris's obituary. For President MacKenzie's letter, see DUA, staff files 188, "Dr. D. Fraser Harris," ASM to Harris, 27 June 1916.

40 *Dalhousie Gazette*, 12 Nov. 1919, by Observer, "The Past and the Present"; ibid., 14 Feb. 1923.

41 Ibid., 21 Nov. 1894; 11 Feb. 1896; 12 Mar. 1897.

10 TOWARDS UNIVERSITY FEDERATION

1 DUA, POC, A-612, "Sir Robert Falconer 1911–1930," ASM to Falconer, 1 Nov. 1920.

2 DUA, staff files, 312, "Archibald MacMechan," MacMechan to ASM, 19 Nov. 1922.

3 *Herald*, 6 Feb. 1920.

4 William S. Learned and Kenneth C.M. Sills, *Education in the Maritime Provinces of Canada* (New York 1922), p. 29; for a judicious and well-balanced modern survey, based upon both the Carnegie and Rockefeller archives, see John G. Reid, "Health, Education, Economy: Philanthropic Foundations in the Atlantic Region in the 1920s and 1930s," *Acadiensis* 14, no. 1 (Autumn 1984), pp. 64–83; see also Reid's *Mount Allison University: A History, to 1963*, vol. II: *1914–1963* (Toronto 1984), pp. 48–53.

5 Learned and Sills, *Education in the Maritime Provinces*, p. 36.

6 POC, A-354, "Carnegie Corporation, 1922," ASM to W.S. Learned, 1 Apr. 1922.

7 Ibid., A-148, "R.B. Bennett, 1912–1928," Bennett to ASM, 22 Nov. 1922, from Calgary; A-612, ASM to Falconer, 20 Mar. 1922, confidential.

8 Learned and Sills, *Education in the Maritime Provinces*, p. 42.

9 *Dalhousie Gazette*, 10 Jan. 1923.

10 POC, A-612, ASM to Falconer, 20 Mar. 1922, confidential.

11 Ibid., A-353, "Carnegie Corporation of New York, 1922," Learned to ASM, 15 Feb. 1922; ASM to Learned, 20 Feb. 1922; Learned to ASM, 23 Feb. 1922.

12 Ibid., ASM to Learned, 2 Mar. 1922, enclosing text of the Dalhousie BOG resolutions of 28 Feb. 1922.

13 Ibid., POC, A-353, "Carnegie Corporation, 1922," ASM to Learned, 8 Mar. 1922.

14 Ibid., POC, A-394, "Confederation of Maritime Universities, 1922," G.F. Pearson to ASM, 9 Apr. 1922.

15 Ibid., ASM to Walter Murray (president of University of Saskatchewan), 13 July 1922.

16 Ibid., A-354, Pearson to Learned, 19 July 1922, confidential.

17 Ibid., Learned to Pearson, 5 Sept. 1922.

18 A full account of this meeting was published. See PANS, vertical file, vol. 312, no. 1, *Minutes of the Second Conference of Representatives of the Universities, Colleges and Governments of the Maritime Provinces and Newfoundland* (Halifax 1922): Judd's intervention is on p. 81. For MacKenzie's private reaction to this debate, see POC, A-1022, "Confederation of Maritime Universities, 1922–1923," ASM to Falconer, 3 Nov. 1922.

19 Ibid., ASM to John H. Bell, 18 Nov. 1922, replying to Bell's of 14 Nov. This is a most useful letter, a summing up, for the benefit of the Prince Edward Island premier, of the current state of financial negotiations.

20 *Minutes of the Second Conference...*, p. 101; BOG Minutes, 29 Jan. 1923; MacKenzie's reflections on this subject are in his New Year's 1923 message to the students (*Dalhousie Gazette*, 10 Jan. 1923) and also in an argument for federation, perhaps set out for a speech, dated 22 Mar. 1923, and from whence the quotations come. See POC, A-1038, "King's College 1922–1938."

21 See *Morning Chronicle*, 19 Feb. 1923; ASM to Learned, 17 Feb. 1923, in Carnegie Corporation Archives, New York, Maritime provinces education federation files, cited in Reid, *Mount Allison University*, p. 54; POC, A-395, ASM to J.C. Webster, 27 Feb. 1923.

22 Ibid., ASM to B.C. Borden, 20 Apr. 1923; ASM to J.C. Webster, 15 Nov. 1923.

23 *Church Work* (Springhill, NS), 15 May 1923; POC, A-706, "King's College, 1920–1925," ASM to T.S. Boyle, 26 May 1923; Boyle to ASM, 29 May 1923; Boyle to ASM, n.d. [1 June 1923], personal; Pearson to Archbishop Clare Worrell, 5 June 1923.

24 POC, A-395, ASM to J.C. Webster, 15 Nov. 1923 (my italics).

25 Ibid., A-706, ASM to Boyle, 13 July 1923.

26 Ibid., Boyle to ASM, Friday, n.d. [received 14 July 1923], personal; ASM to King's College *Record*, 9 Jan. 1924.

27 Ibid., Minutes of Special meeting of BOG executive with King's, 26 Feb. 1925. H.E. Mahon, Alumni representative on the Dalhousie board, explained about the Birchdale lease. For the text of the Agreement of Association between Dalhousie University and the University of King's College, see Appendix 2.

28 POC, A-395, J.C. Webster to ASM, 20 Oct. 1923; 30 Apr. 1926.

29 Reid, *Mount Allison*, pp. 68–81, has a judicious account of this process.

30 POC, A-373, "Central Advisory Committee, 1923–1930," Pearson to F.P. Keppel, 29, 31 Dec. 1923. The Learned and Sills report mentions Newfoundland in the context of federation (p. 48), with reference also to a possible junior college at St John's.

31 POC, A-373, ASM to Keppel, 14 Feb., 17 Mar. 1924; Keppel to ASM, 7 Apr. 1924; ASM to Keppel, 21 May, 13 June 1924. For Newfoundland, see F.W. Rowe, *A History of Newfoundland and Labrador* (Toronto 1980), pp. 379–81; for Memorial, see Malcolm Macleod, *A Bridge Built Halfway: A History of Memorial University College, 1925–1950* (Montreal and Kingston 1990), pp. 19–21. According to Macleod, until the autumn of 1924 hope for a Carnegie subsidy was only that, a hope; but evidence in the Central Advisory Committee papers at Dalhousie suggests that the matter was decided in principle in February 1924. See POC, A-373, V.P. Burke to F.P. Keppel, 15 Mar. 1924, from St John's, with reference to Keppel's letter of 6 Feb. 1924, copy.

32 POC, A-373, ASM to Keppel, 1 Nov. 1924; ASM to F.W. Patterson, 29 Oct. 1924; Macleod, *Memorial College*, pp. 21, 202.

33 POC, A-355 "Carnegie Corporation, 1923–1927," ASM to Pearson, 7 Nov. 1924, telegram; Pearson to ASM, 7 Nov. 1924, telegram; ASM to Keppel, 8 Nov. 1924.

34 Ibid., A-356, "Carnegie Corporation, 1927–1932," Robert M. Lester to ASM, 22 Oct., 18 Nov. 1929; Lester to ASM, 4 June 1930; ASM to Lester, 7 June 1930.

35 *Novascotian*, 16 Apr. 1849, reporting Howe's speech in the Assembly debates for Saturday, 24 Feb. 1849.

36 Vice-President Denis Stairs, Dalhousie's Rhodes scholar for 1961, has made pertinent suggestions to the last pages of this chapter.

37 This wicked Oxford aphorism was put by Fyfe less pungently, "imitation pearls before genuine swine." This paragraph owes much to Frederick W. Gibson, *Queen's University 1917–1961: To Serve and Yet Be Free* (Kingston and Montreal, 1983), especially pp. 110, 128–30.

Index

At the beginning of each chapter there is an outline table of contents. Hence the index entry under Dalhousie College and University is narrowly focused.

D. = Dalhousie